A Butterfly's Journey

FACES OF RESILIENCE

A modern showcase
of an ageless experience

BARBARA J. HOPKINSON

LYNDA CHELDELIN FELL

INTRODUCTION BY
BARBARA J. HOPKINSON
Founder & CEO, A Butterfly's Journey

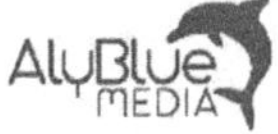

Faces of Resilience – 1ˢᵗ ed.
Barbara J. Hopkinson/Lynda Cheldelin Fell
A Butterfly's Journey www.abutterflysjourney.org

Cover Design by AlyBlue Media, LLC
Cover Photo by Renee Mckenna
Interior Design by AlyBlue Media LLC
Interior Photos by Barbara J. Hopkinson, Lynda Cheldelin Fell, Renee Hopkinson, Patti Rae Milliotis, James Stewart, Mark Yates protected by copyright © and may not be reproduced, distributed or transmitted in any form or by any means without prior written permission of A Butterfly's Journey.

Published by AlyBlue Media, LLC
Copyright © 2019 by AlyBlue Media and A Butterfly's Journey. All rights reserved. No part of this publication may be reproduced, distributed or transmitted in any form or by any means, without prior written permission of the publisher.

ISBN: 978-1-944328-71-9
AlyBlue Media, LLC
Ferndale, WA 98248
www.AlyBlueMedia.com

This book is designed to provide informative photos and narratives to readers. It is sold with the understanding that the models, writers, authors or publisher is not engaged to render any type of psychological, legal, or any other kind of professional advice. The content is the sole expression and opinion of the models. No warranties or guarantees are expressed or implied by the choice to include any of the content in this book. Neither the publisher nor the author or writers shall be liable for any physical, psychological, emotional, financial, or commercial damages including but not limited to special, incidental, consequential or other damages. Our views and rights are the same: You are responsible for your own choices, actions and results.

PRINTED IN THE UNITED STATES OF AMERICA

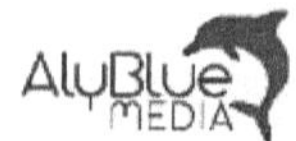

TESTIMONIALS

"CORNERSTONE . . . Resilience is the cornerstone for surviving a significant loss intact—it is the cornerstone for surviving life." —MITCH CARMODY, author, speaker, grief educator

"HEALING . . . I remember not wanting to remove the ink and went to the Saturday banquet dinner without changing my clothes. I sat at a table not knowing a single person, but a conversation began with my ink and continued through the evening. It literally became a support group meeting and ended with hugs. The experience is one of the most healing I have ever had and it continues every time I see my photo as well as the others." —BARBARA J. ROBERATTI

"INCREDIBLE . . . This was such an incredible experience for me!" —KARLA ROBINSON

"PEACE . . . The photos of us will be a reminder for years to come. It helps symbolize our healing. My daughter has since adopted a butterfly as a loved symbol of freedom, transformation and peace. We are so grateful! —HOLLY SHINSKY

"EVOKING . . . Barbara and her photographer take emotion-evoking photos as people write their feelings about their loved ones. Everyone who experiences it finds it so absolutely healing." —ALAN PEDERSEN

"LIFE-CHANGING . . . Your work is so life-changing. Keep going." —ELIZABETH FOSTER

FACES OF RESILIENCE

DEDICATION

In memory of our loved ones

Photography is truth.

JEAN-LUC GODARD
*

BY BARBARA J. HOPKINSON

INTRODUCTION

As I walked into my son's hospital room on that last evening of May, I remember thinking, "How can I be losing another son?" It was 2002, and I couldn't believe what I was seeing. My twenty-one-year-old son Brent, an Arizona State University Army ROTC student, lay perfectly still, hooked up to life support. Other than all the monitors and tubes, he looked strong, handsome, and perfectly fine, as if he was just sleeping. Fifteen years prior, I had birthed a full-term stillborn son, Robbie, and had a miscarriage before that. This couldn't possibly be happening again.

My husband Bob received a phone message that morning from our oldest son's commanding officer. He said Brent had been in a motorcycle accident, it was bad, and we should come to Arizona as quickly as possible. Our younger son, Brad, barely nineteen, had just walked in after being out all night at his senior prom. It was pure coincidence both Bob and Brad were home at the same time, as neither one had planned to be there.

Out of town on a business trip, I had no clue what was happening. It took four hours of tremendous effort full of mishaps for Bob and Brad to track me down. We met at the Newark airport and boarded a flight to Arizona, uncertain of Brent's fate. He was pronounced braindead while we were in the air.

We arrived at the hospital and spent the night at Brent's bedside. The next morning we sought second and third opinions. That afternoon, we made the agonizing decision to remove our son from life support.

The next week was a flurry of activities. We had to sort Brent's belongings in Arizona and then fly his body and belongings home to Boston. Over the next three days, we attended Brad's high school graduation followed by Brent's wake and then his funeral.

The next twelve months were hell. My marriage of thirty years fell apart, Brad struggled in college, and I attempted suicide.

Thankfully, I didn't complete my suicide attempt. In the final moments, I realized I just couldn't do that to my only remaining child, Brad. That was the turning point when I began to help others to heal myself.

I started a local support chapter of The Compassionate Friends for bereaved families. As we grieved together, I learned a tremendous amount from these people, many of whom became good friends.

In 2006, I met and married my second husband, Jim. We shared twelve wonderful years together until one morning he left for work and never returned. A quarter mile from home, Jim suffered a widow-maker heart attack. I think he knew something was wrong because he turned his car around in a small parking lot before passing out at the wheel. Thankfully, a parked car and boat trailer stopped Jim's vehicle from going into the street and oncoming traffic.

A nearby store owner and policeman witnessed the event. They pulled Jim from the car and started CPR until medics arrived. Despite their efforts, Jim couldn't be revived. I received a call from the hospital saying there had been an accident, and I should come immediately. When I arrived, they asked me to wait for a doctor. I knew then Jim hadn't survived.

Grieving as a widow was entirely different from grieving as a bereaved mother. And both were entirely different from grieving my parents. I was thirty-two when my father died, and forty-seven when my mother died. I also grieved losing sight in my right eye from a fall in a gym, and again when the eye had to be removed.

I feel like a student of grief, but that's not all bad. I've learned a tremendous amount from my journeys. It's made me stronger, reminded me what's important, made me more tolerant, patient and grateful. It forced me to grow as a person, and I've met many wonderful people I wouldn't have known otherwise. Wanting to help grievers beyond our local support group, I started a nonprofit, A Butterfly's Journey, to help people facing loss by offering online resources, action-based tools, and self-expression opportunities.

I created Faces of Resilience photoshoots to encourage open expressions of grief, loss and love. It's using art as a healing modality. These people are resilient. As we write a meaningful expression on their skin and take their photo, I cherish hearing their stories. People tell me how cathartic it feels to express their emotions and honor loved ones. When they receive their photos, many show them to others and talk more about their loss, and in the process a little healing takes place.

I am so grateful to have met Lynda Cheldelin Fell in New York City while filming Open To Hope TV about our respective journeys on child loss. Lynda and I hit it off immediately and co-hosted two shoots on the West coast. We then decided to do a photobook together as a way to help others not feel so alone. What better way than having the company named after Lynda's daughter, AlyBlue Media, publish these photos along with having Patti Rae Miliotis, a bereaved mother as our staff photographer? We're moms on a mission. Perfect!

With love,

Barbara J. Hopkinson

FOUNDER, A BUTTERFLY'S JOURNEY
CREATOR, FACES OF RESILIENCE
abutterflysjourney.org
facesofresilience.org

Your love gave me the wings to be an angel.

BRENT DELIBERO
*

BY LYNDA CHELDELIN FELL

PREFACE

One night in 2007, I had a vivid dream. I was the front passenger in a car and my teen daughter Aly was sitting behind the driver. Suddenly, the car missed a curve in the road and sailed into a lake. The driver and I escaped the sinking car, but Aly did not. I dove again and again into the murky water searching desperately for my daughter. But I failed to find her. She was gone. My beloved daughter was gone, leaving nothing but an open book floating on the water where she disappeared.

Two years later that horrible nightmare became reality when Aly died as a backseat passenger in a car accident on August 5, 2009. Returning home from a swim meet, the car carrying Aly was T-boned by a father coming home from work. My beautiful fifteen-year-old daughter took the brunt of the impact and died instantly. She was the only fatality.

Just when I thought life couldn't get any worse, it did. My dear sweet hubby buried his grief in the sand. He escaped into eighty-hour workweeks, more wine, more food, and less talking. His blood pressure shot up, his cholesterol went off the chart, and the perfect storm arrived on June 4, 2012. Suddenly, he began drooling and couldn't speak. My 46-year-old soulmate was having a major stroke.

My husband survived the stroke but couldn't speak, read, or write, and his right side was paralyzed. Still reeling from the loss of our daughter, I found myself again thrust into a fog of grief so thick I couldn't see through the storm. Adrenaline and autopilot resumed their familiar place at the helm.

As I fought to restore balance to my world, I discovered that helping others was a powerful way to heal my own heart. Grief Diaries was born and built on this belief. By writing books narrating our journeys, our written words become a portable support group for others. When we swap stories, we feel less alone. It's comforting to know someone else understands.

Which brings us to this photobook. I first met Barbara Hopkinson while filming a segment of Open to Hope TV in Manhattan. Admiring one another's projects, we became immediate friends and soon discovered a mutual passion for modernizing grief using likeminded philosophies. Both driven to help the bereaved find comfort and understanding through different platforms of expression, we collaborated and created this book as one of those platforms.

They say one picture is worth a thousand words because it captures complex emotions in a single shot. Barbara's concept of portraying an experience as old as mankind and turning it into art is brilliant. Pairing visual art with self-expression offers not only a powerful healing tool for the bereaved, it also reveals a stunning gallery showcasing both the commonality and individuality of our journeys.

It's our hope that this influential collection tells a story better than written words, and serves as an agent of change by stimulating conversations about a universal experience through love, loss, heartbreak, resilience and—ultimately—hope.

Warm regards,

Lynda Cheldelin Fell

CREATOR, GRIEF DIARIES
www.lyndafell.com

GALLERY

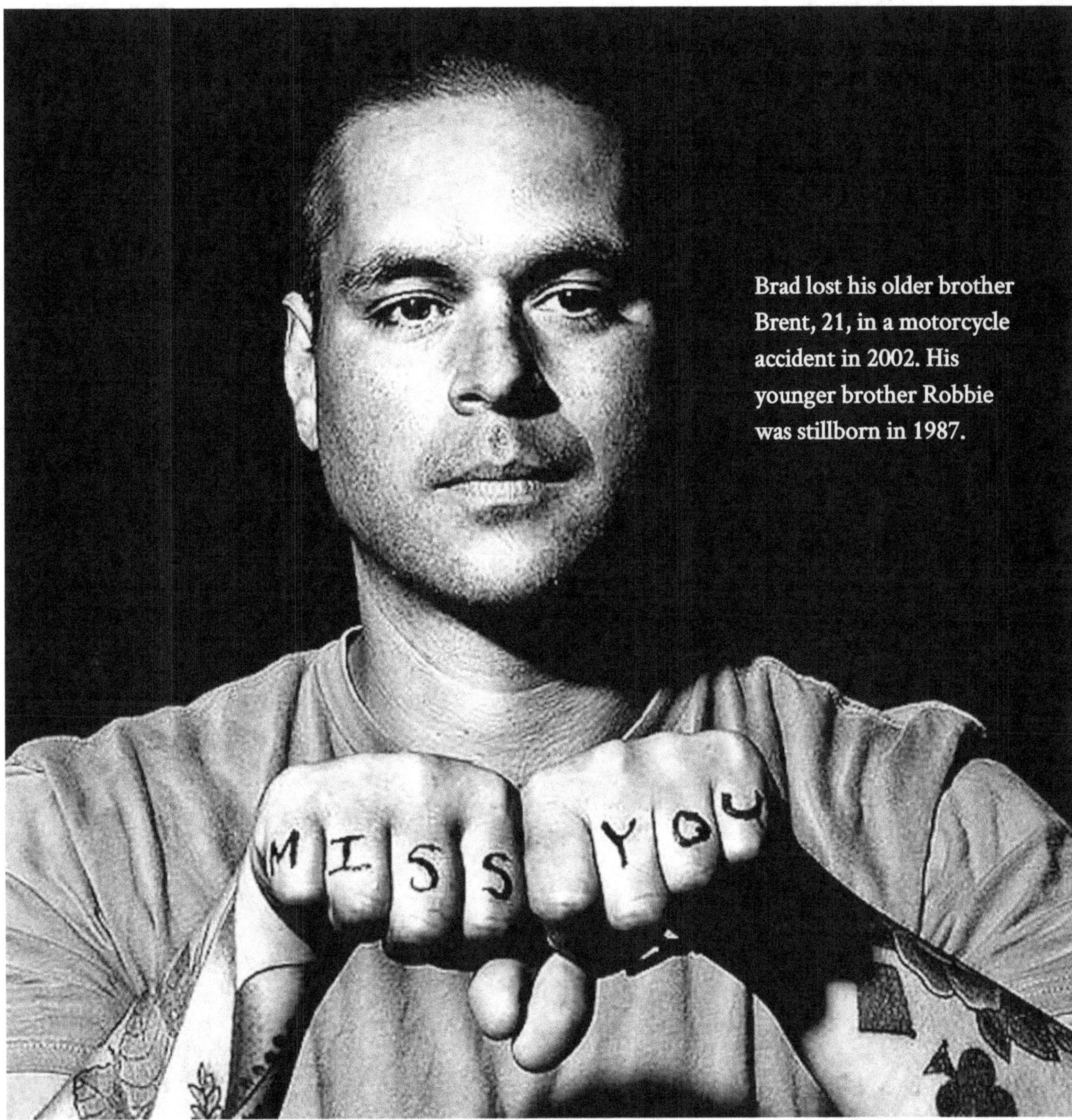

Brad lost his older brother Brent, 21, in a motorcycle accident in 2002. His younger brother Robbie was stillborn in 1987.

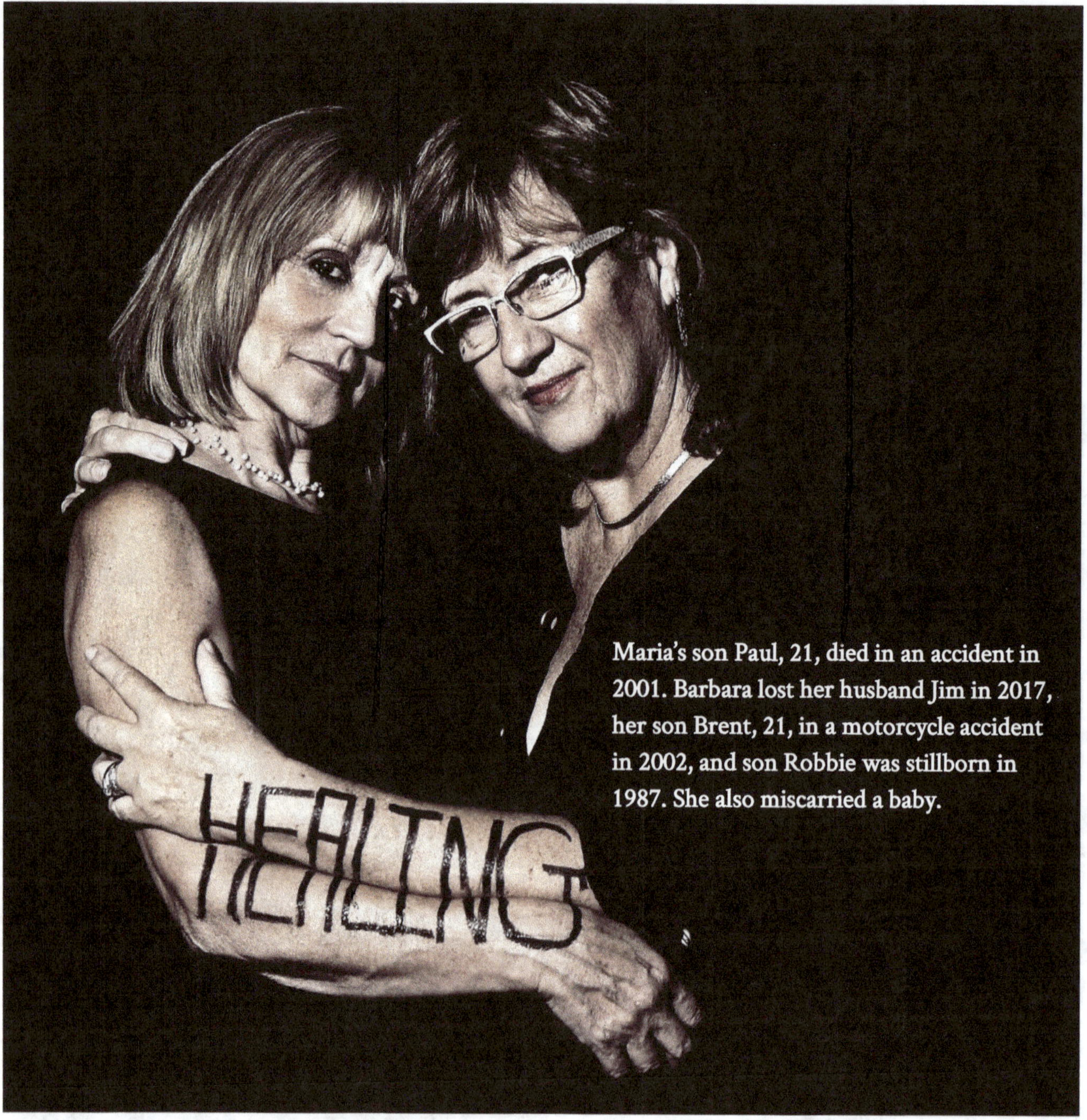

Maria's son Paul, 21, died in an accident in 2001. Barbara lost her husband Jim in 2017, her son Brent, 21, in a motorcycle accident in 2002, and son Robbie was stillborn in 1987. She also miscarried a baby.

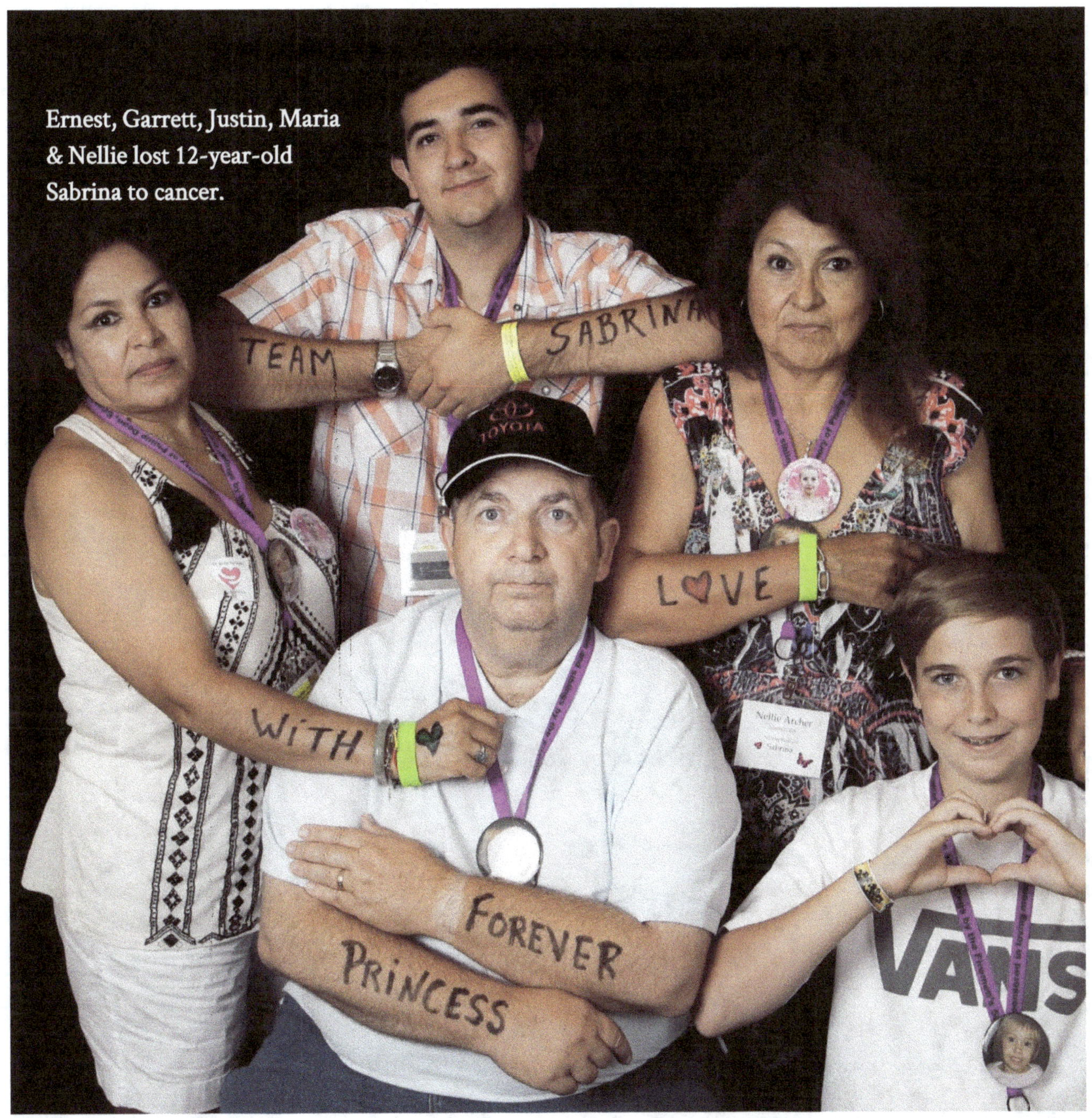

Ernest, Garrett, Justin, Maria & Nellie lost 12-year-old Sabrina to cancer.

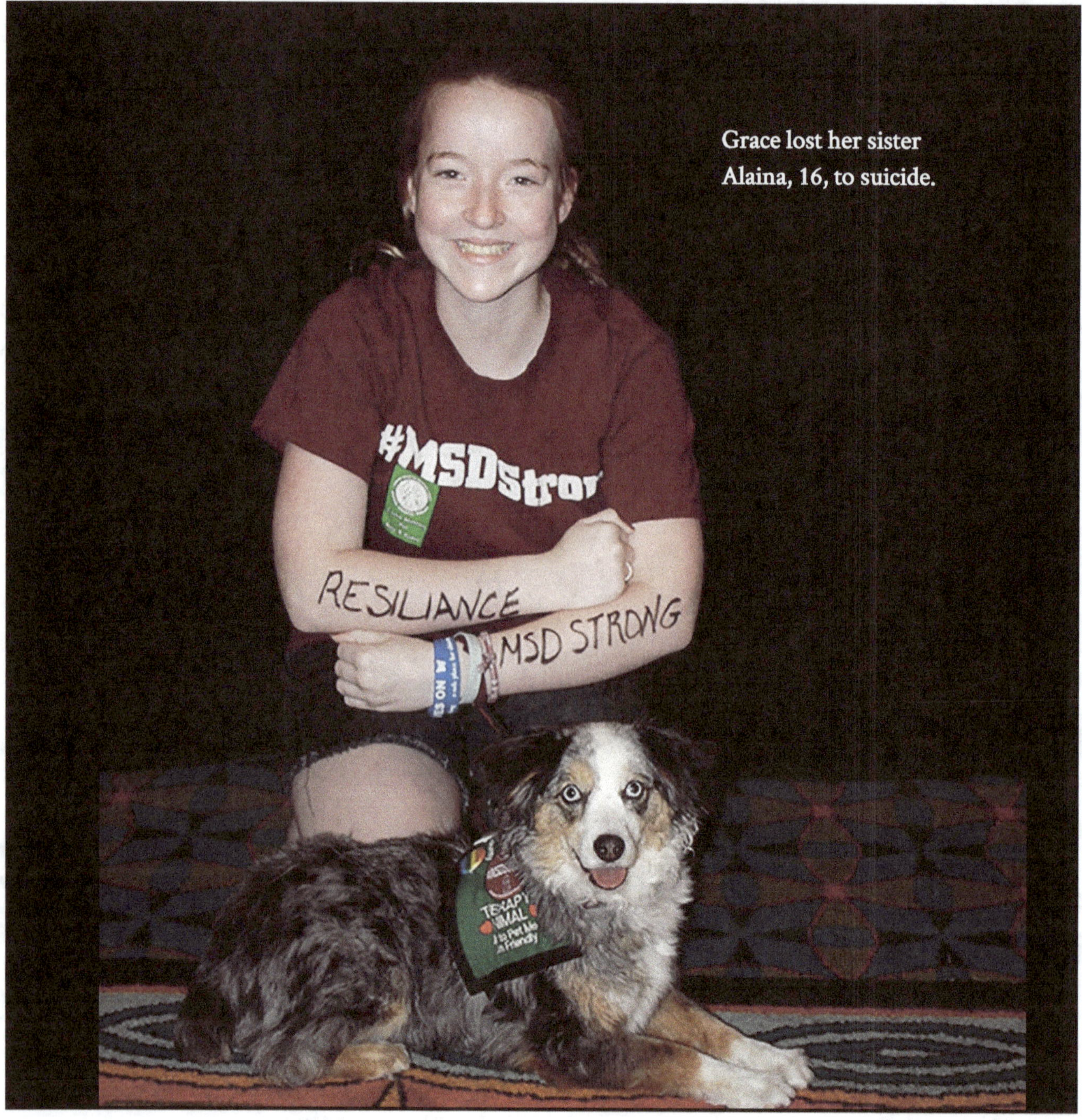

Grace lost her sister Alaina, 16, to suicide.

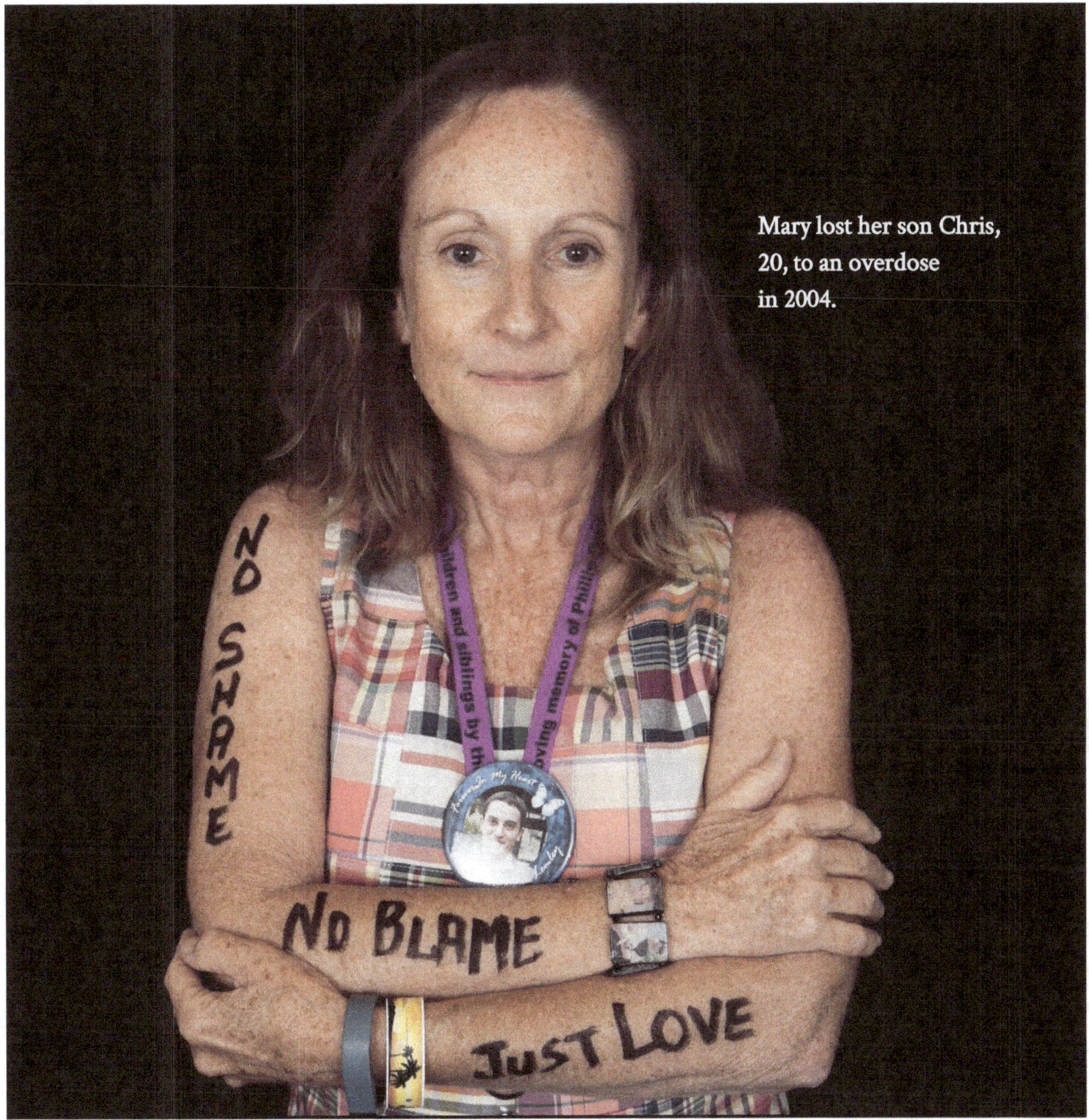

Mary lost her son Chris,
20, to an overdose
in 2004.

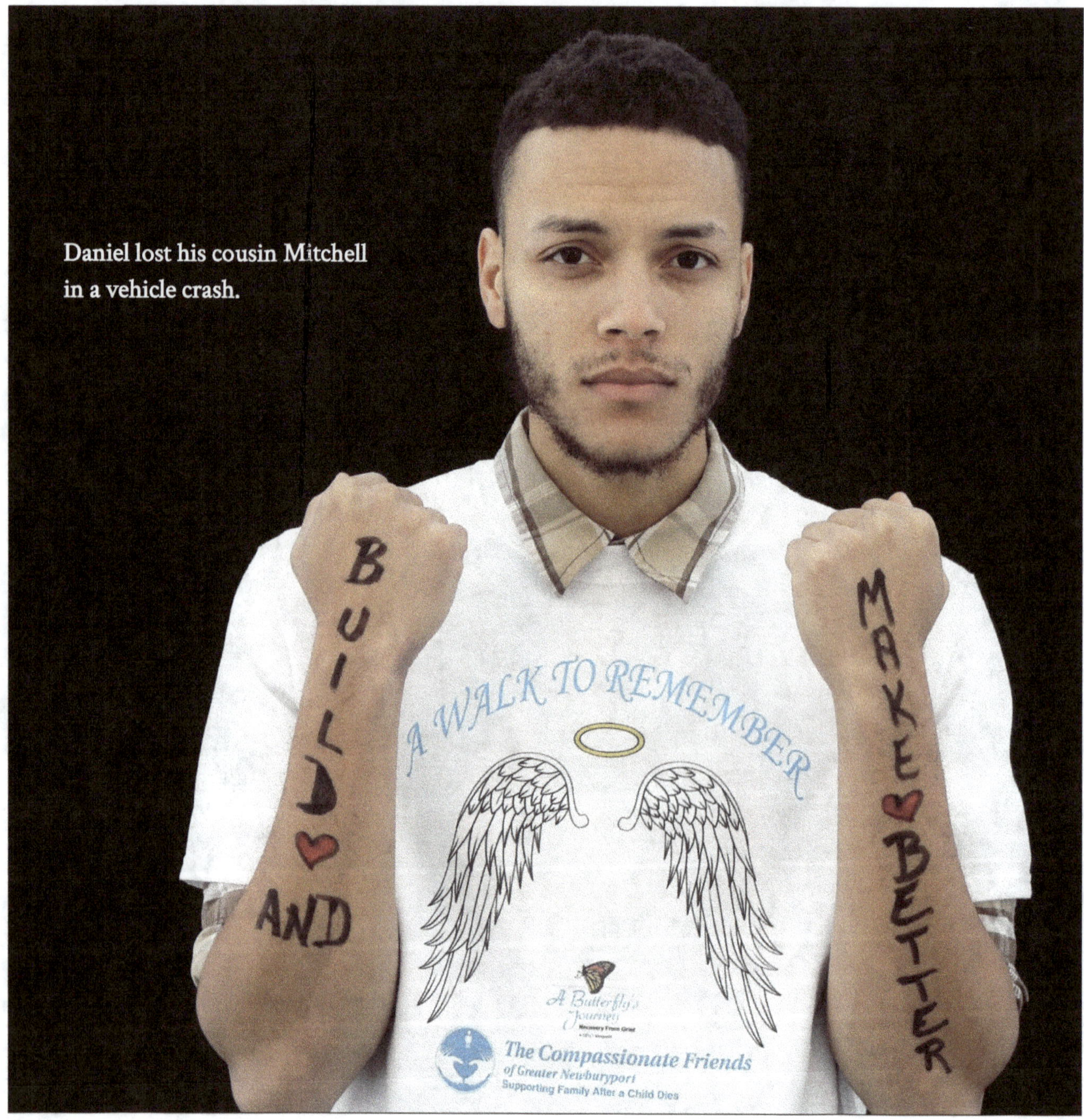

Daniel lost his cousin Mitchell
in a vehicle crash.

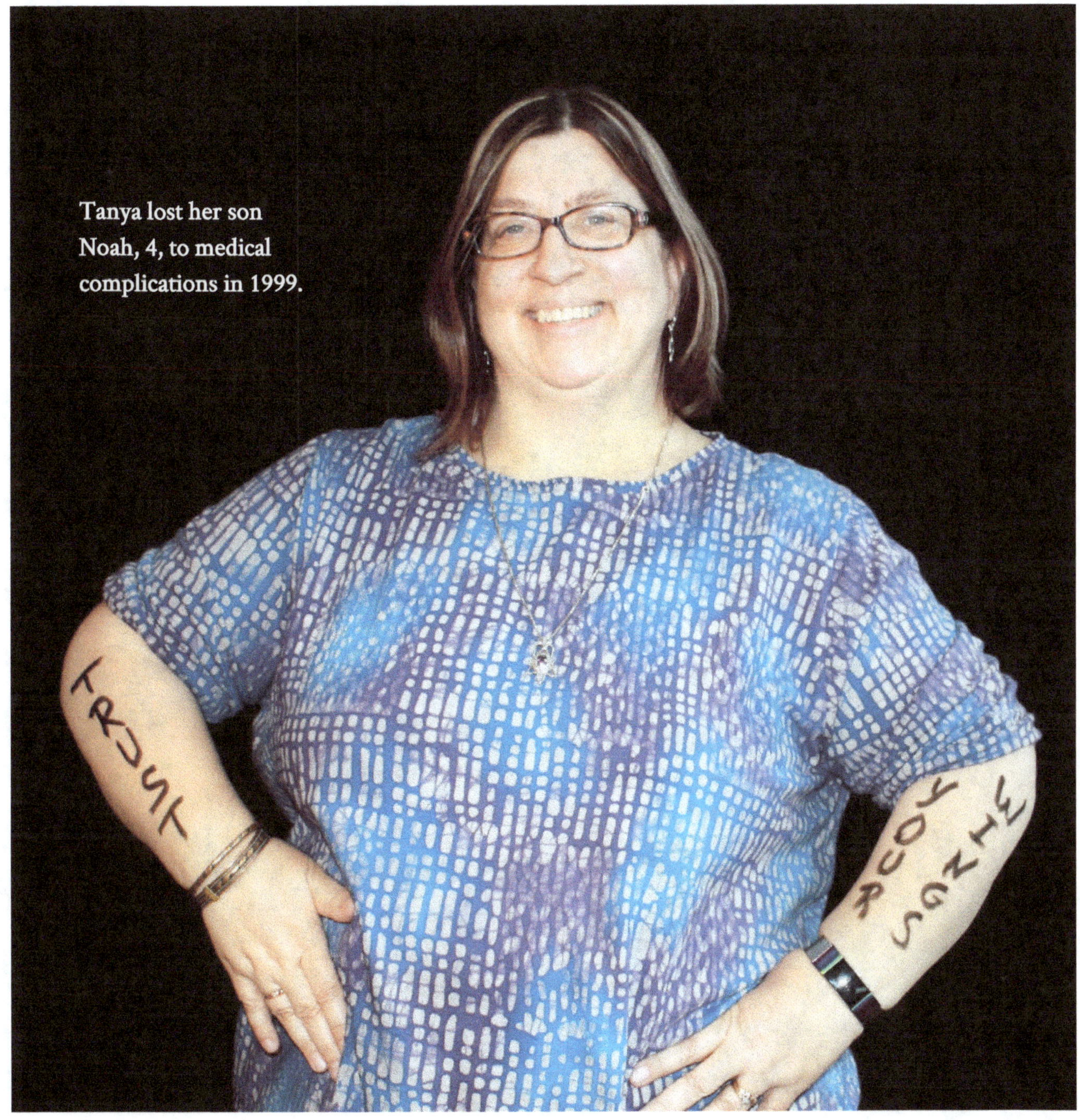

Tanya lost her son
Noah, 4, to medical
complications in 1999.

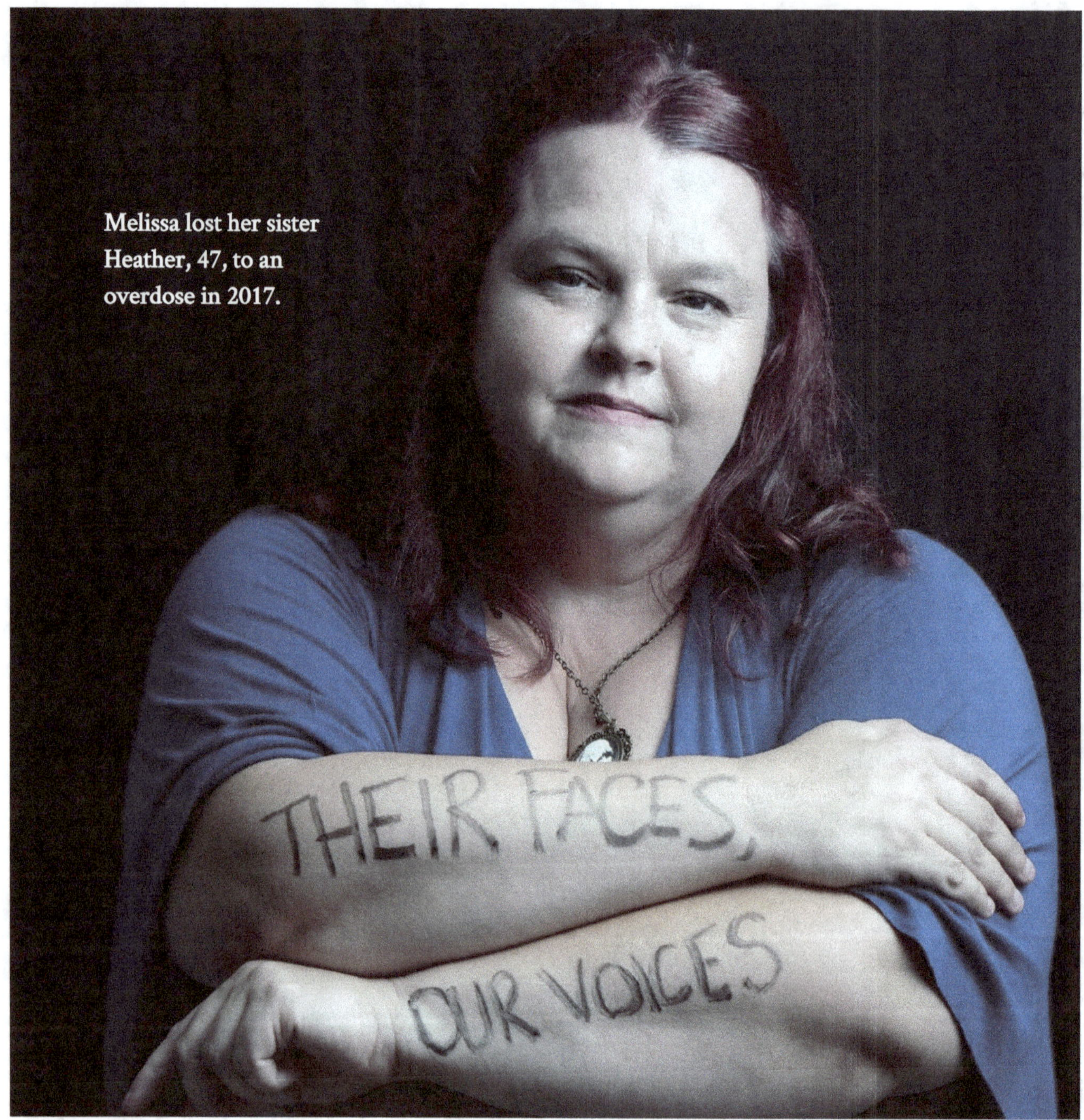

Melissa lost her sister Heather, 47, to an overdose in 2017.

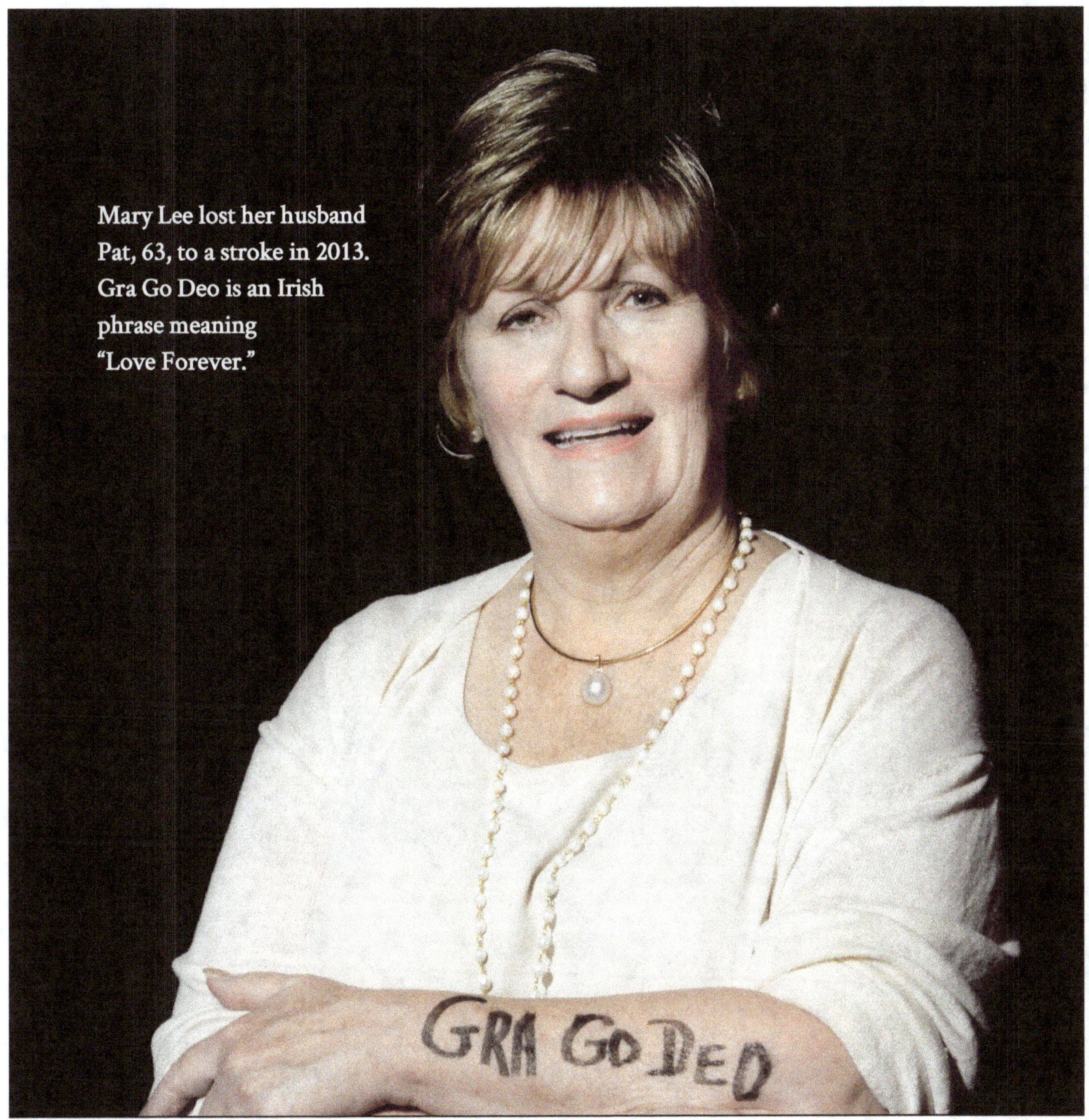

Mary Lee lost her husband Pat, 63, to a stroke in 2013. Gra Go Deo is an Irish phrase meaning "Love Forever."

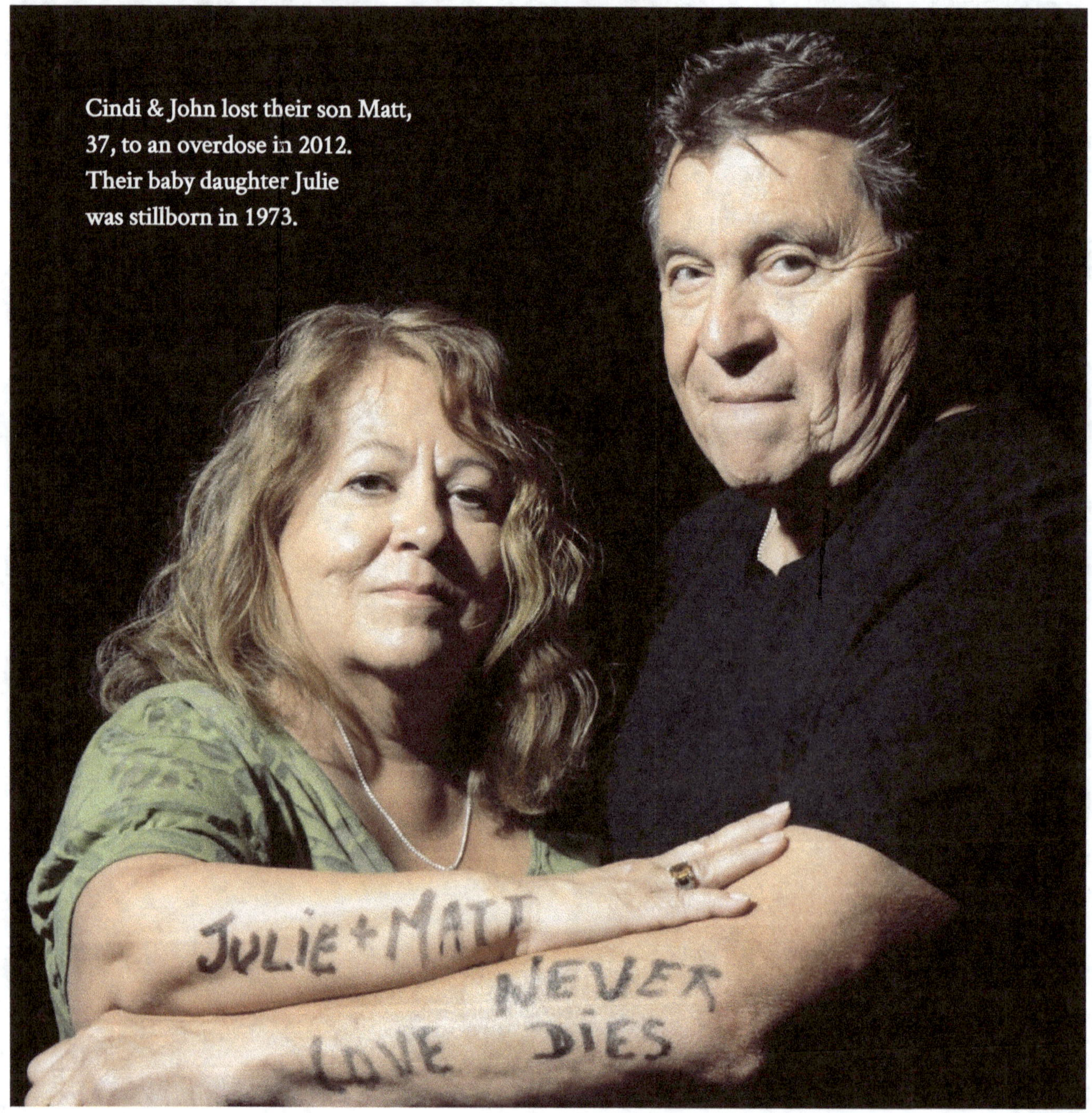

Cindi & John lost their son Matt,
37, to an overdose in 2012.
Their baby daughter Julie
was stillborn in 1973.

JULIE+MATT
LOVE NEVER DIES

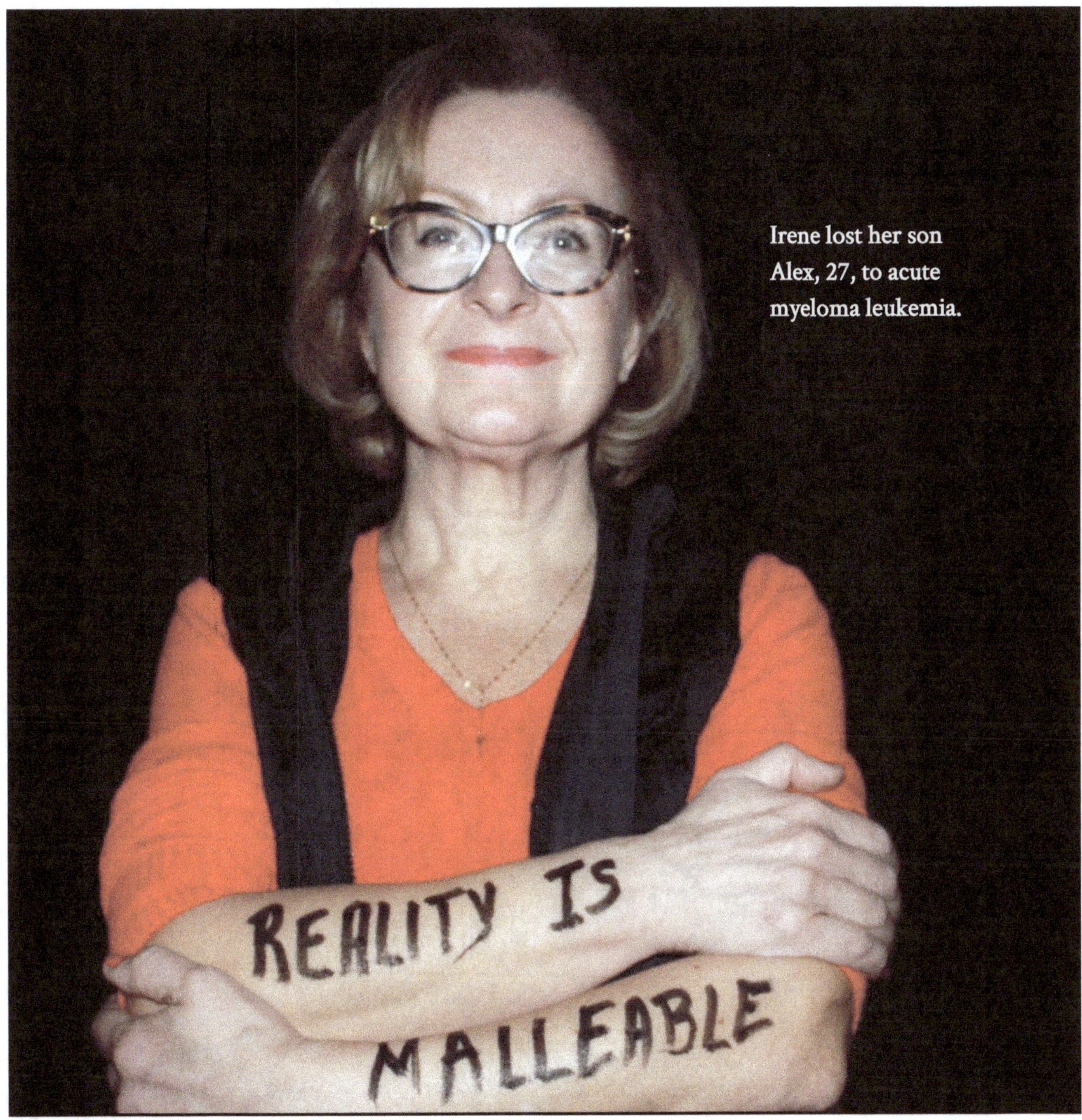

Irene lost her son
Alex, 27, to acute
myeloma leukemia.

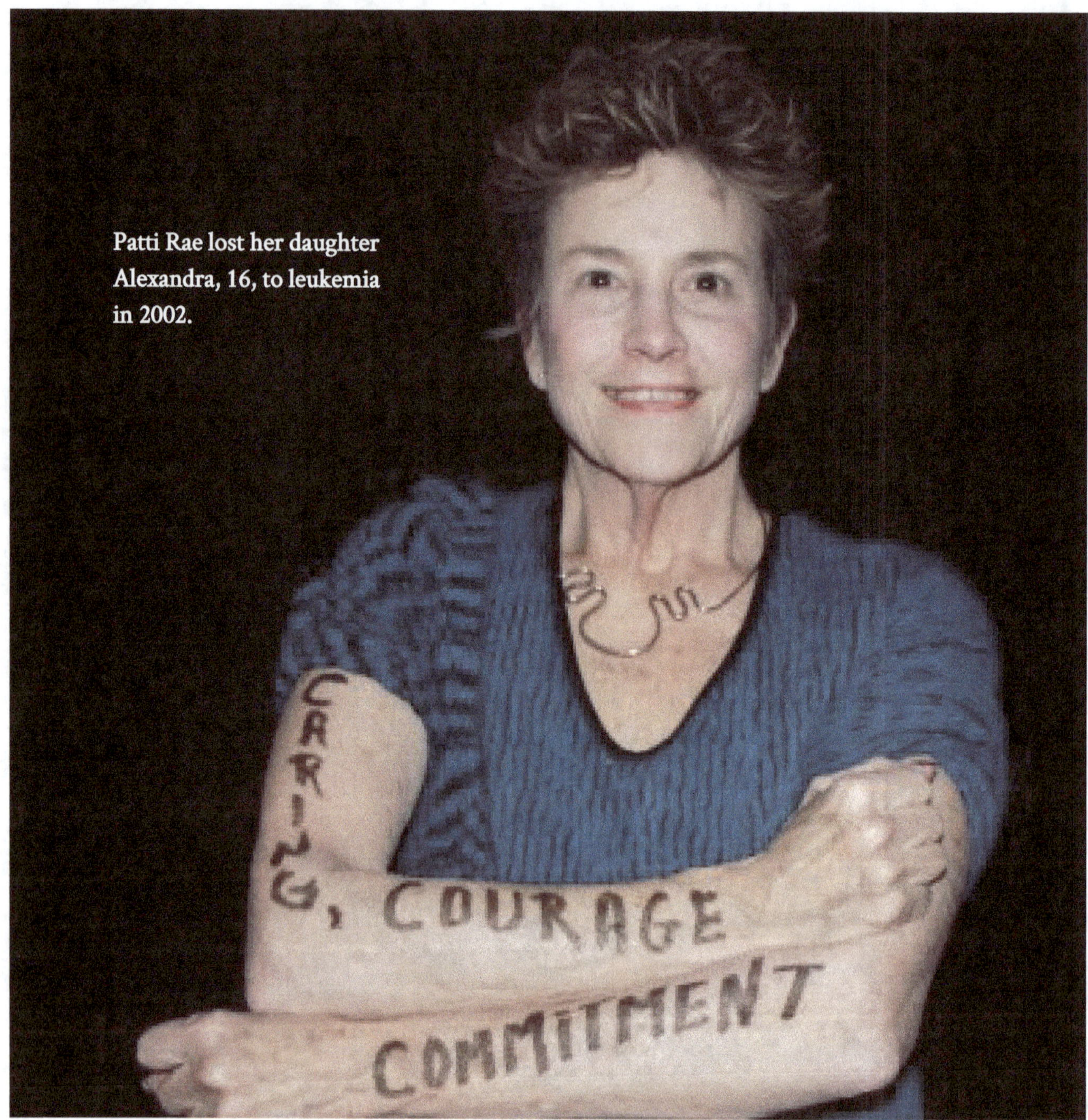

Patti Rae lost her daughter Alexandra, 16, to leukemia in 2002.

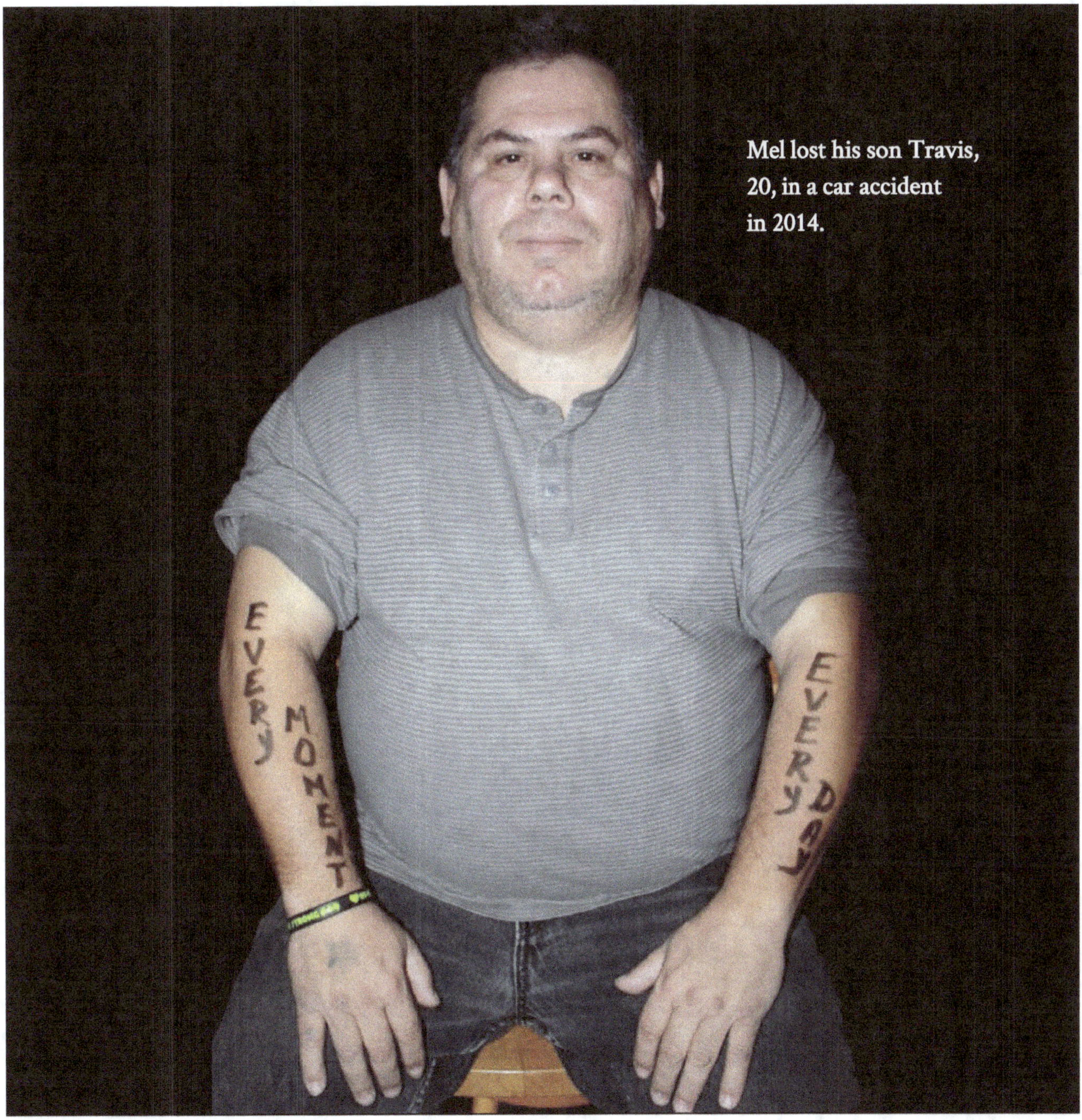

Mel lost his son Travis,
20, in a car accident
in 2014.
EVERY MOMENT
EVERY DAY

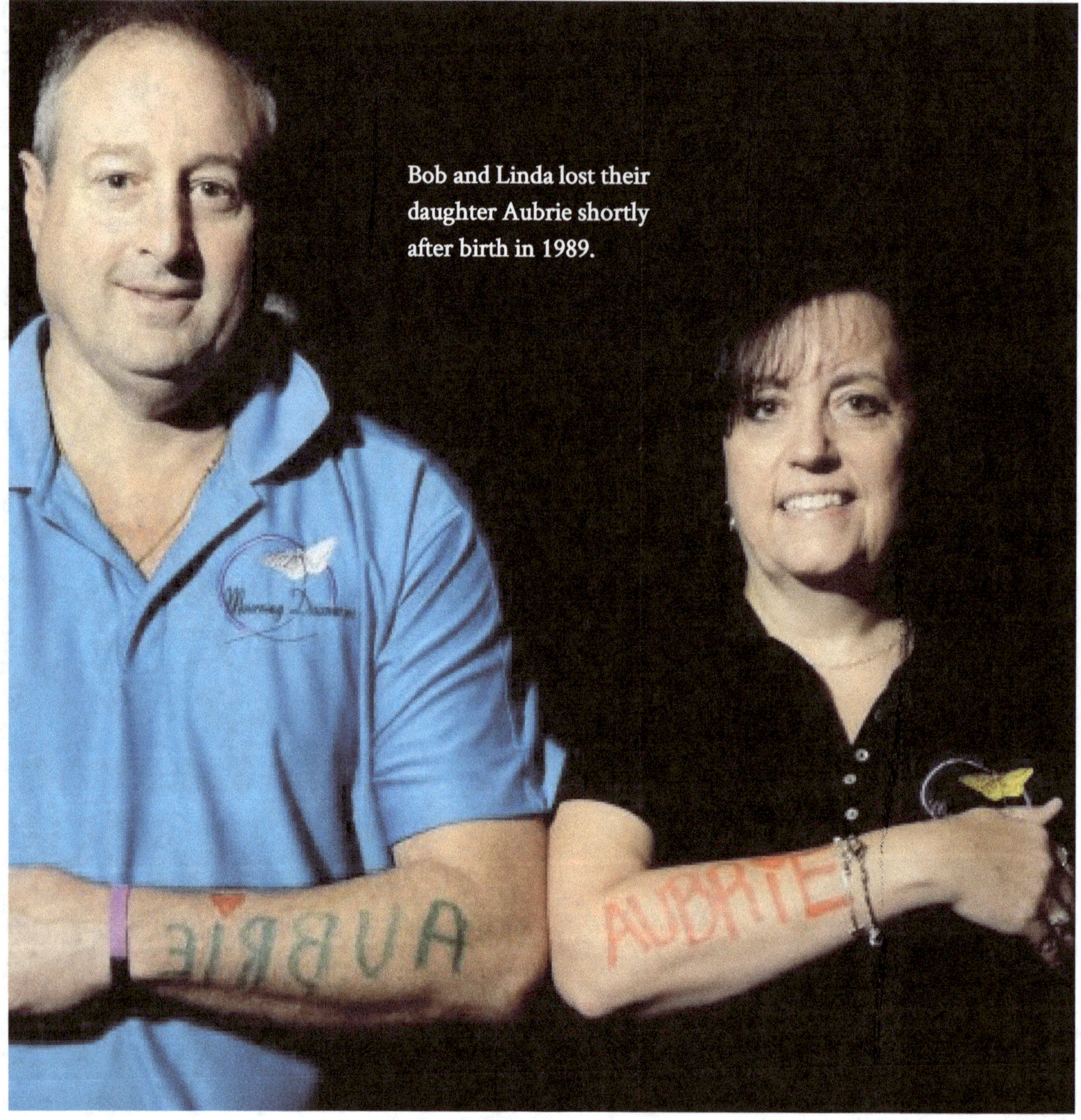

Bob and Linda lost their daughter Aubrie shortly after birth in 1989.

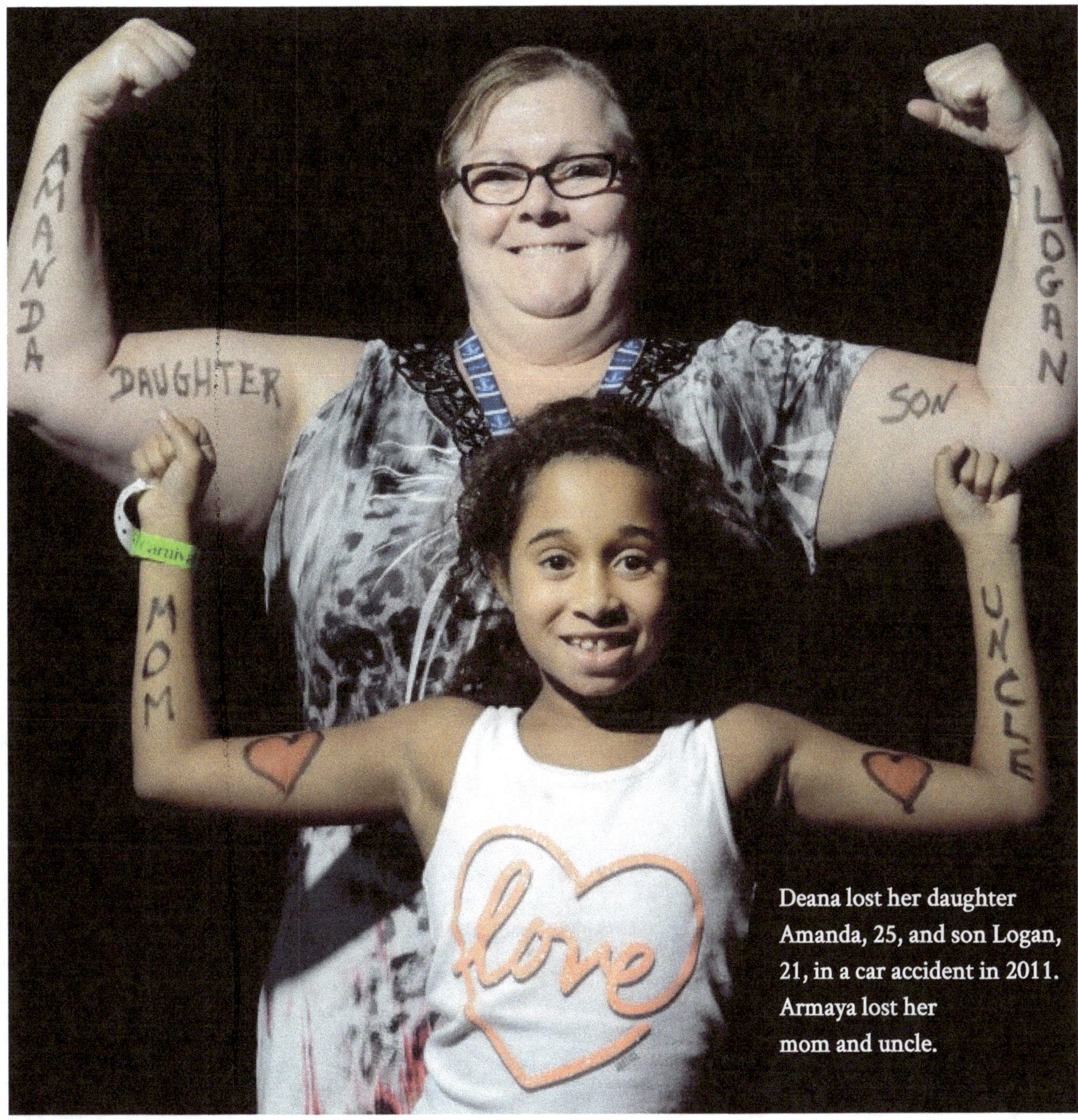

Deana lost her daughter Amanda, 25, and son Logan, 21, in a car accident in 2011. Armaya lost her mom and uncle.

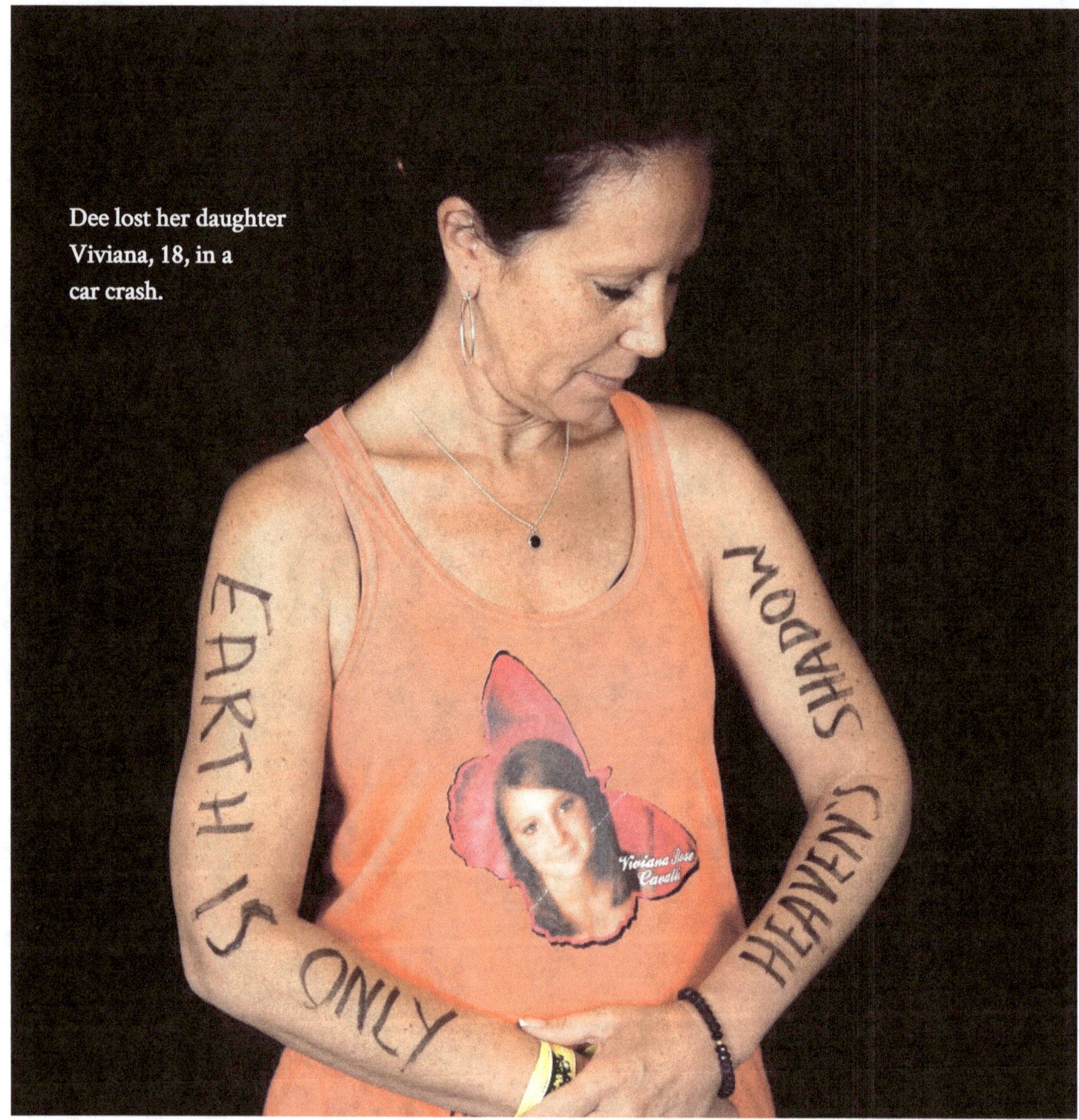

Dee lost her daughter Viviana, 18, in a car crash.

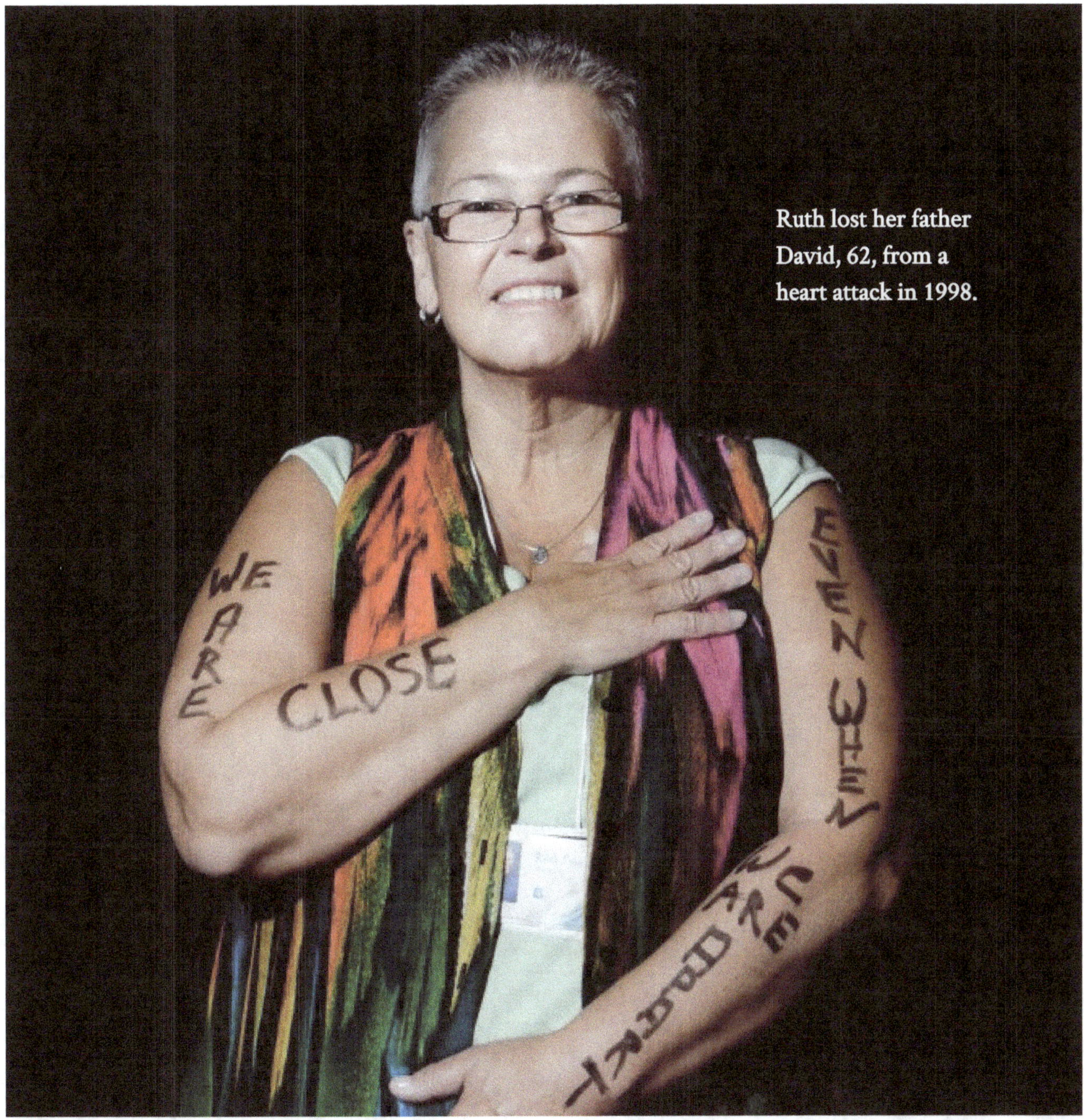

Ruth lost her father David, 62, from a heart attack in 1998.

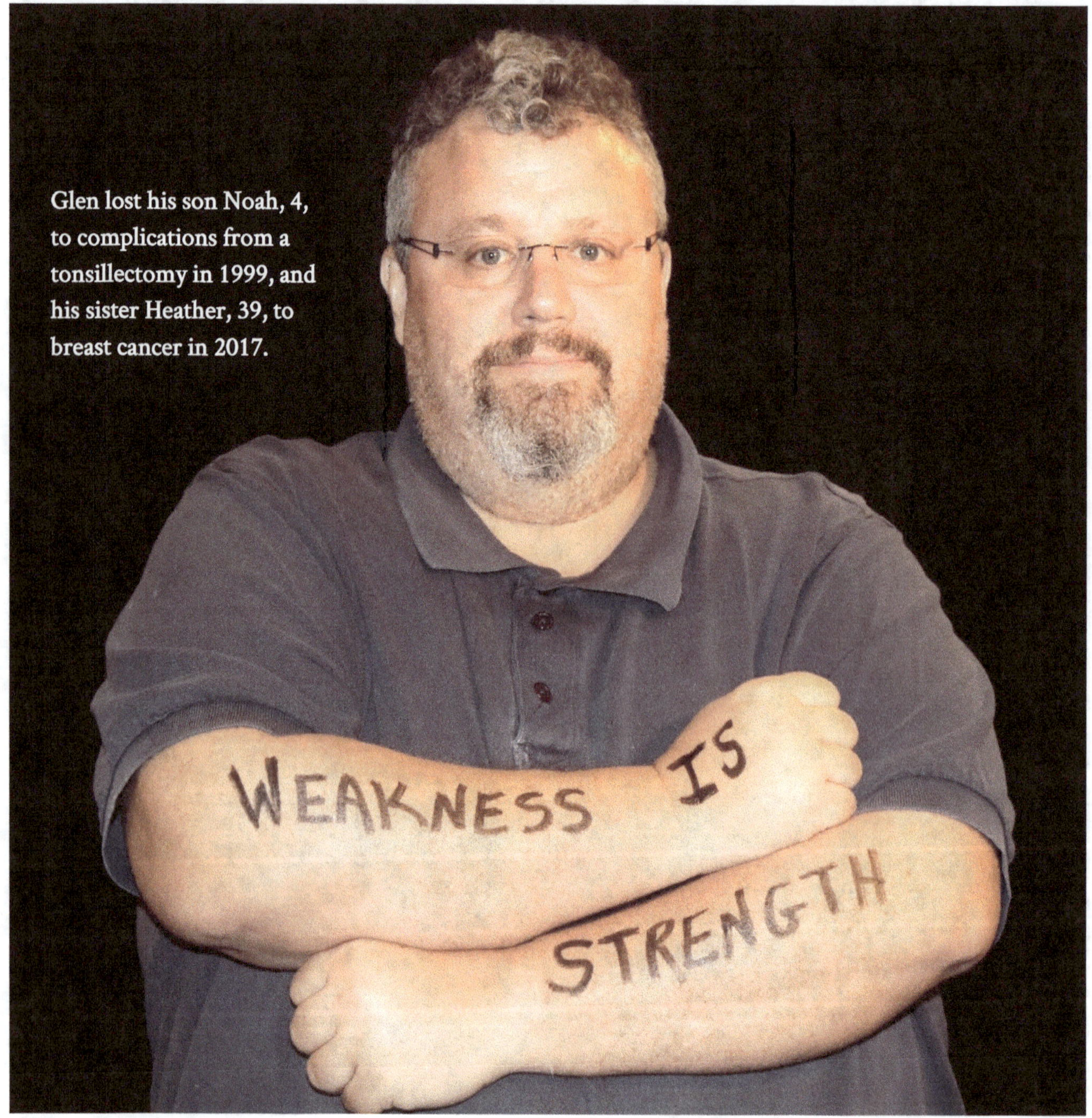

Glen lost his son Noah, 4, to complications from a tonsillectomy in 1999, and his sister Heather, 39, to breast cancer in 2017.

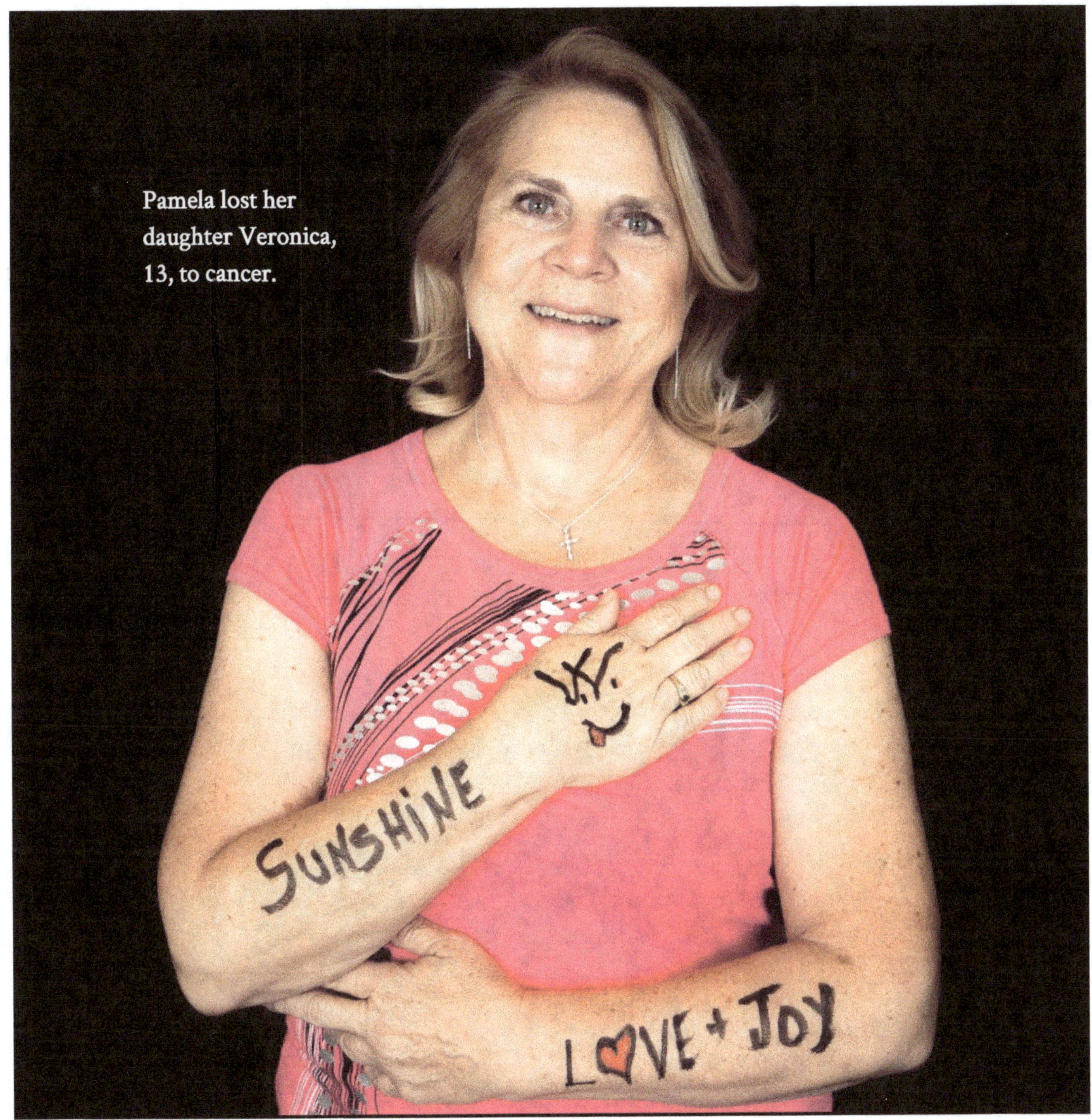

Pamela lost her daughter Veronica, 13, to cancer.

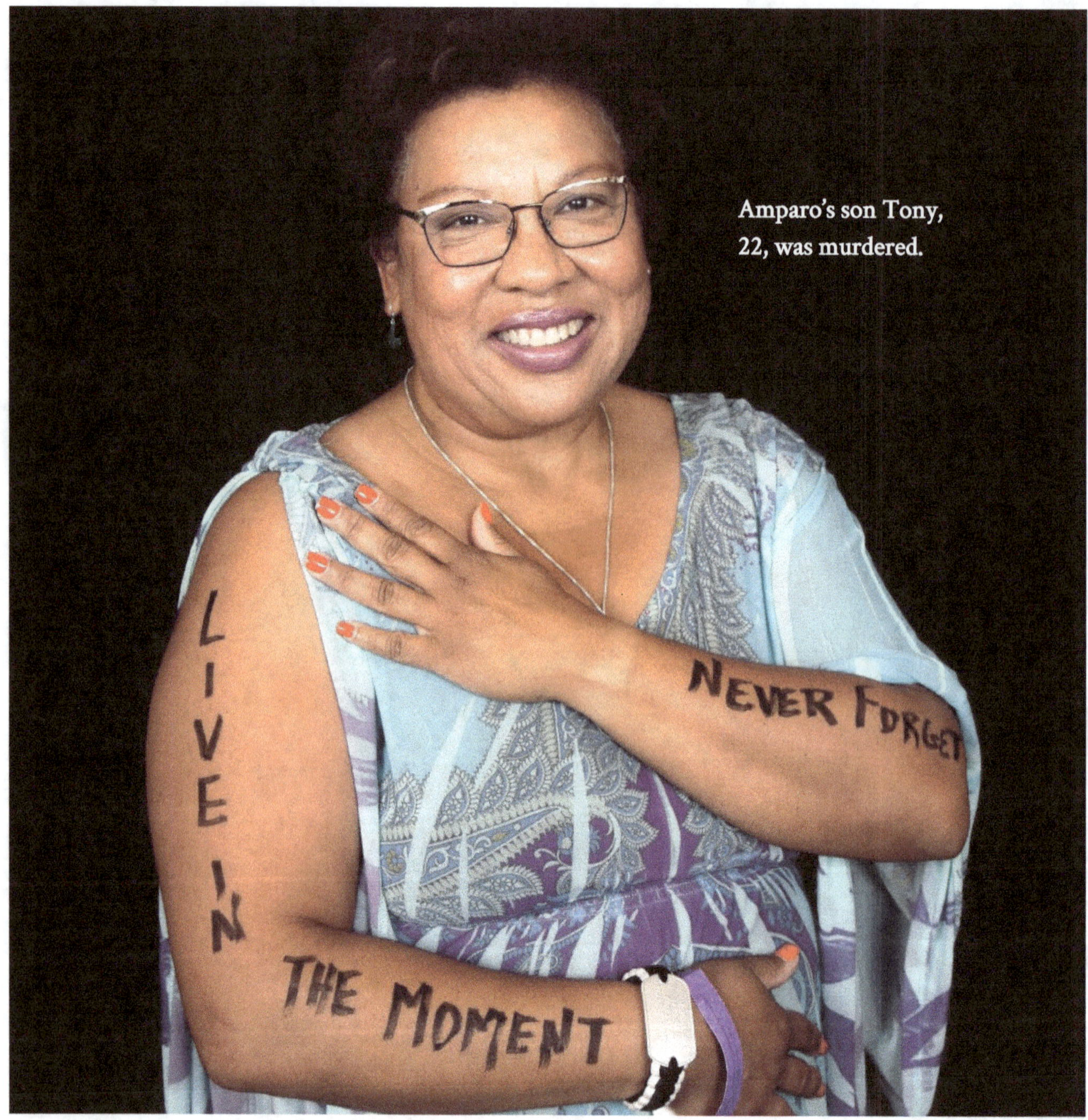

Amparo's son Tony, 22, was murdered.

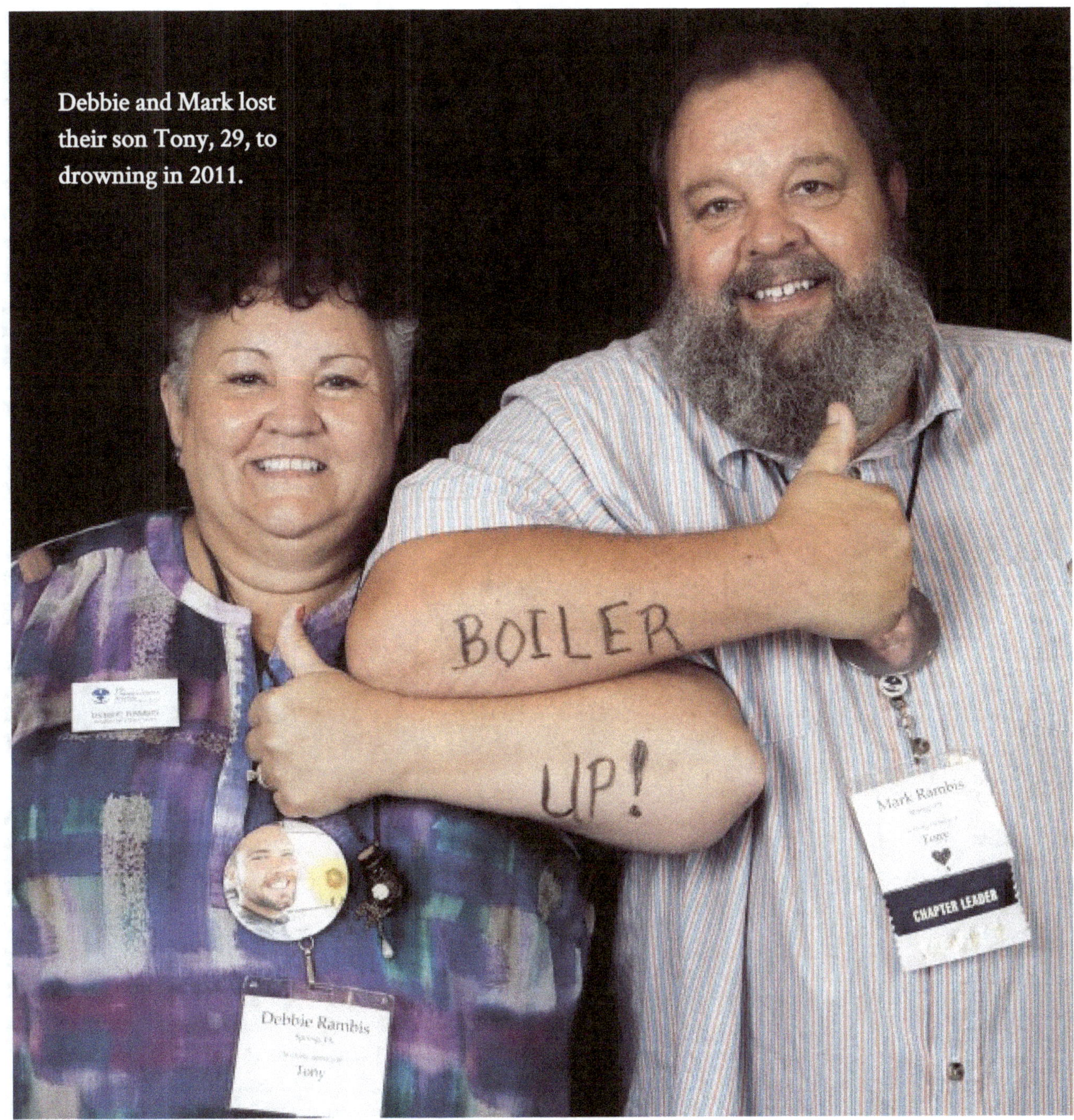

Debbie and Mark lost their son Tony, 29, to drowning in 2011.

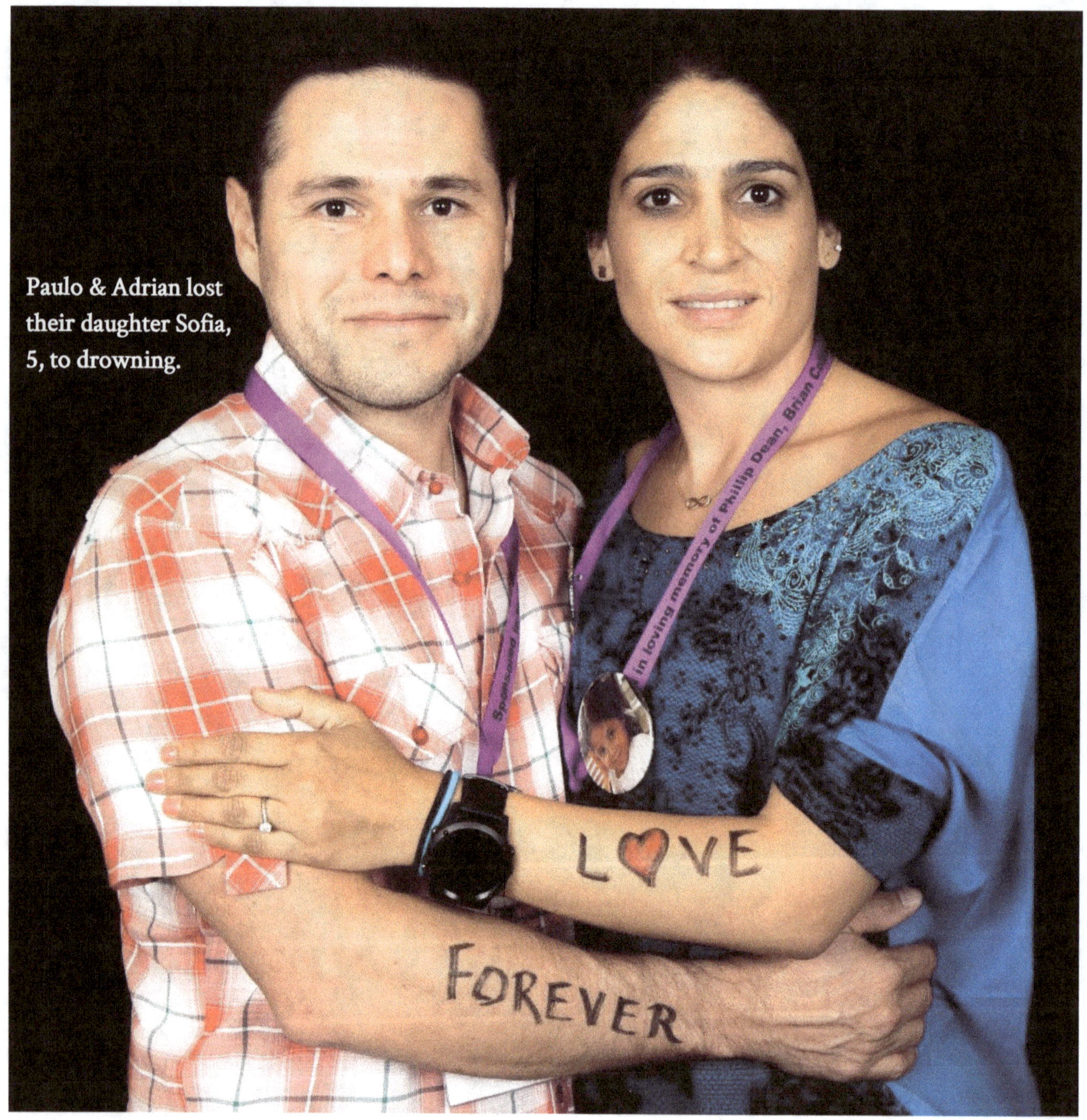

Paulo & Adrian lost their daughter Sofia, 5, to drowning.

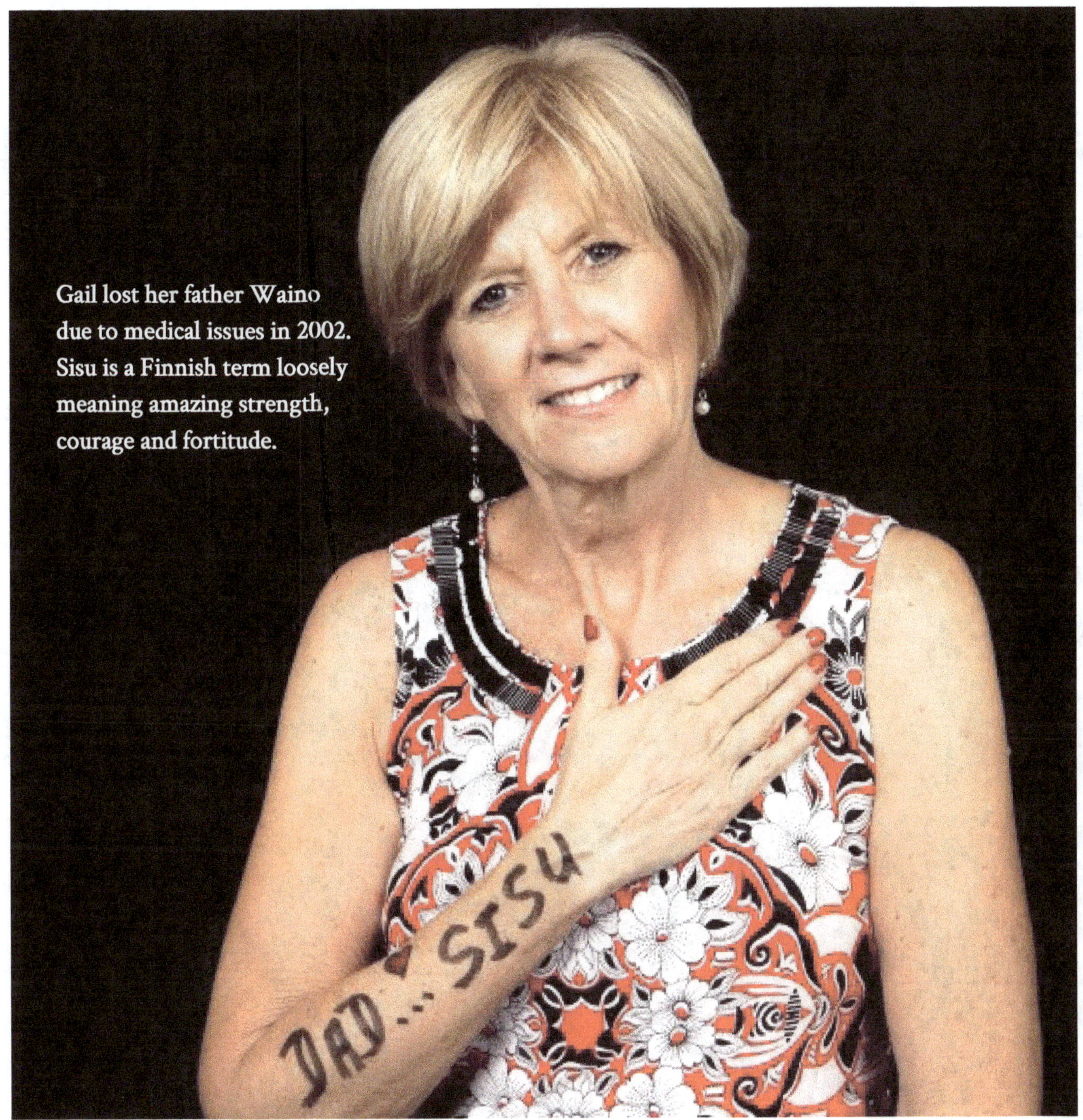

Gail lost her father Waino due to medical issues in 2002. Sisu is a Finnish term loosely meaning amazing strength, courage and fortitude.

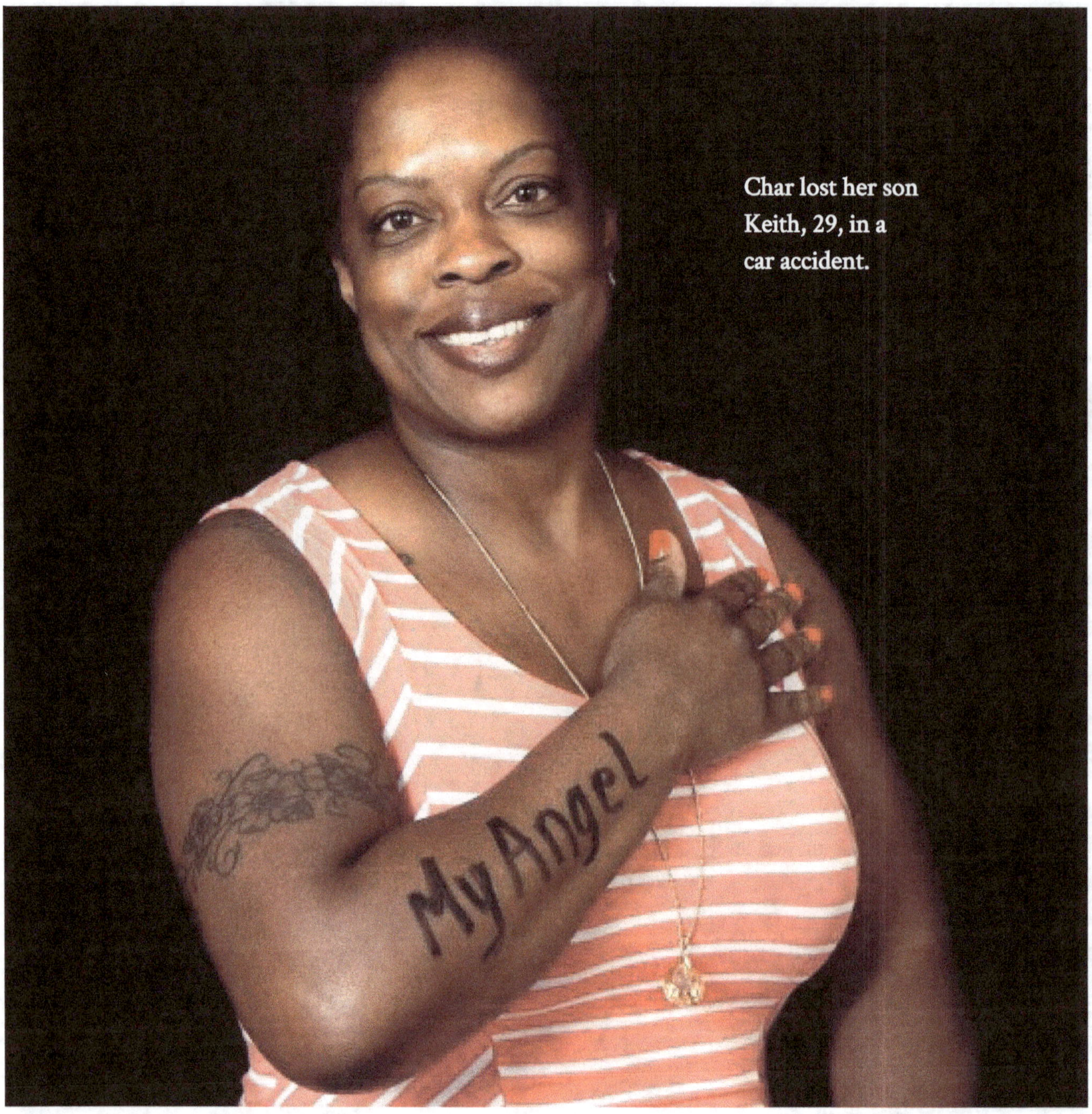

Char lost her son Keith, 29, in a car accident.

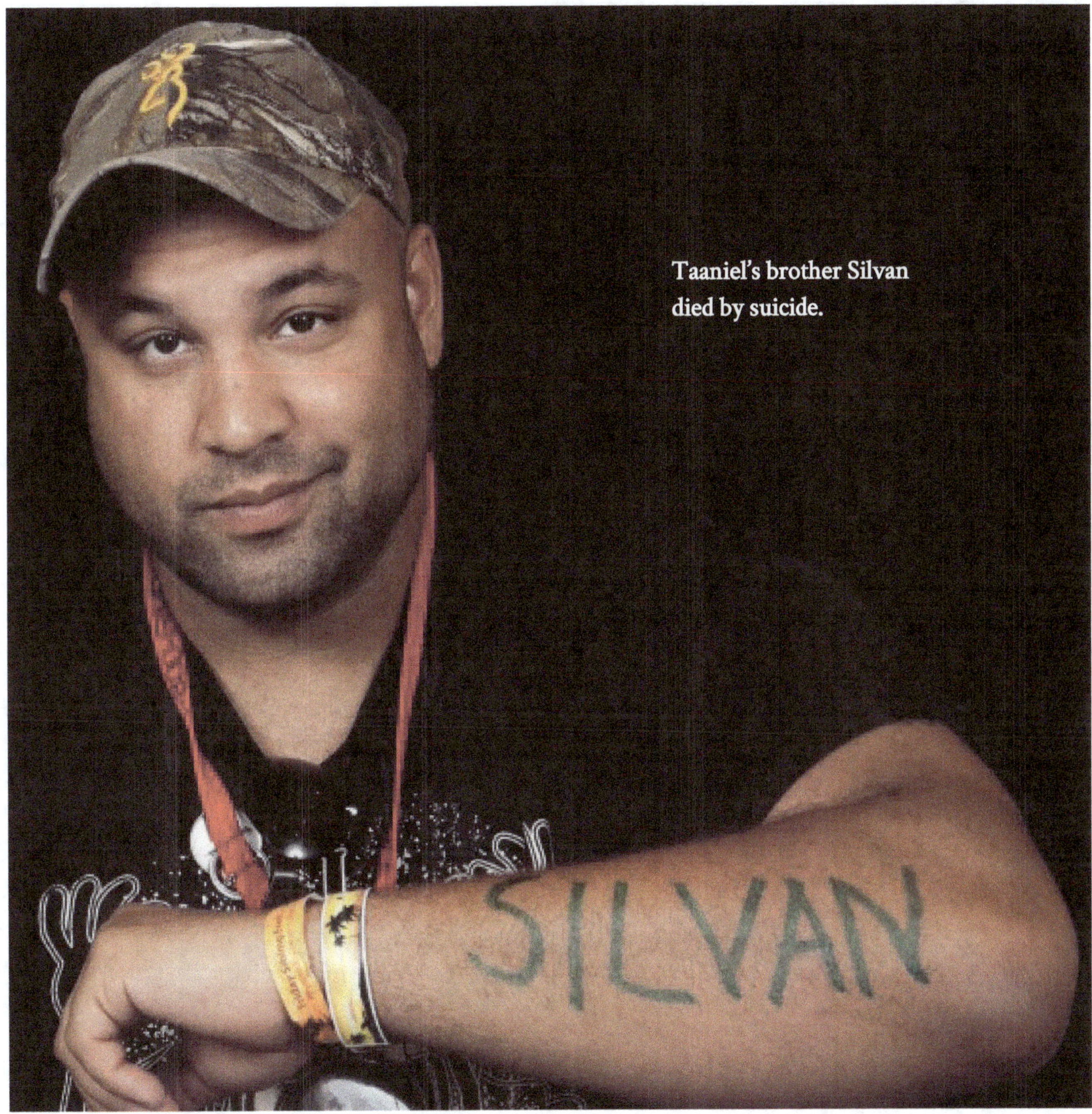
Taaniel's brother Silvan
died by suicide.

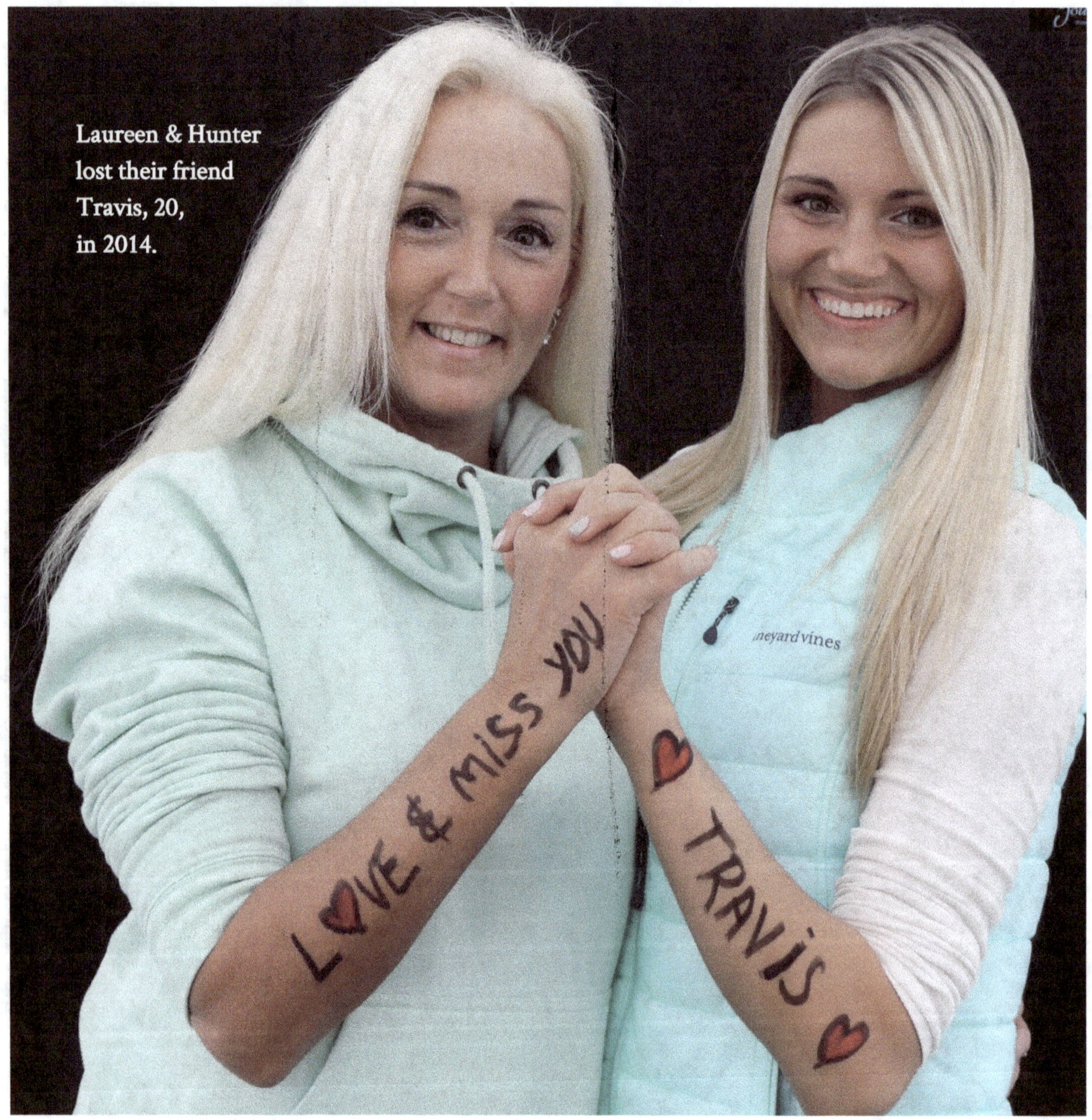
Laureen & Hunter
lost their friend
Travis, 20,
in 2014.
LOVE & miss YOU
TRAVIS

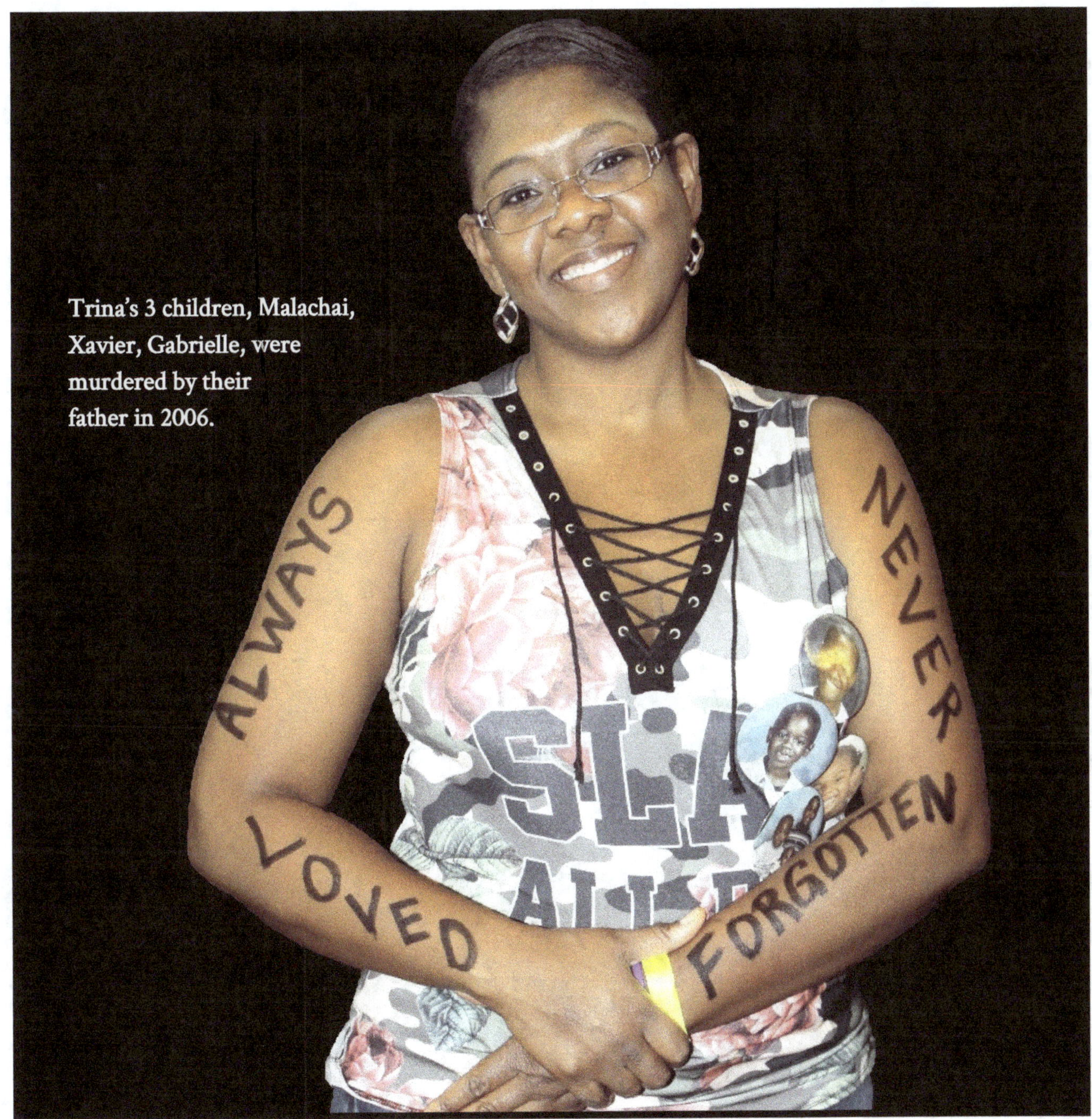

Trina's 3 children, Malachai, Xavier, Gabrielle, were murdered by their father in 2006.

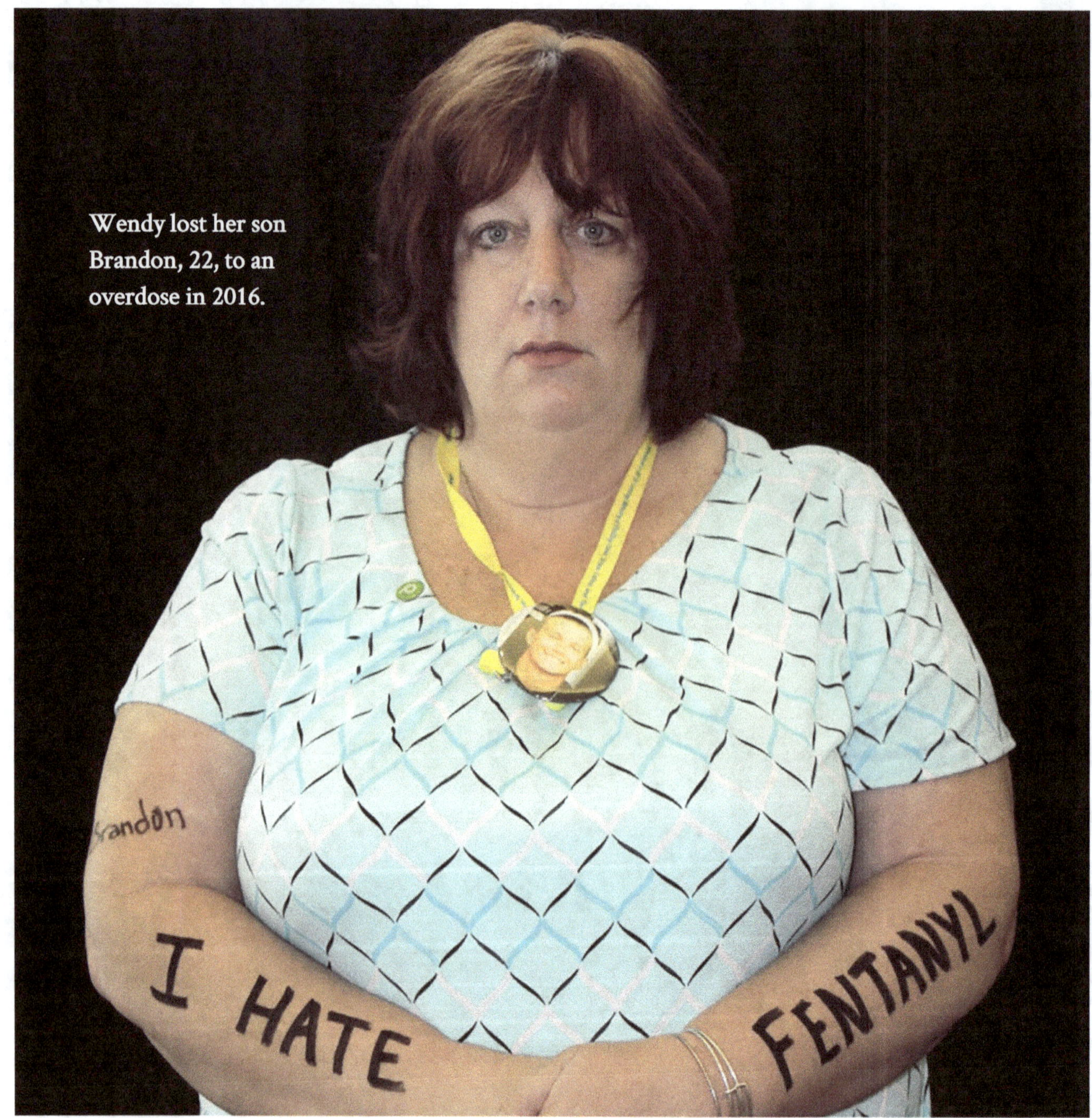

Wendy lost her son
Brandon, 22, to an
overdose in 2016.

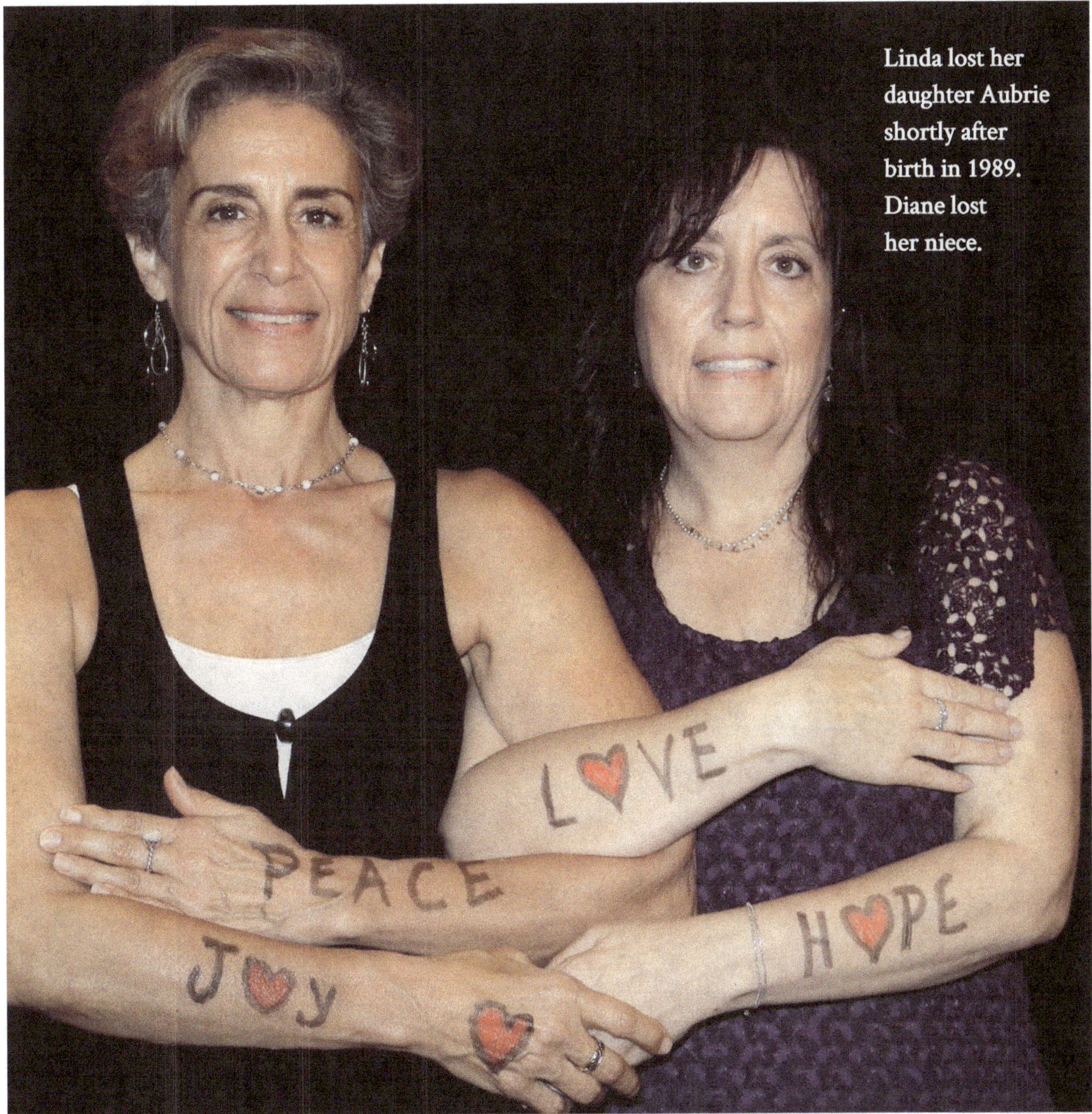

Linda lost her daughter Aubrie shortly after birth in 1989. Diane lost her niece.

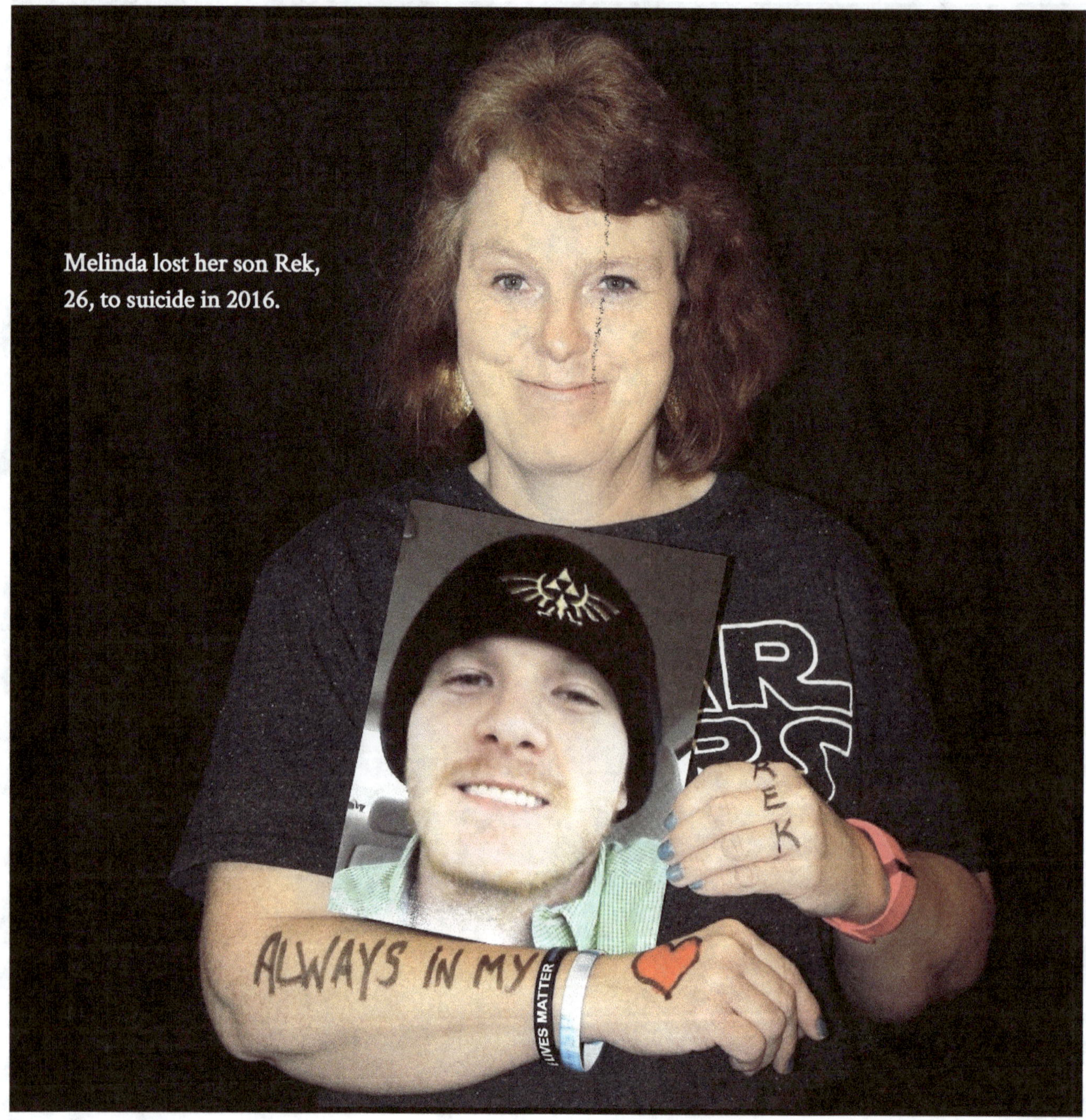

Melinda lost her son Rek, 26, to suicide in 2016.

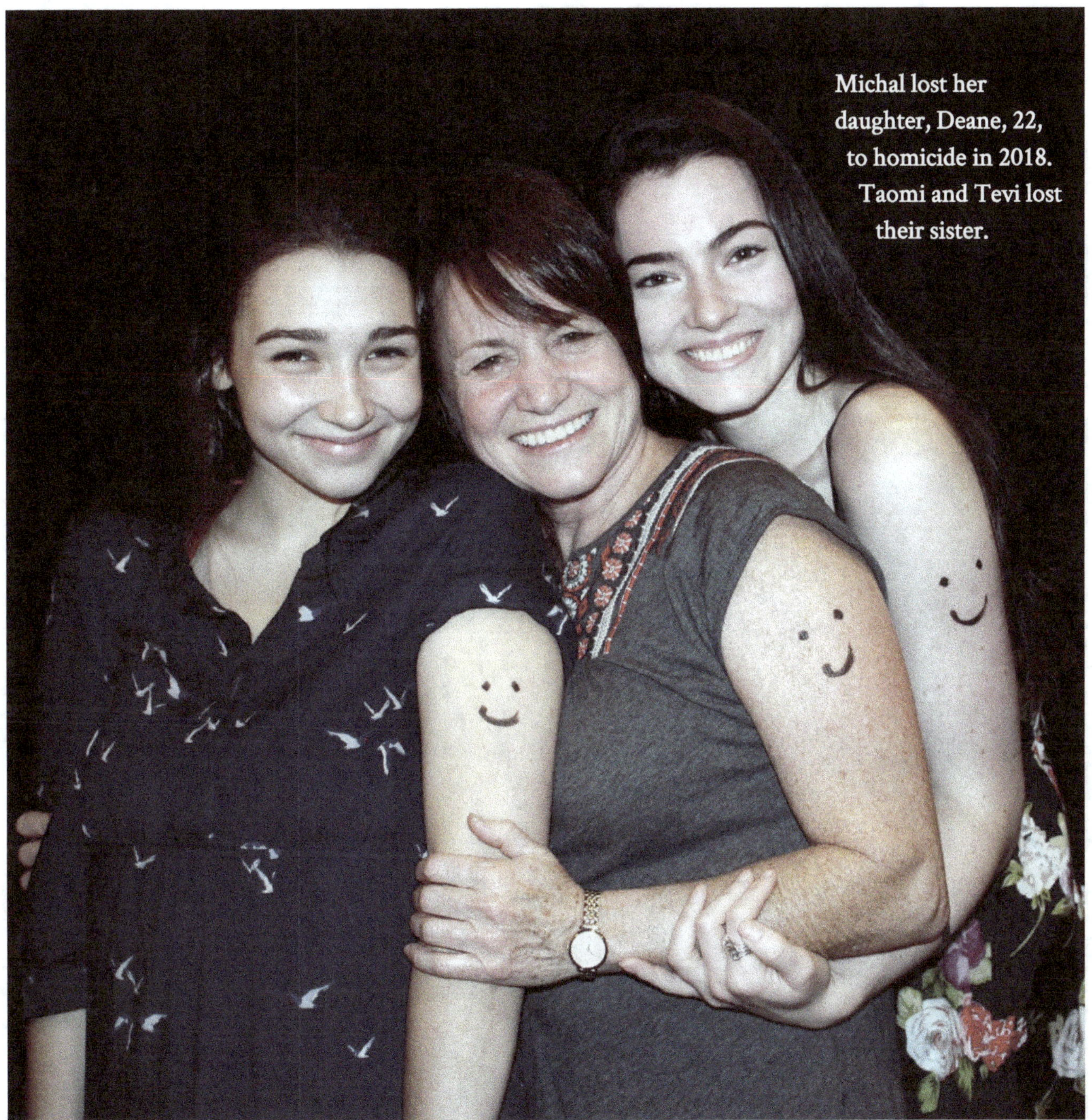

Michal lost her daughter, Deane, 22, to homicide in 2018. Taomi and Tevi lost their sister.

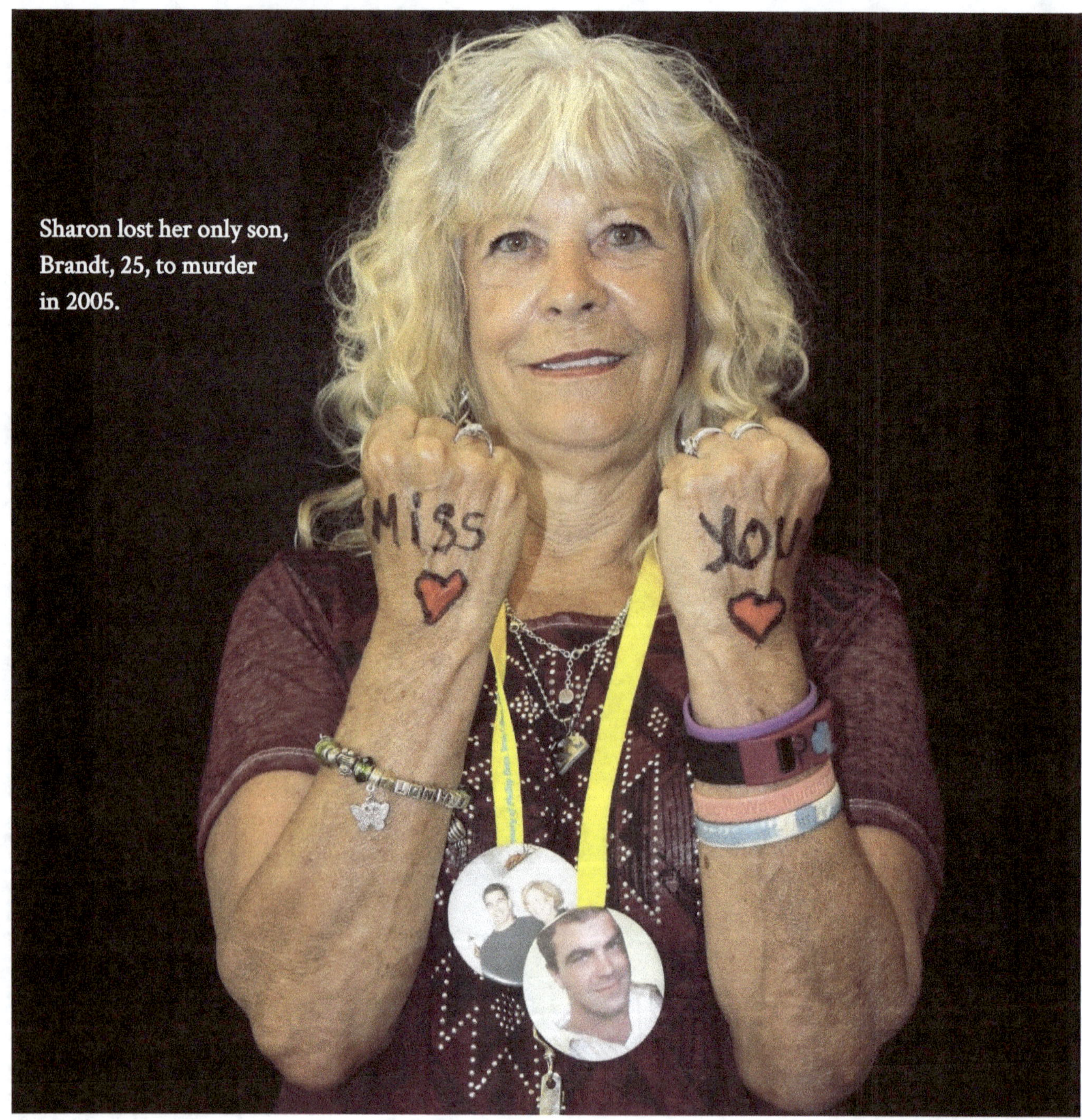

Sharon lost her only son, Brandt, 25, to murder in 2005.

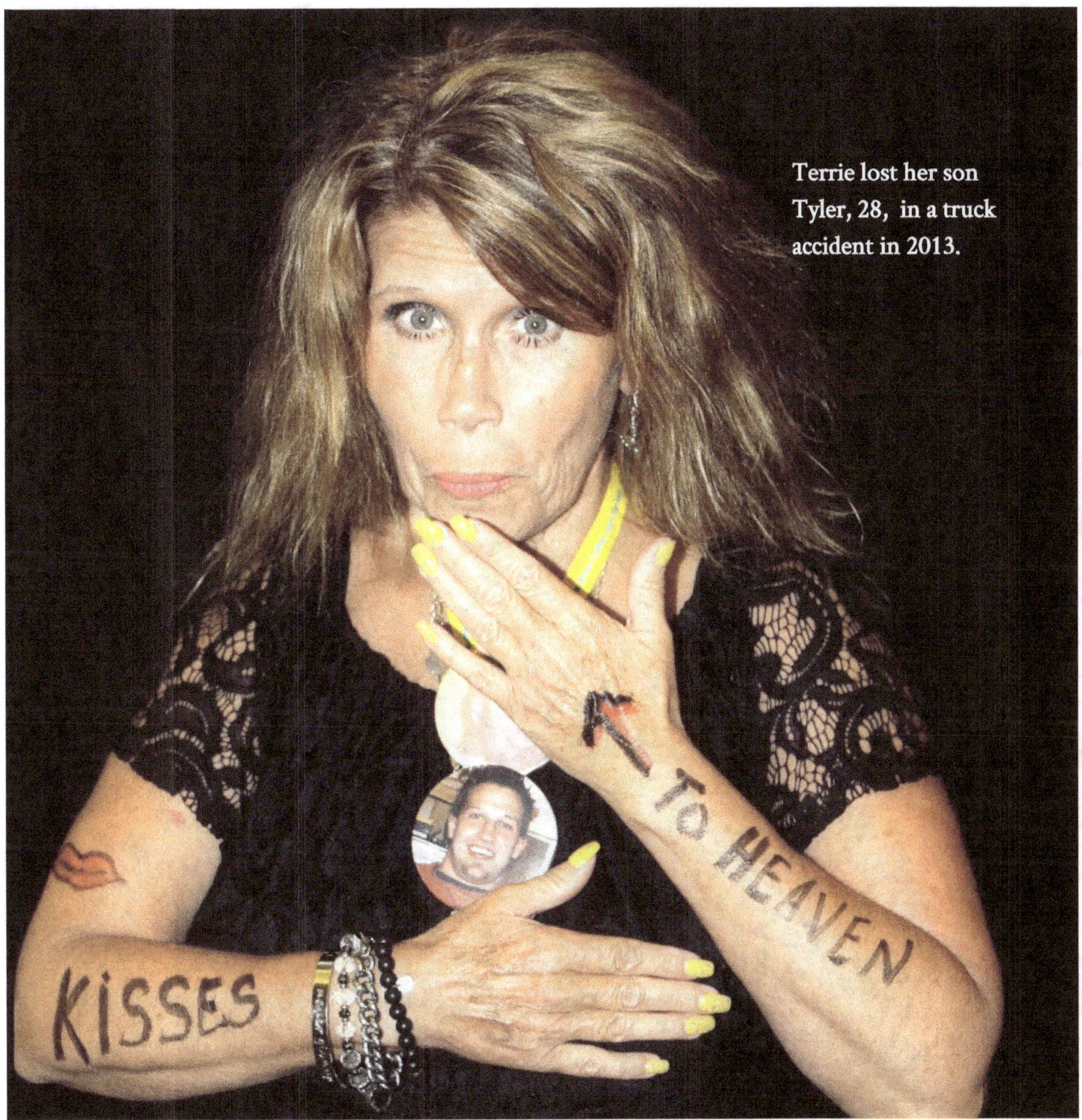

Terrie lost her son Tyler, 28, in a truck accident in 2013.

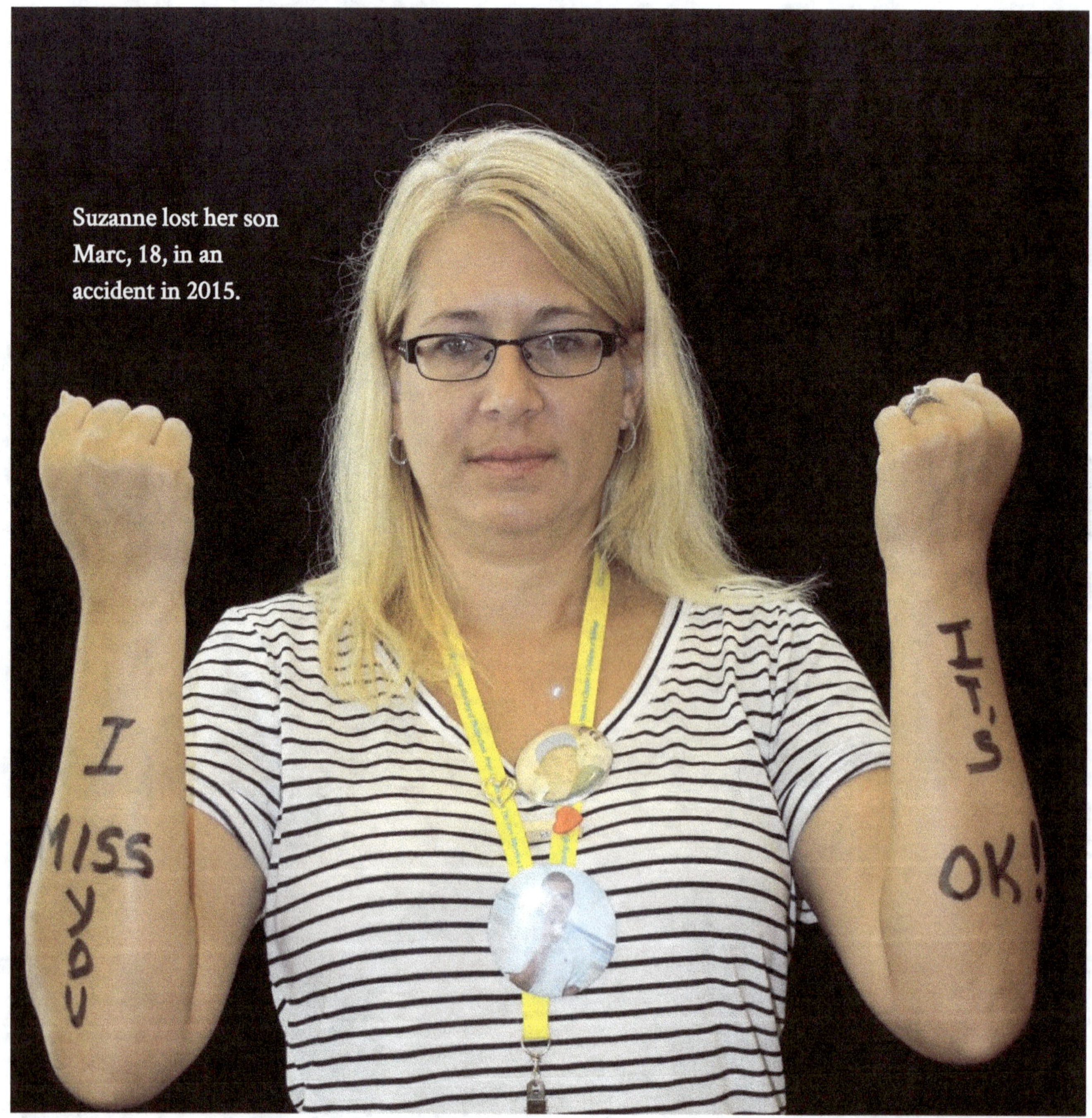
Suzanne lost her son
Marc, 18, in an
accident in 2015.
I
MISS
YOU
It's
OK!

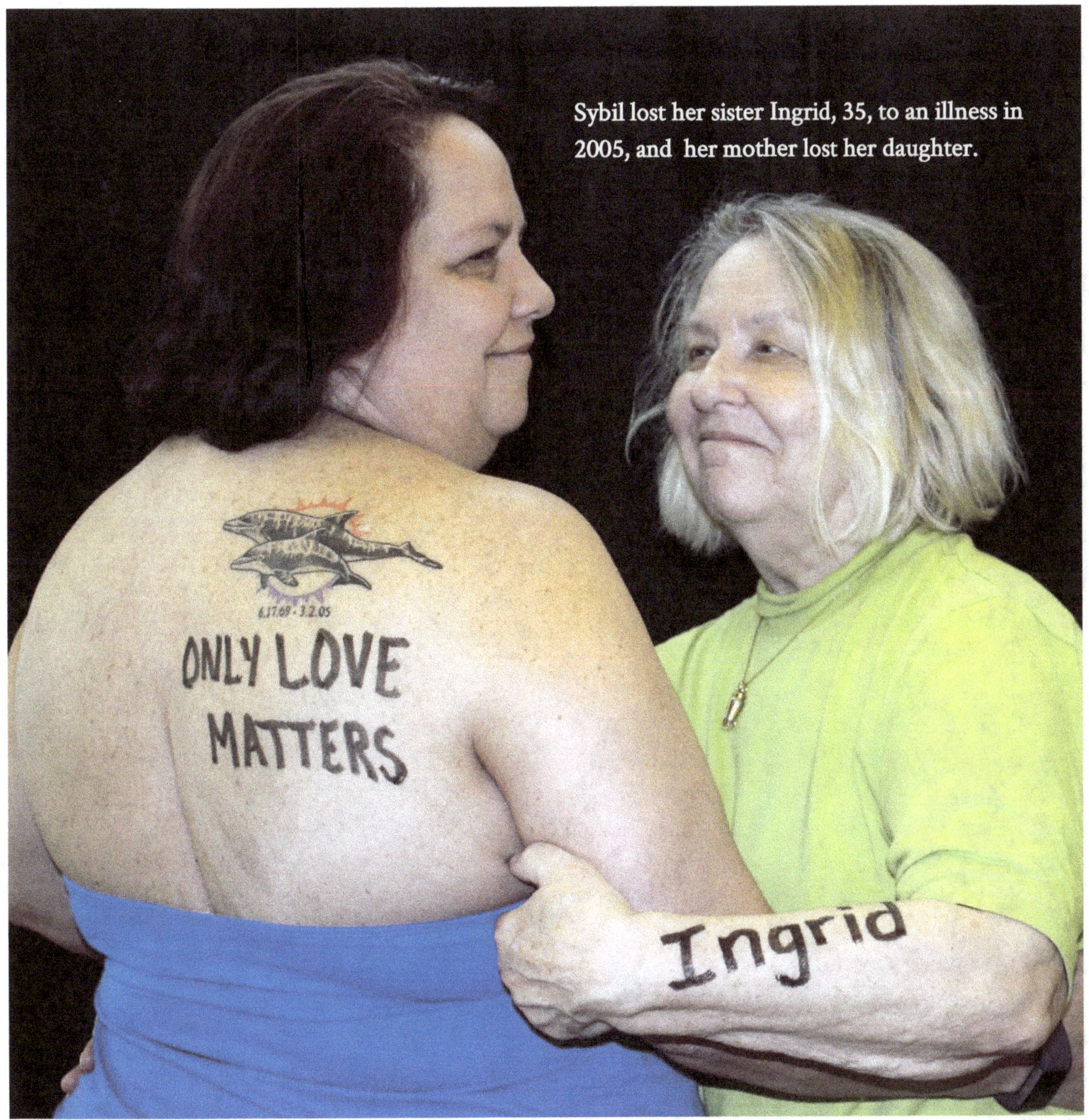

Sybil lost her sister Ingrid, 35, to an illness in 2005, and her mother lost her daughter.

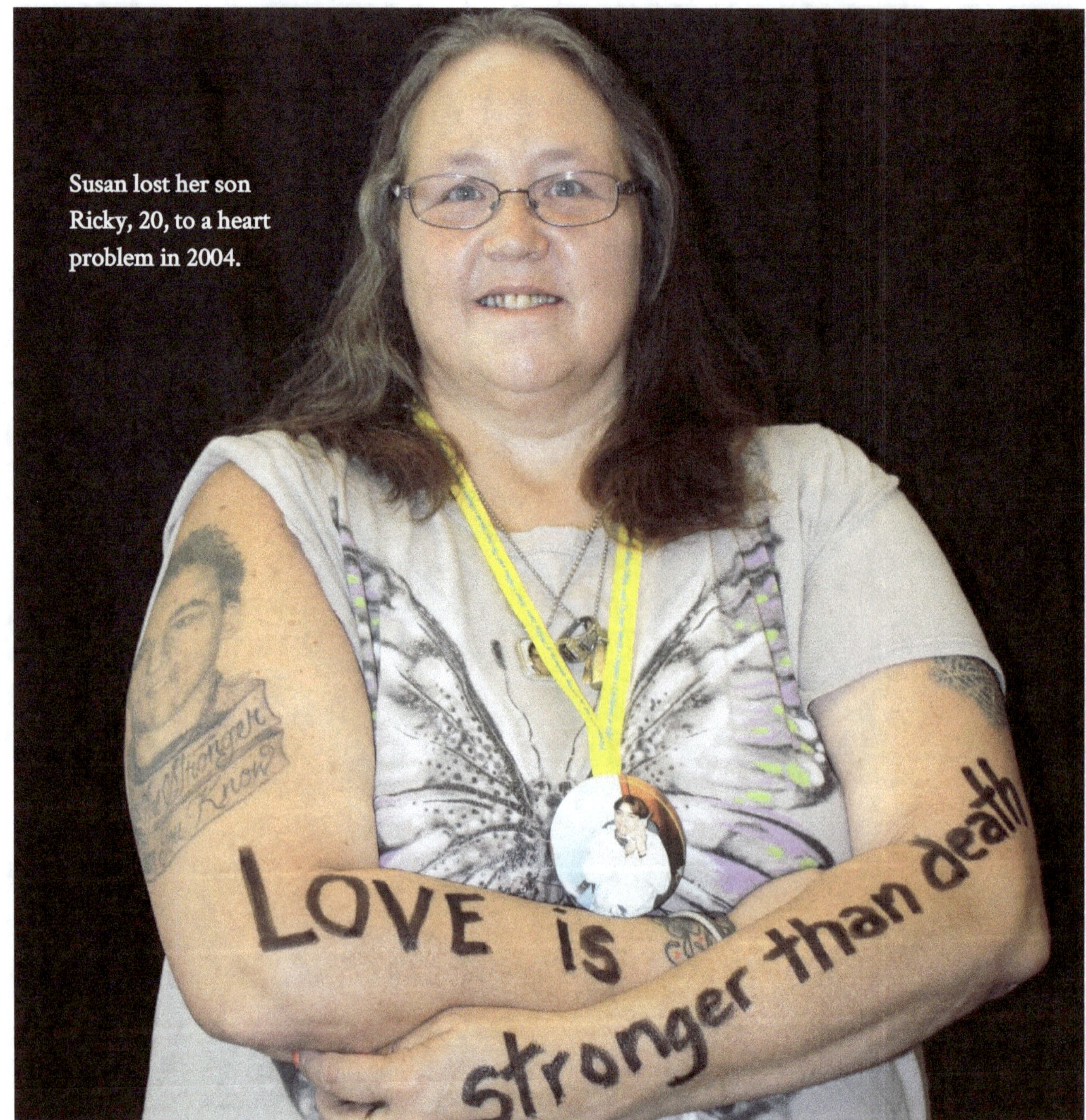

Susan lost her son
Ricky, 20, to a heart
problem in 2004.

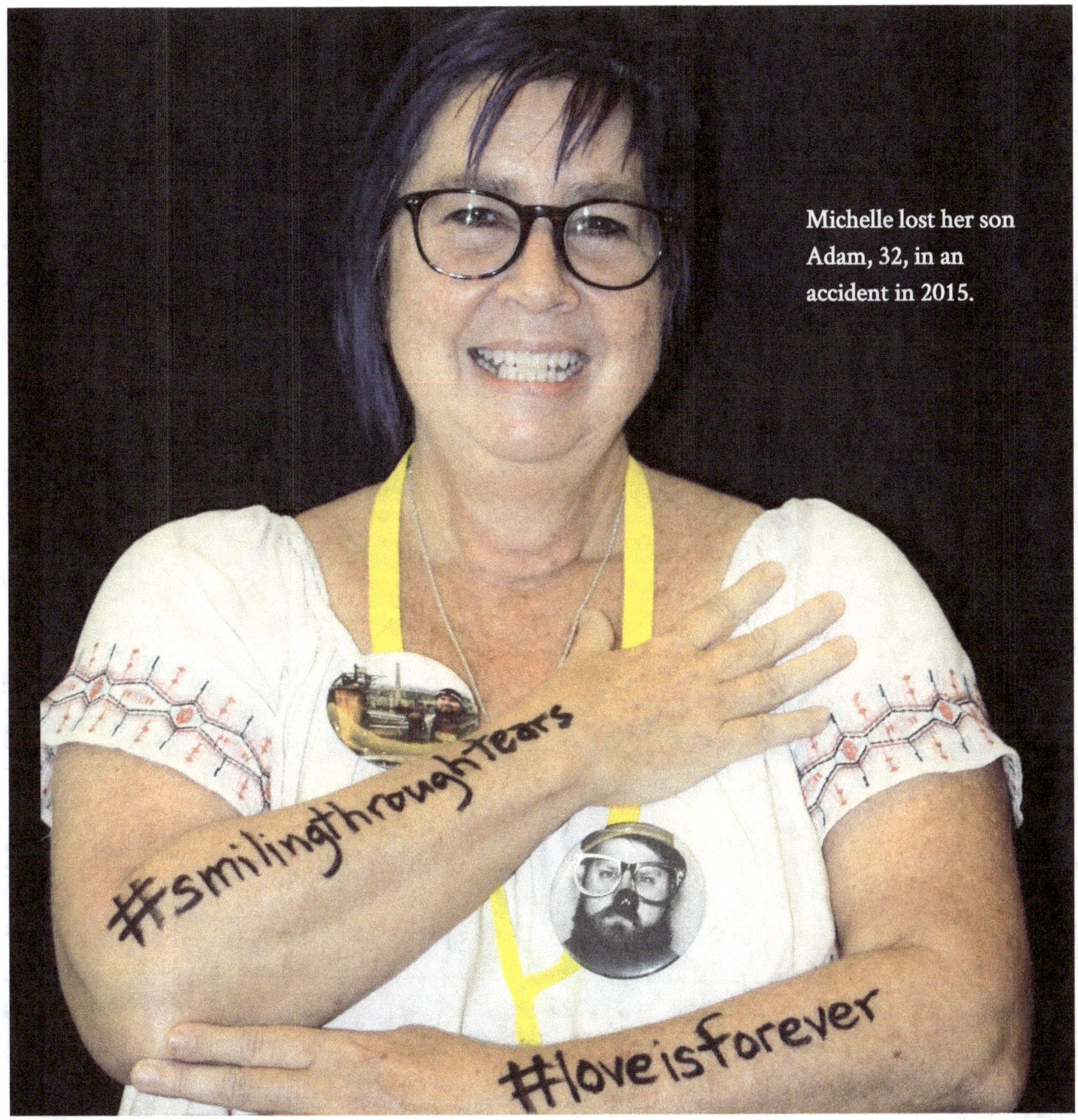

Michelle lost her son Adam, 32, in an accident in 2015.

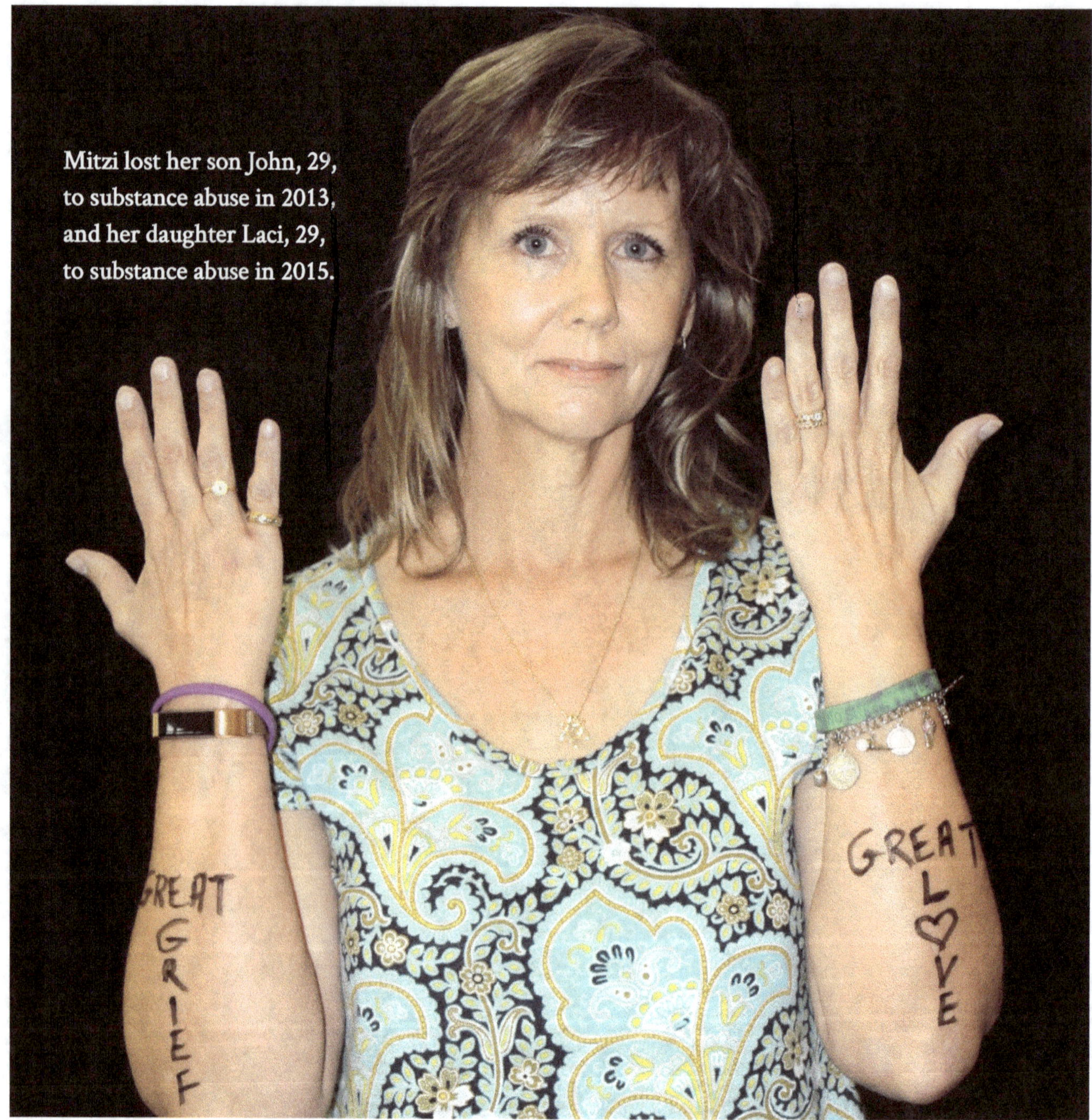

Mitzi lost her son John, 29, to substance abuse in 2013, and her daughter Laci, 29, to substance abuse in 2015.

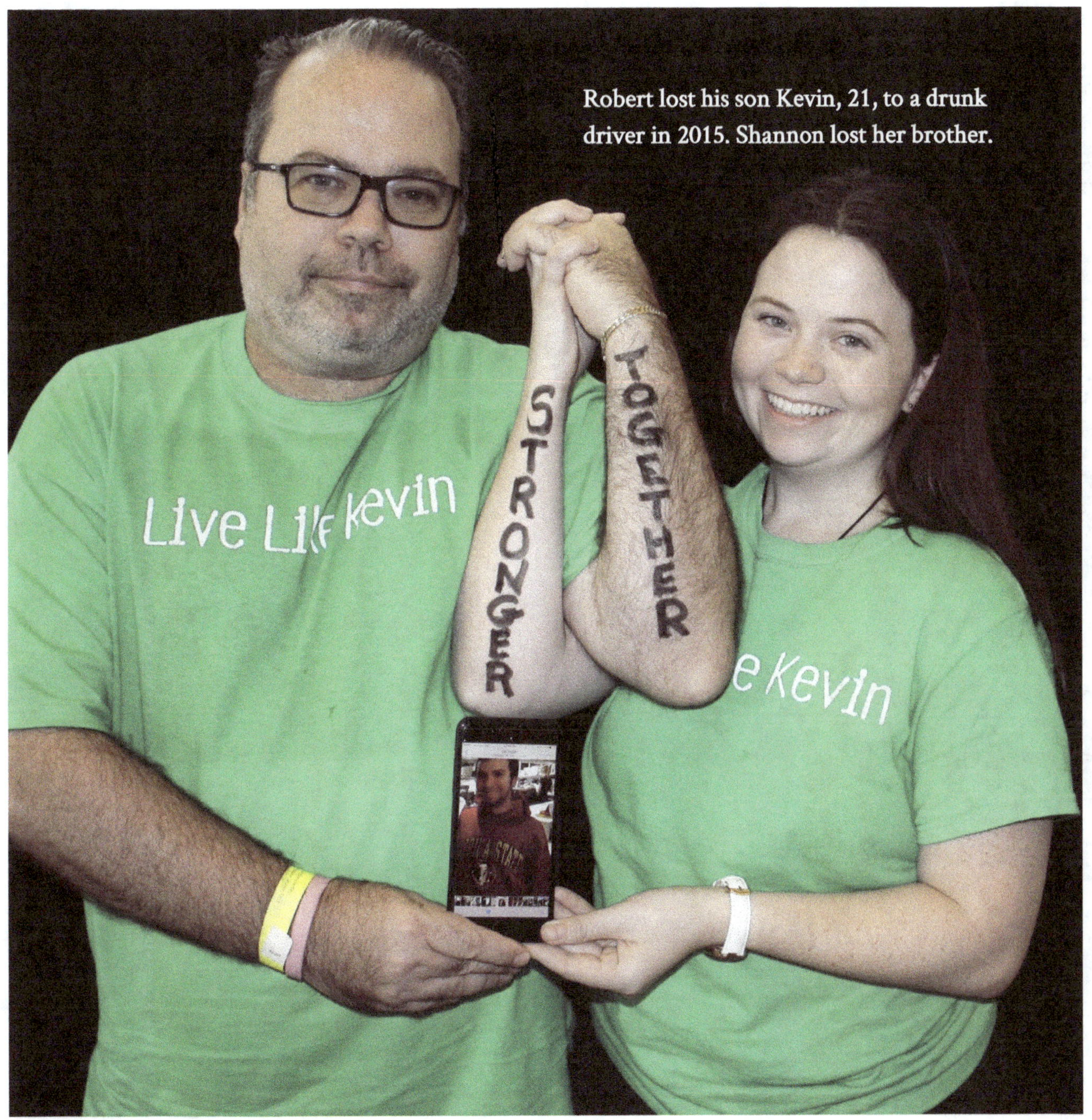

Robert lost his son Kevin, 21, to a drunk driver in 2015. Shannon lost her brother.

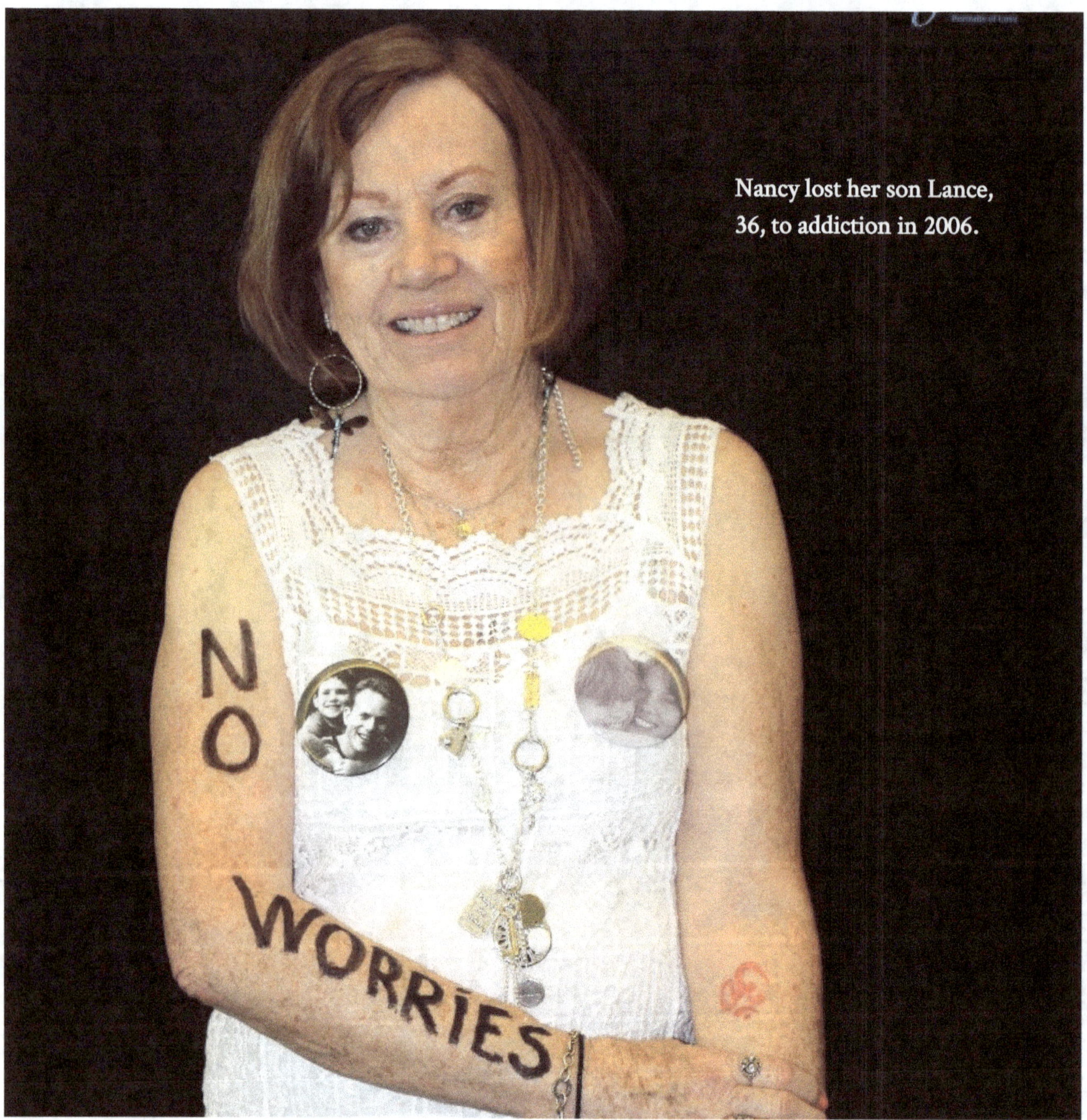

Nancy lost her son Lance, 36, to addiction in 2006.

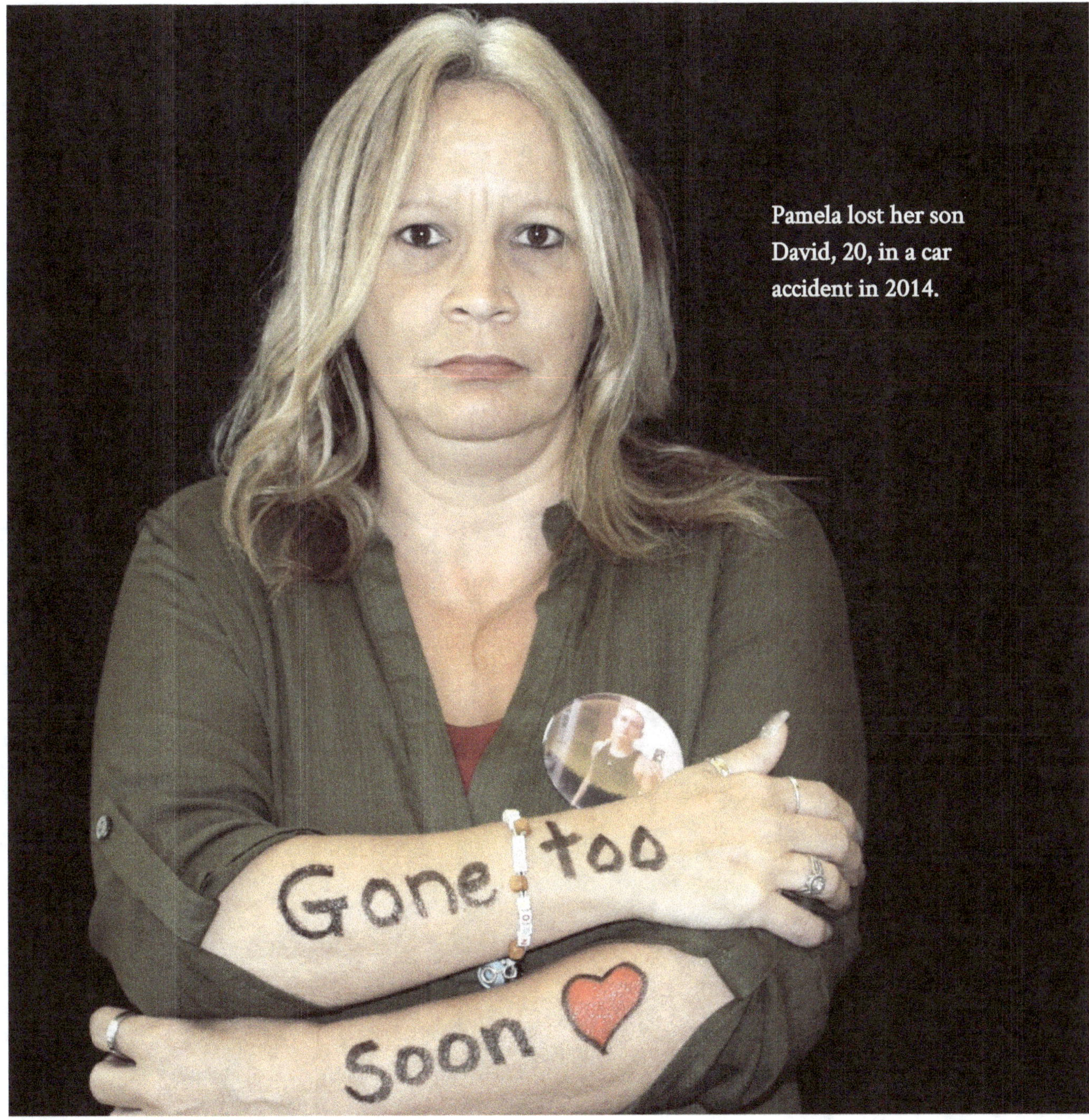

Pamela lost her son David, 20, in a car accident in 2014.

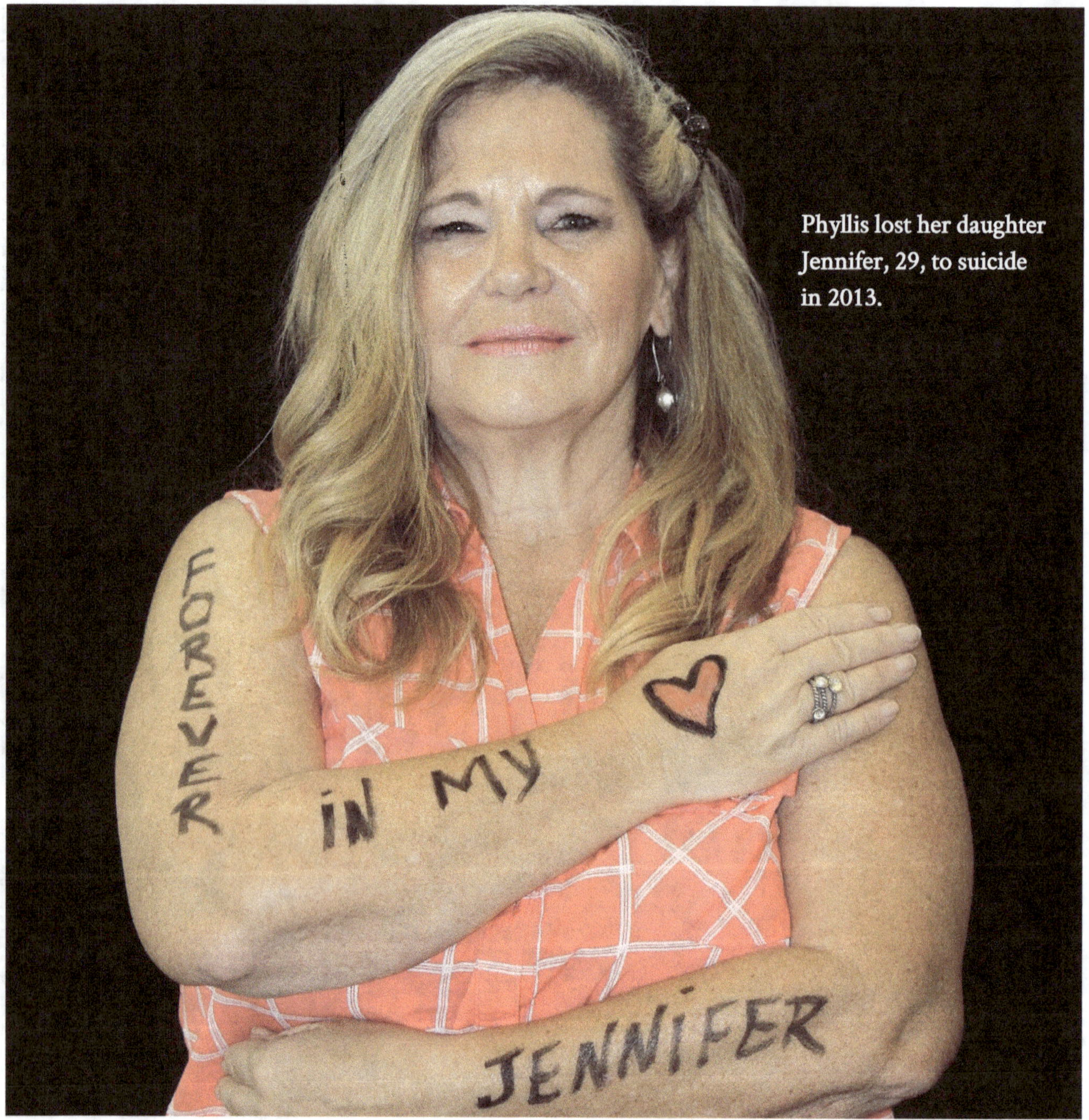

Phyllis lost her daughter Jennifer, 29, to suicide in 2013.

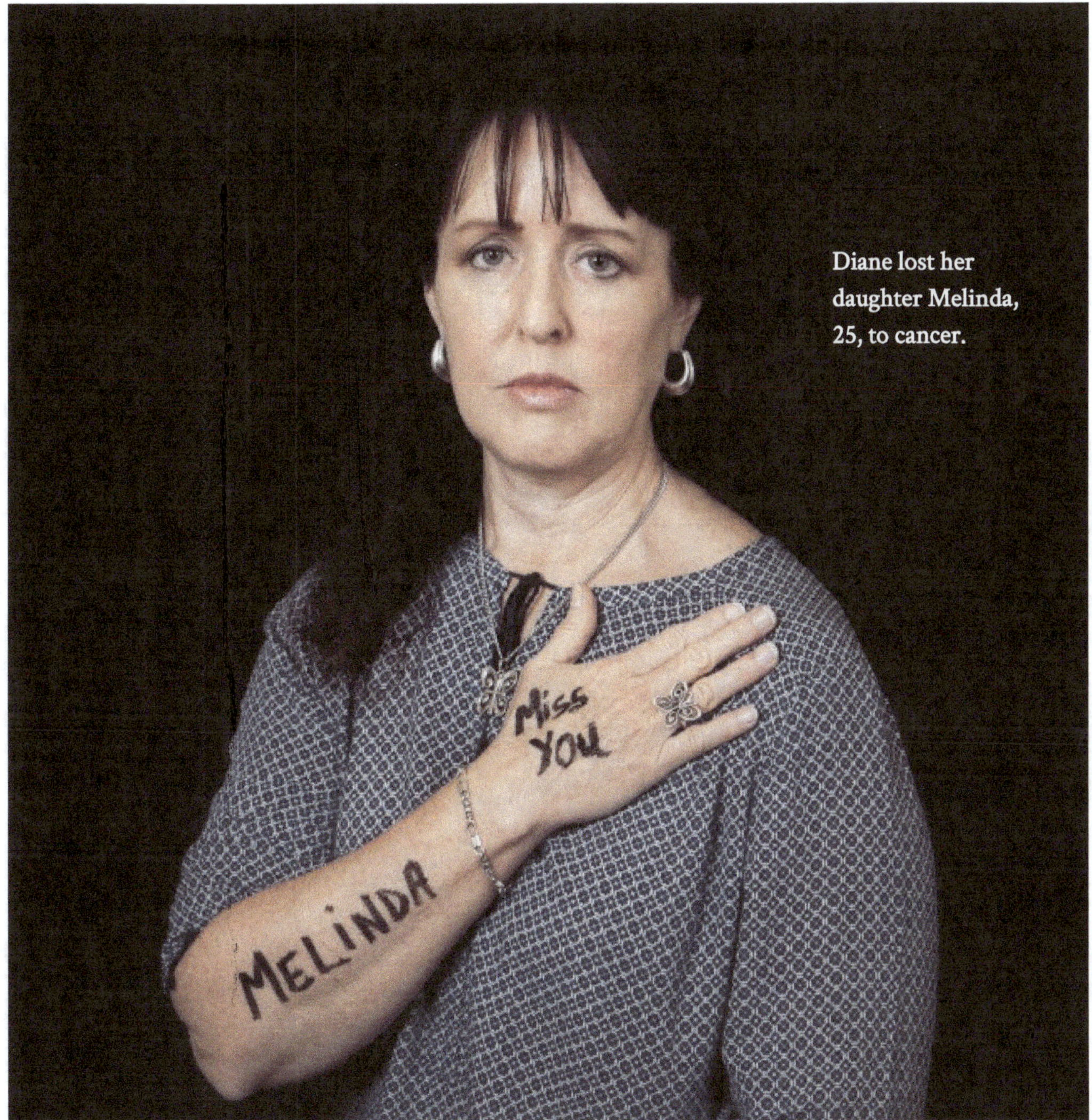

Diane lost her daughter Melinda, 25, to cancer.

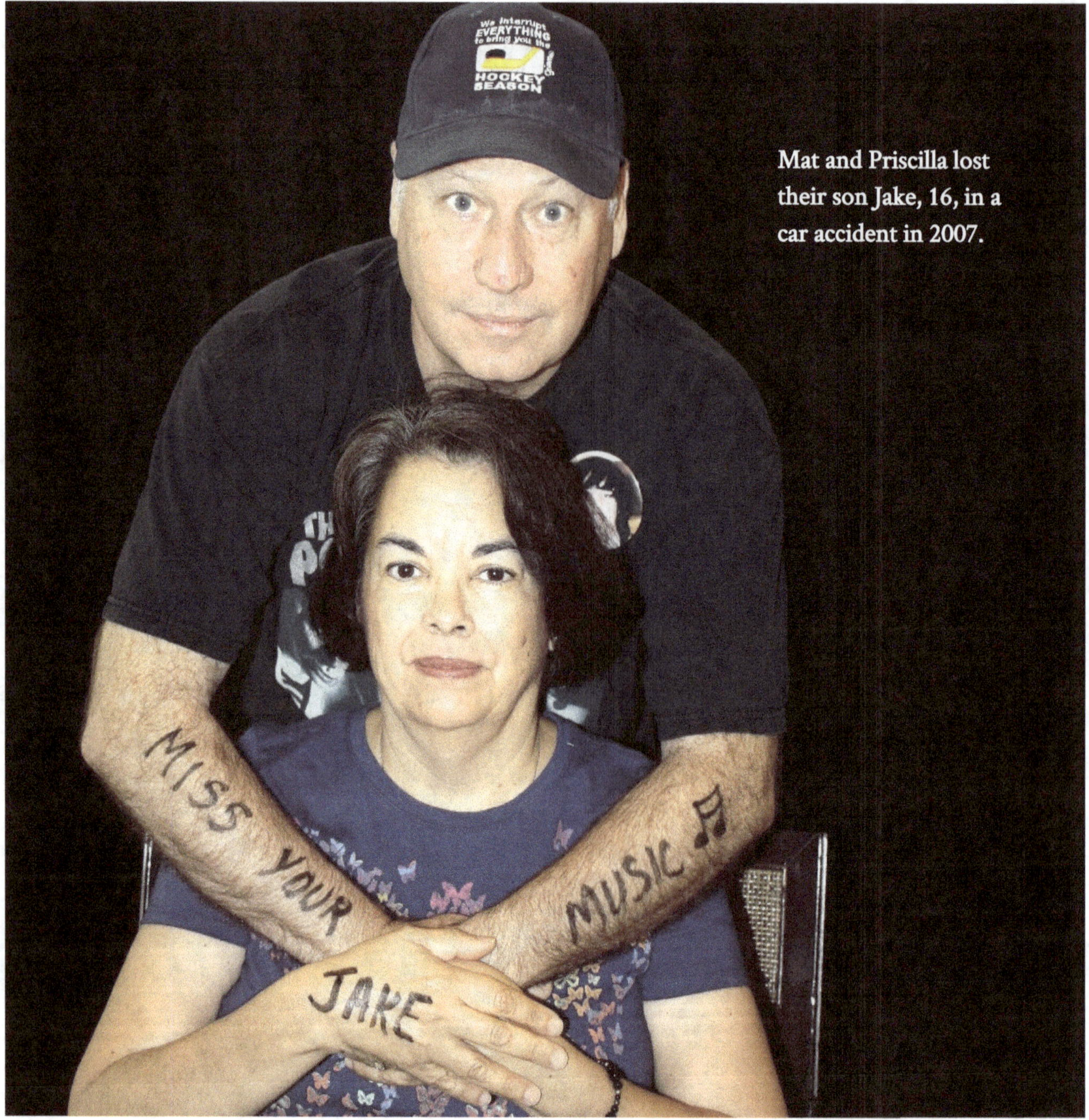

Mat and Priscilla lost their son Jake, 16, in a car accident in 2007.

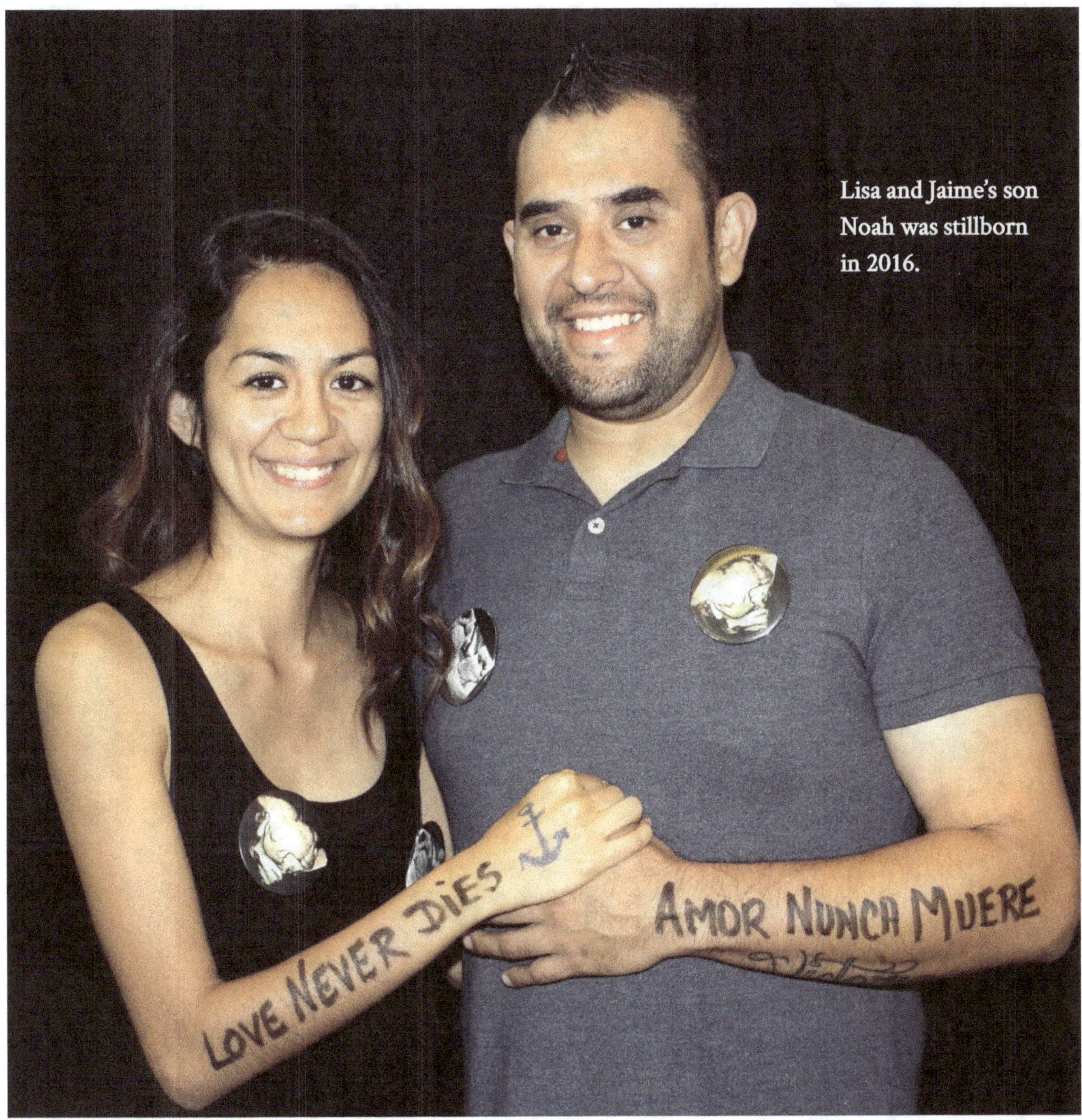

Lisa and Jaime's son Noah was stillborn in 2016.

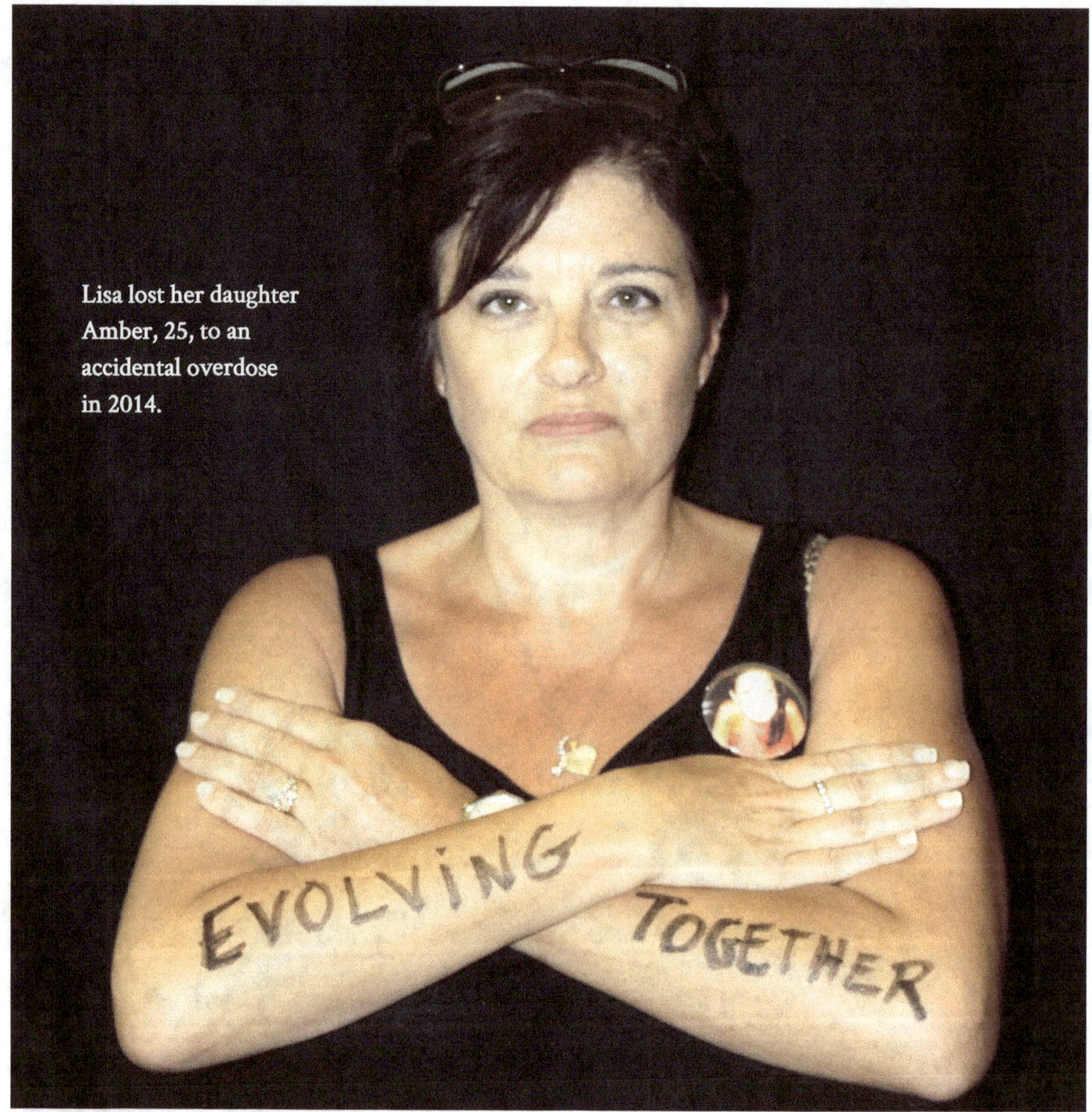

Lisa lost her daughter
Amber, 25, to an
accidental overdose
in 2014.

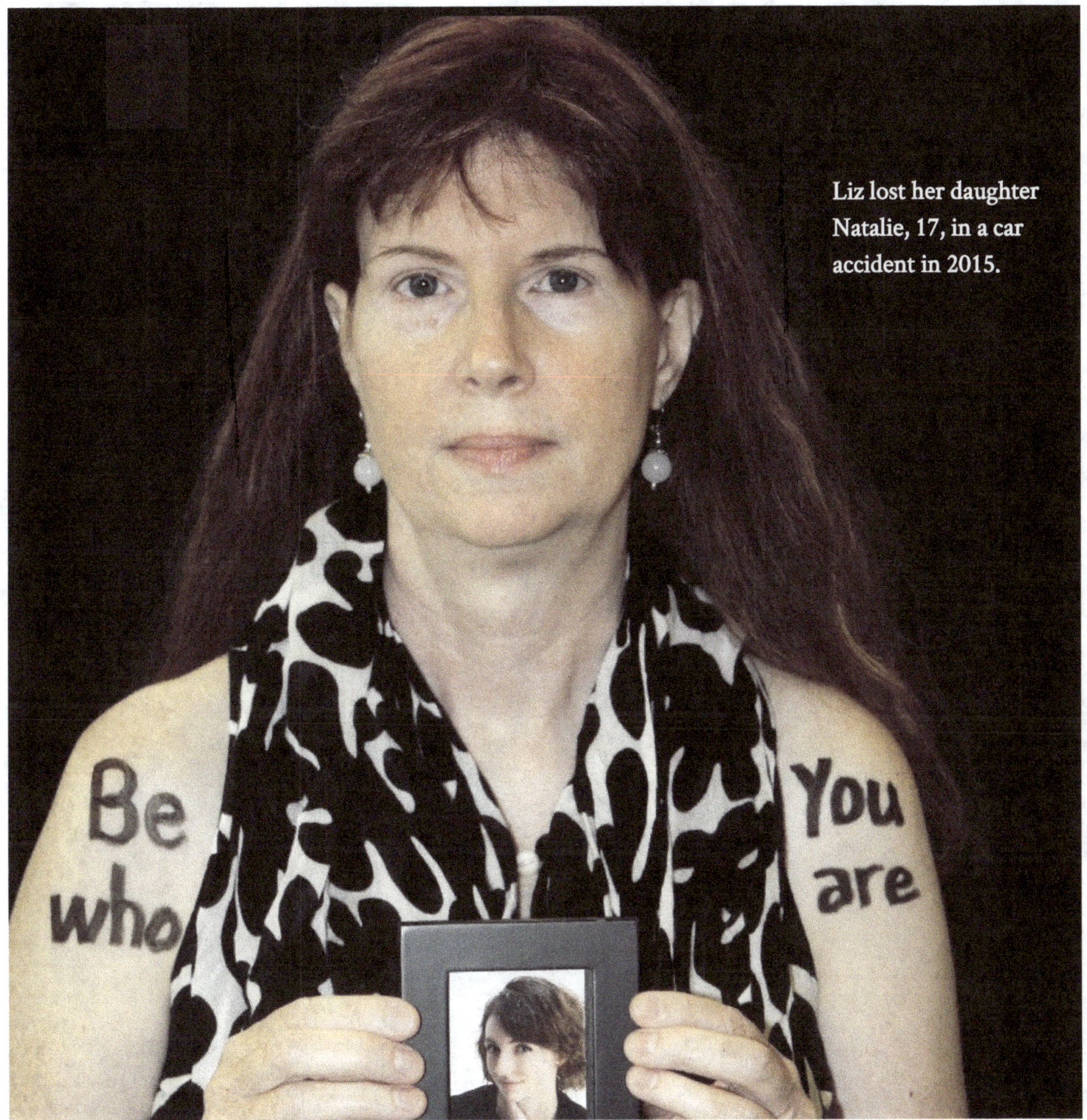
Liz lost her daughter
Natalie, 17, in a car
accident in 2015.
Be
who
You
are

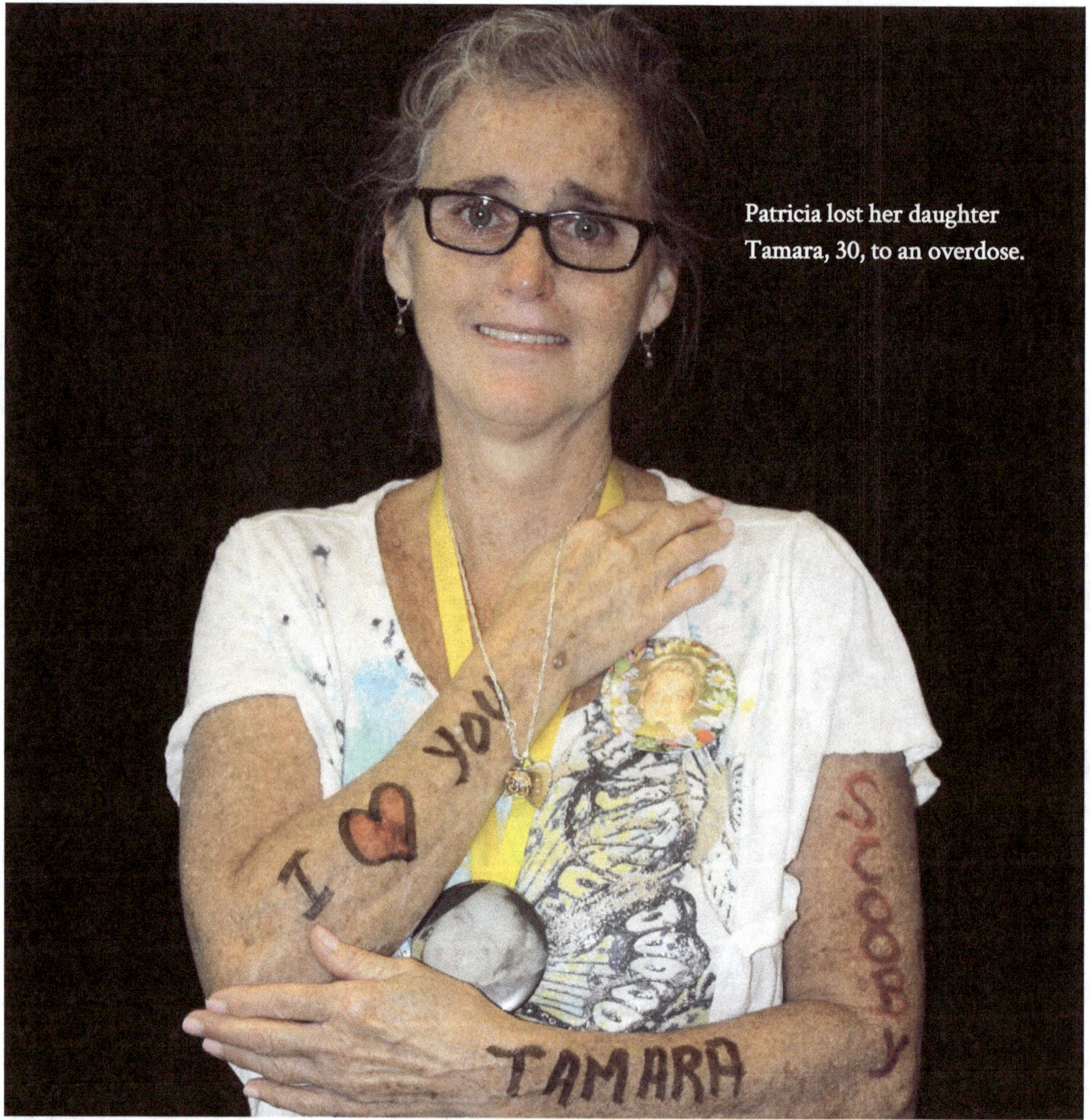

Patricia lost her daughter Tamara, 30, to an overdose.

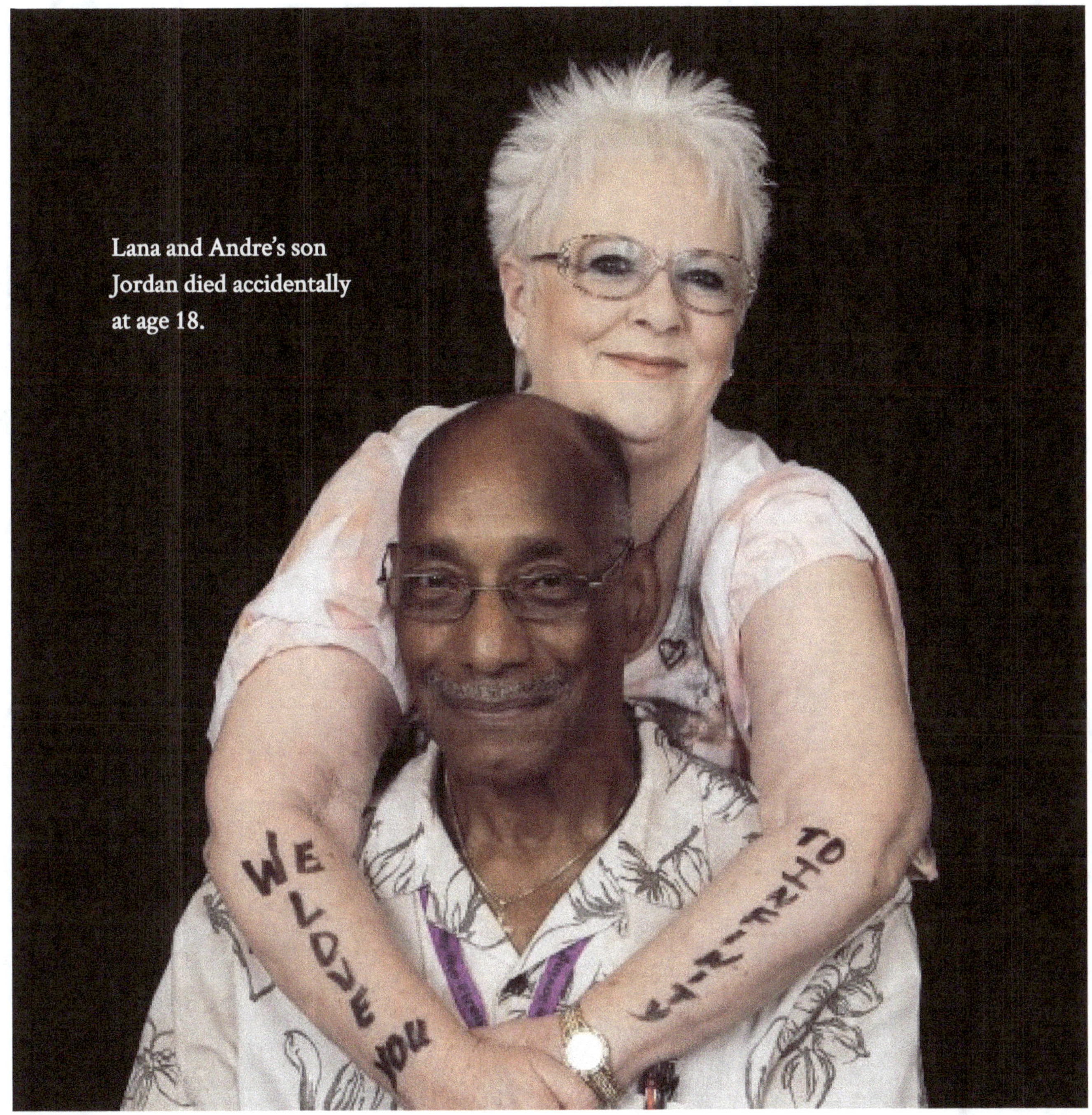

Lana and Andre's son Jordan died accidentally at age 18.

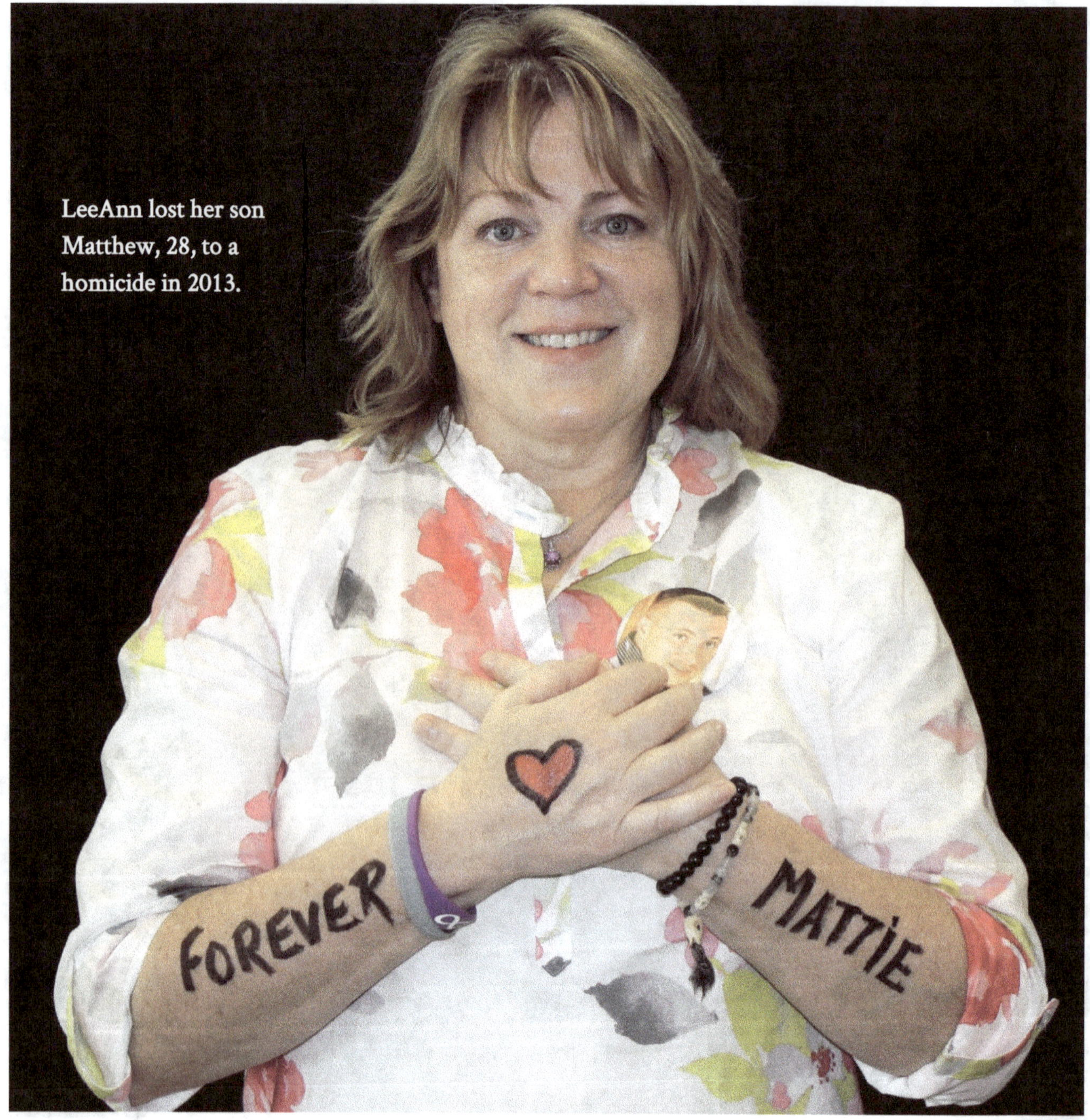

LeeAnn lost her son Matthew, 28, to a homicide in 2013.

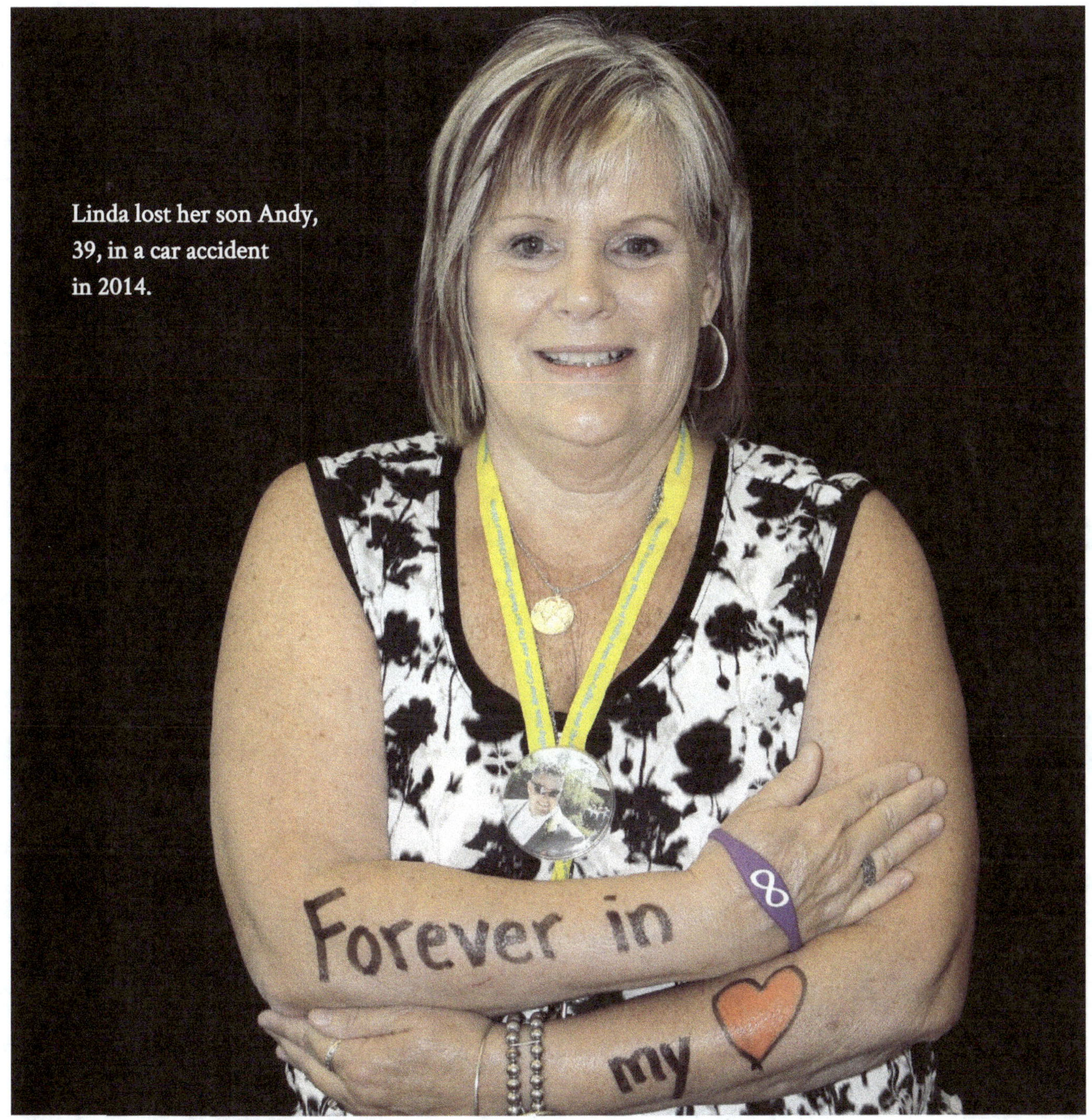

Linda lost her son Andy,
39, in a car accident
in 2014.

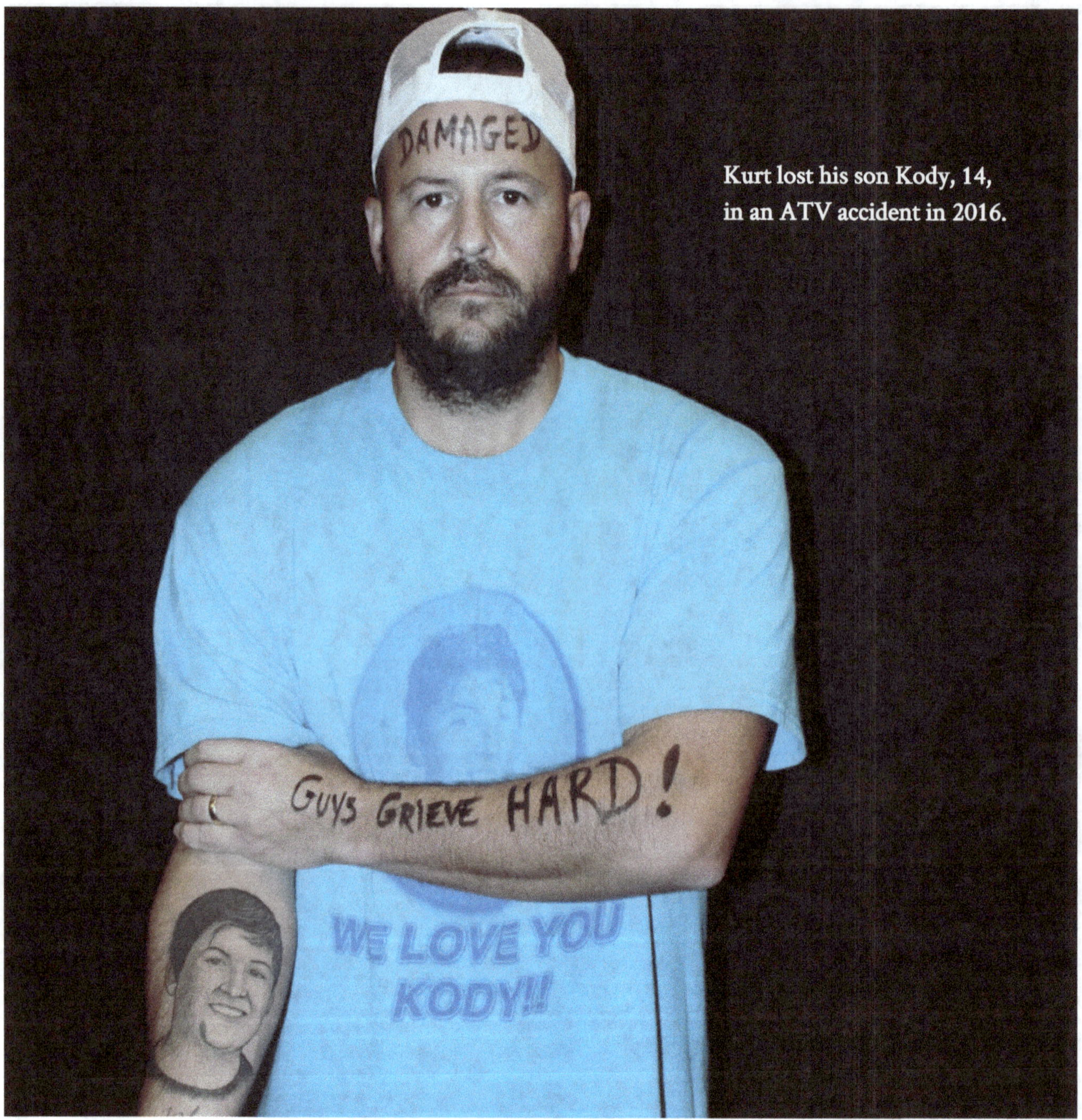

Kurt lost his son Kody, 14,
in an ATV accident in 2016.

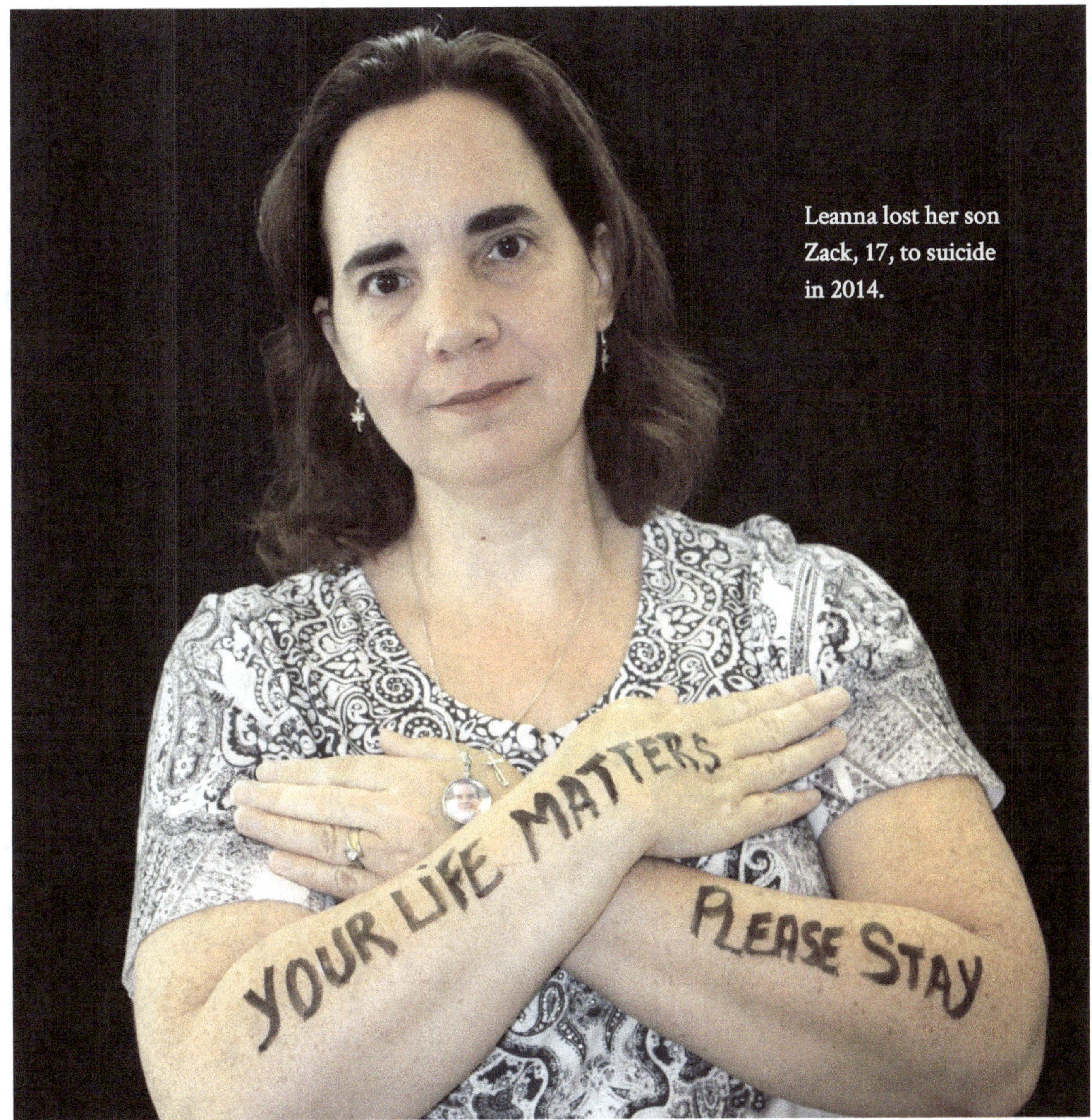

Leanna lost her son
Zack, 17, to suicide
in 2014.

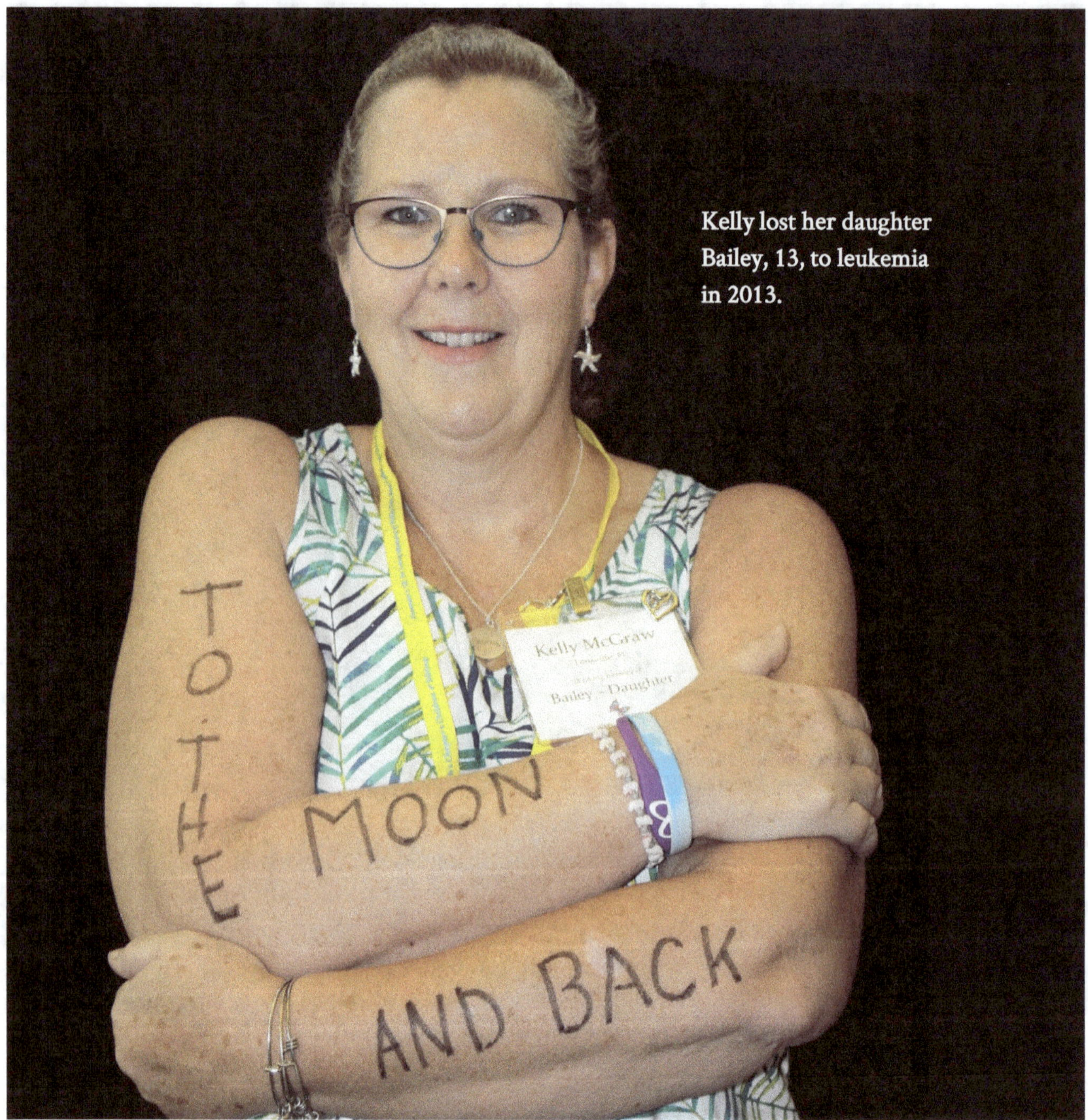

Kelly lost her daughter Bailey, 13, to leukemia in 2013.

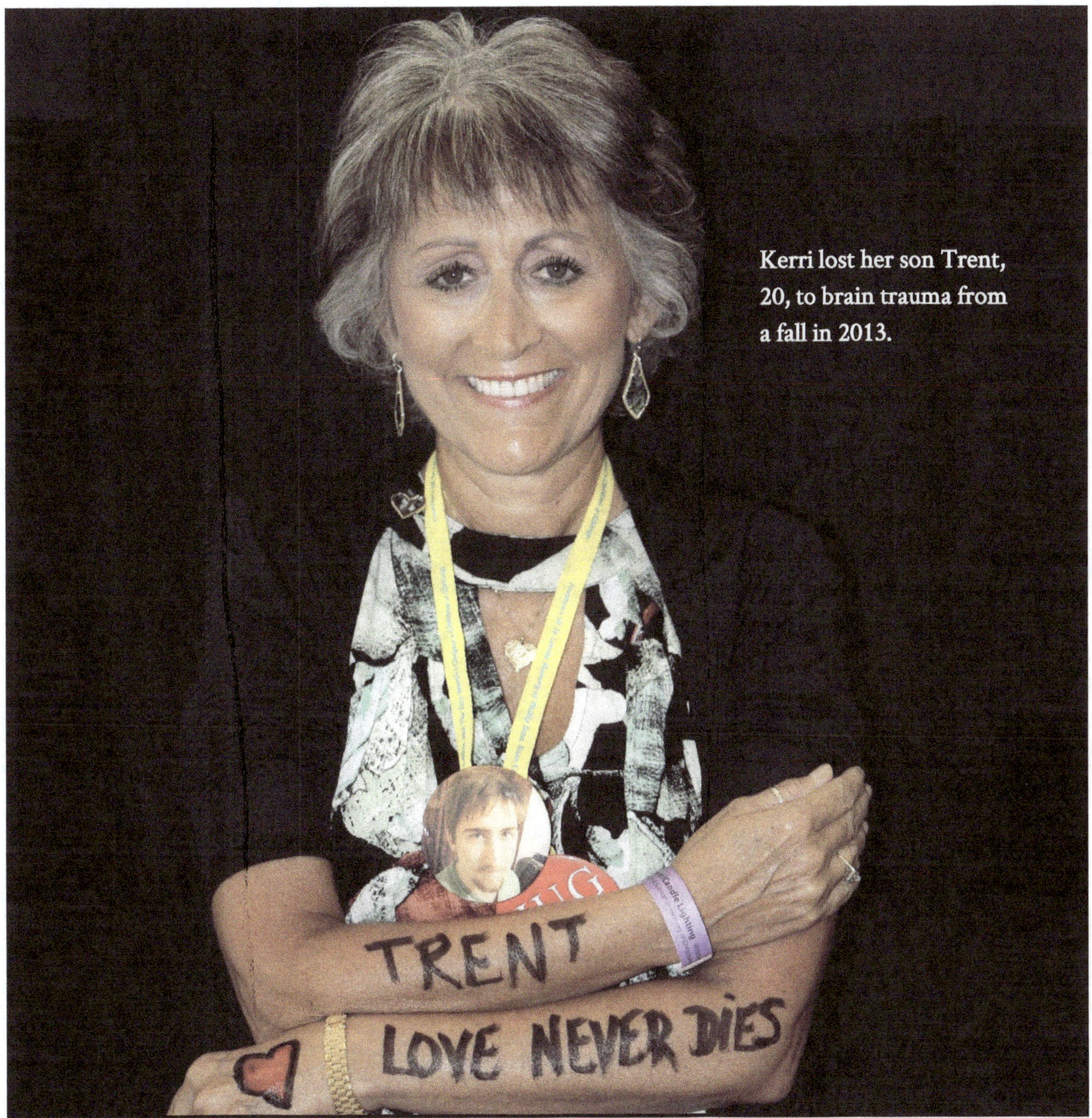

Kerri lost her son Trent, 20, to brain trauma from a fall in 2013.

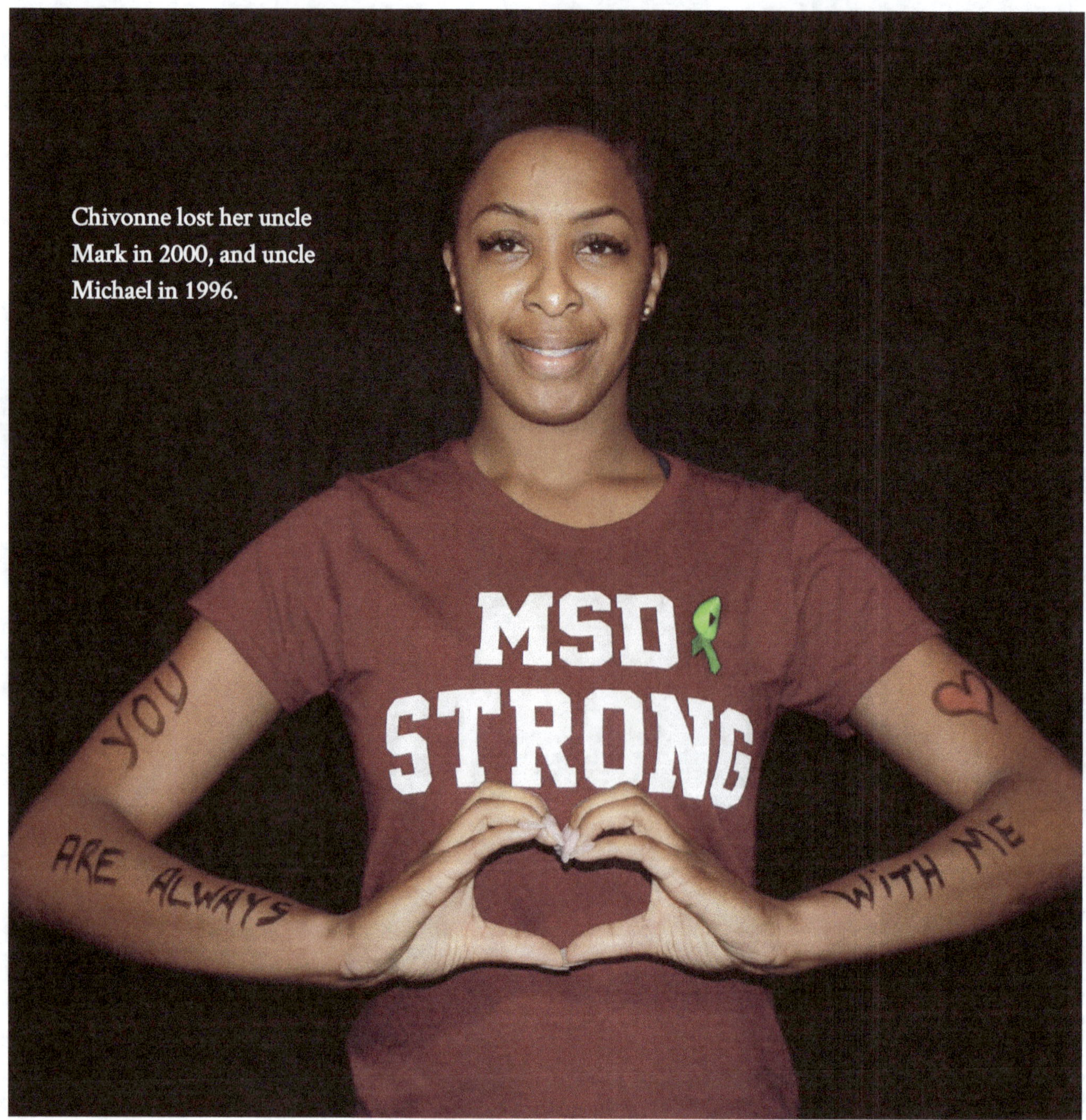

Chivonne lost her uncle Mark in 2000, and uncle Michael in 1996.

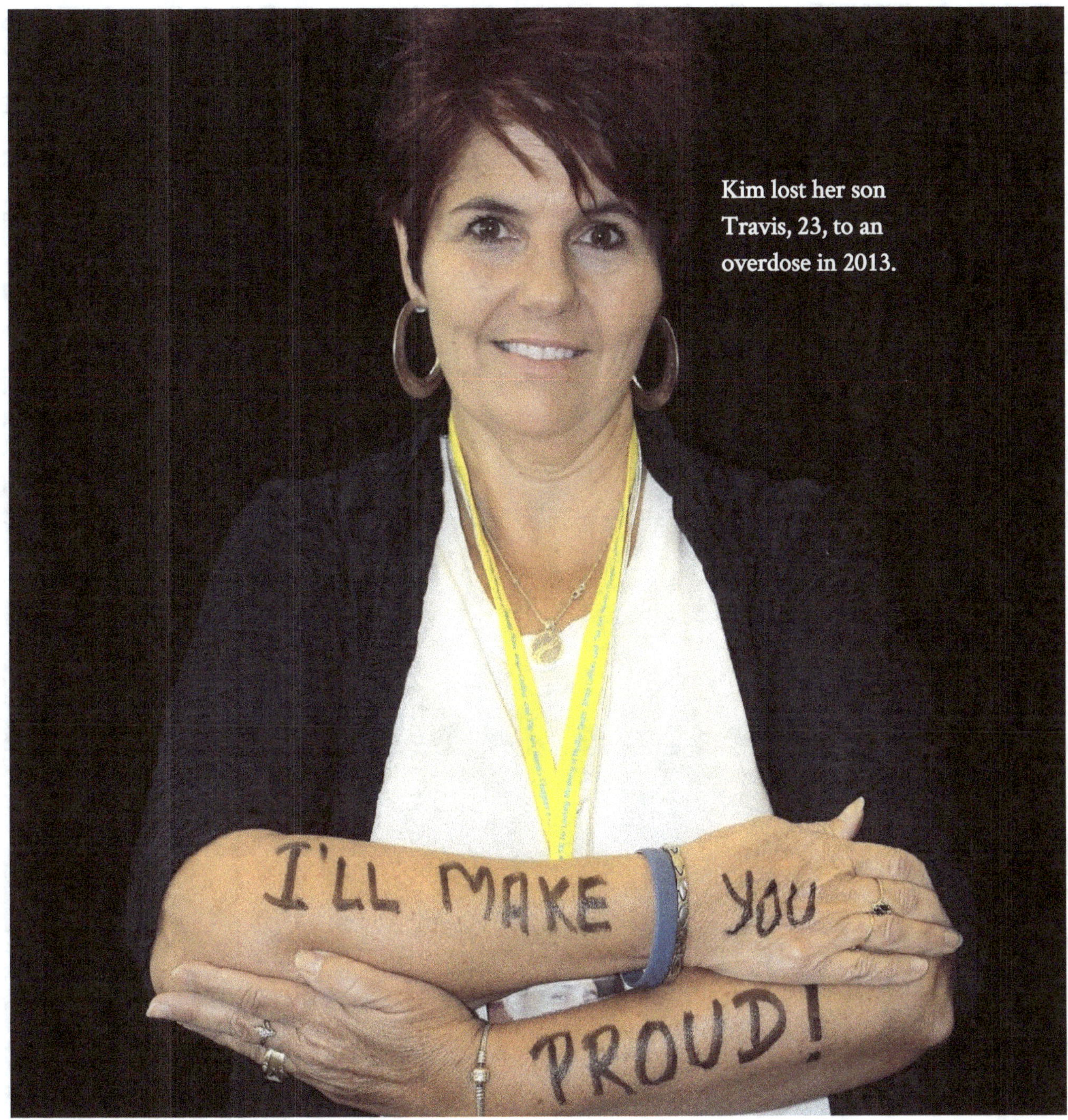

Kim lost her son
Travis, 23, to an
overdose in 2013.

I'LL MAKE YOU
PROUD!

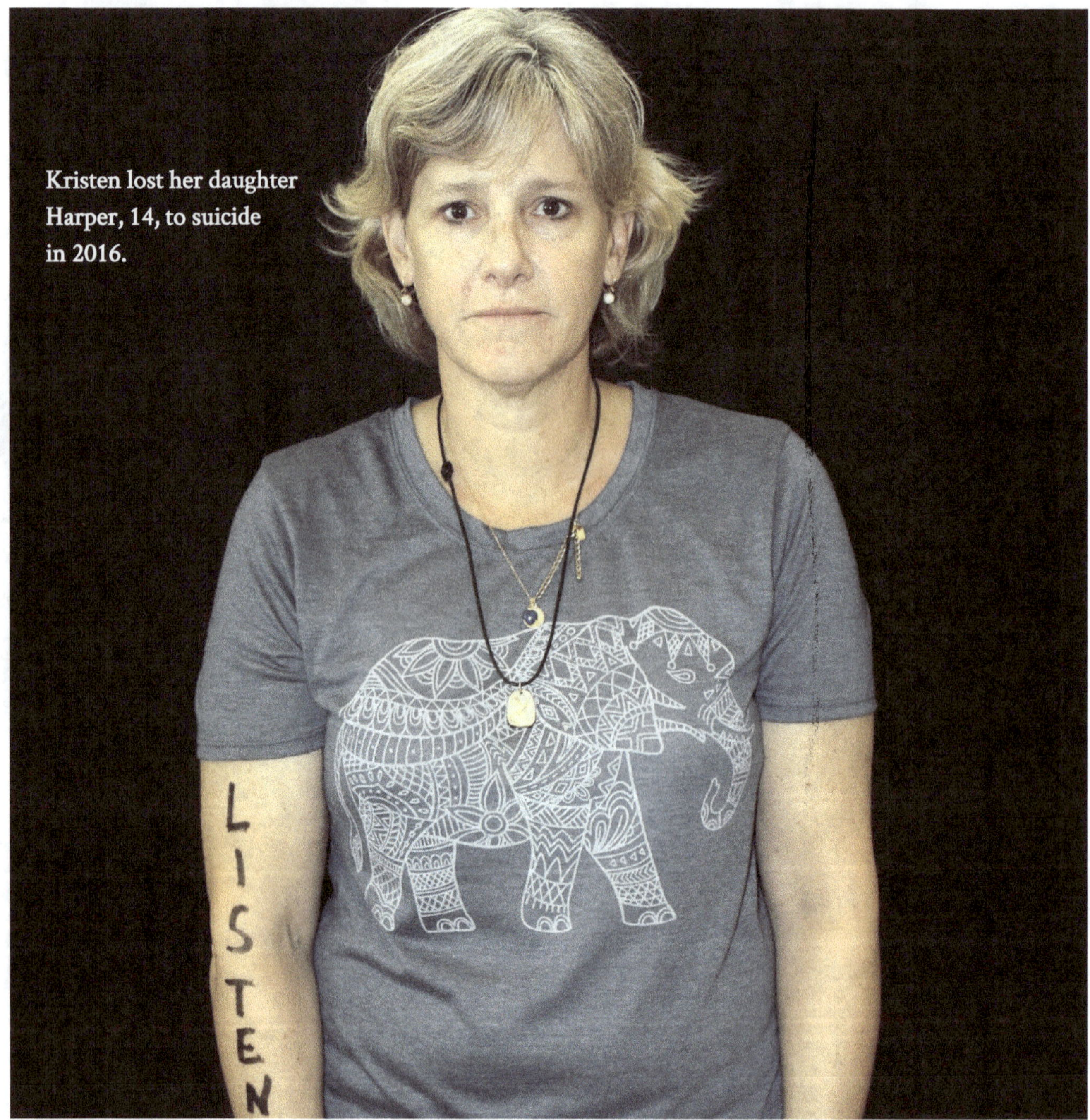

Kristen lost her daughter Harper, 14, to suicide in 2016.

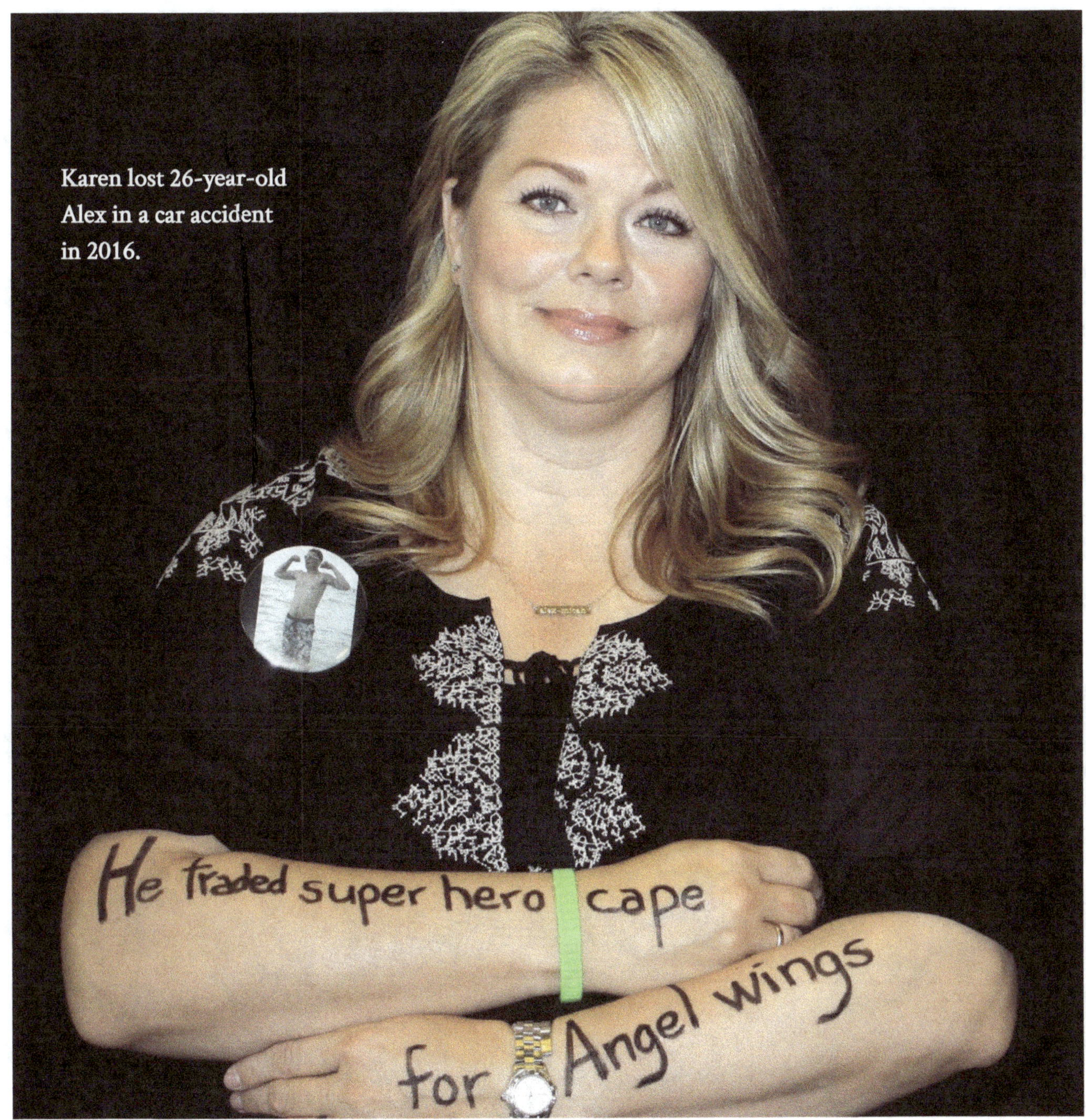

Karen lost 26-year-old Alex in a car accident in 2016.

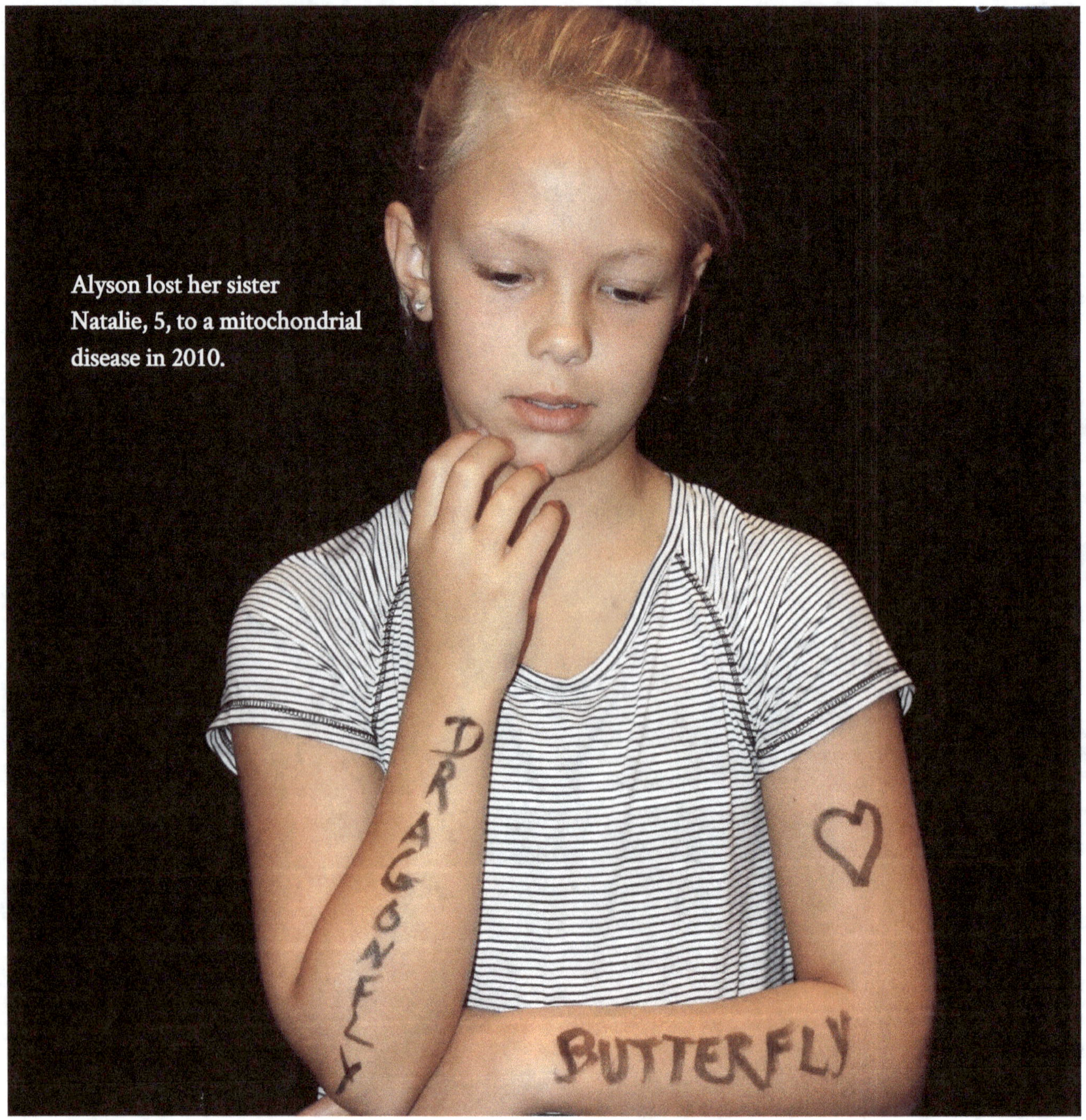

Alyson lost her sister Natalie, 5, to a mitochondrial disease in 2010.

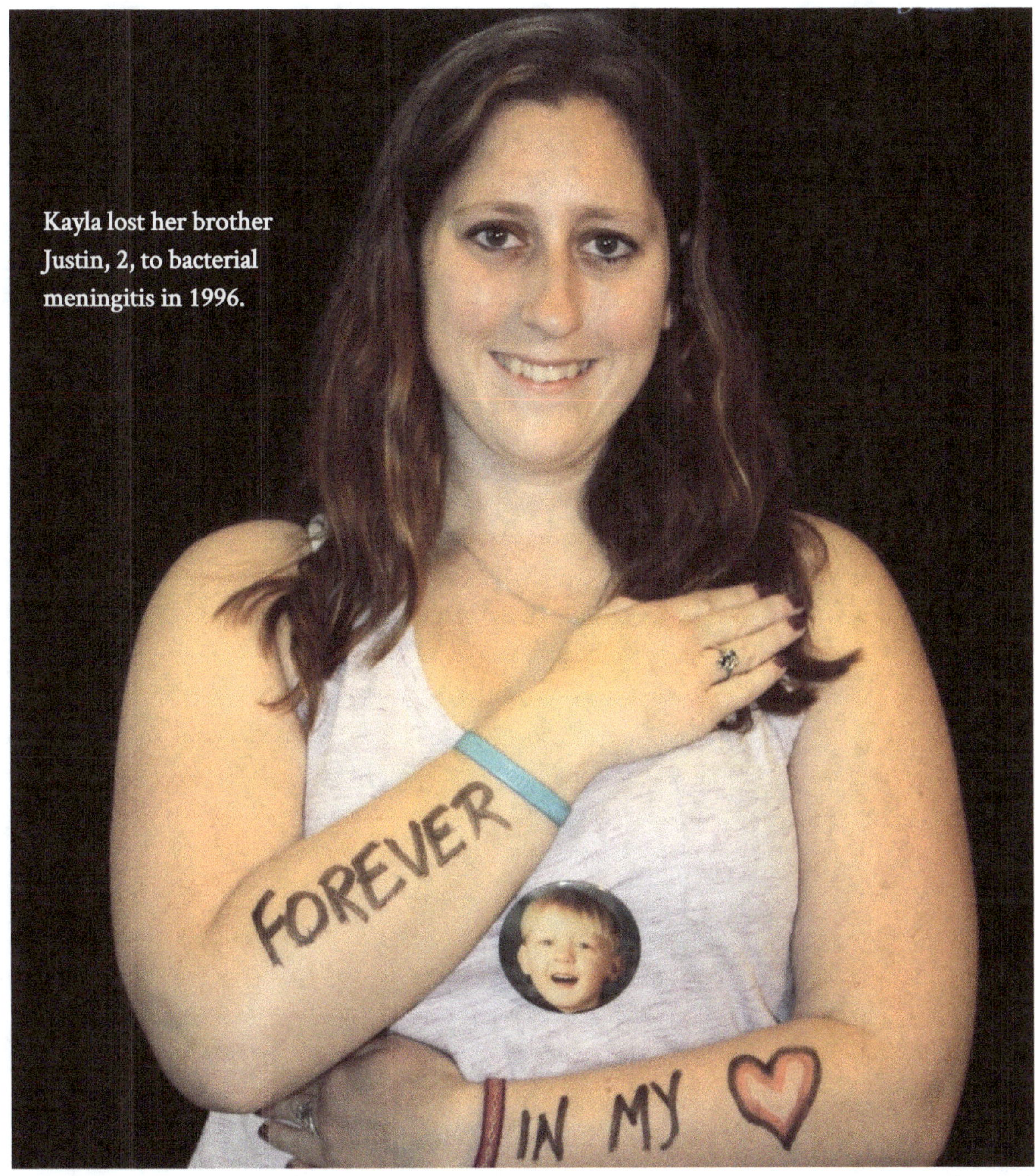

Kayla lost her brother Justin, 2, to bacterial meningitis in 1996.

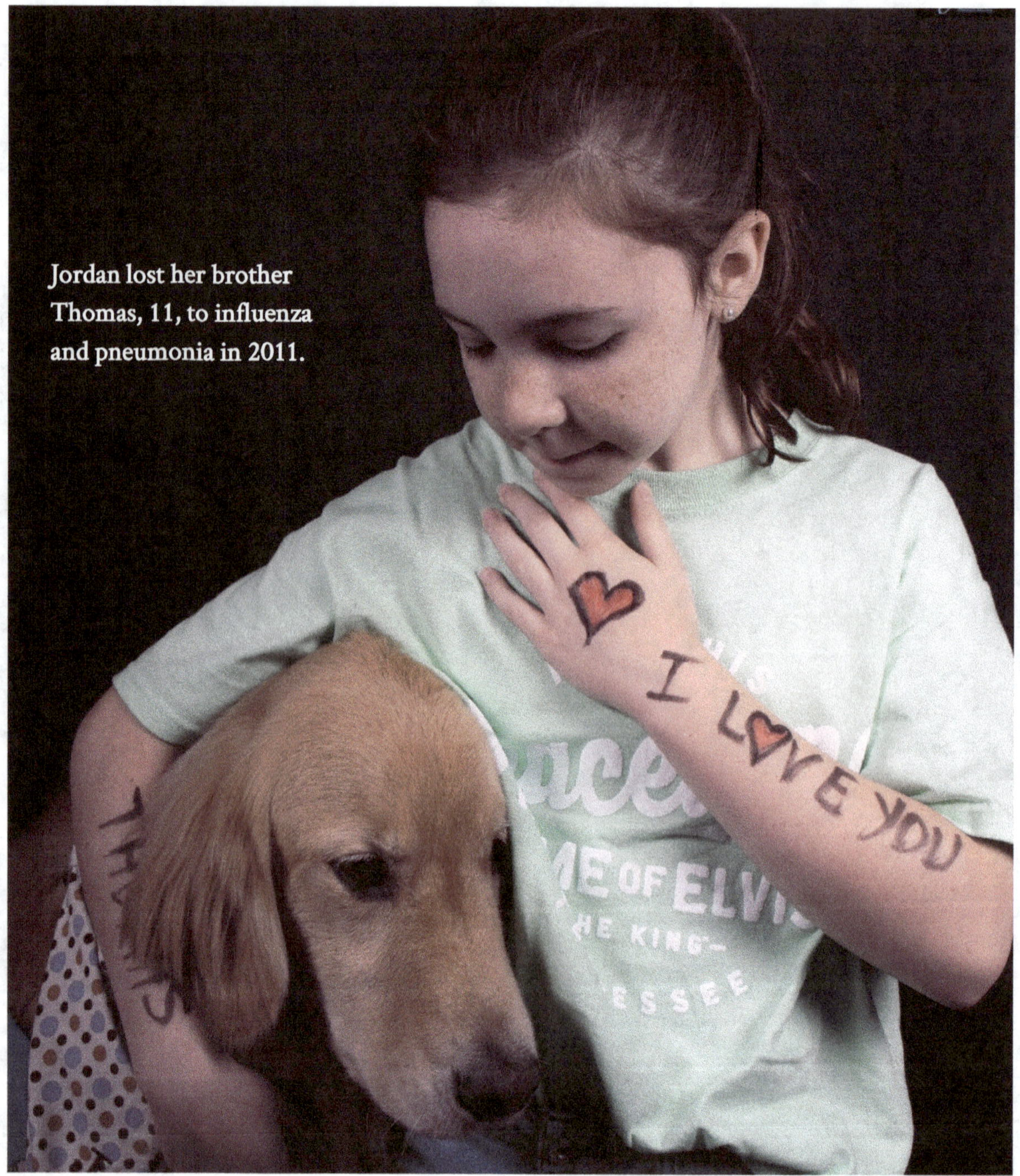
Jordan lost her brother
Thomas, 11, to influenza
and pneumonia in 2011.

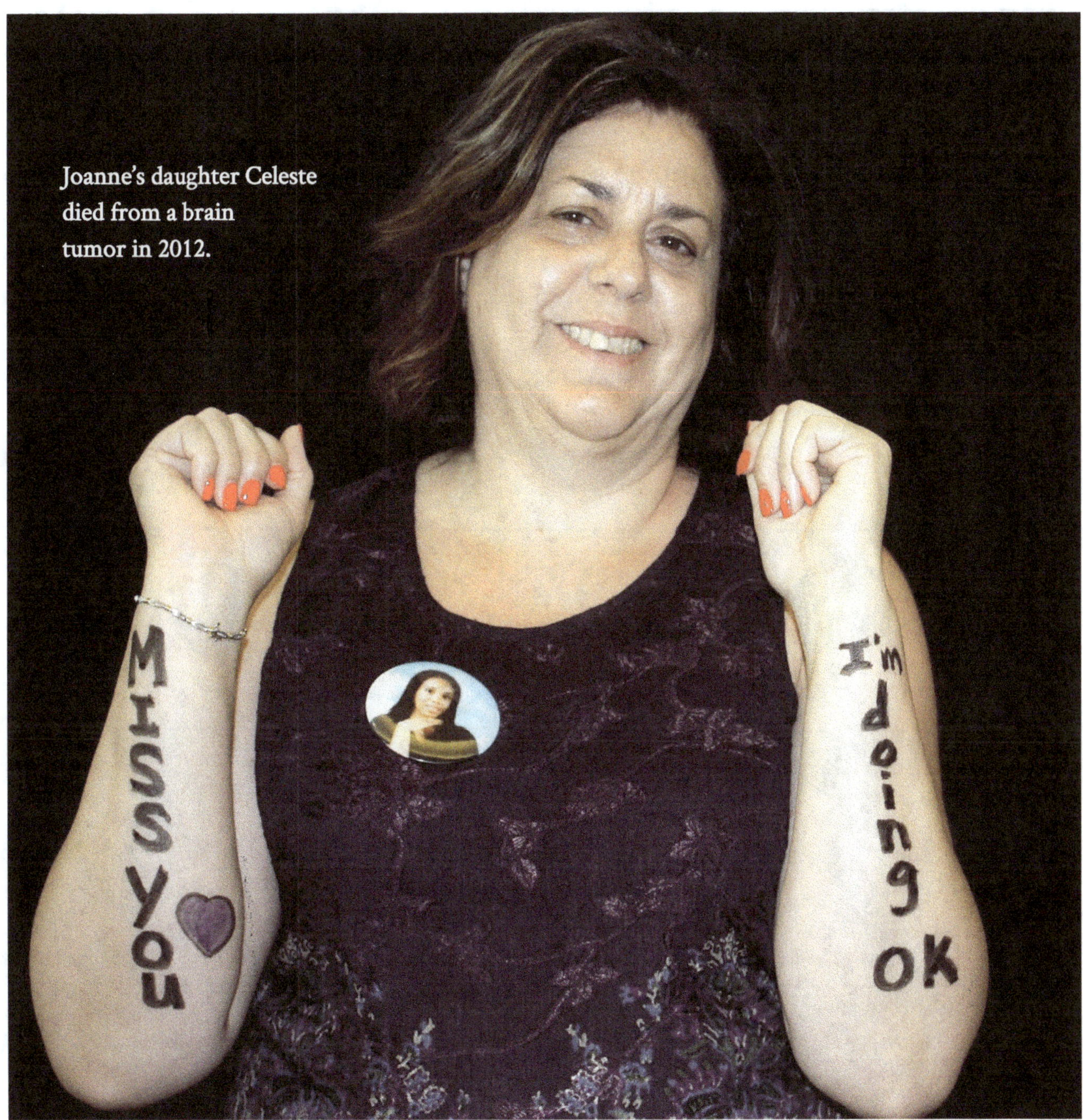
Joanne's daughter Celeste
died from a brain
tumor in 2012.
MISS YOU
I'm doing OK

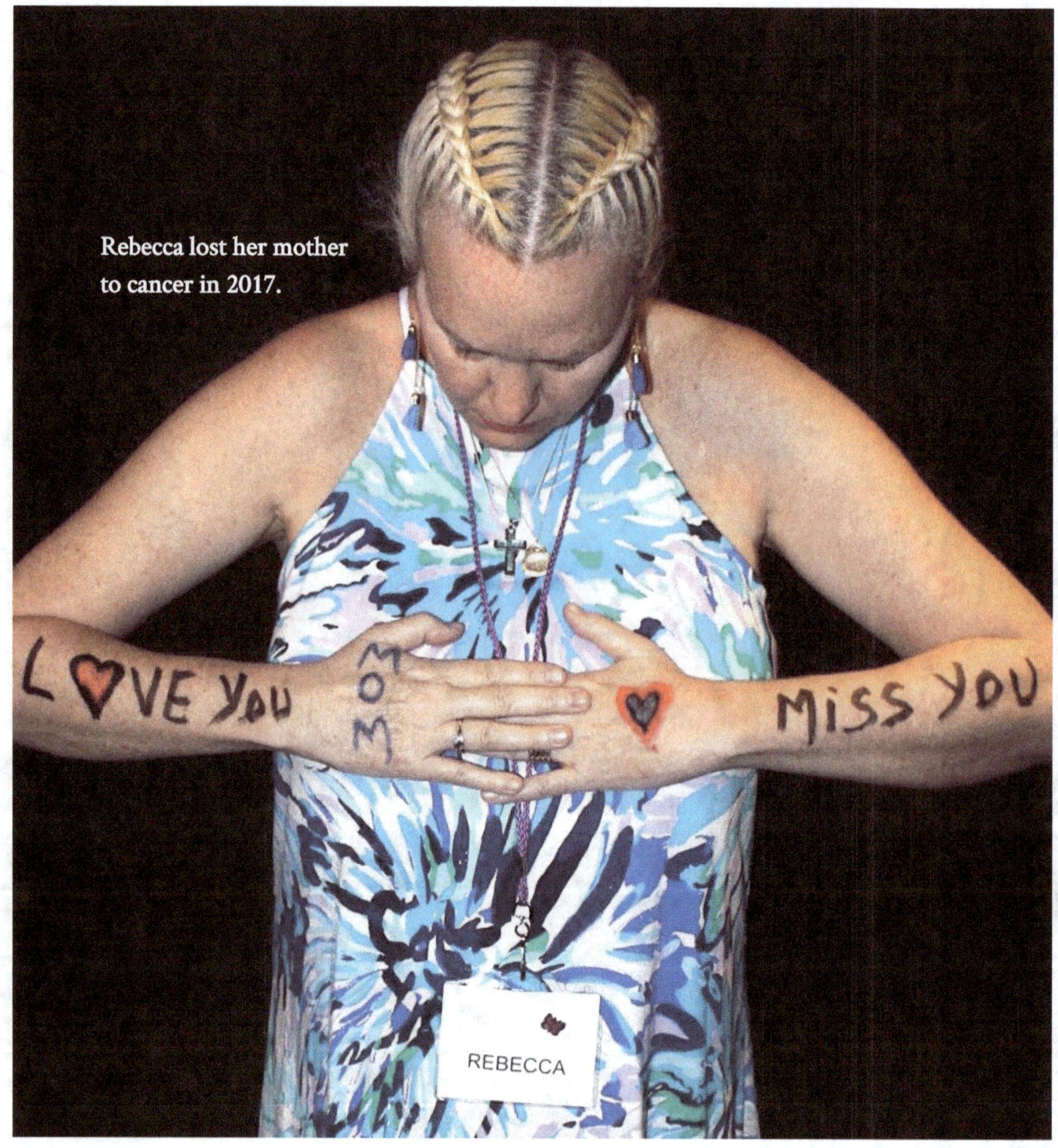

Rebecca lost her mother
to cancer in 2017.

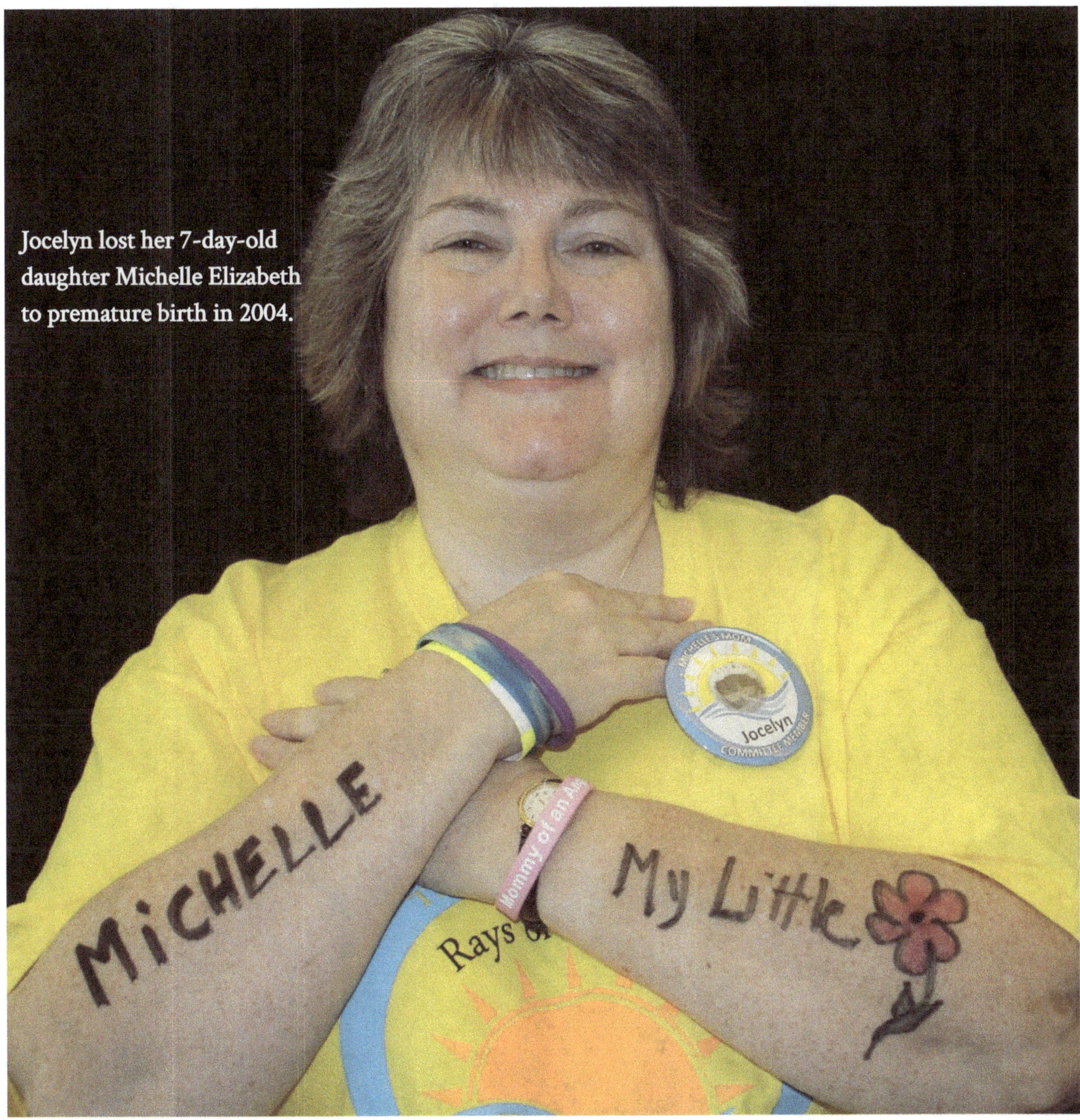

Jocelyn lost her 7-day-old daughter Michelle Elizabeth to premature birth in 2004.

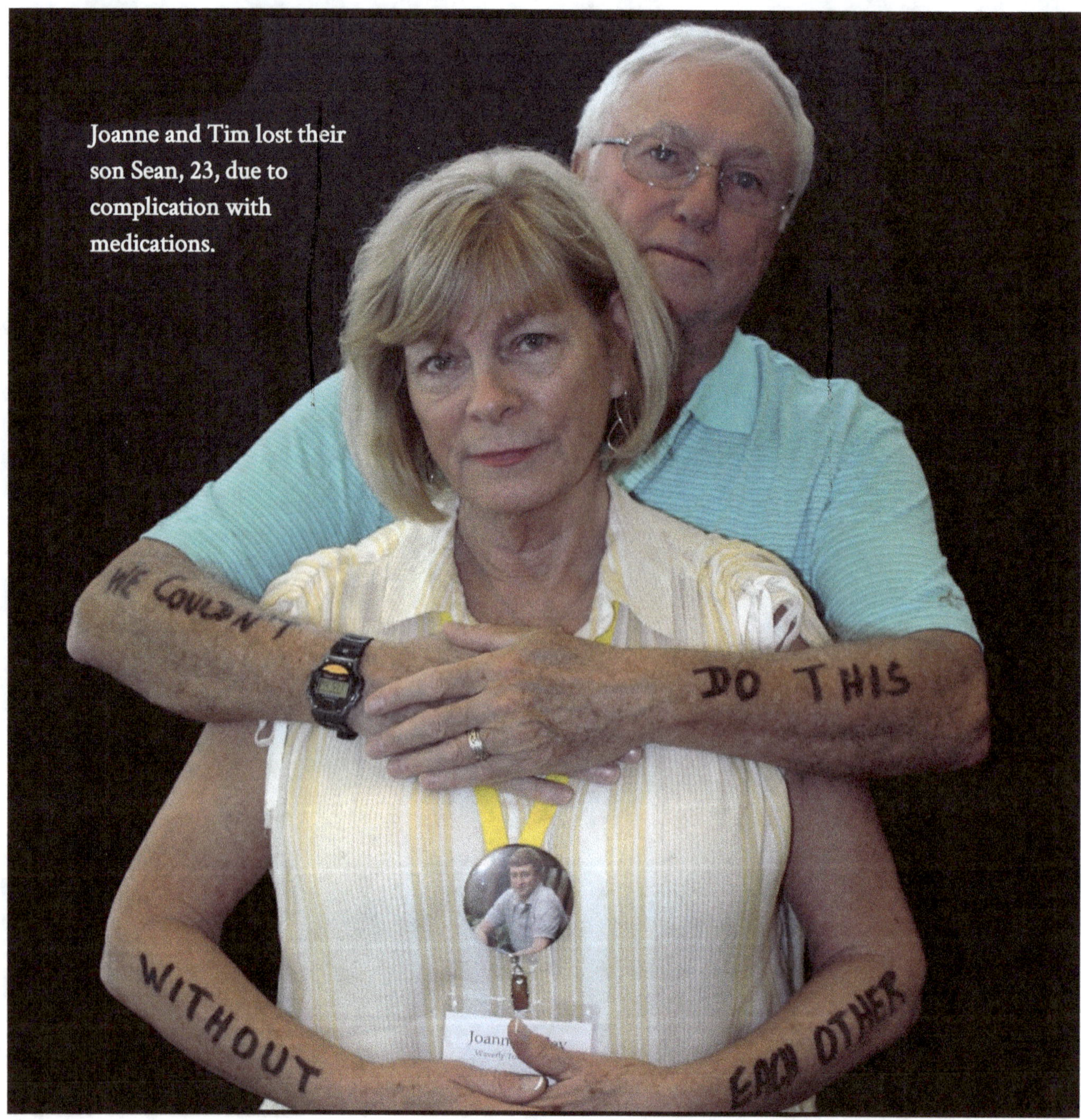

Joanne and Tim lost their son Sean, 23, due to complication with medications.

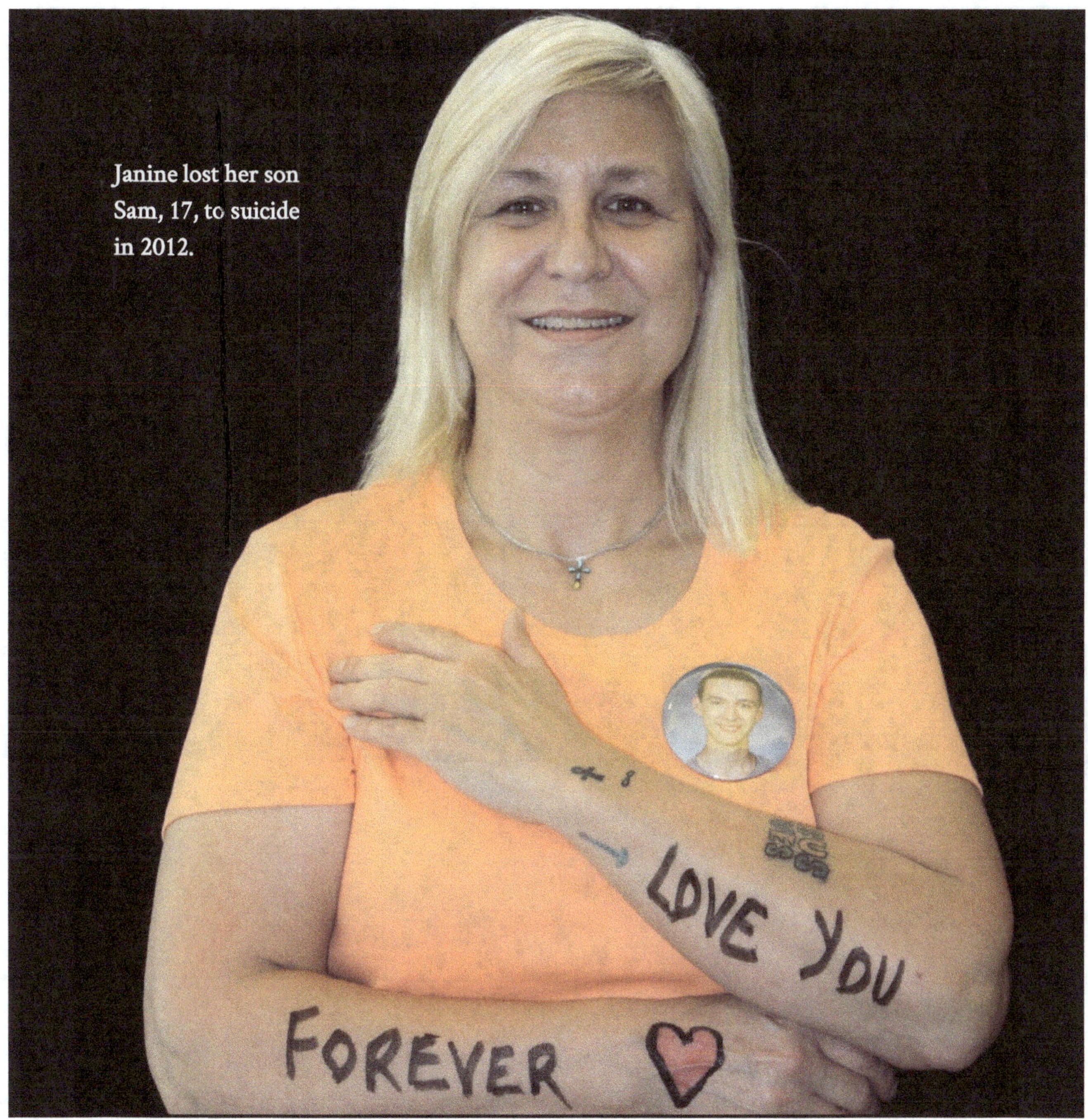

Janine lost her son
Sam, 17, to suicide
in 2012.

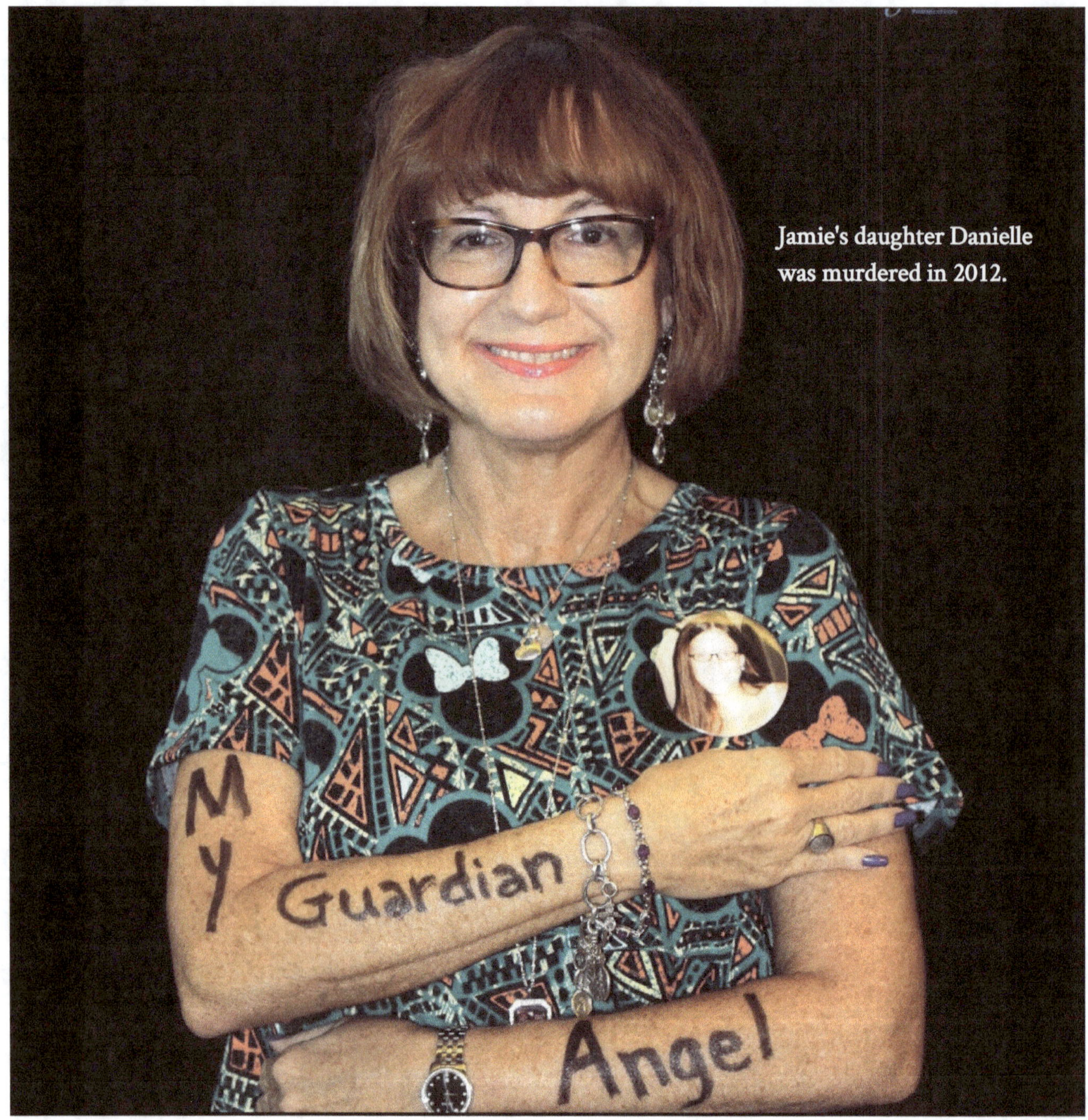

Jamie's daughter Danielle was murdered in 2012.

My
Guardian
Angel

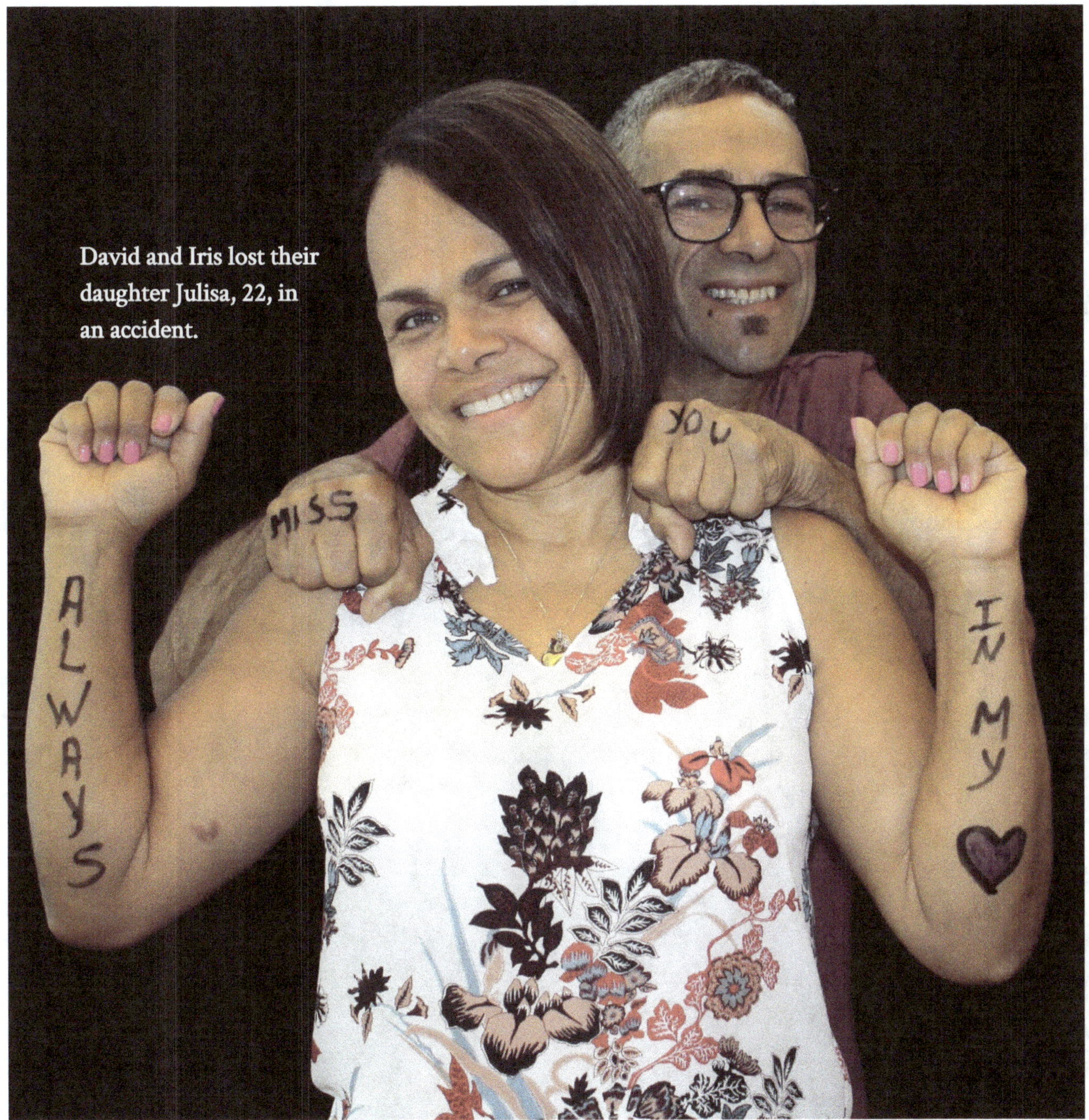

David and Iris lost their daughter Julisa, 22, in an accident.

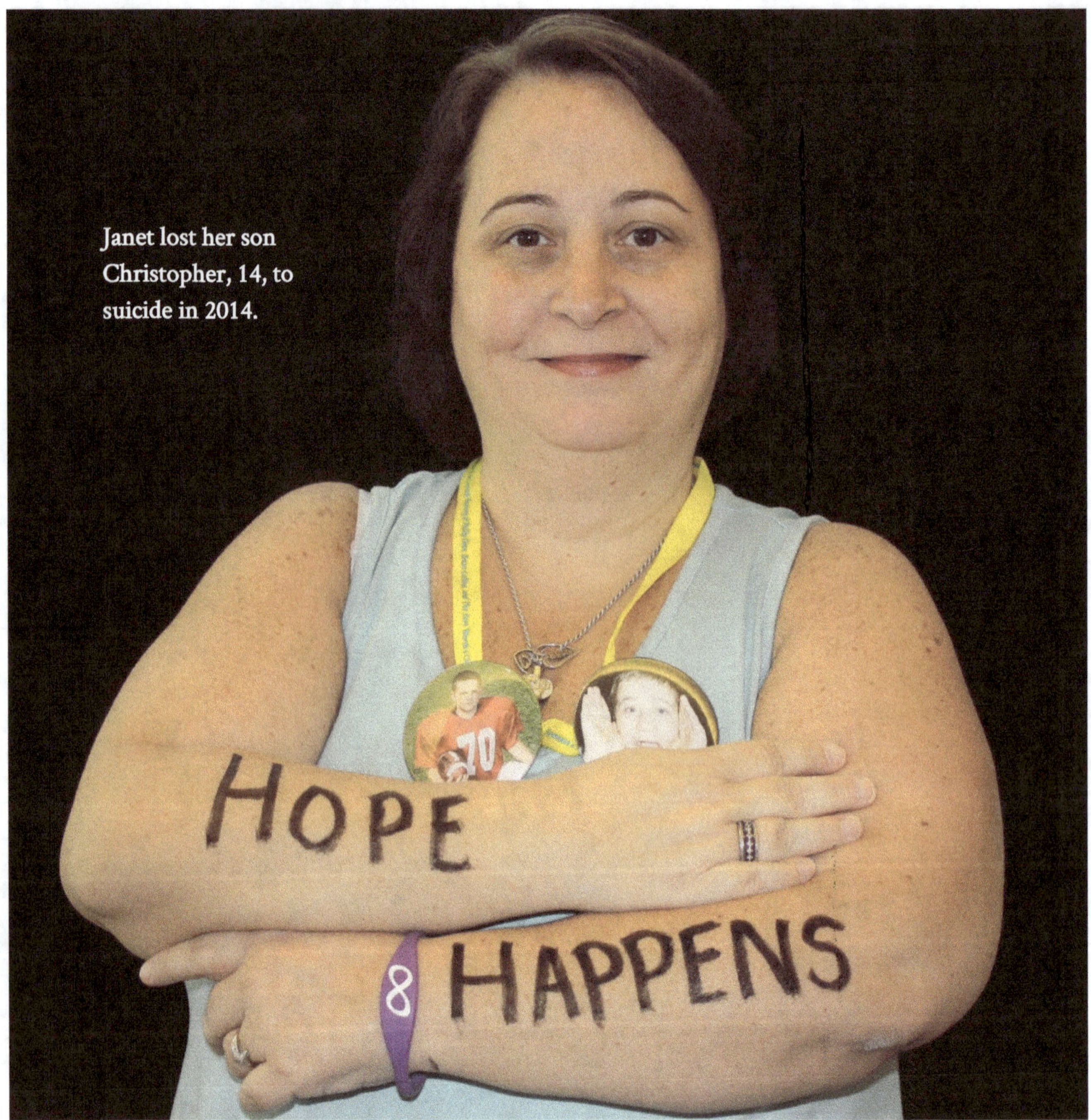

Janet lost her son Christopher, 14, to suicide in 2014.

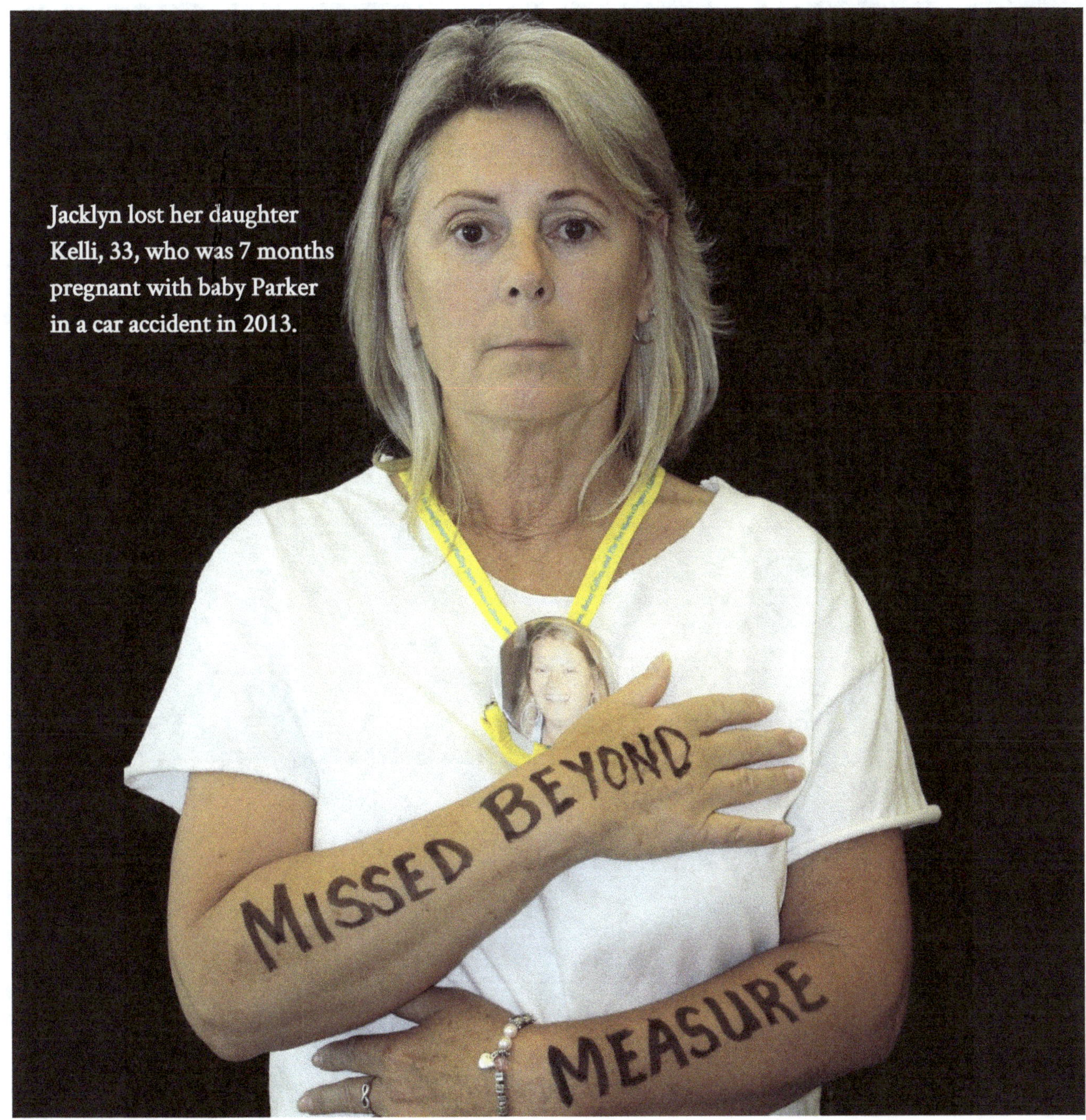

Jacklyn lost her daughter
Kelli, 33, who was 7 months
pregnant with baby Parker
in a car accident in 2013.

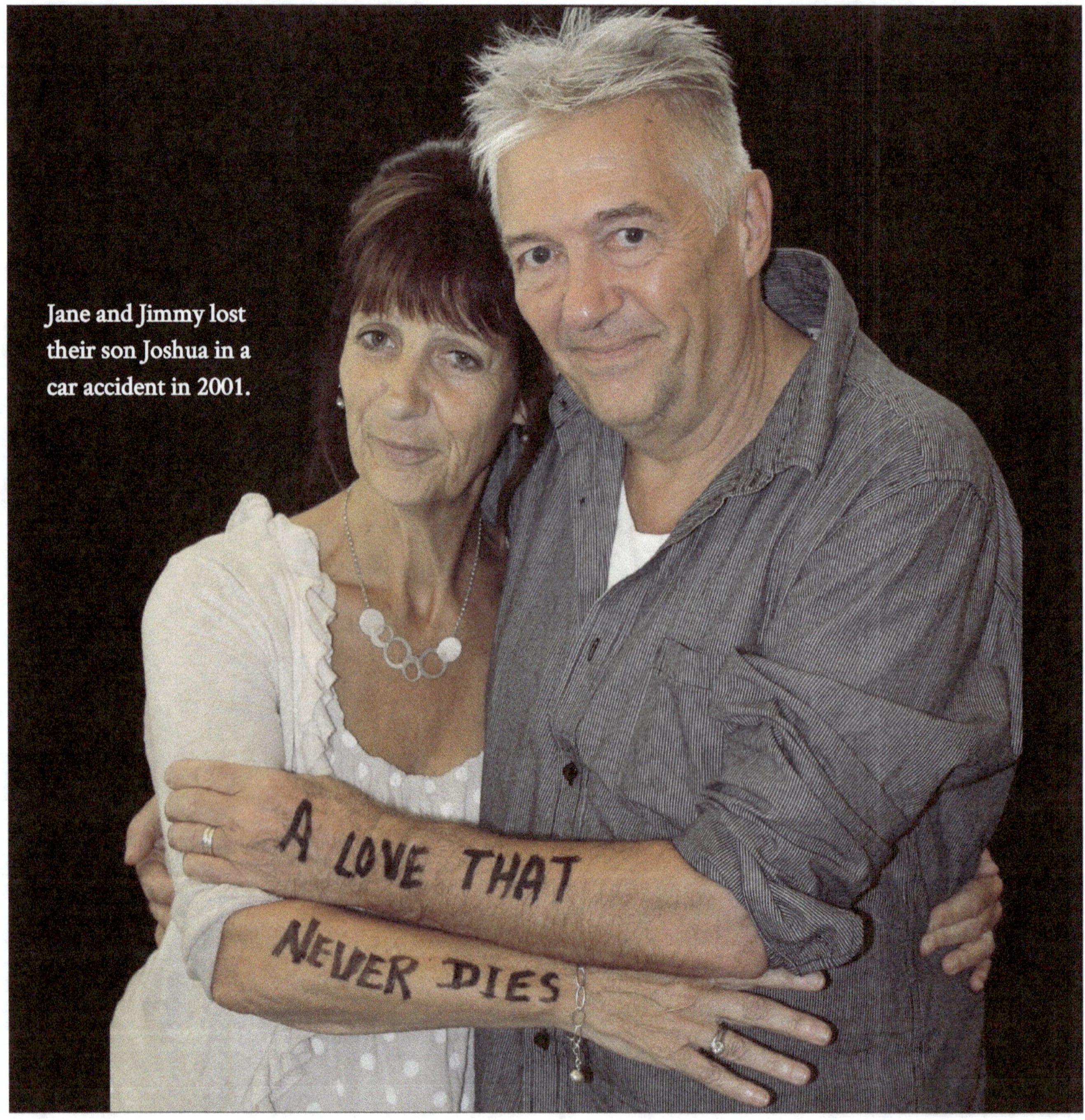

Jane and Jimmy lost
their son Joshua in a
car accident in 2001.

A LOVE THAT
NEVER DIES

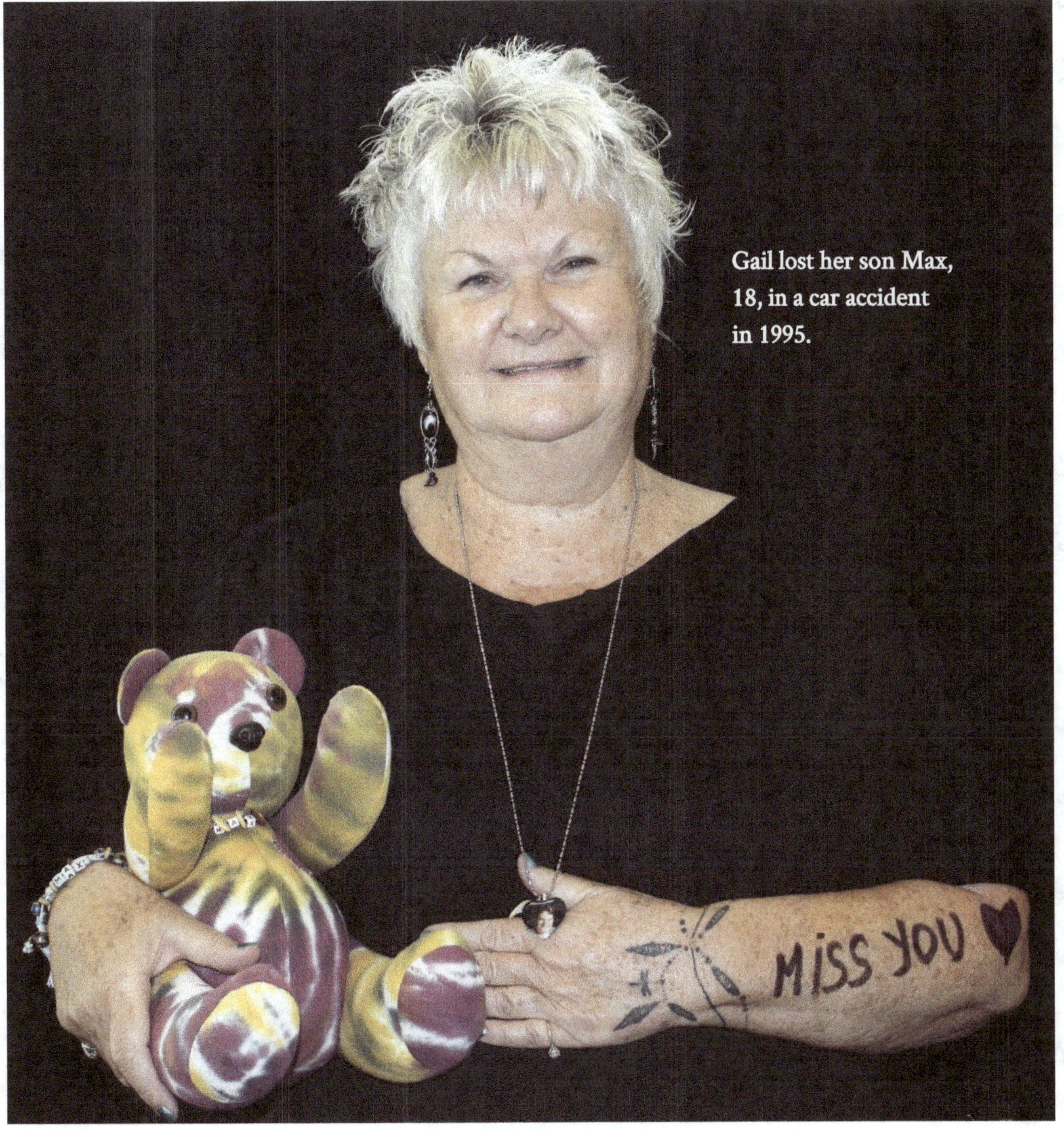

Gail lost her son Max, 18, in a car accident in 1995.

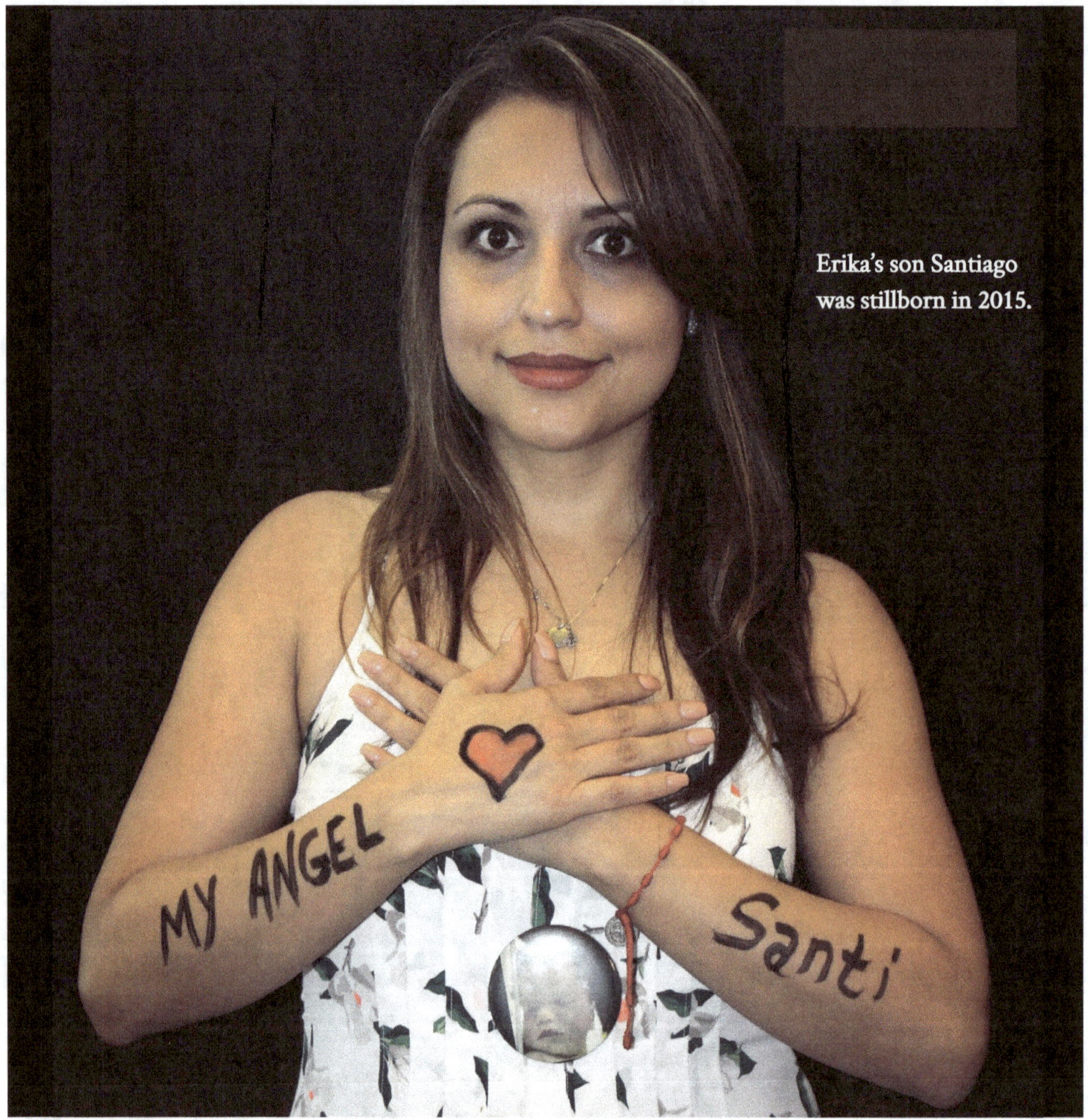

Erika's son Santiago was stillborn in 2015.

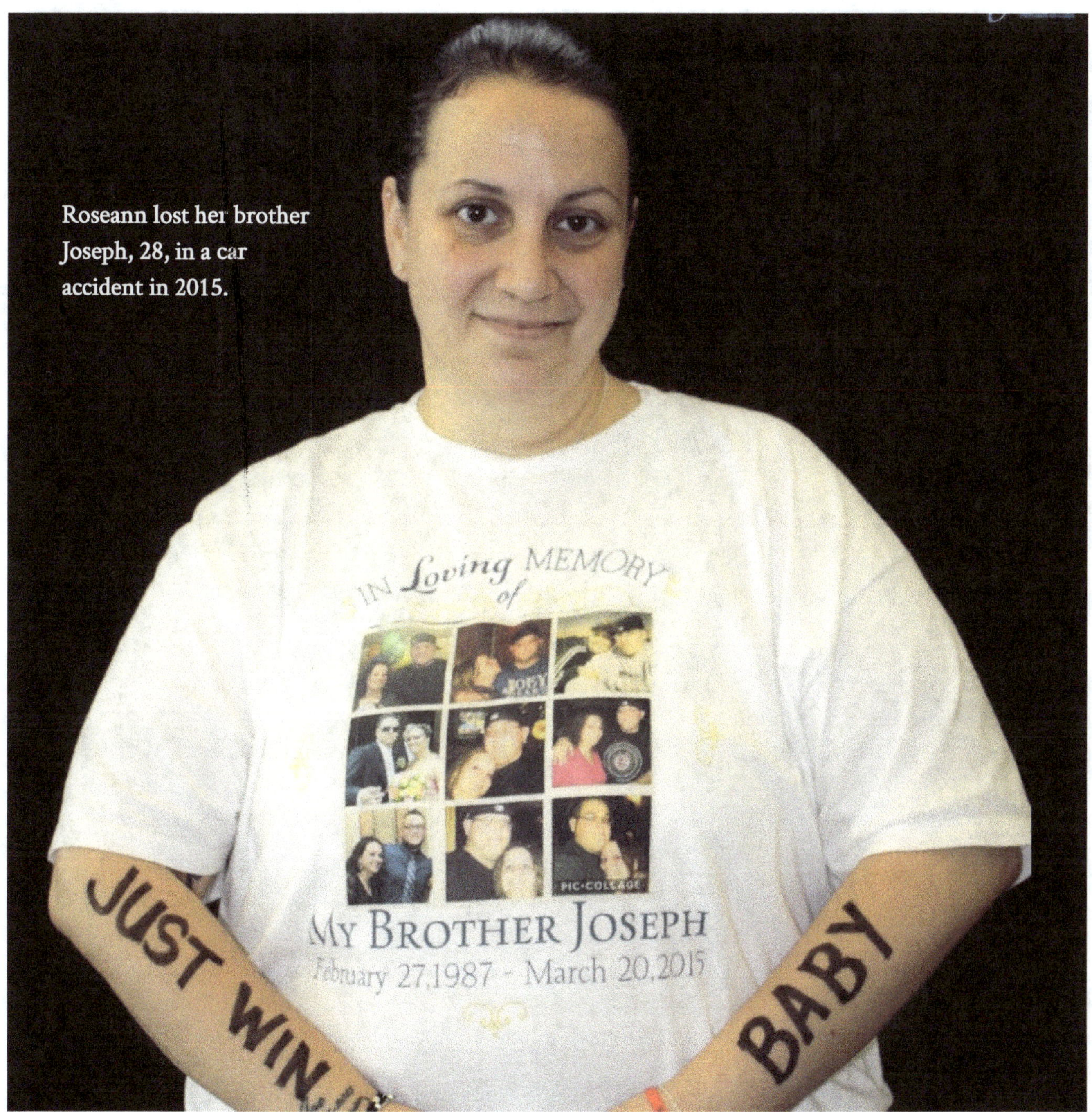

Roseann lost her brother Joseph, 28, in a car accident in 2015.

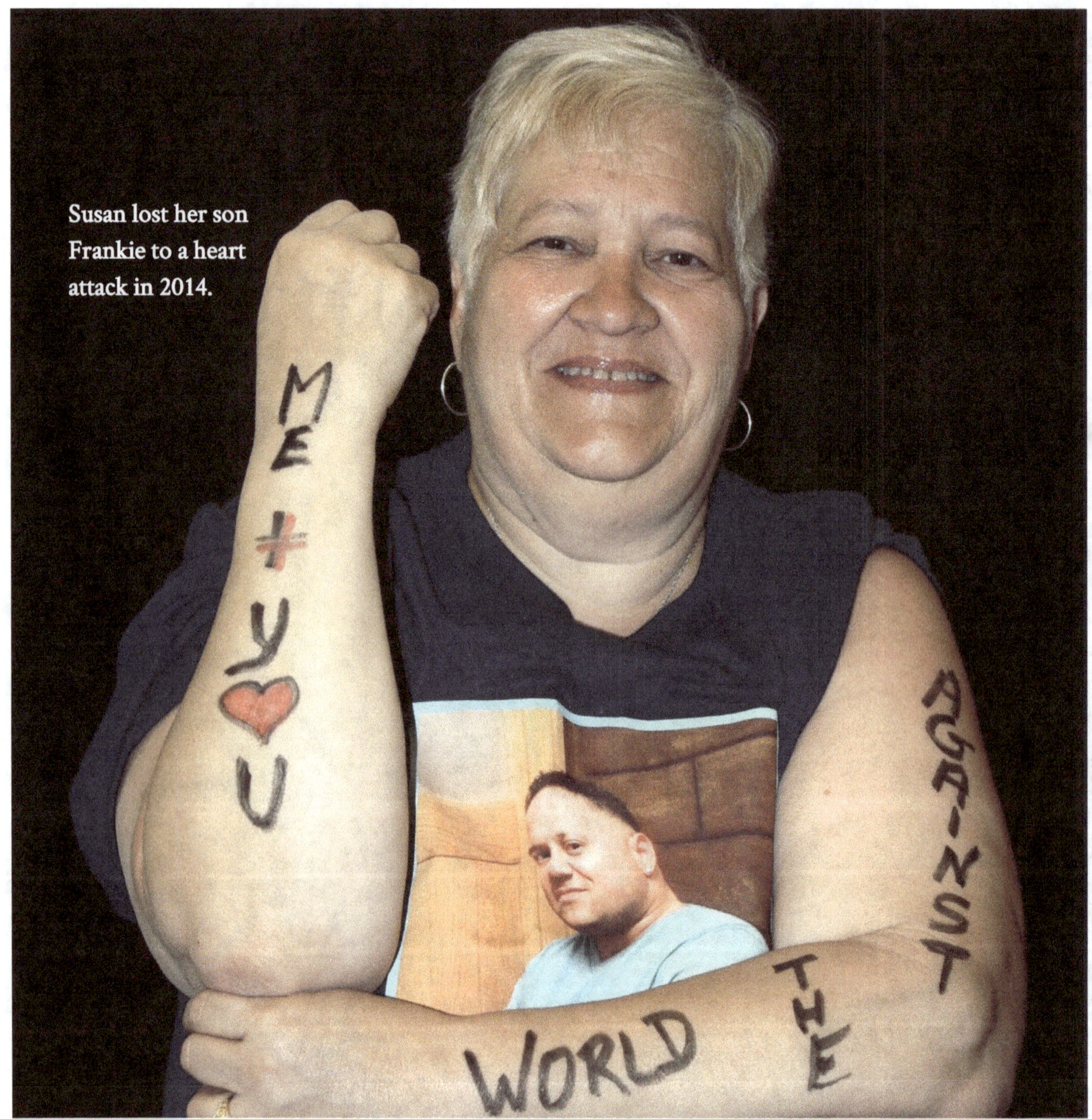

Susan lost her son Frankie to a heart attack in 2014.

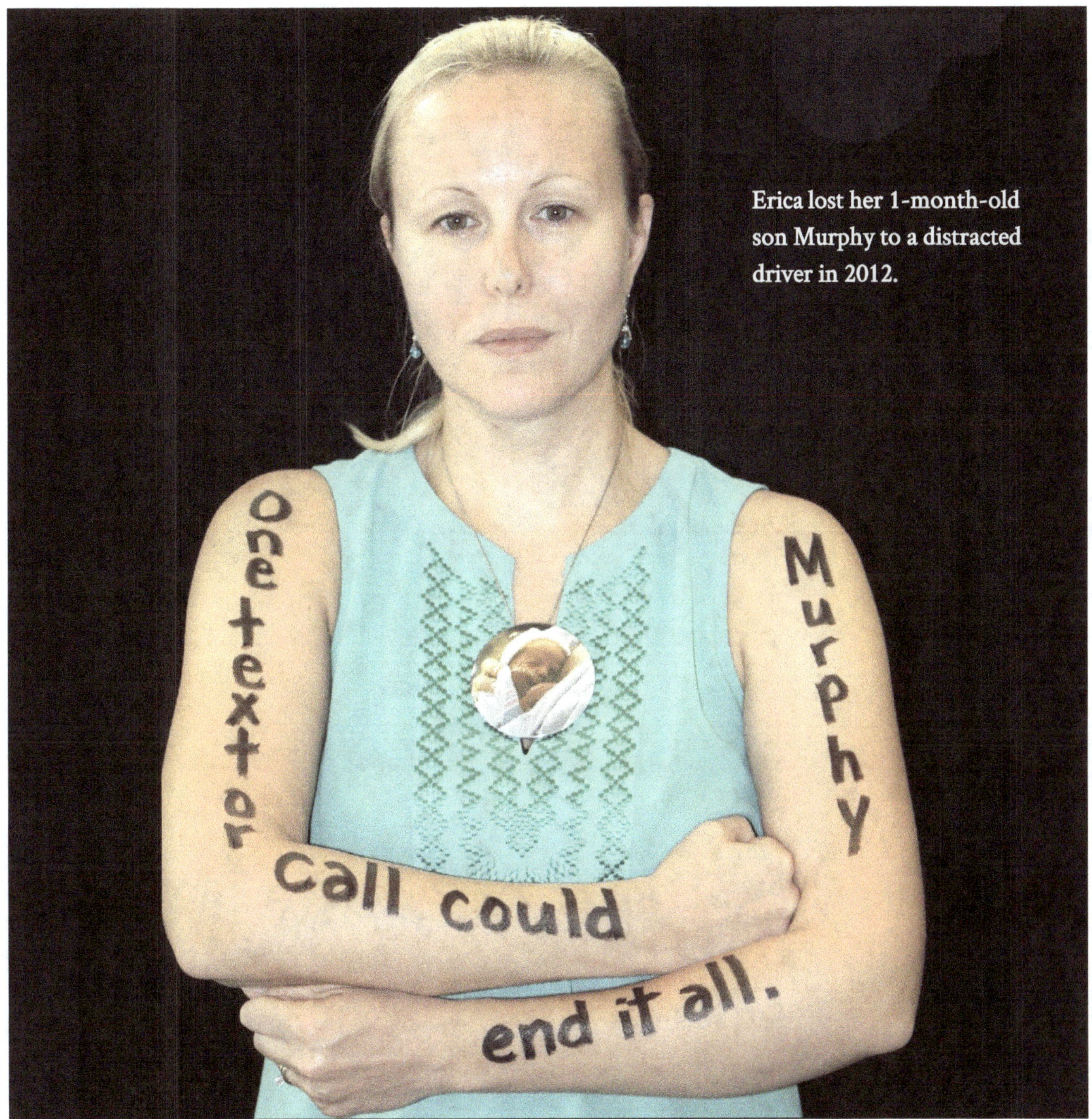

Erica lost her 1-month-old son Murphy to a distracted driver in 2012.

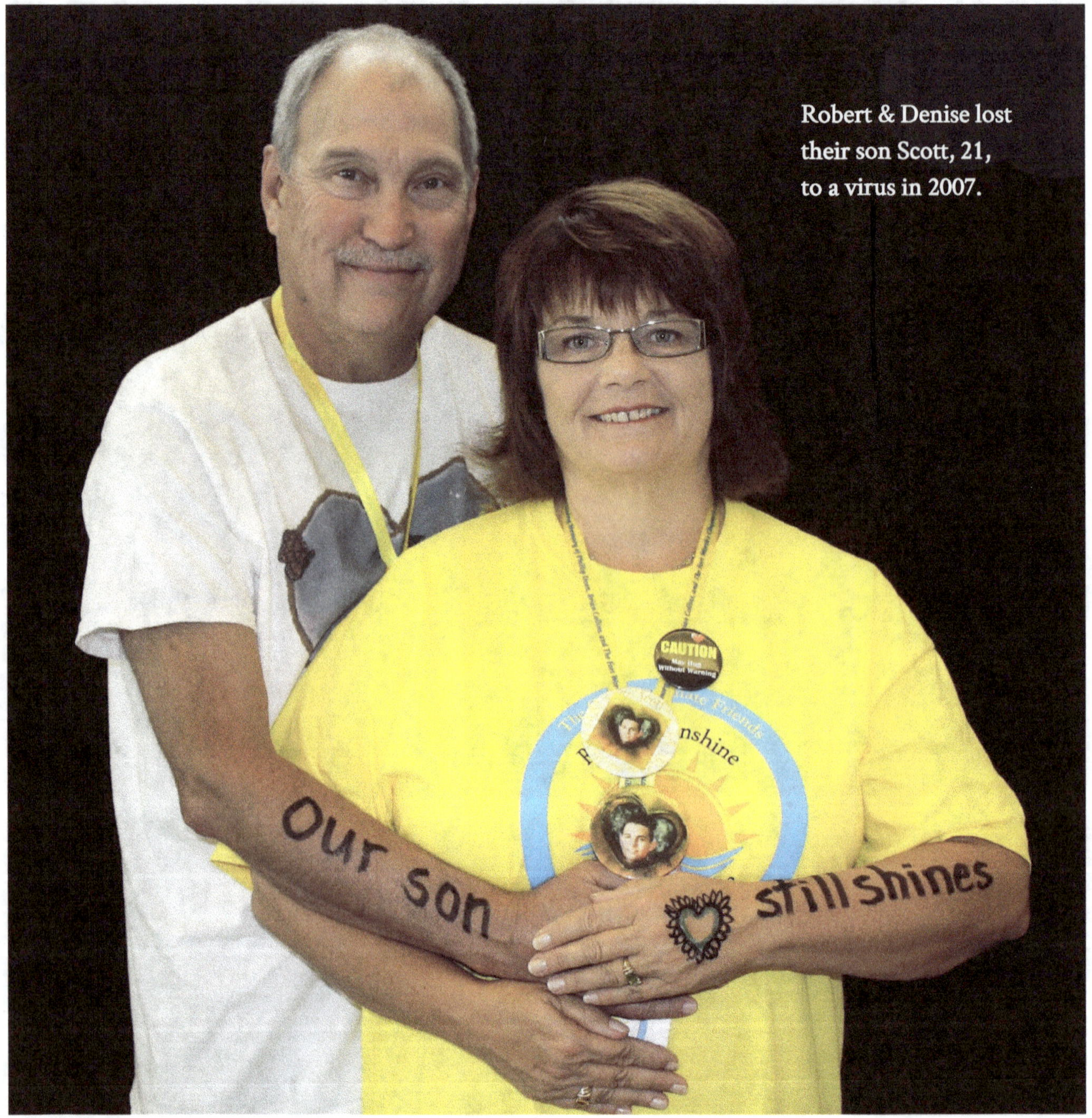

Robert & Denise lost
their son Scott, 21,
to a virus in 2007.
CAUTION
Our son
still shines

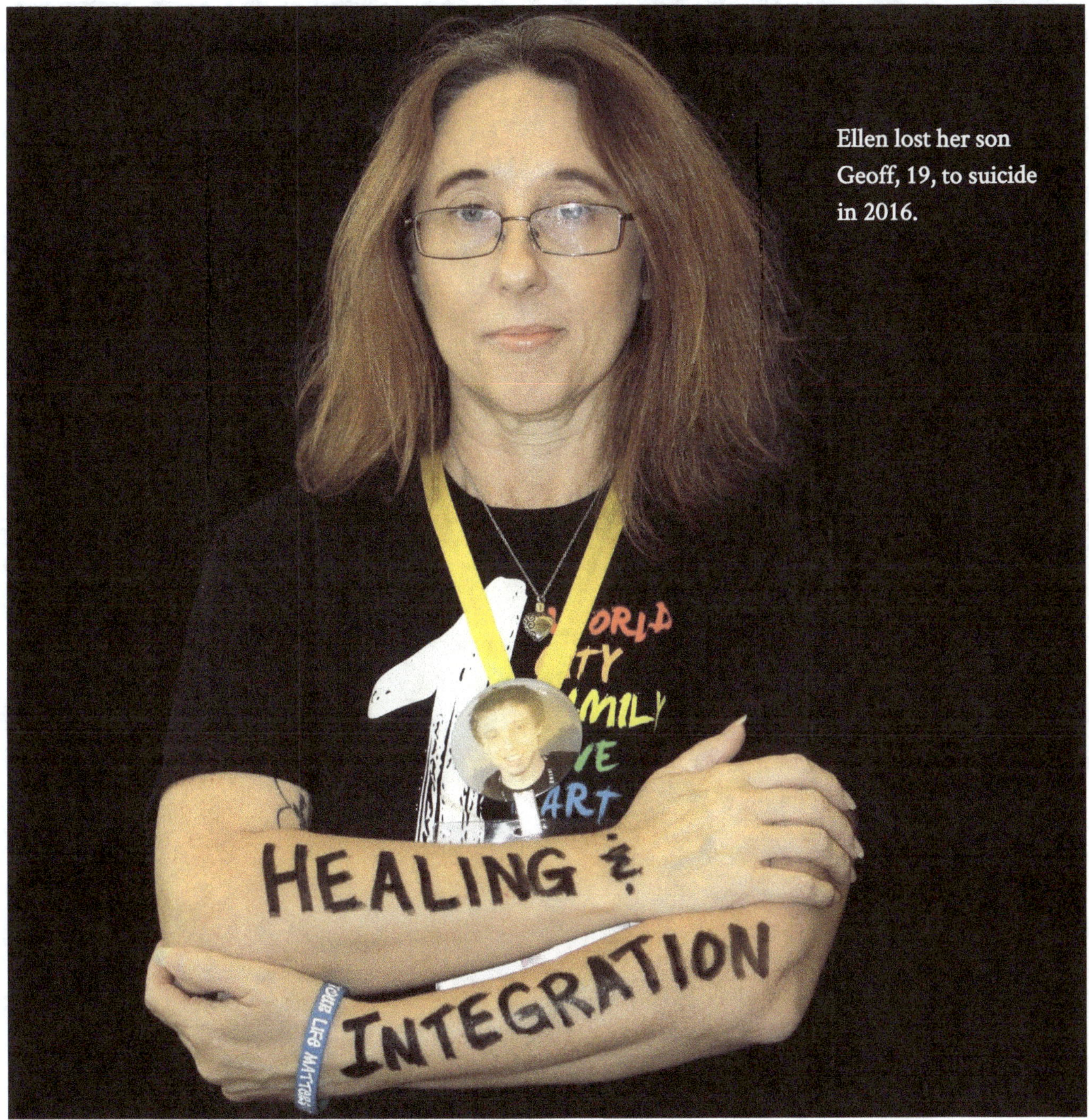

Ellen lost her son Geoff, 19, to suicide in 2016.

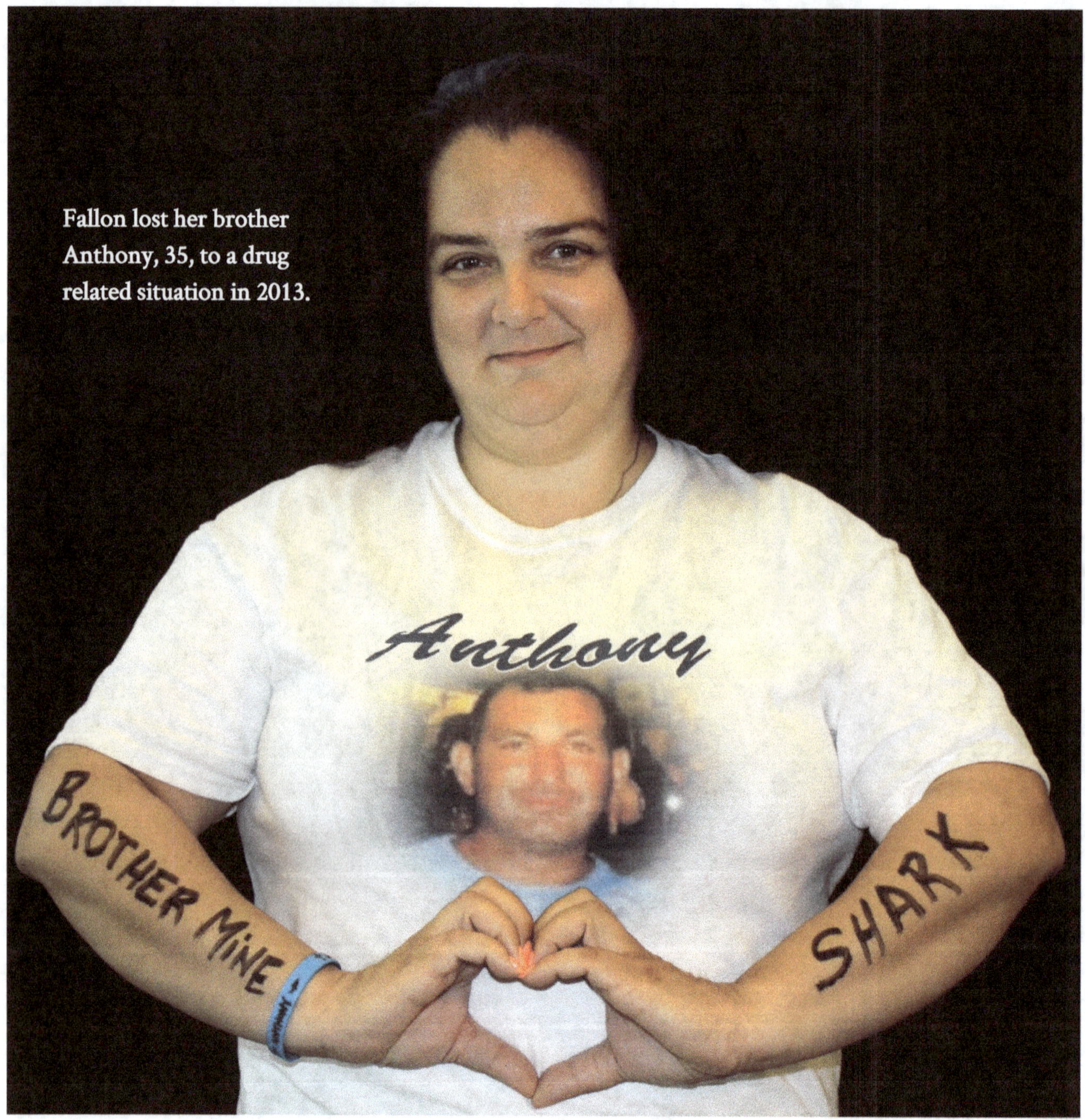

Fallon lost her brother Anthony, 35, to a drug related situation in 2013.

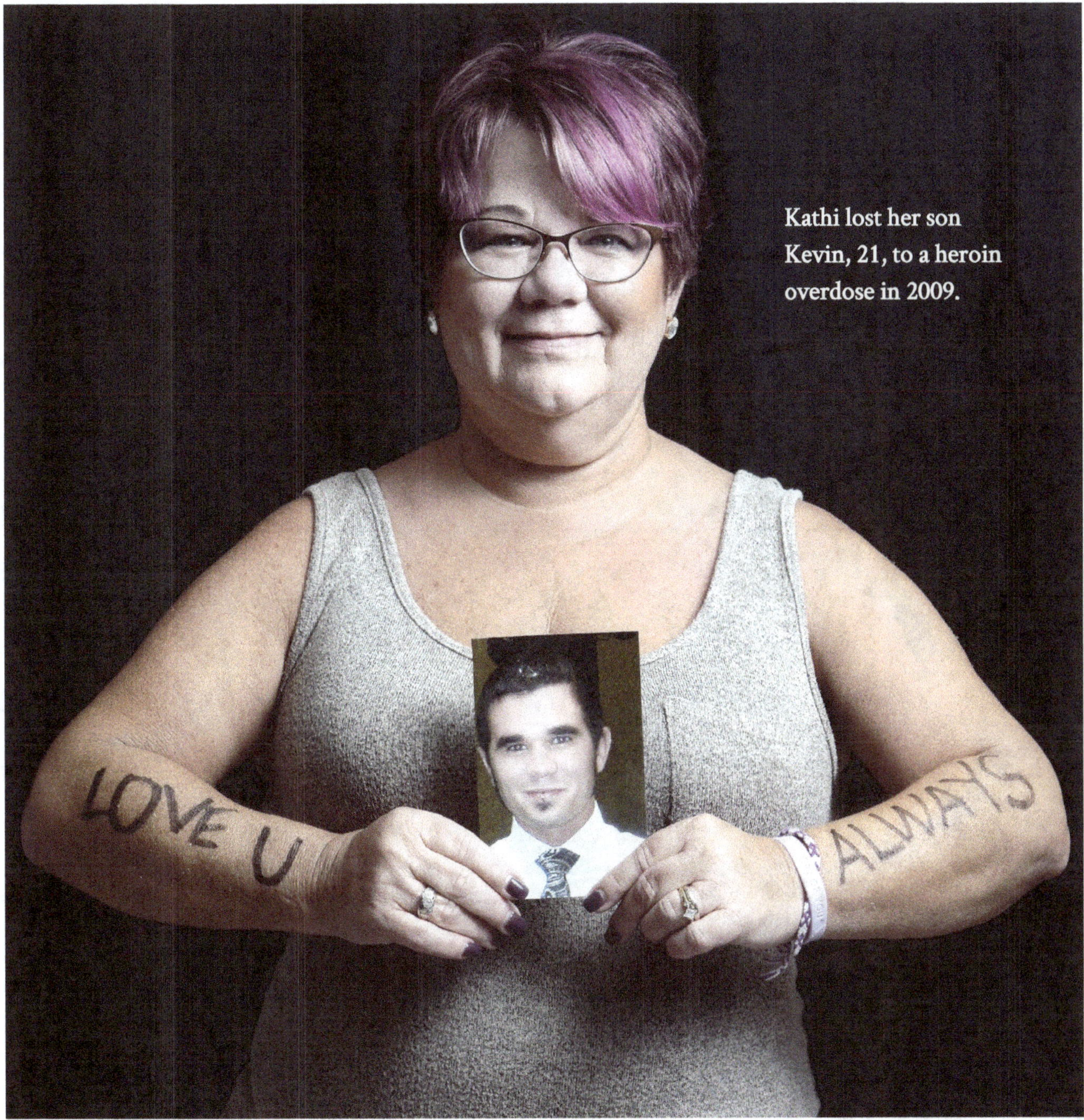

Kathi lost her son
Kevin, 21, to a heroin
overdose in 2009.

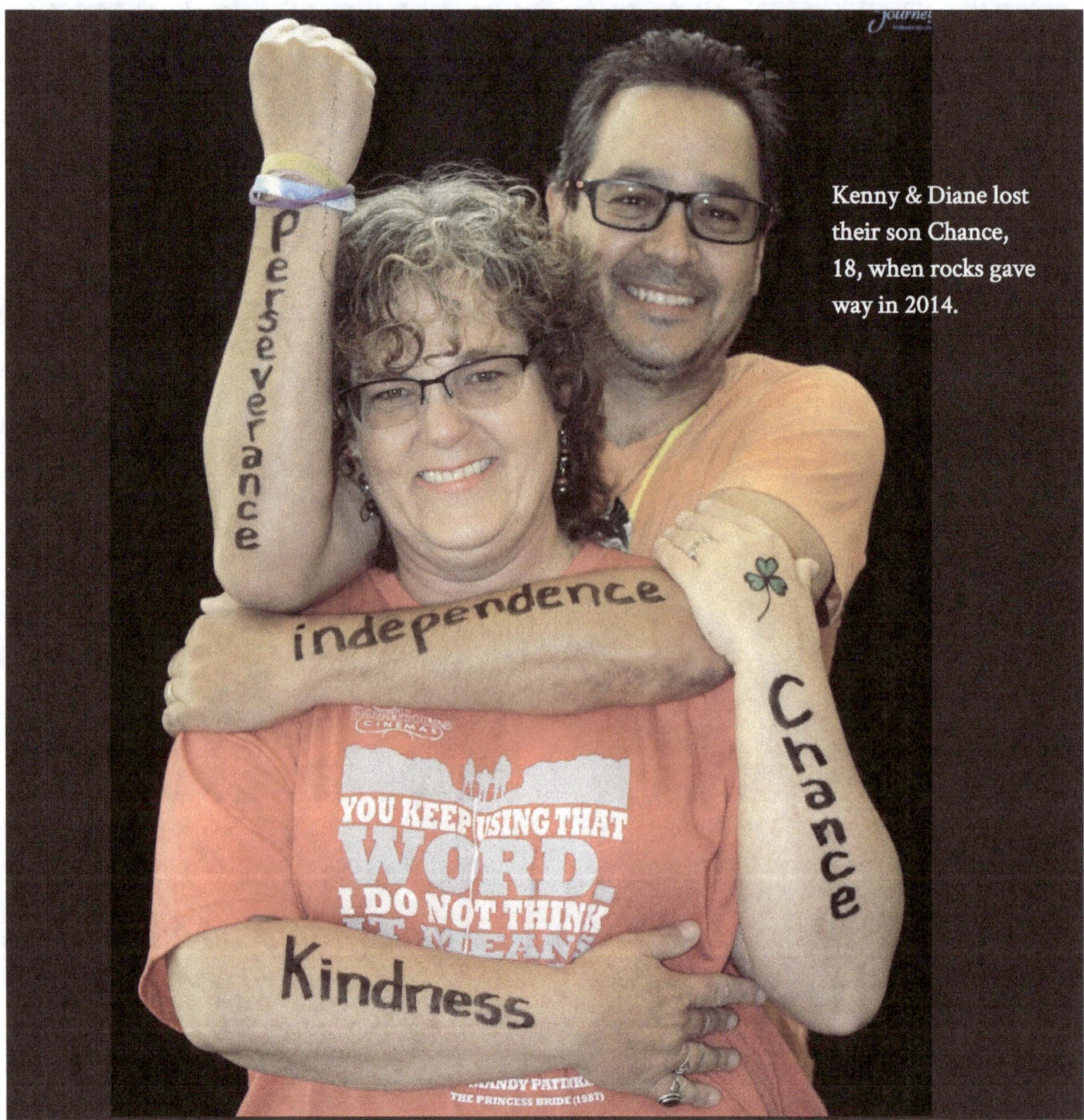

Kenny & Diane lost their son Chance, 18, when rocks gave way in 2014.

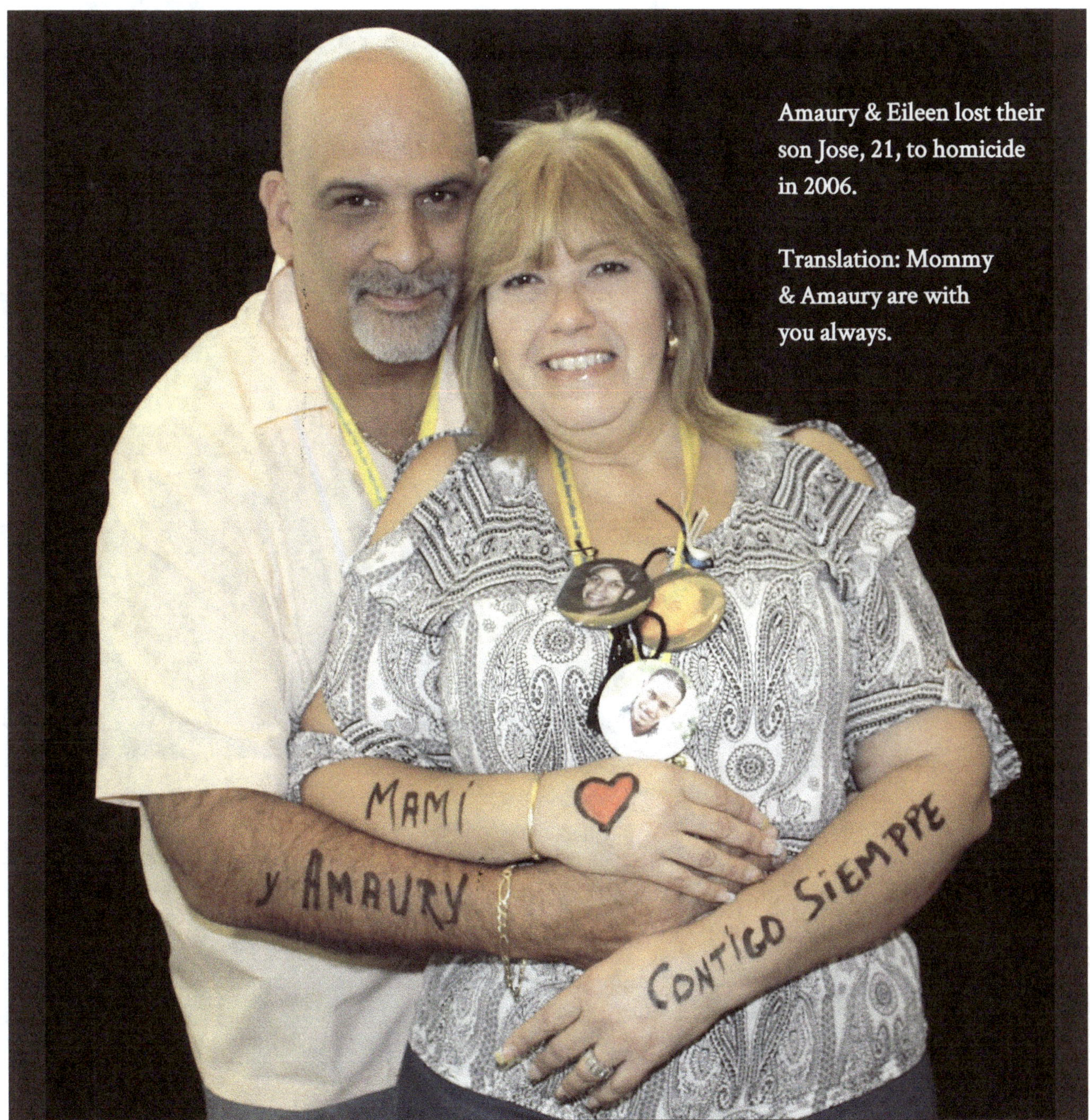

Amaury & Eileen lost their son Jose, 21, to homicide in 2006.

Translation: Mommy & Amaury are with you always.

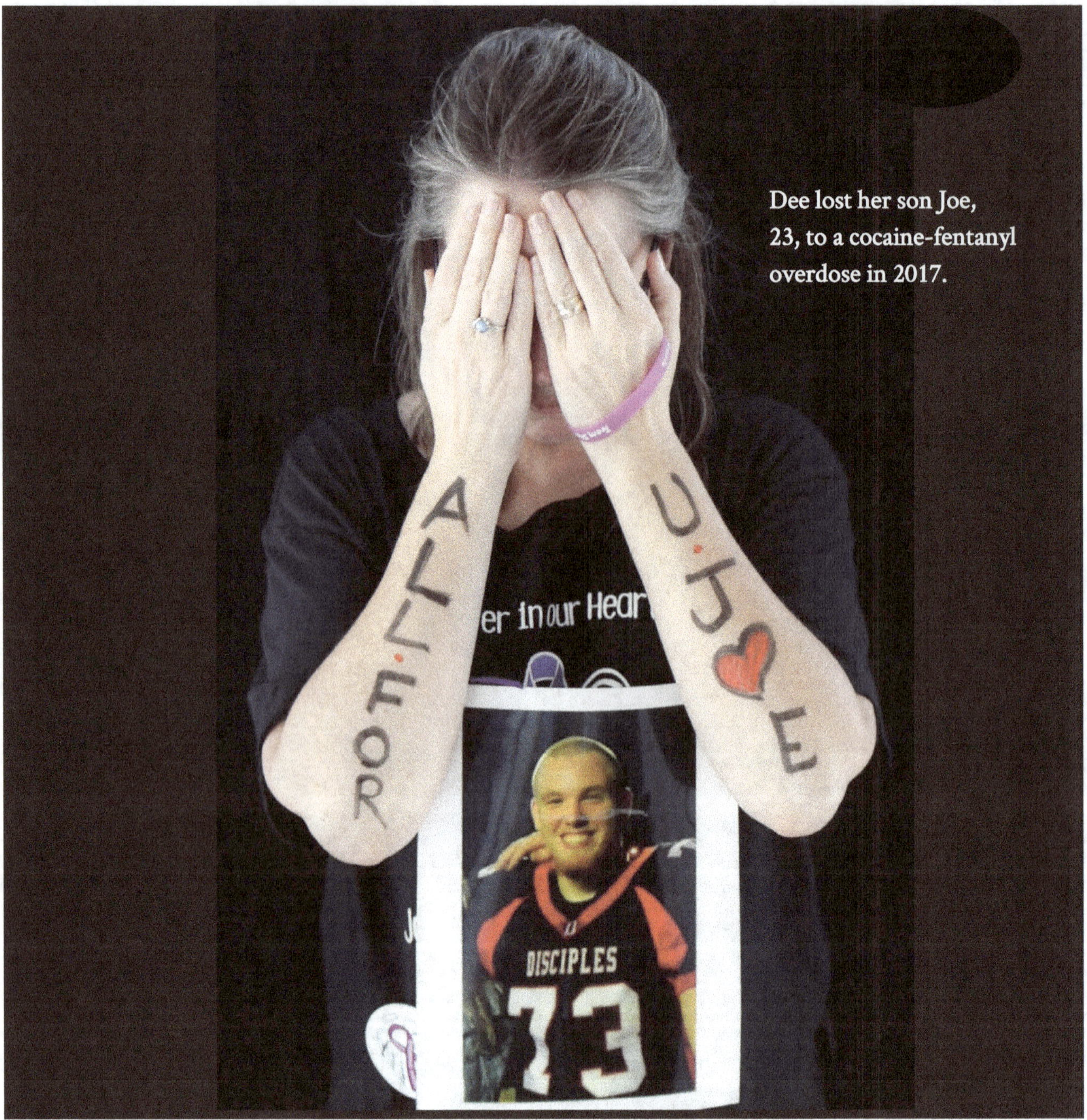

Dee lost her son Joe, 23, to a cocaine-fentanyl overdose in 2017.

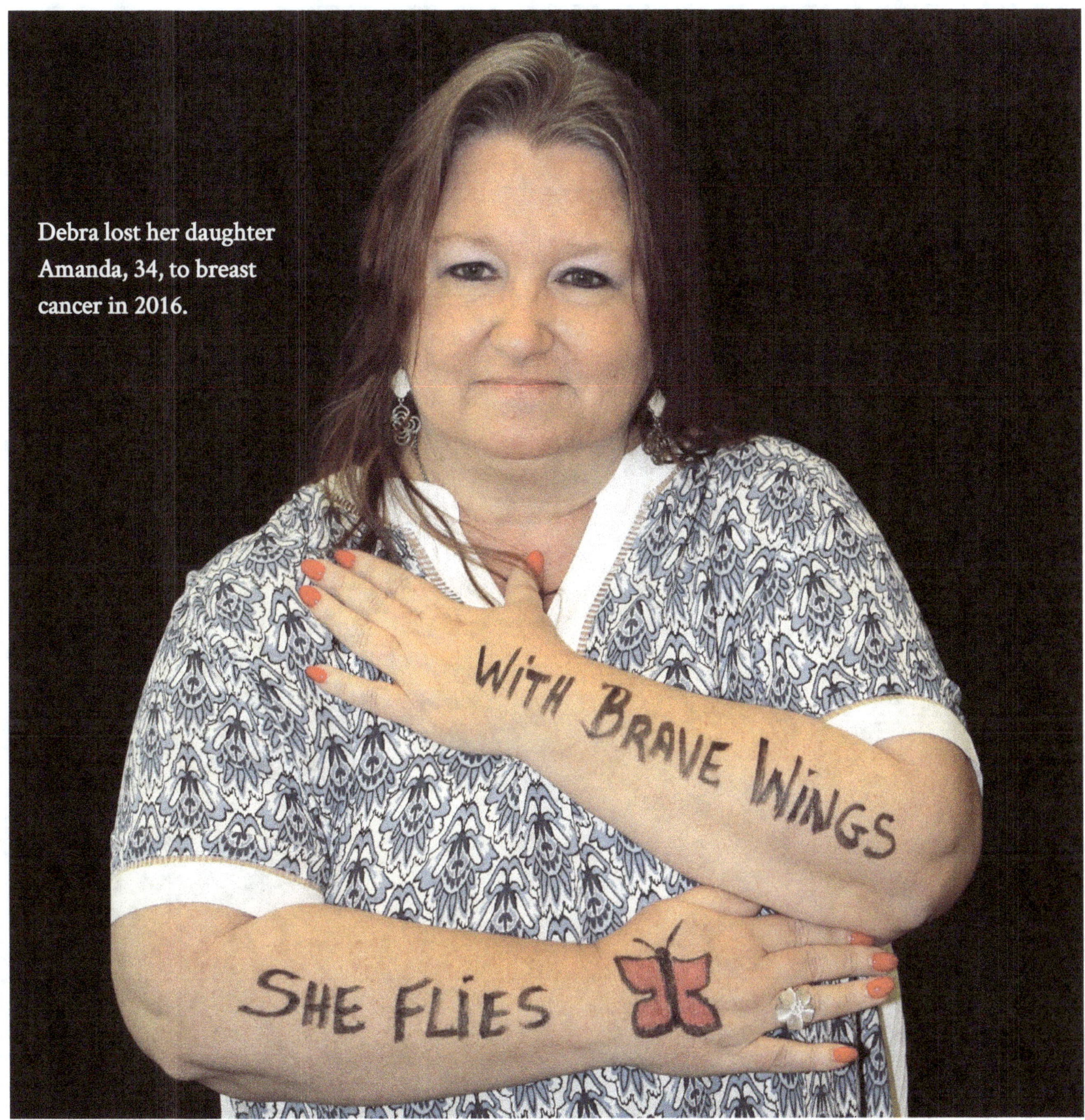

Debra lost her daughter Amanda, 34, to breast cancer in 2016.

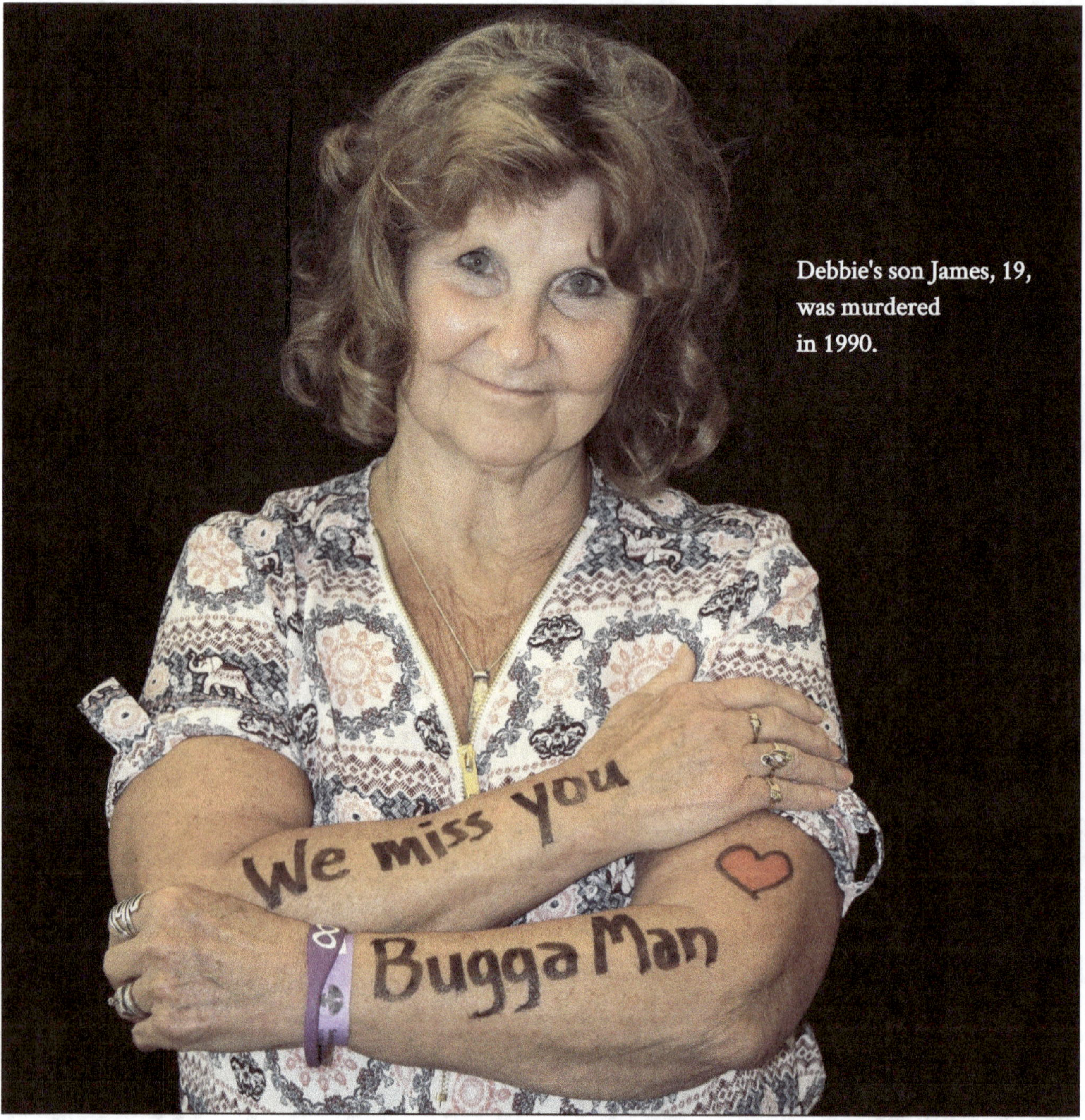

Debbie's son James, 19, was murdered in 1990.

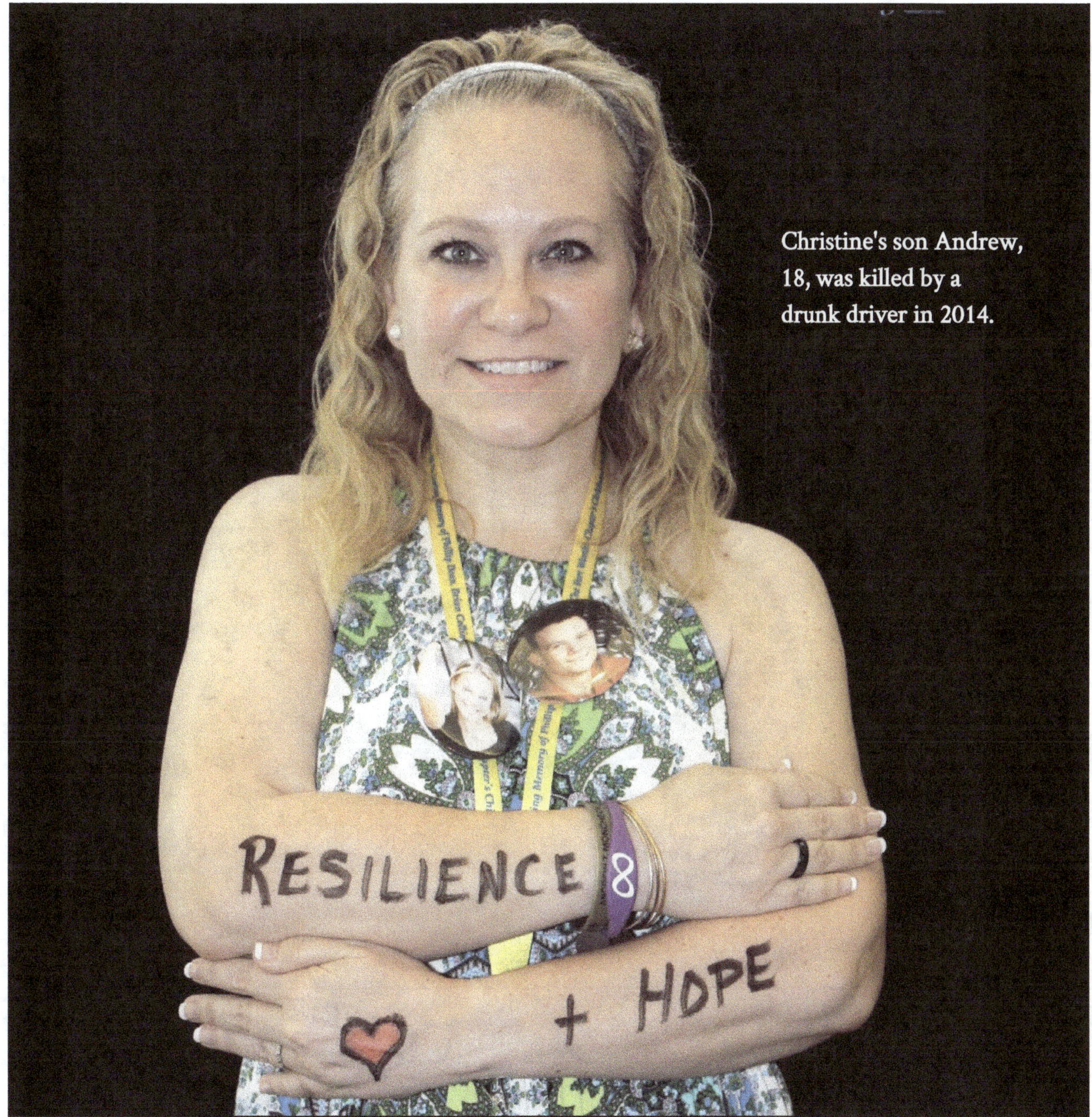

Christine's son Andrew, 18, was killed by a drunk driver in 2014.

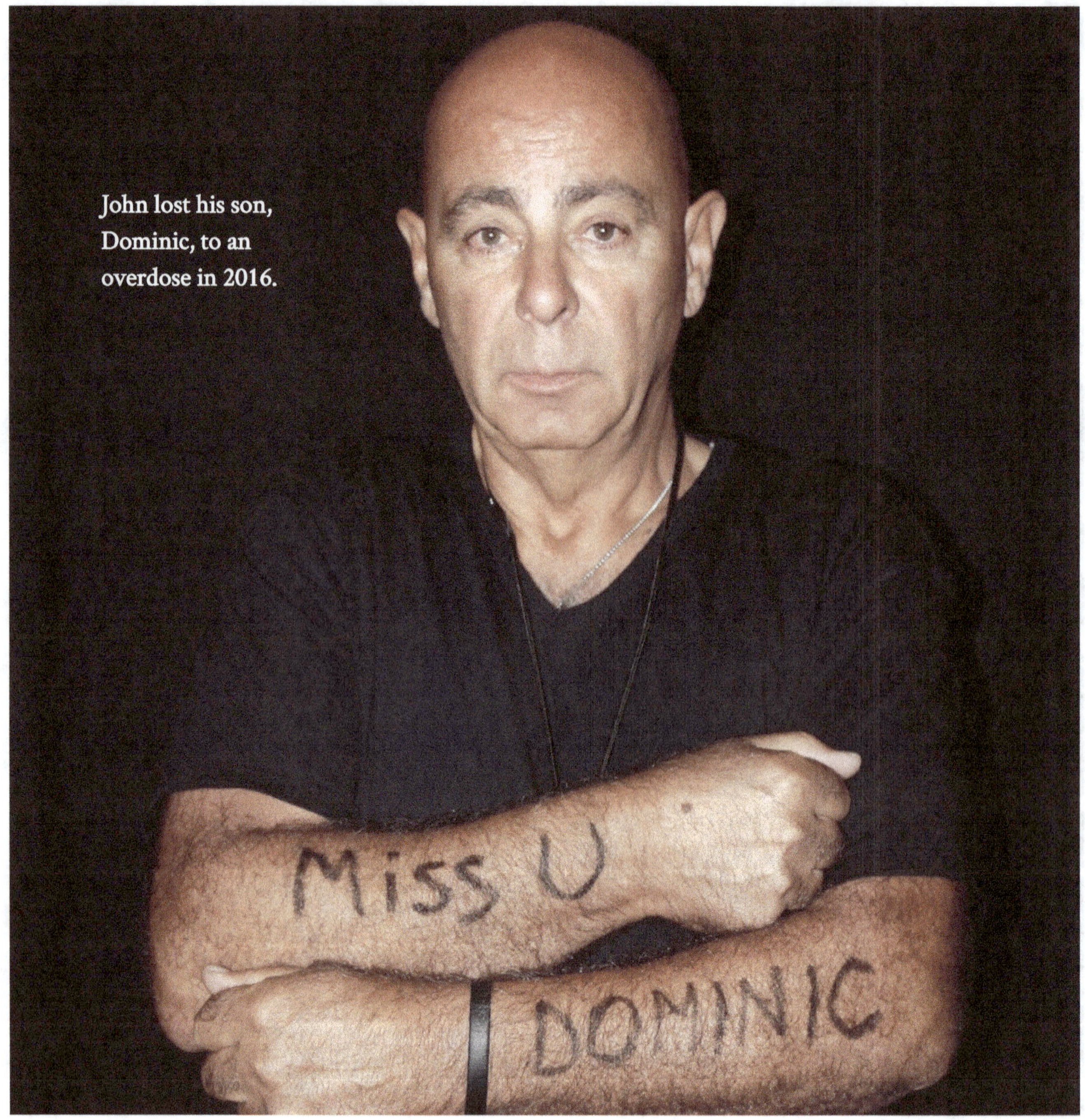

John lost his son, Dominic, to an overdose in 2016.

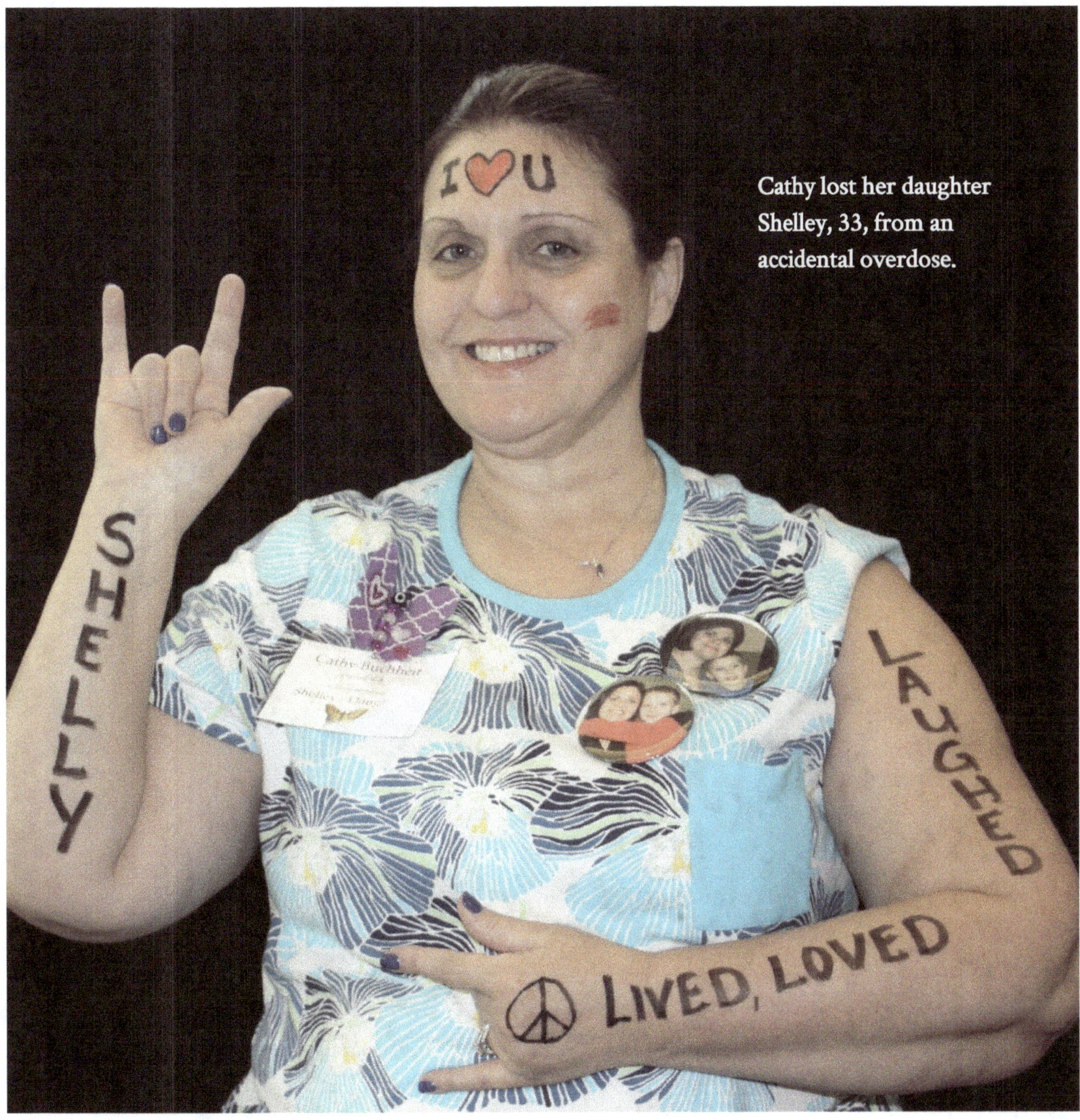

Cathy lost her daughter Shelley, 33, from an accidental overdose.

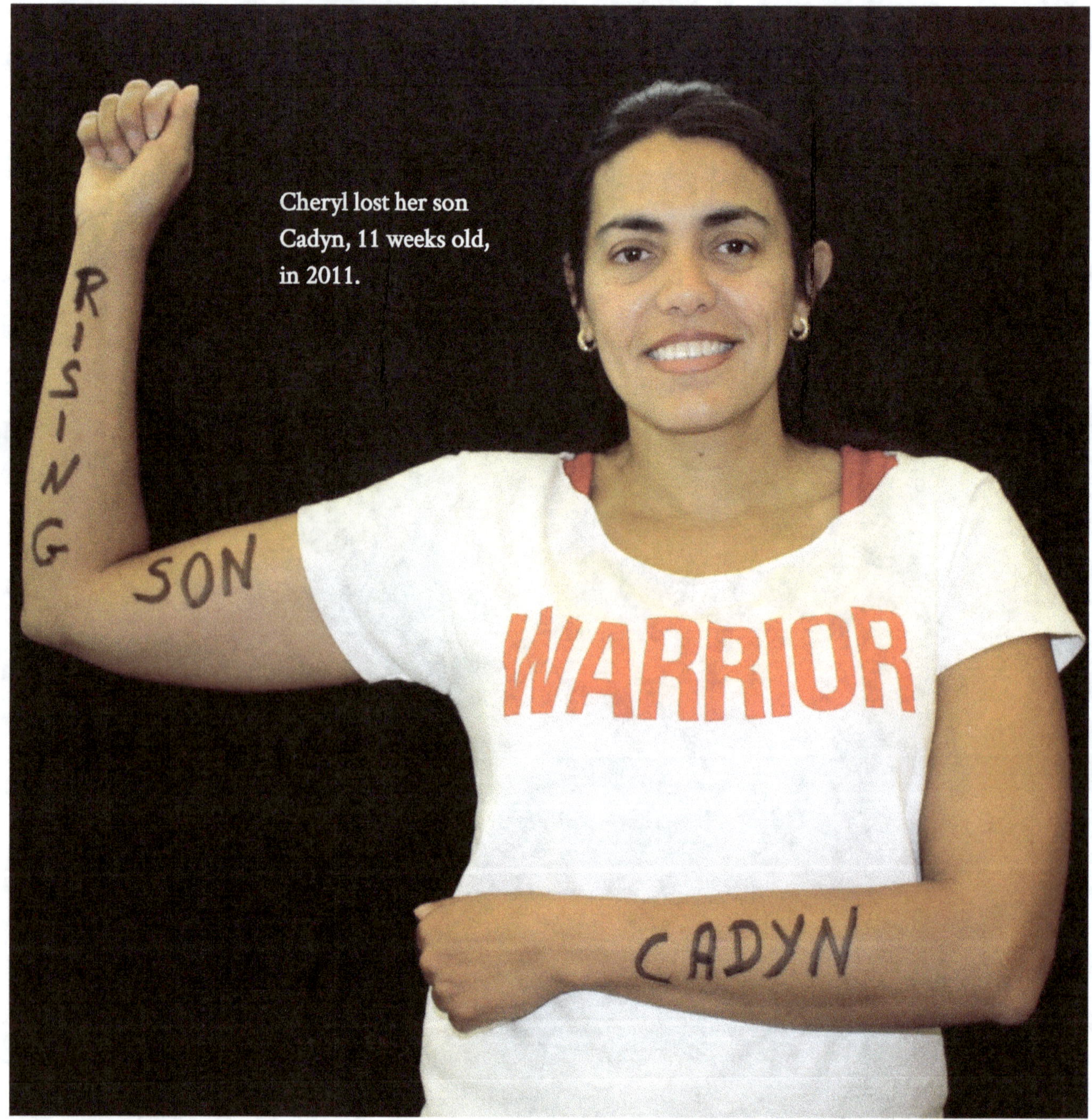

Cheryl lost her son
Cadyn, 11 weeks old,
in 2011.

RISING
SON
WARRIOR
CADYN

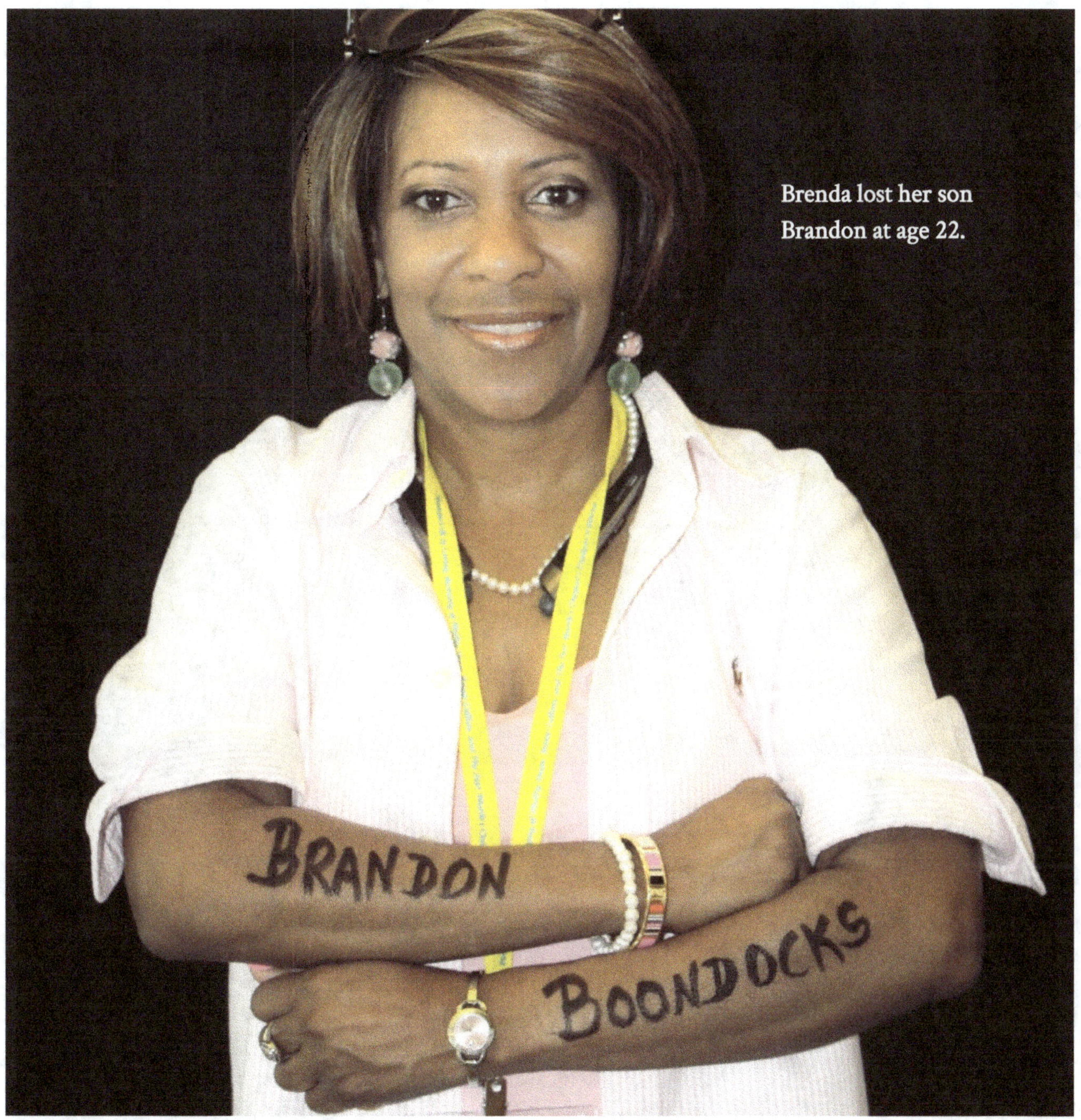

Brenda lost her son
Brandon at age 22.

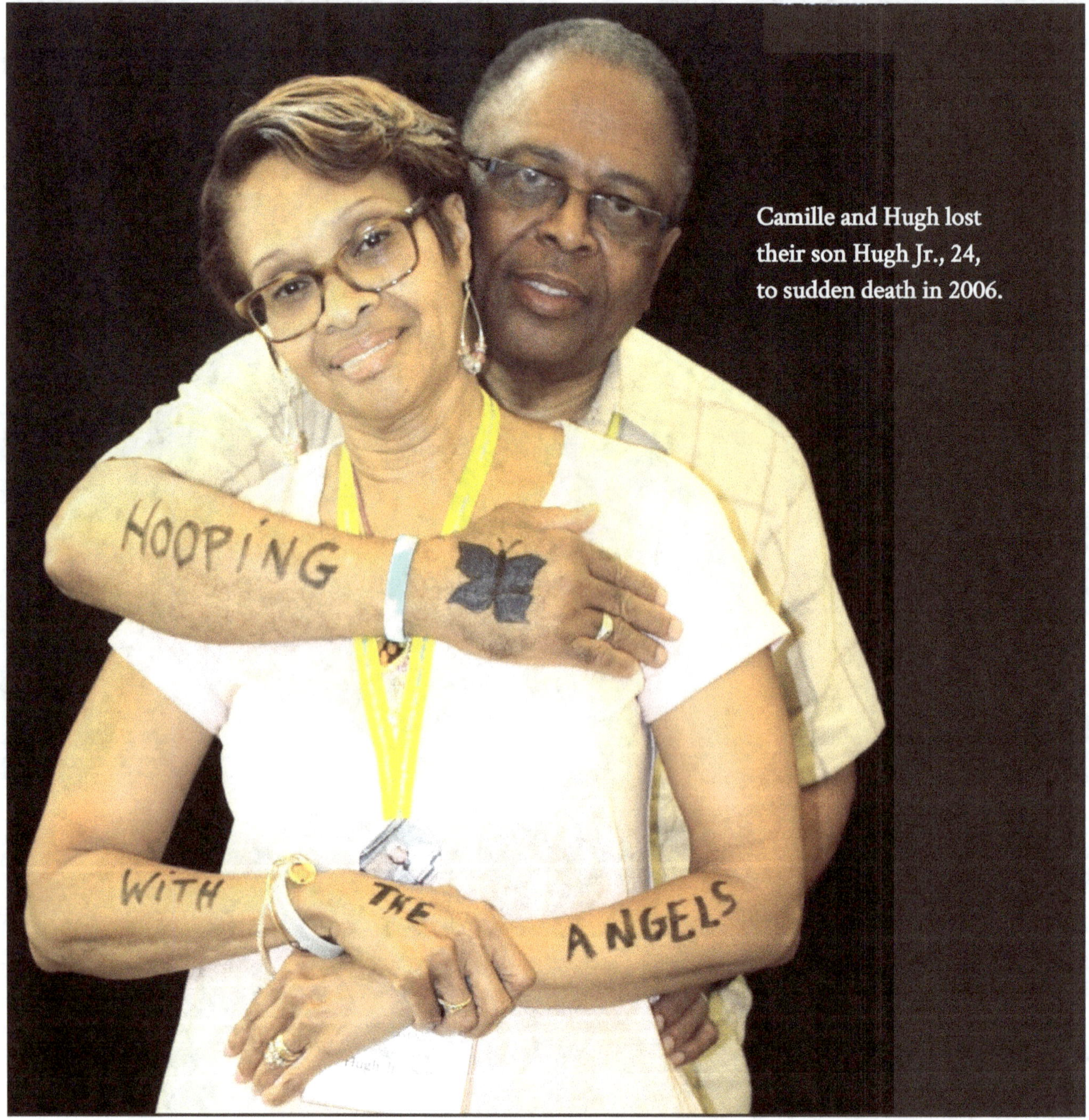

Camille and Hugh lost their son Hugh Jr., 24, to sudden death in 2006.

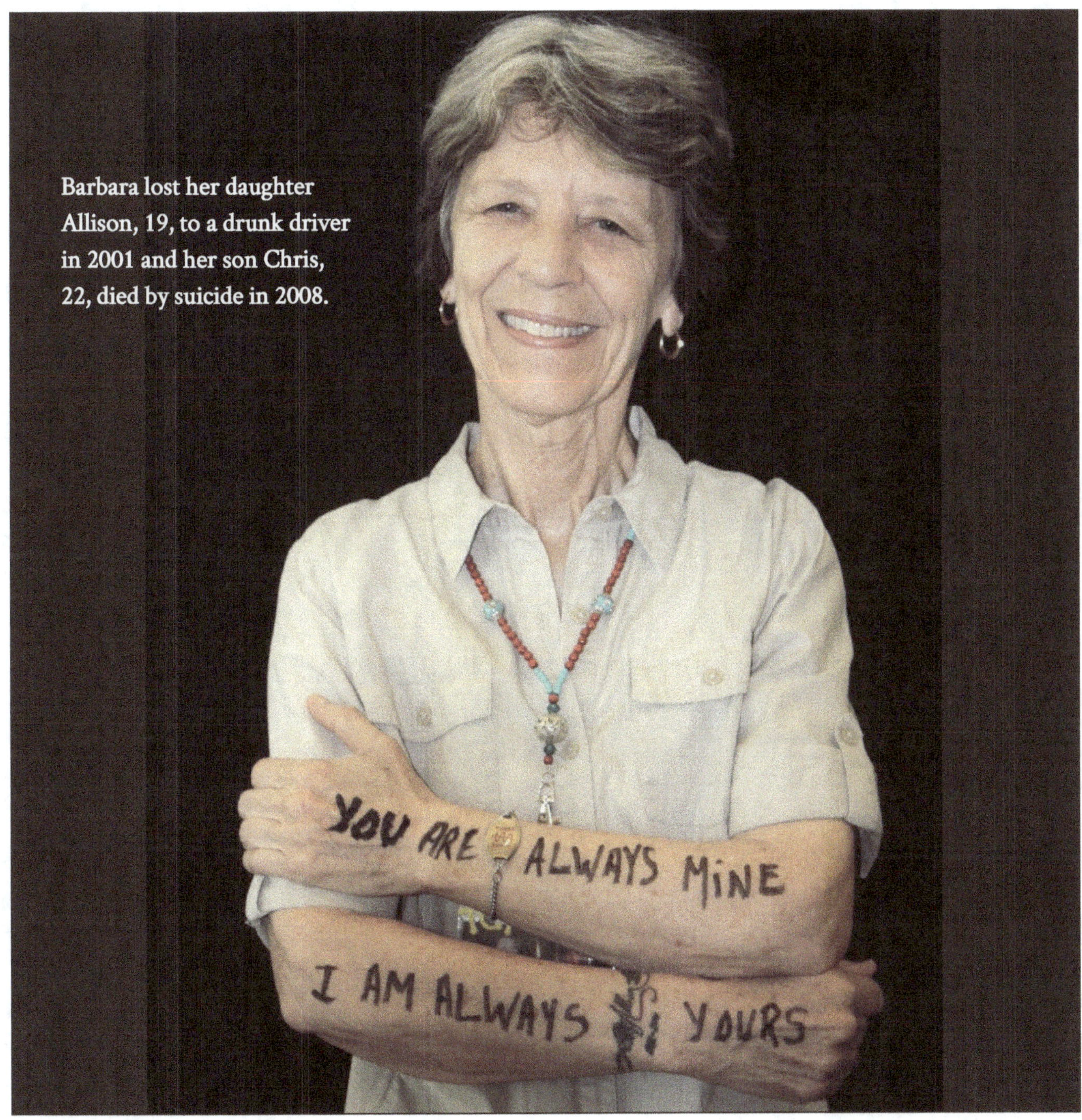

Barbara lost her daughter Allison, 19, to a drunk driver in 2001 and her son Chris, 22, died by suicide in 2008.

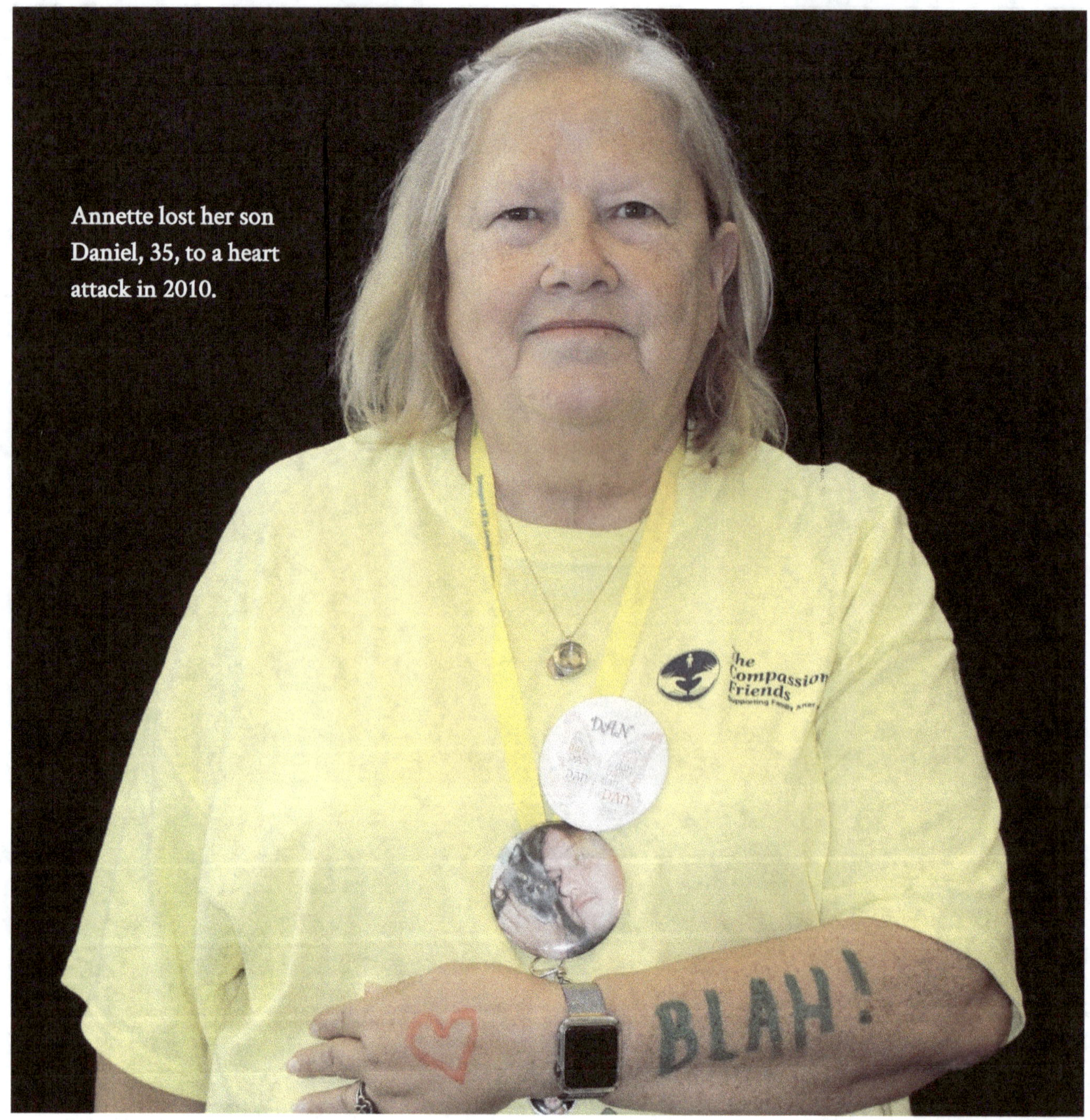

Annette lost her son Daniel, 35, to a heart attack in 2010.

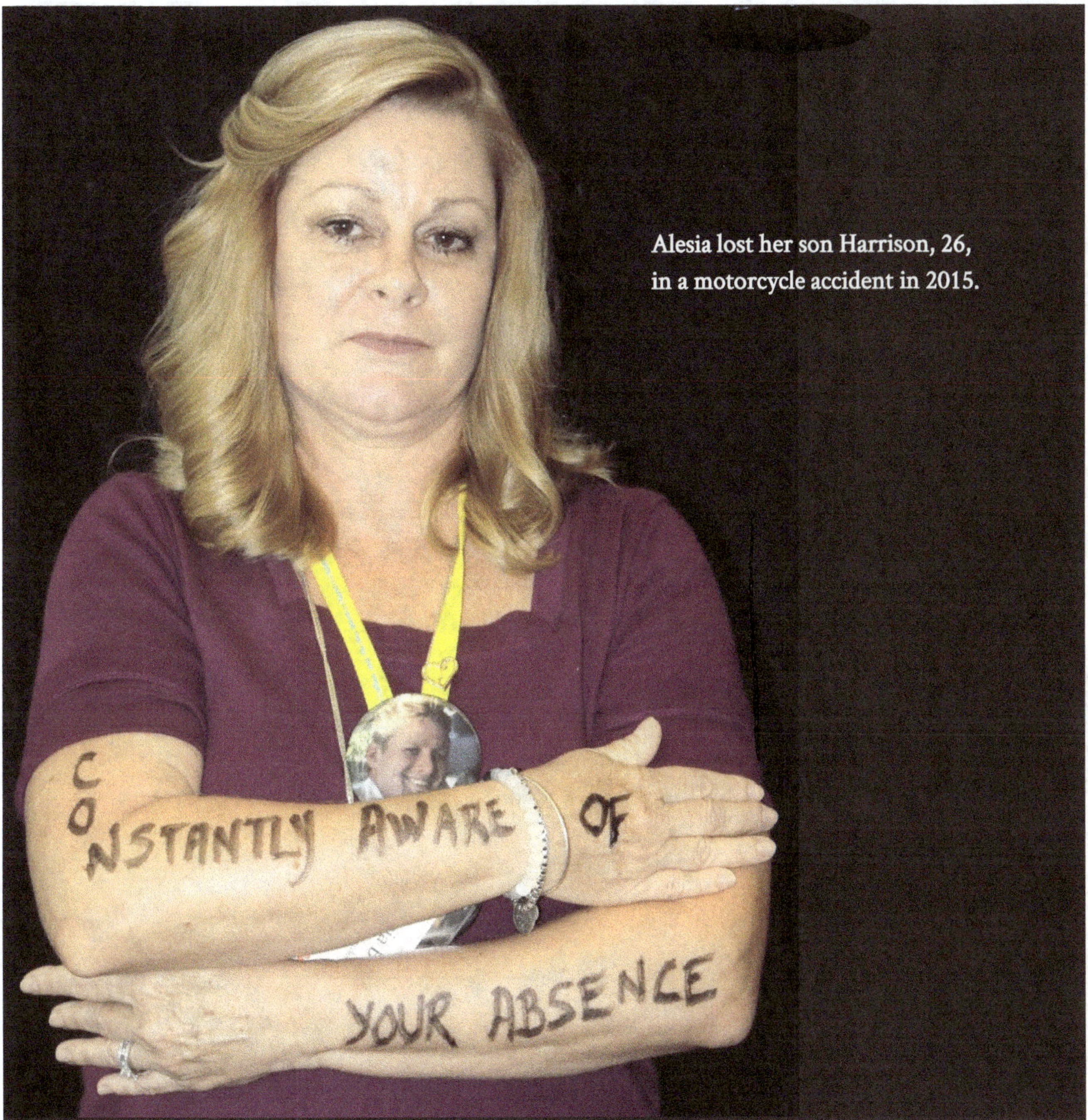

Alesia lost her son Harrison, 26, in a motorcycle accident in 2015.

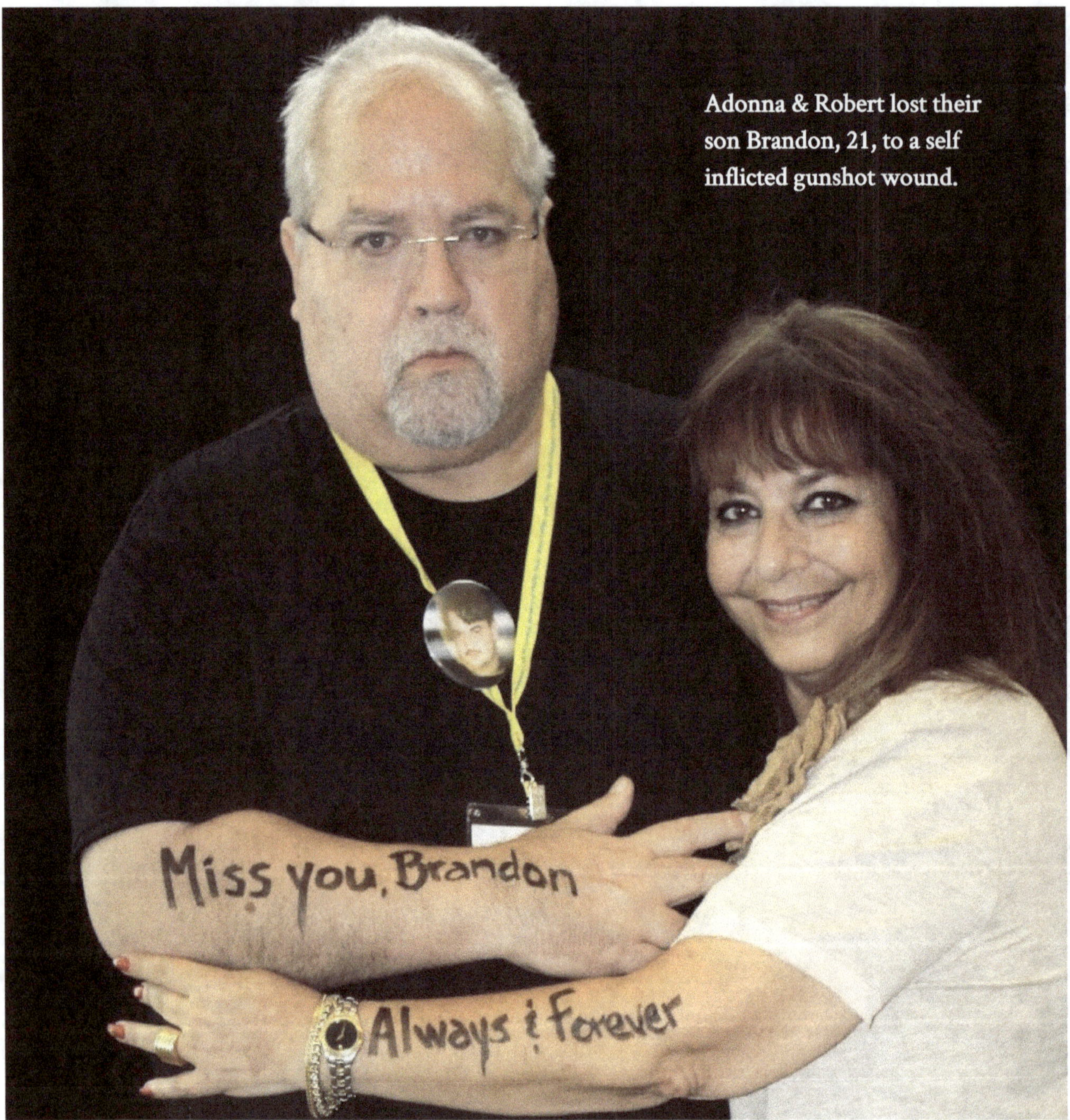

Adonna & Robert lost their son Brandon, 21, to a self inflicted gunshot wound.

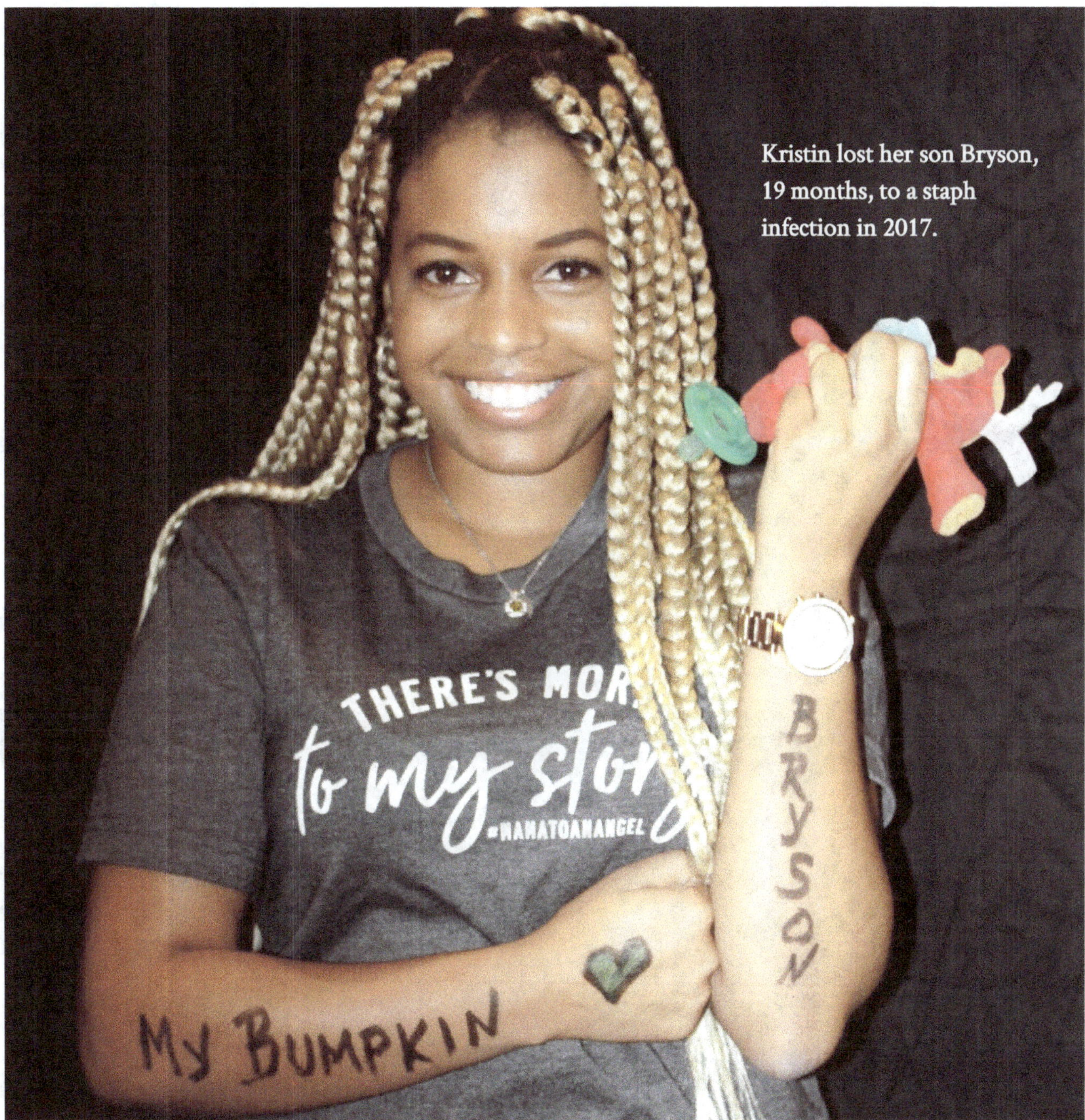

Kristin lost her son Bryson, 19 months, to a staph infection in 2017.

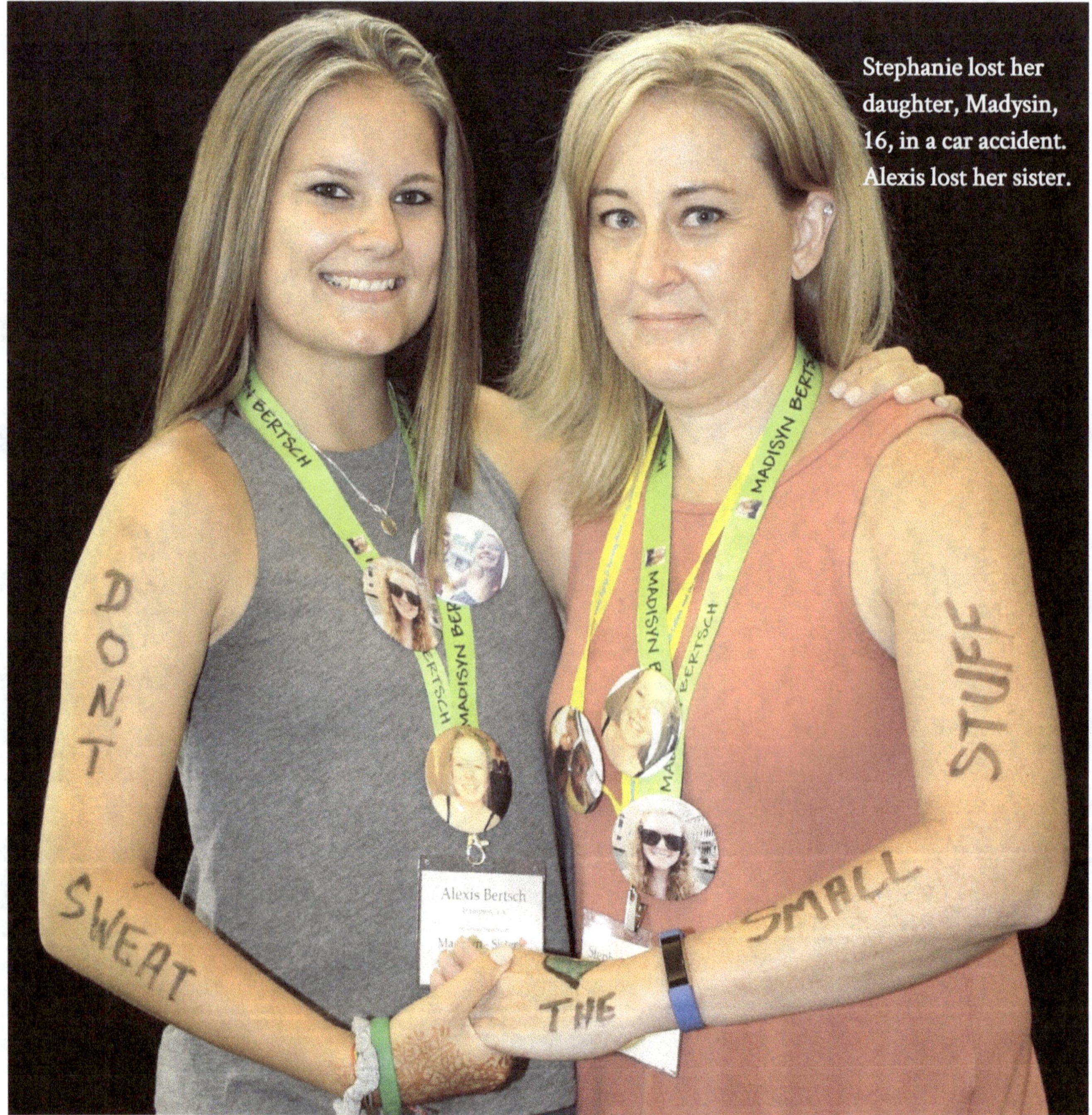

Stephanie lost her daughter, Madysin, 16, in a car accident. Alexis lost her sister.

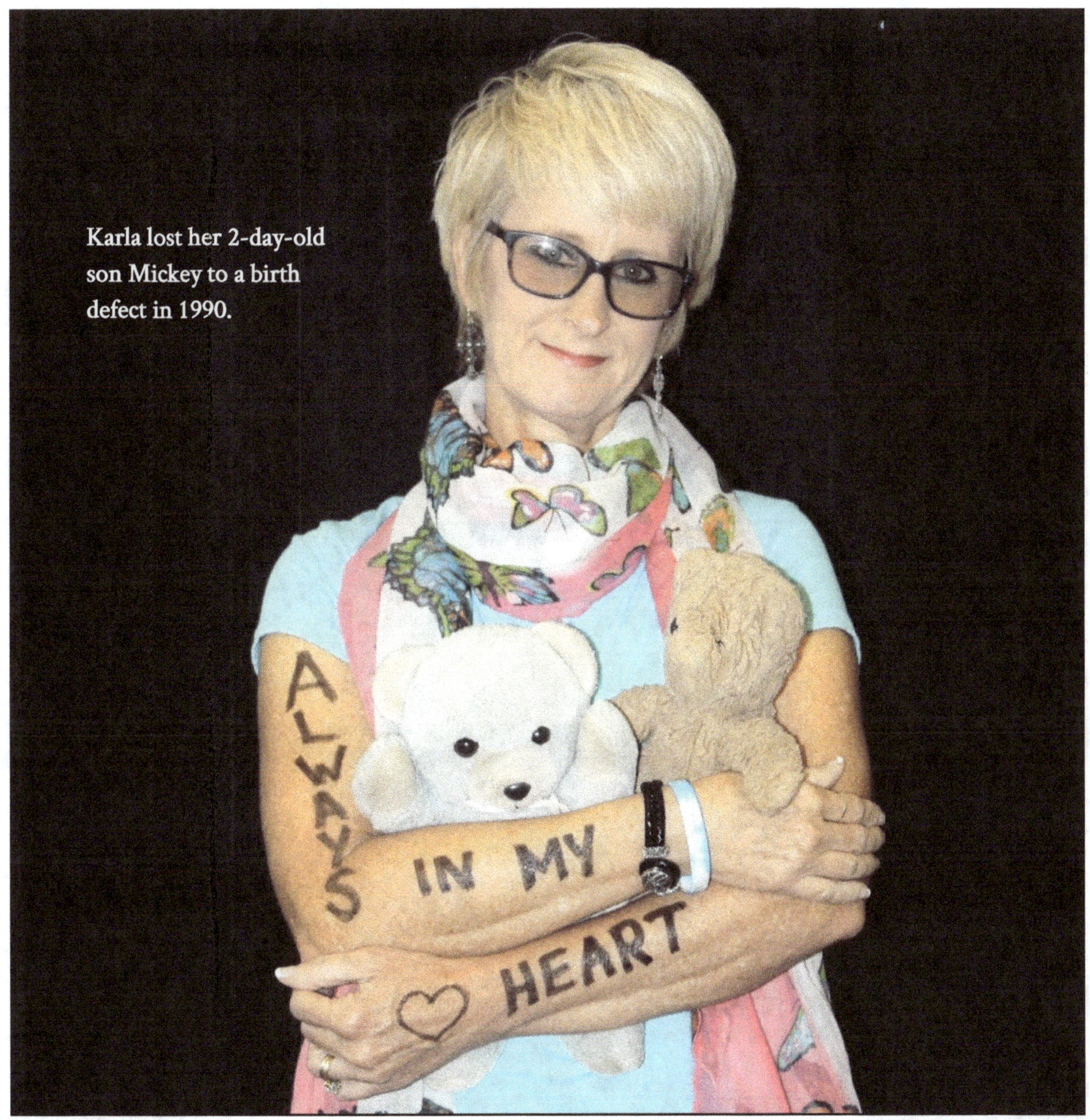

Karla lost her 2-day-old son Mickey to a birth defect in 1990.

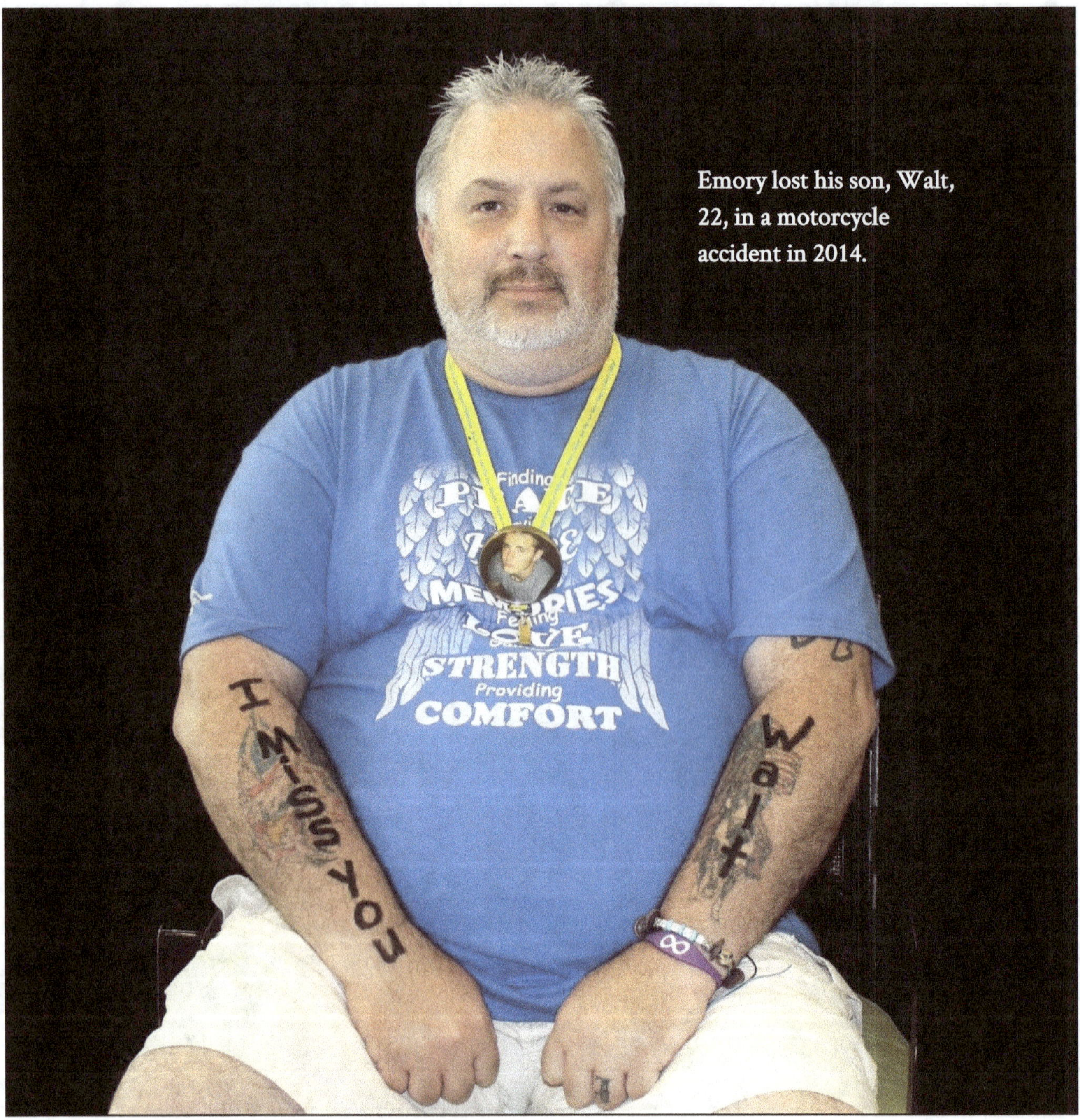

Emory lost his son, Walt, 22, in a motorcycle accident in 2014.

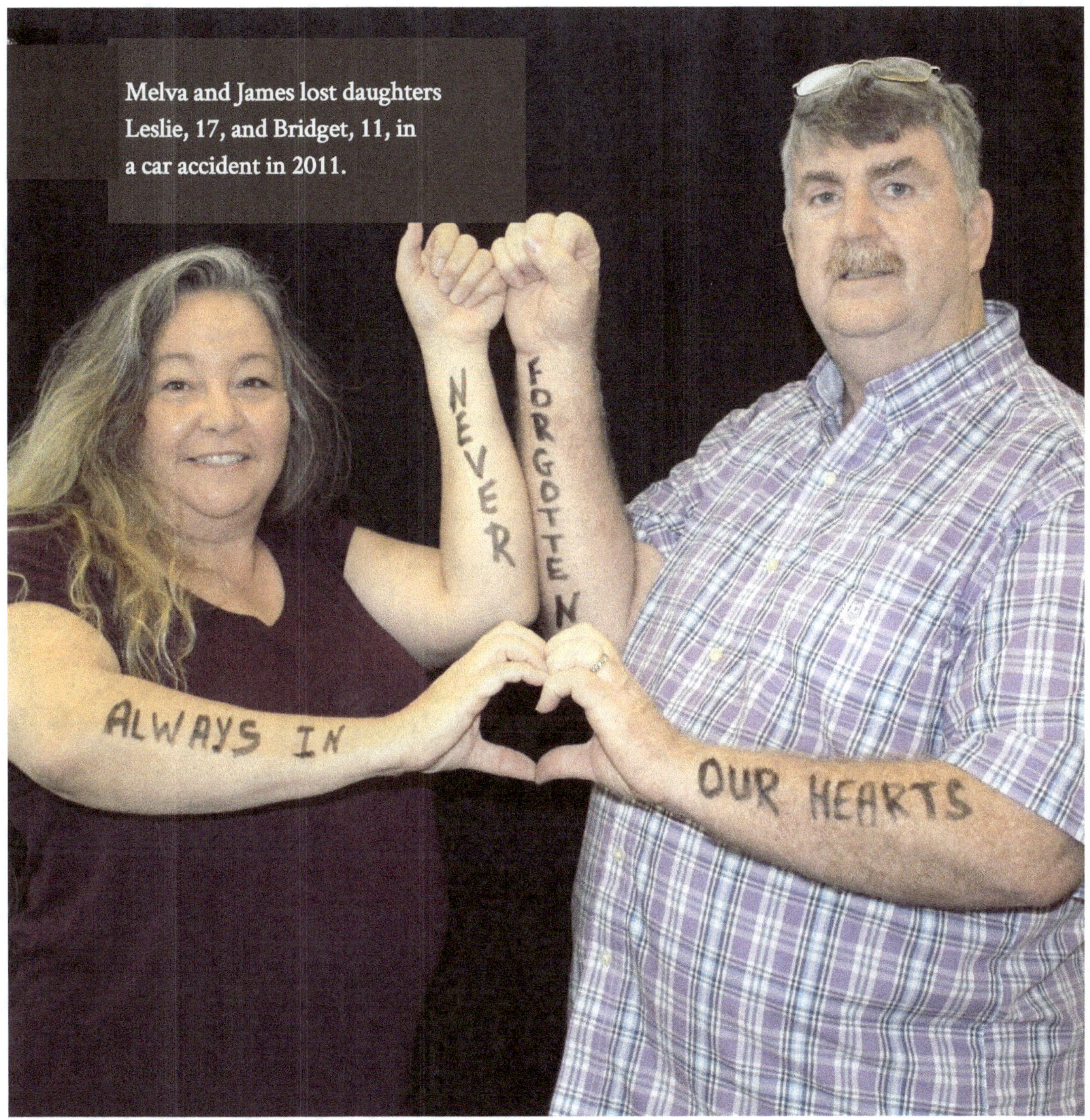
Melva and James lost daughters
Leslie, 17, and Bridget, 11, in
a car accident in 2011.
NEVER
FORGOTTEN
ALWAYS IN
OUR HEARTS

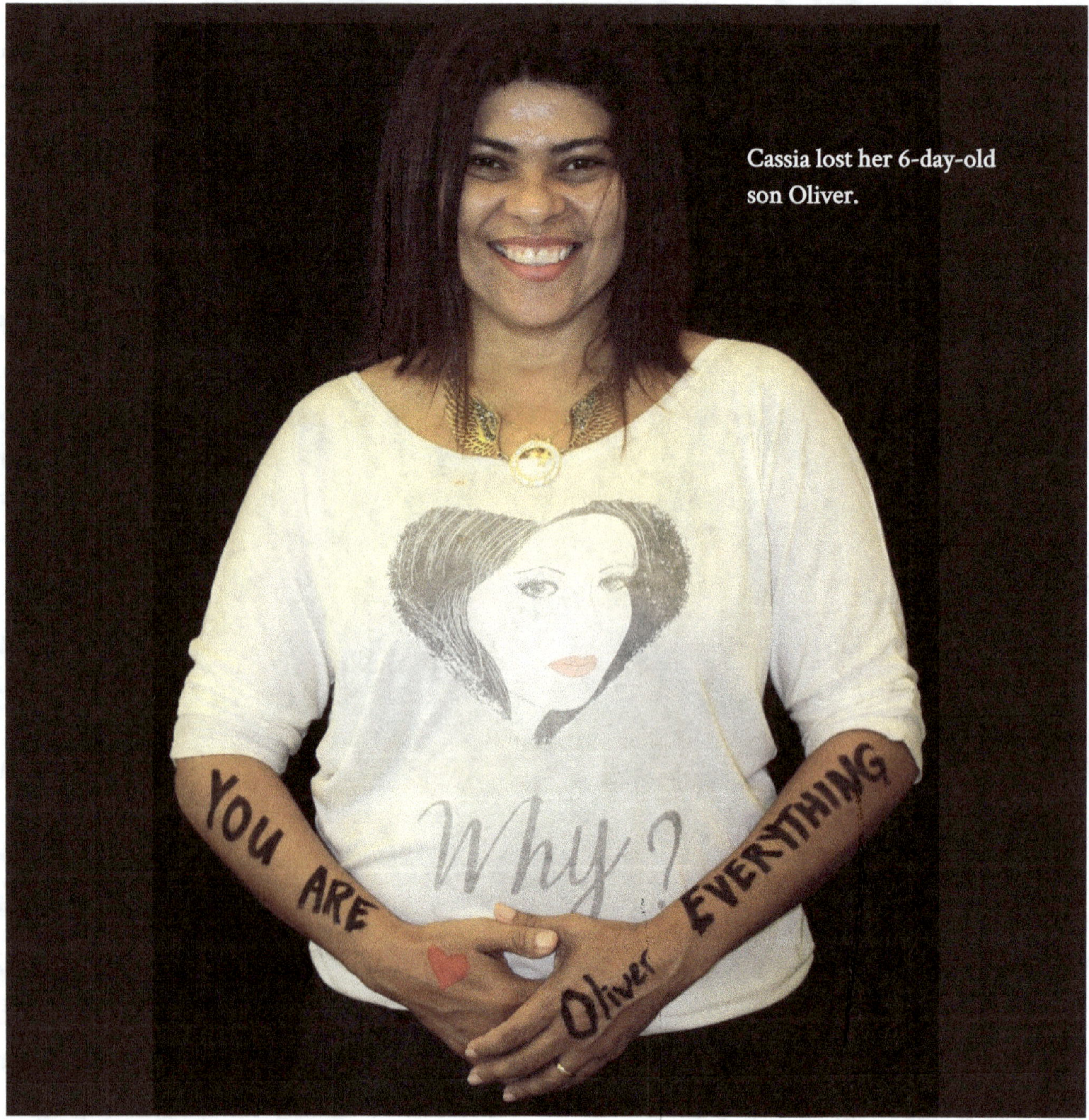

Cassia lost her 6-day-old son Oliver.

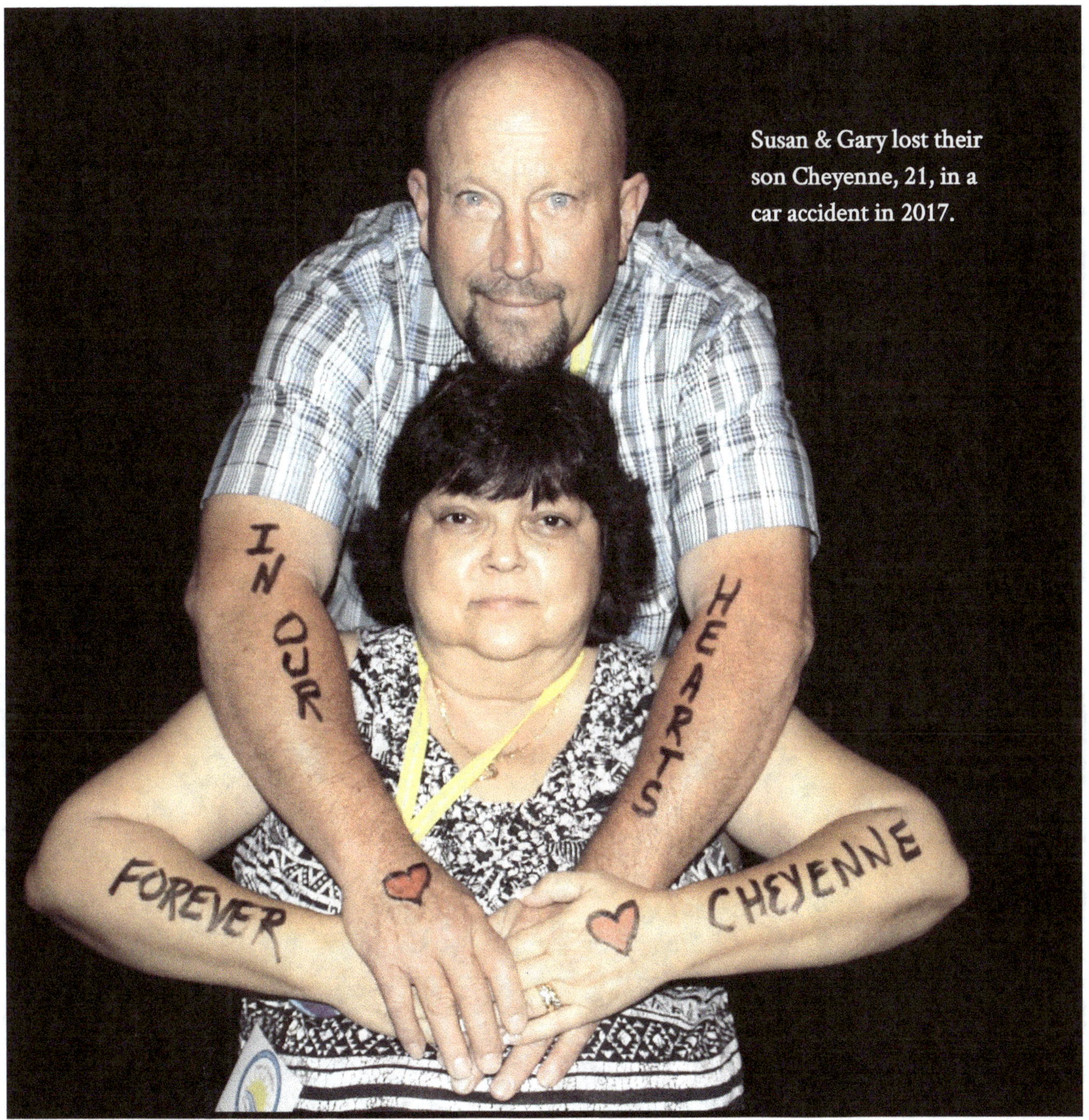

Susan & Gary lost their son Cheyenne, 21, in a car accident in 2017.

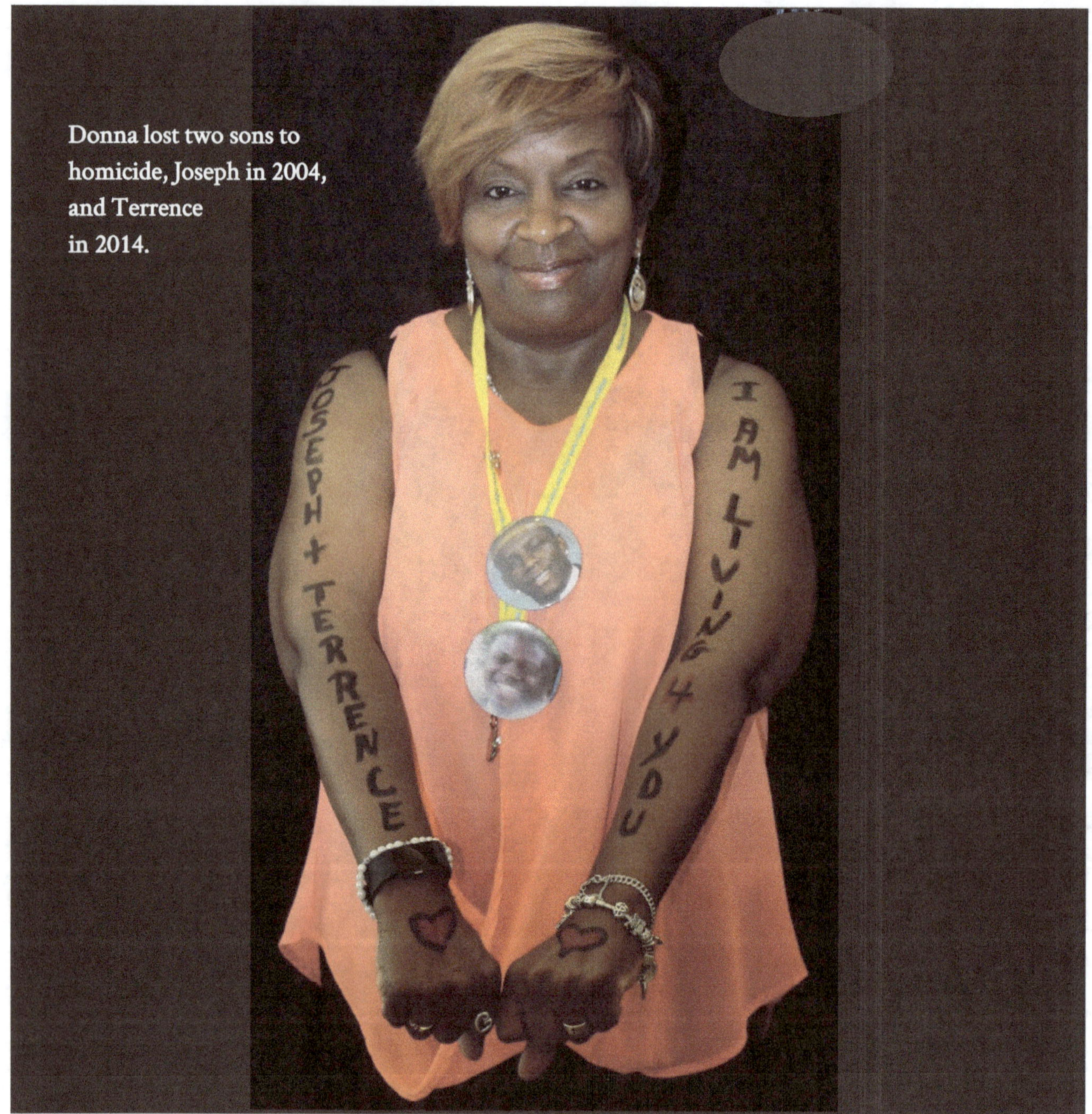

Donna lost two sons to homicide, Joseph in 2004, and Terrence in 2014.

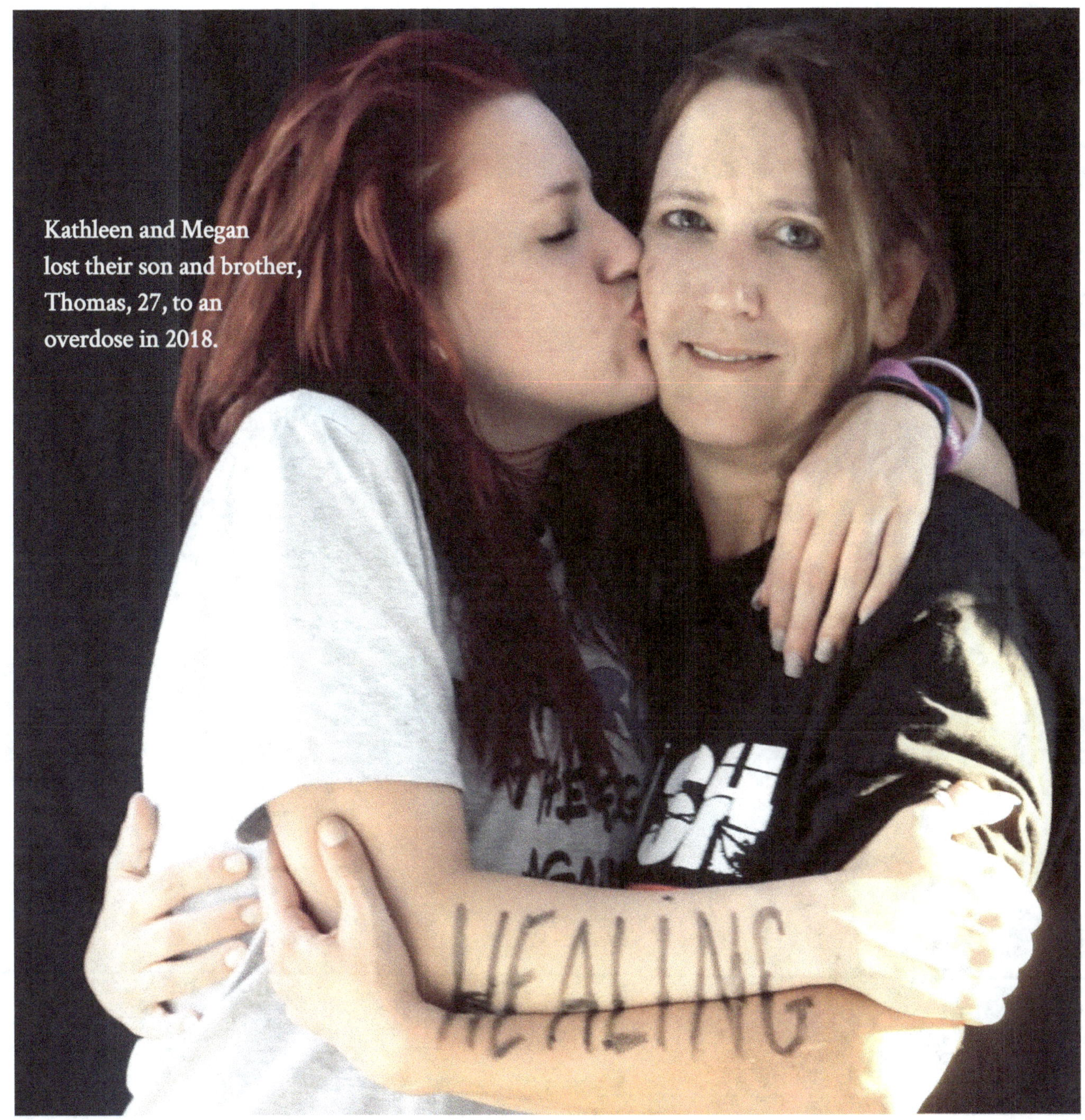

Kathleen and Megan
lost their son and brother,
Thomas, 27, to an
overdose in 2018.

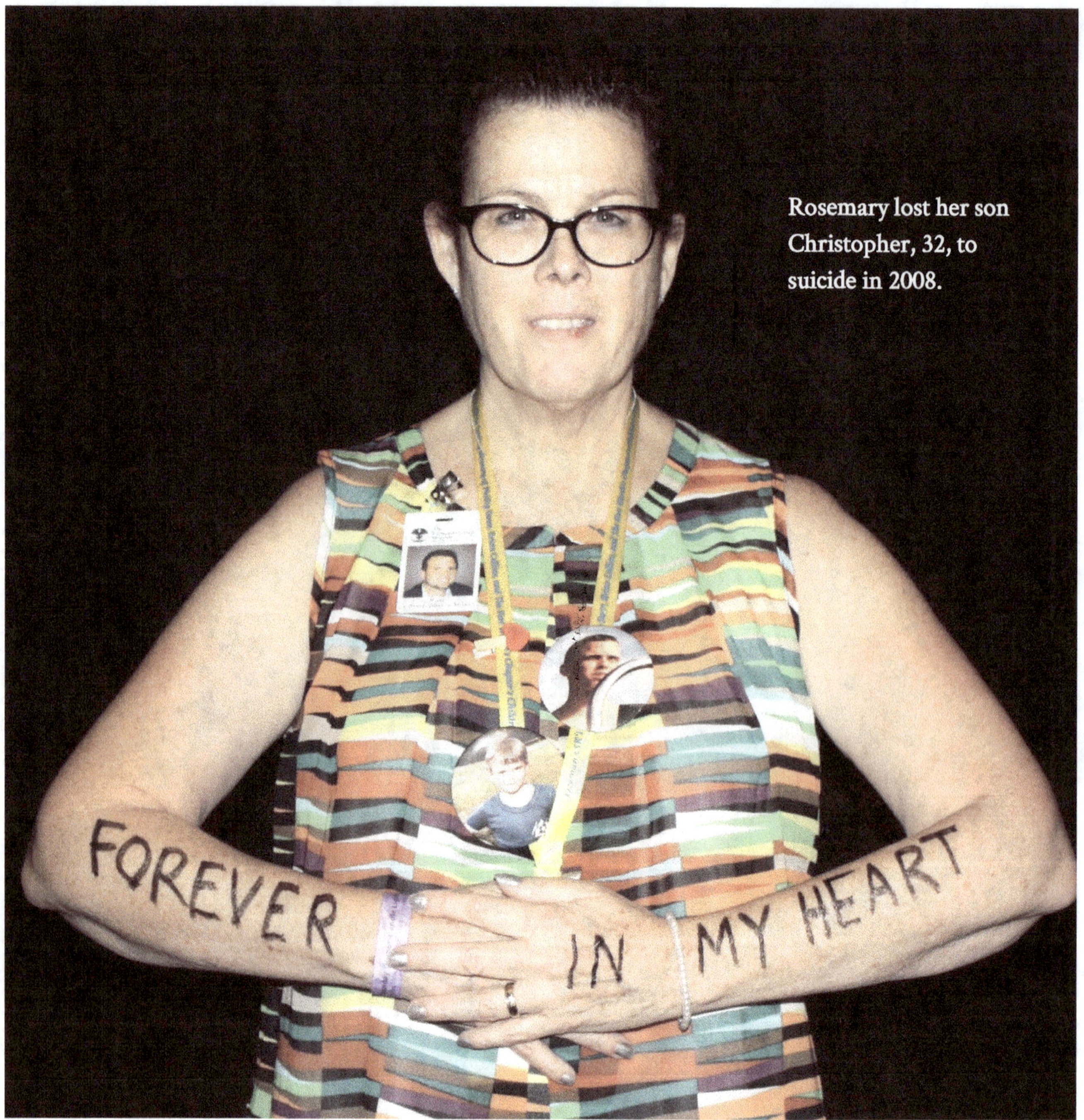

Rosemary lost her son Christopher, 32, to suicide in 2008.

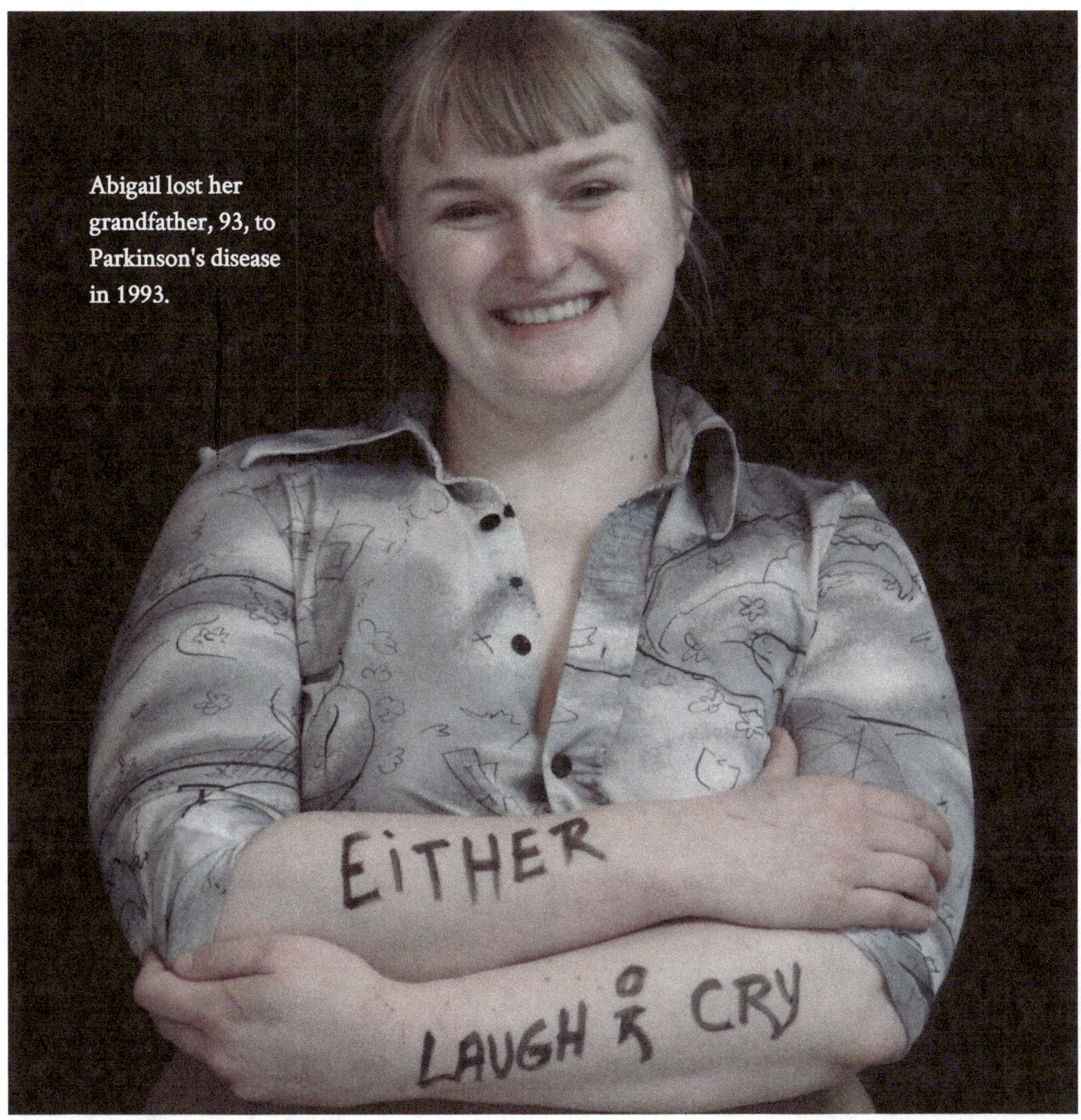

Abigail lost her grandfather, 93, to Parkinson's disease in 1993.

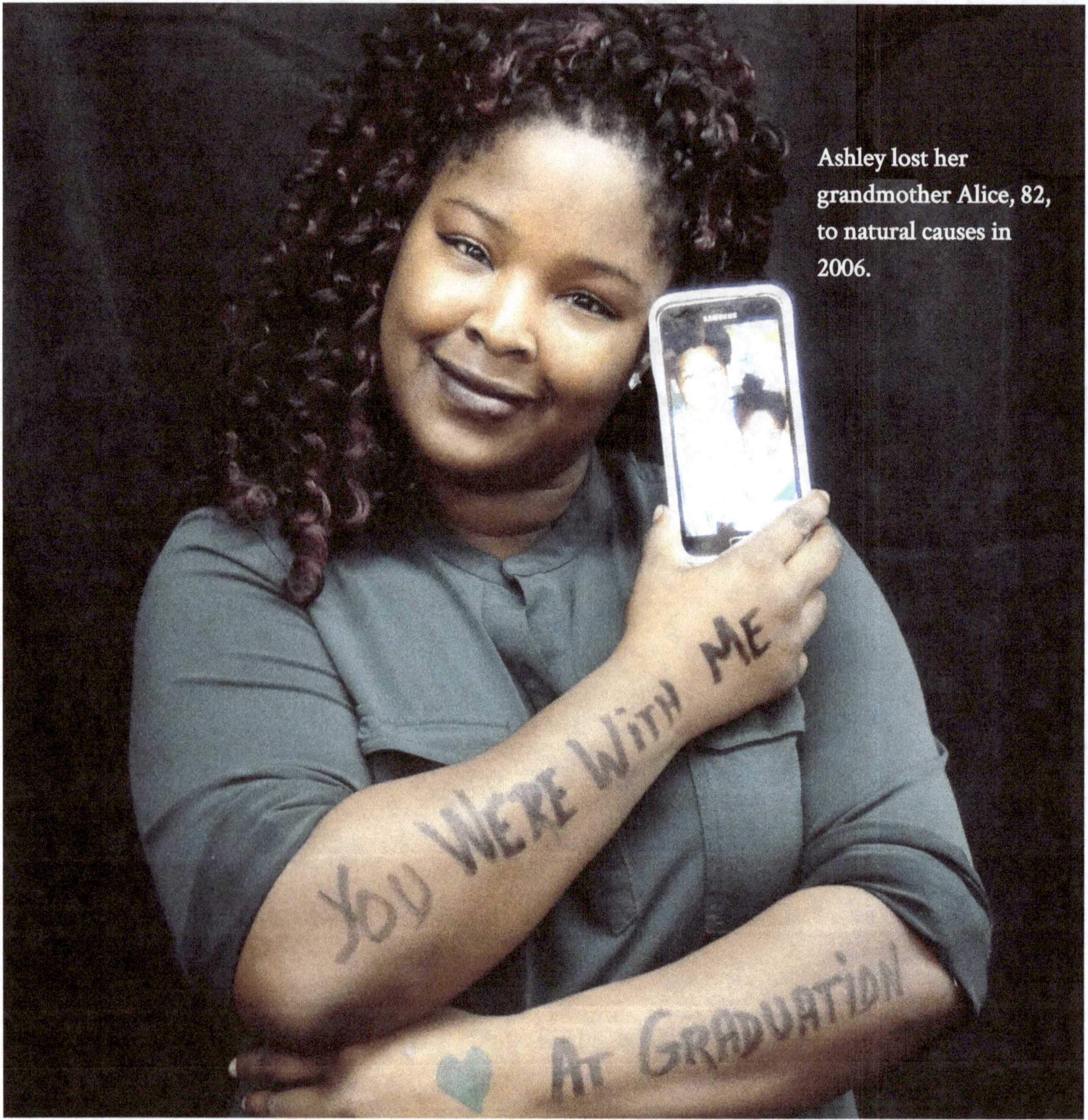

Ashley lost her grandmother Alice, 82, to natural causes in 2006.

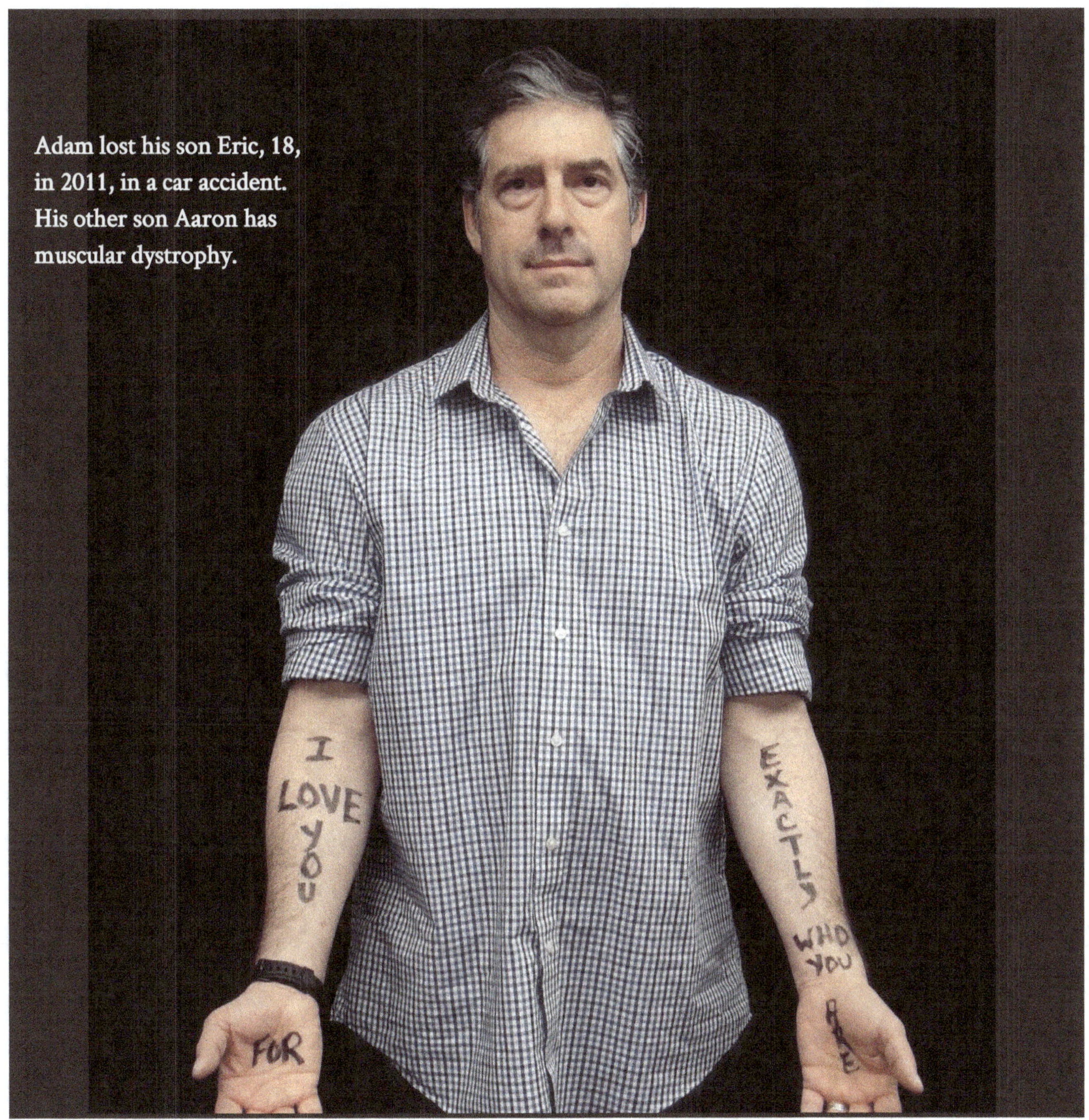

Adam lost his son Eric, 18, in 2011, in a car accident. His other son Aaron has muscular dystrophy.

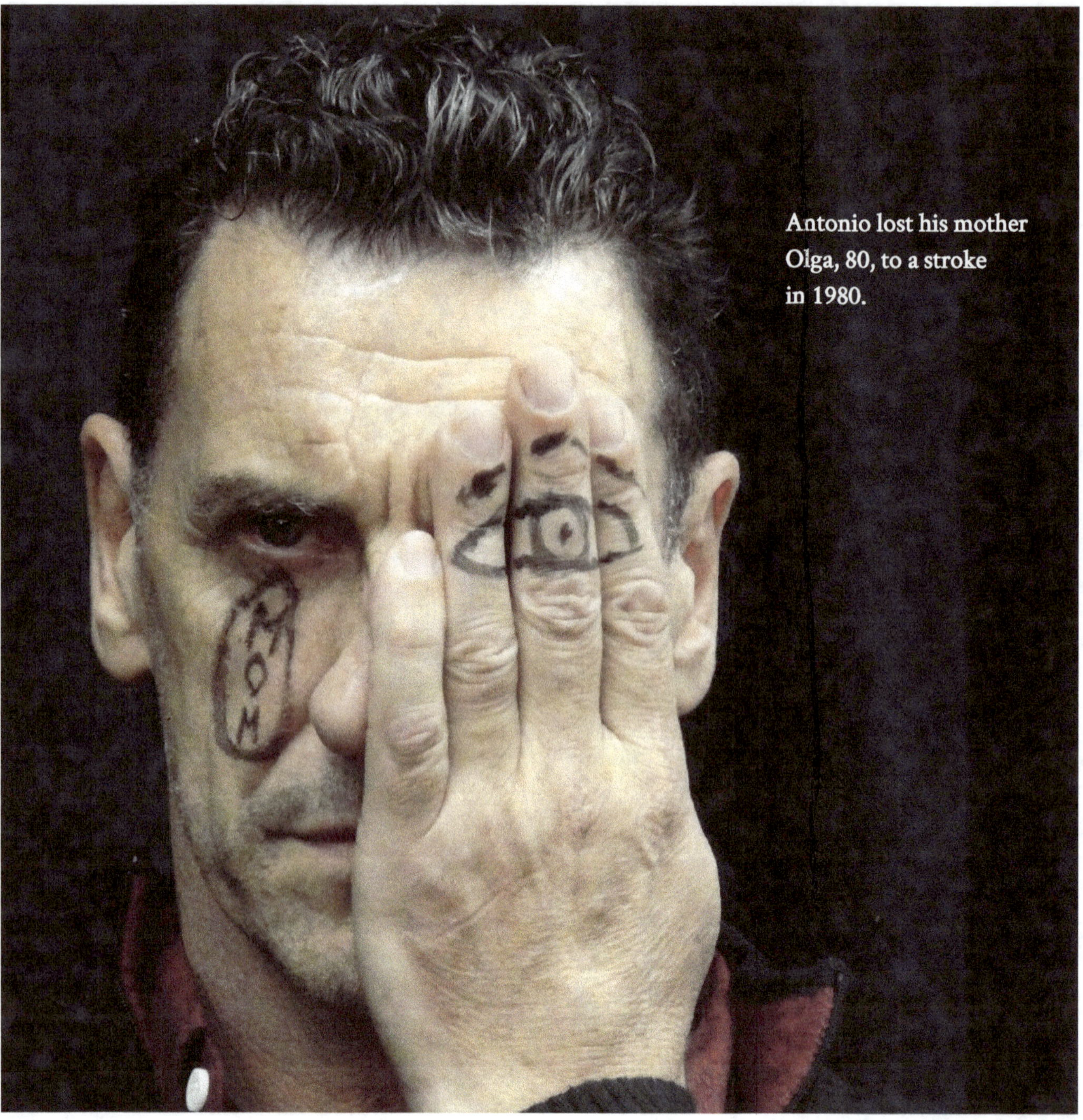
Antonio lost his mother
Olga, 80, to a stroke
in 1980.

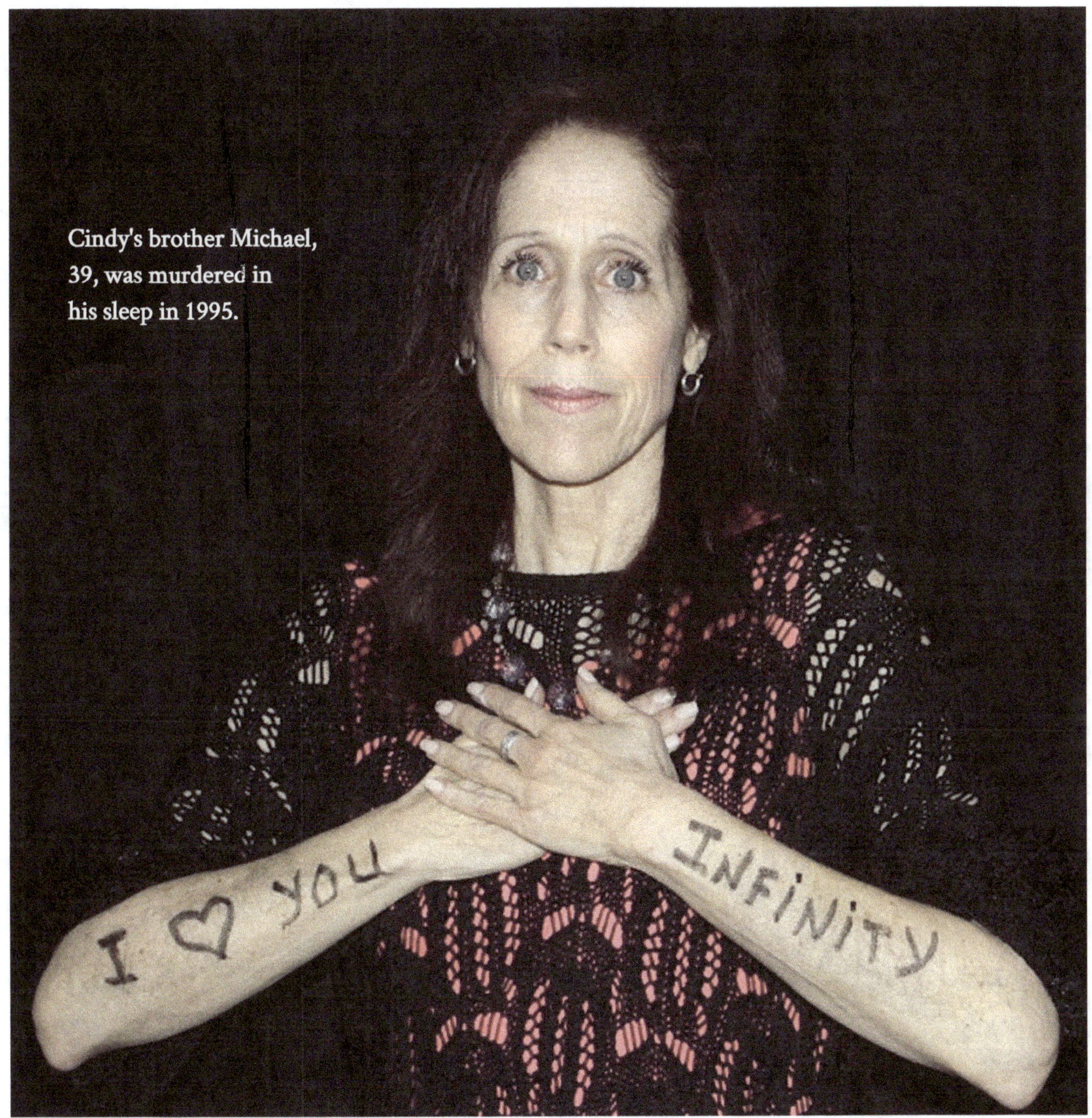

Cindy's brother Michael, 39, was murdered in his sleep in 1995.

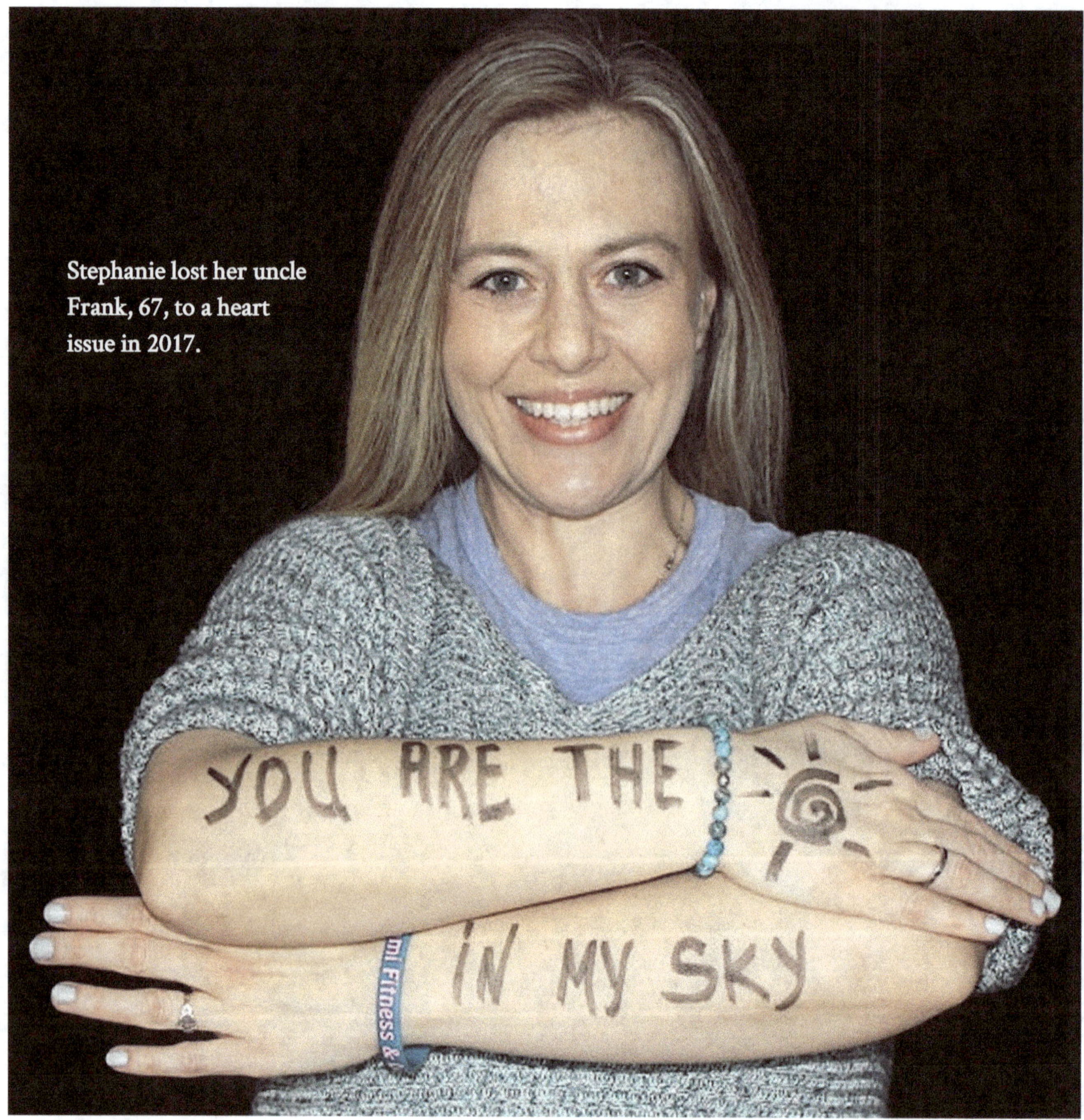

Stephanie lost her uncle Frank, 67, to a heart issue in 2017.

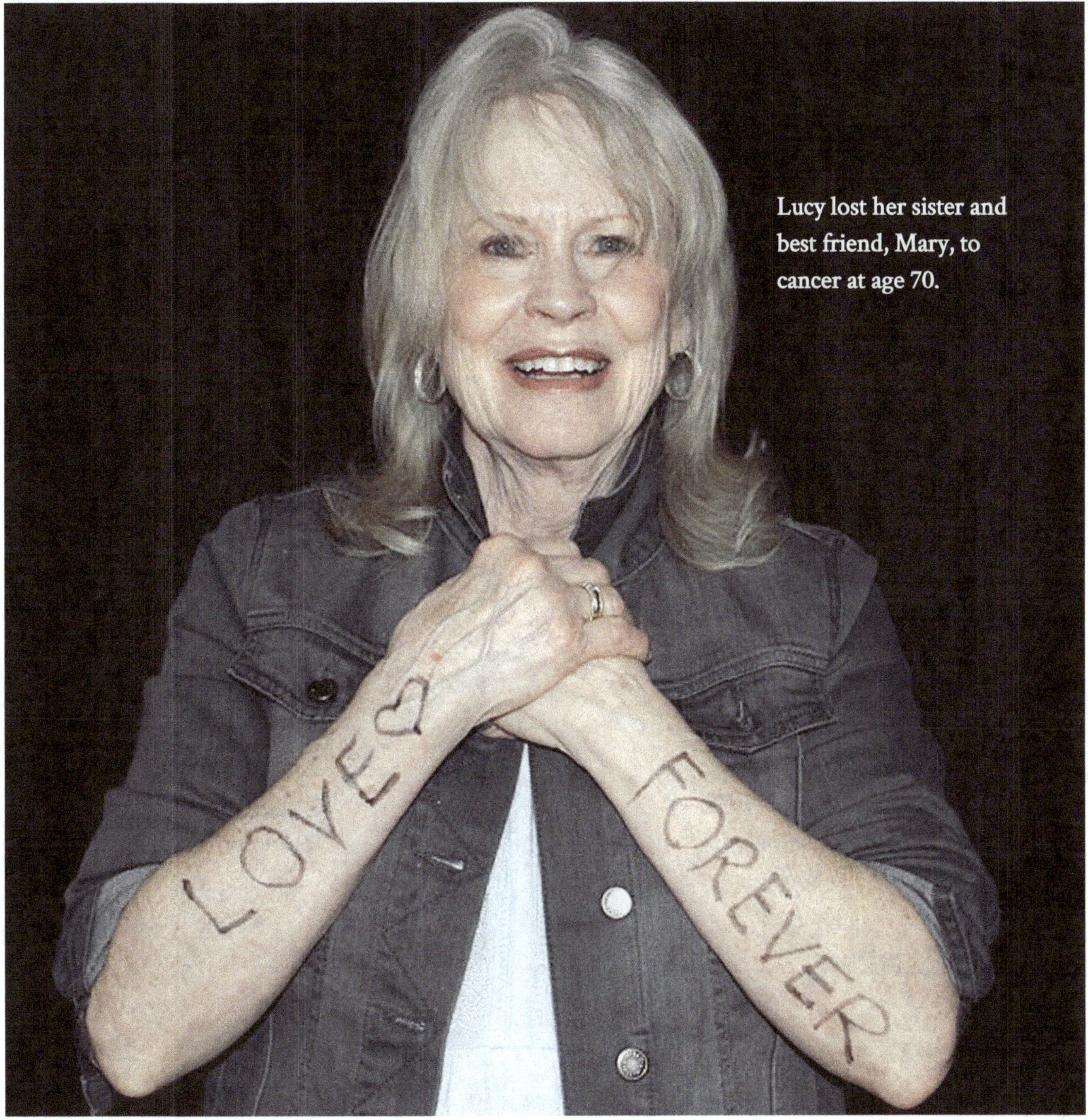

Lucy lost her sister and best friend, Mary, to cancer at age 70.

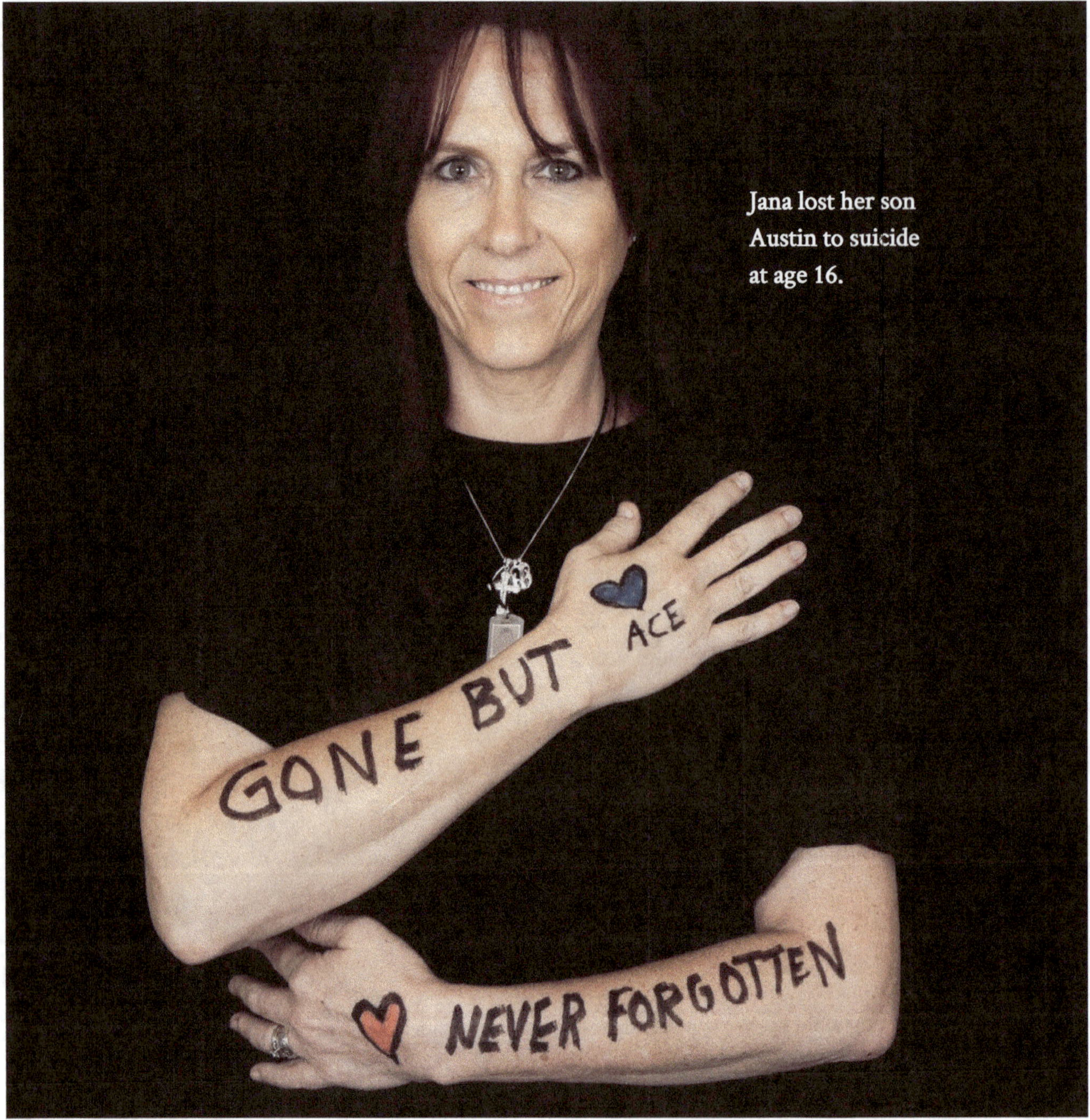

Jana lost her son Austin to suicide at age 16.

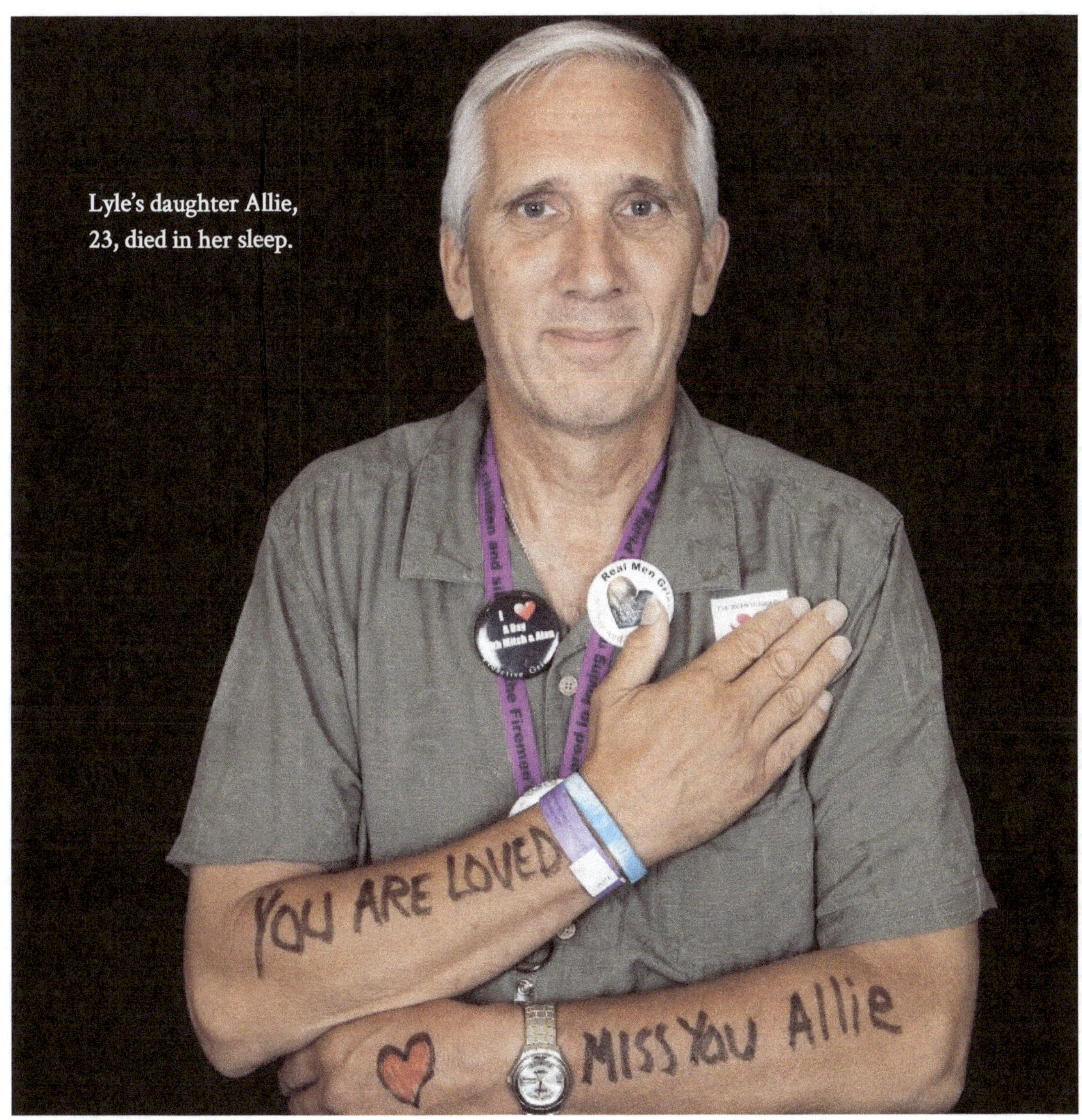

Lyle's daughter Allie,
23, died in her sleep.

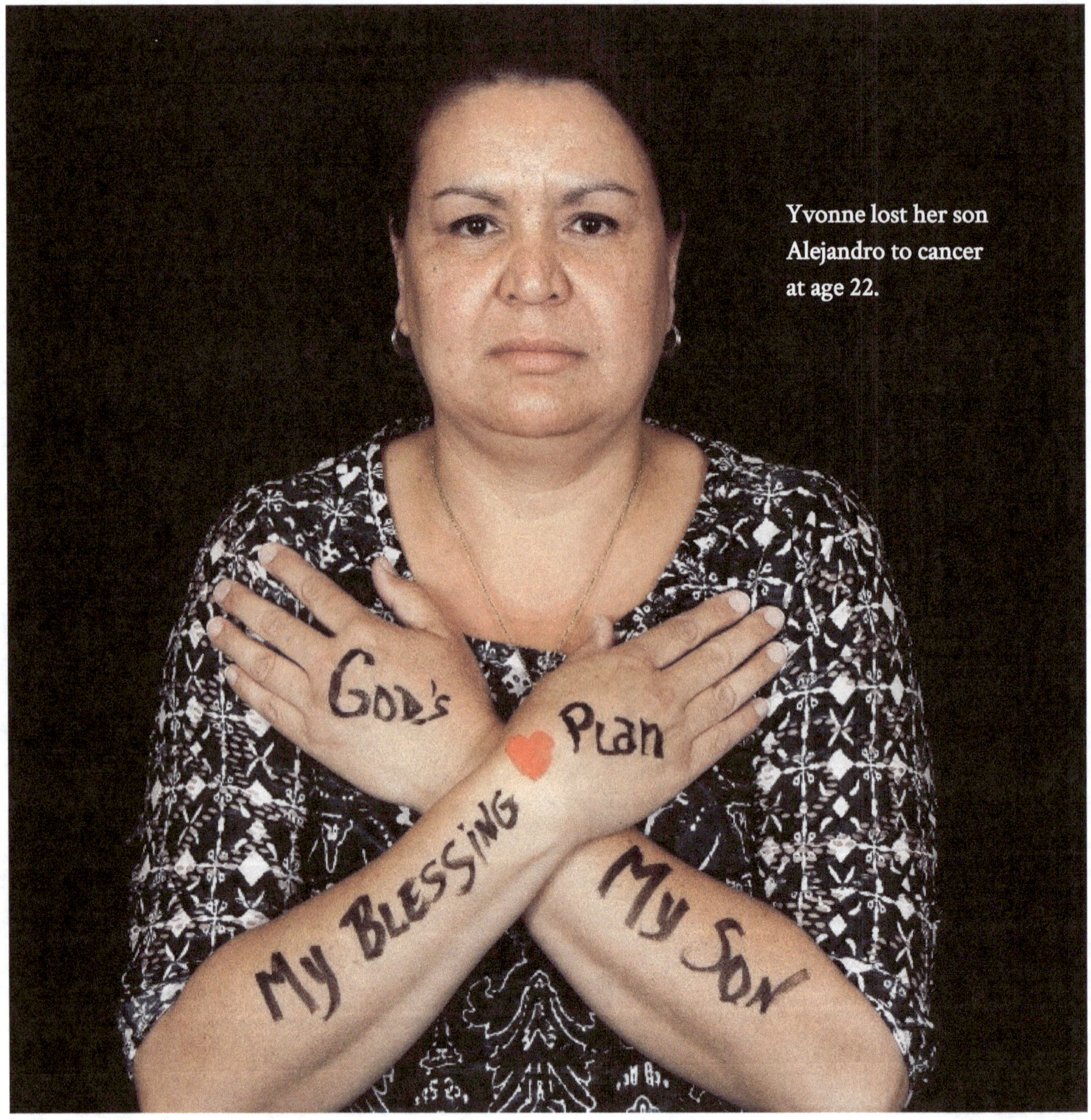

Yvonne lost her son Alejandro to cancer at age 22.

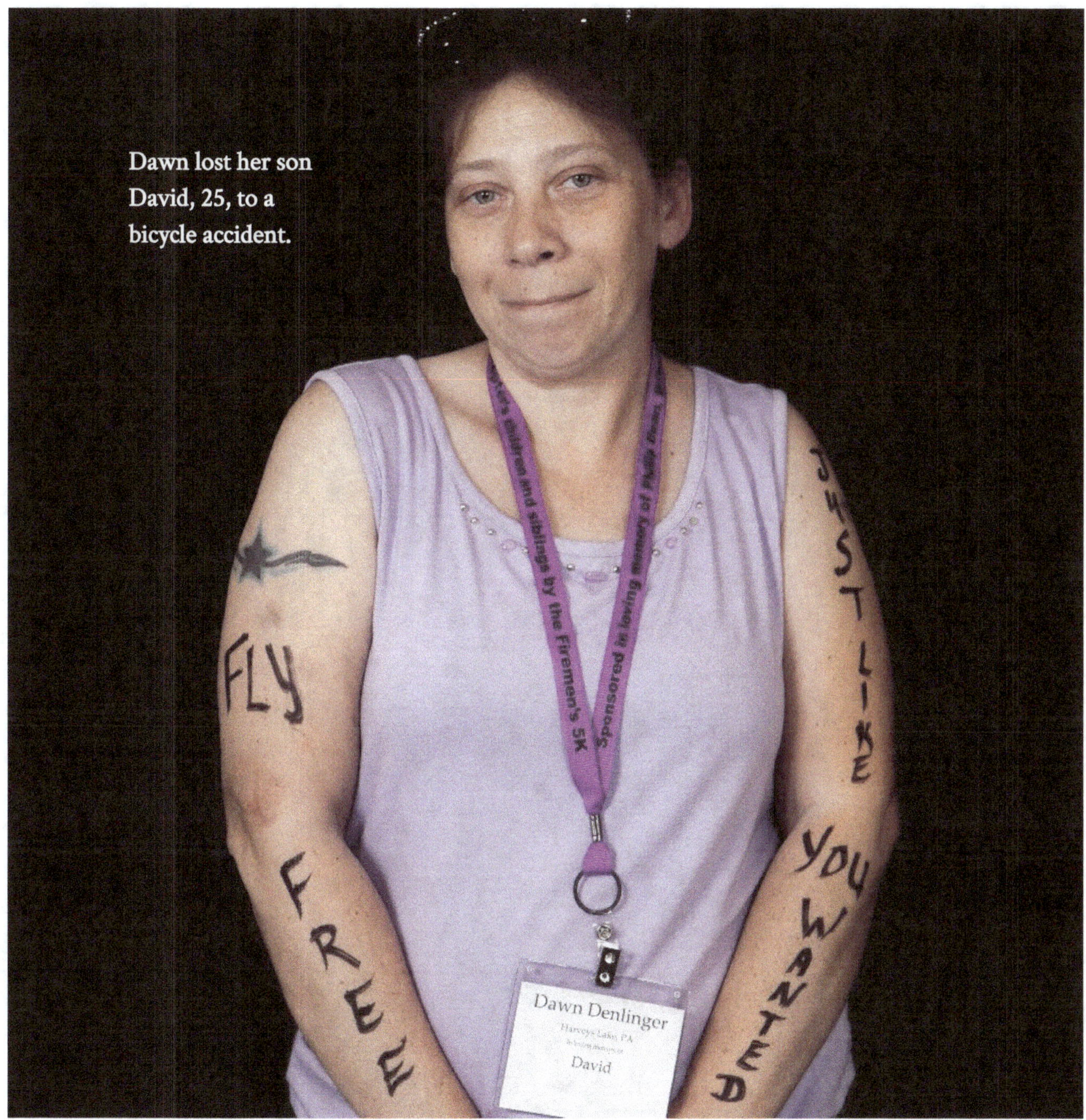
Dawn lost her son
David, 25, to a
bicycle accident.

FLY
FREE
JUST LIKE
YOU WANTED

Dawn Denlinger
Harveys Lake, PA
David

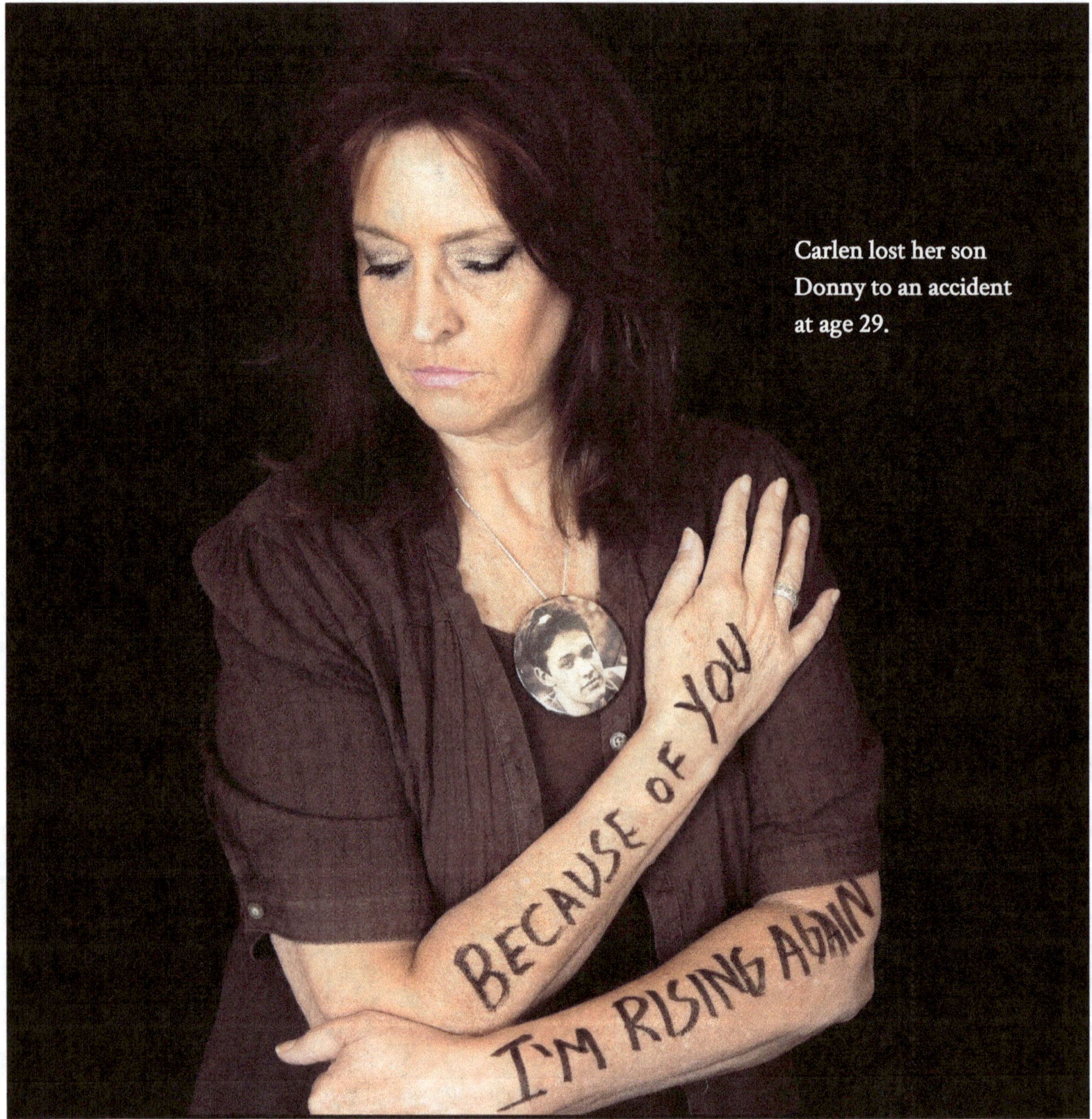

Carlen lost her son
Donny to an accident
at age 29.

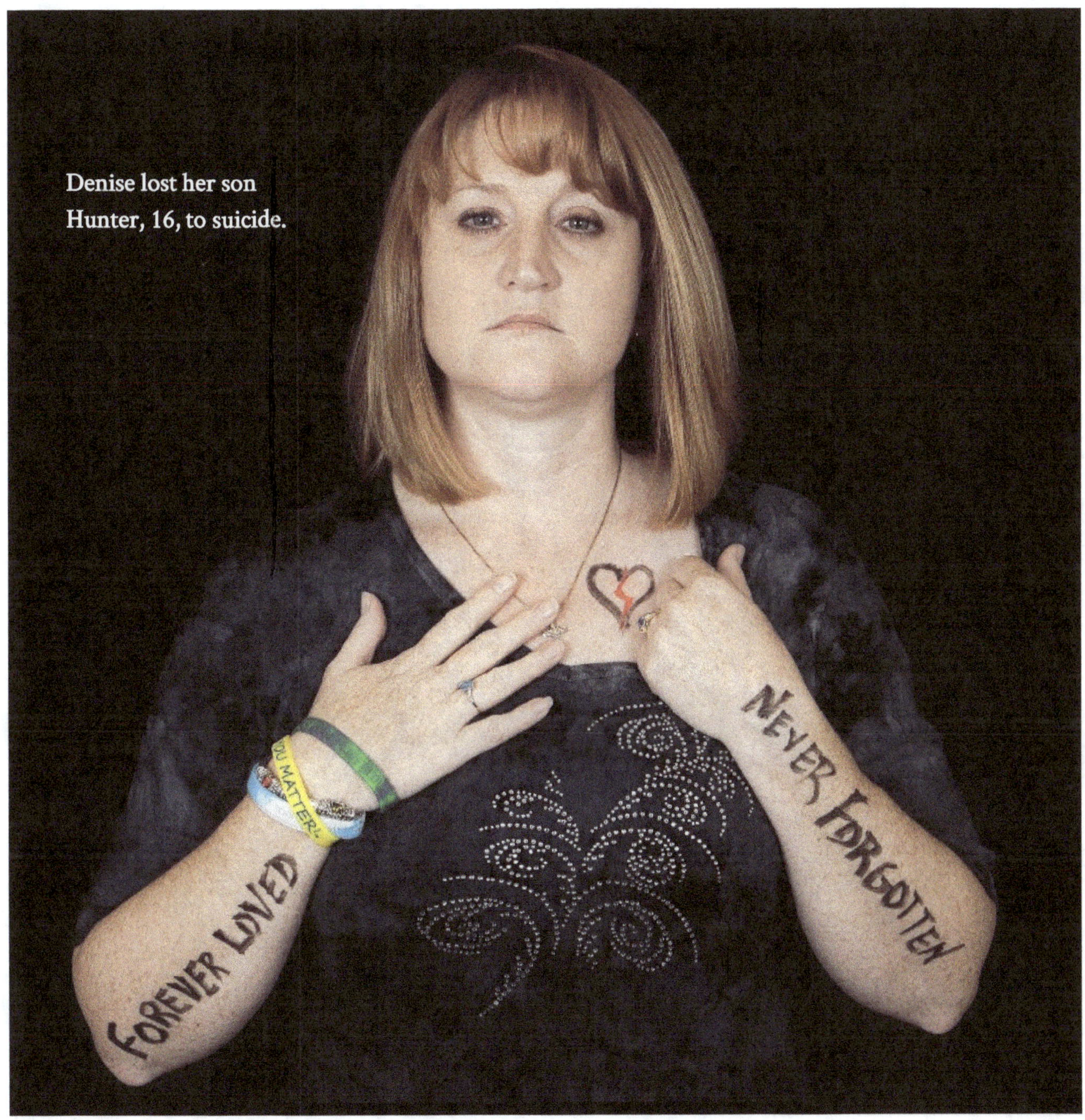

Denise lost her son
Hunter, 16, to suicide.

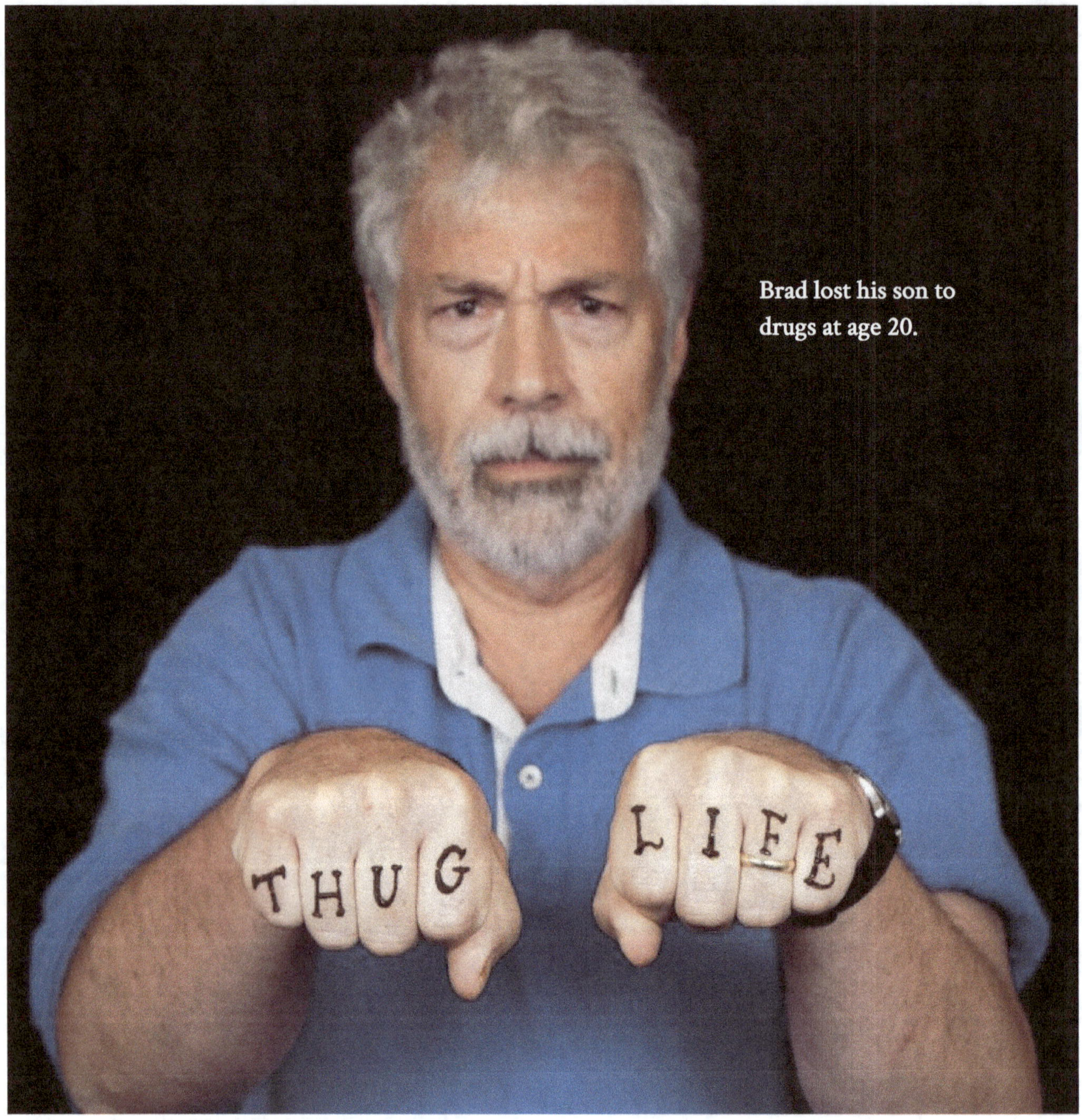

Brad lost his son to
drugs at age 20.

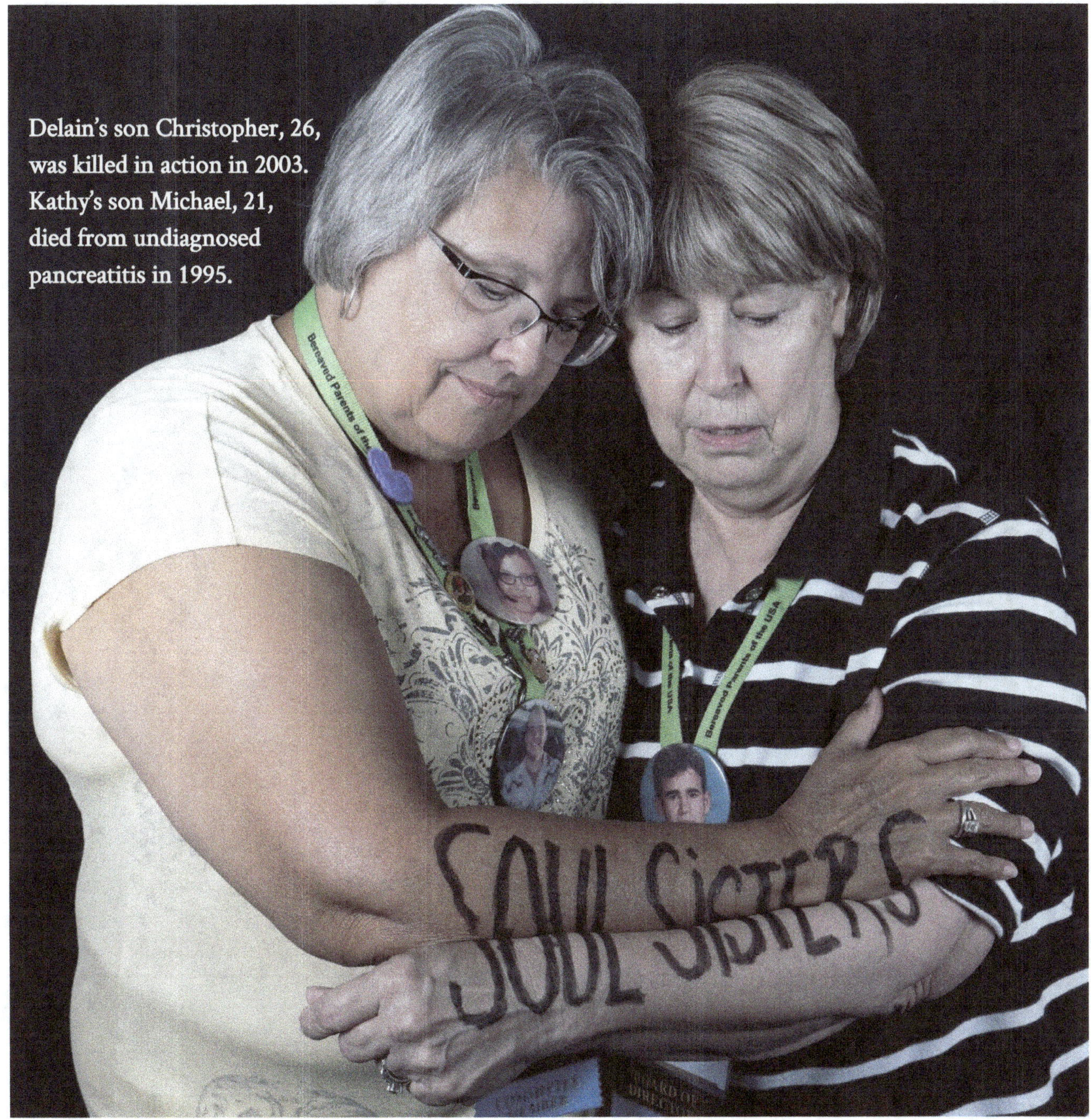

Delain's son Christopher, 26, was killed in action in 2003. Kathy's son Michael, 21, died from undiagnosed pancreatitis in 1995.

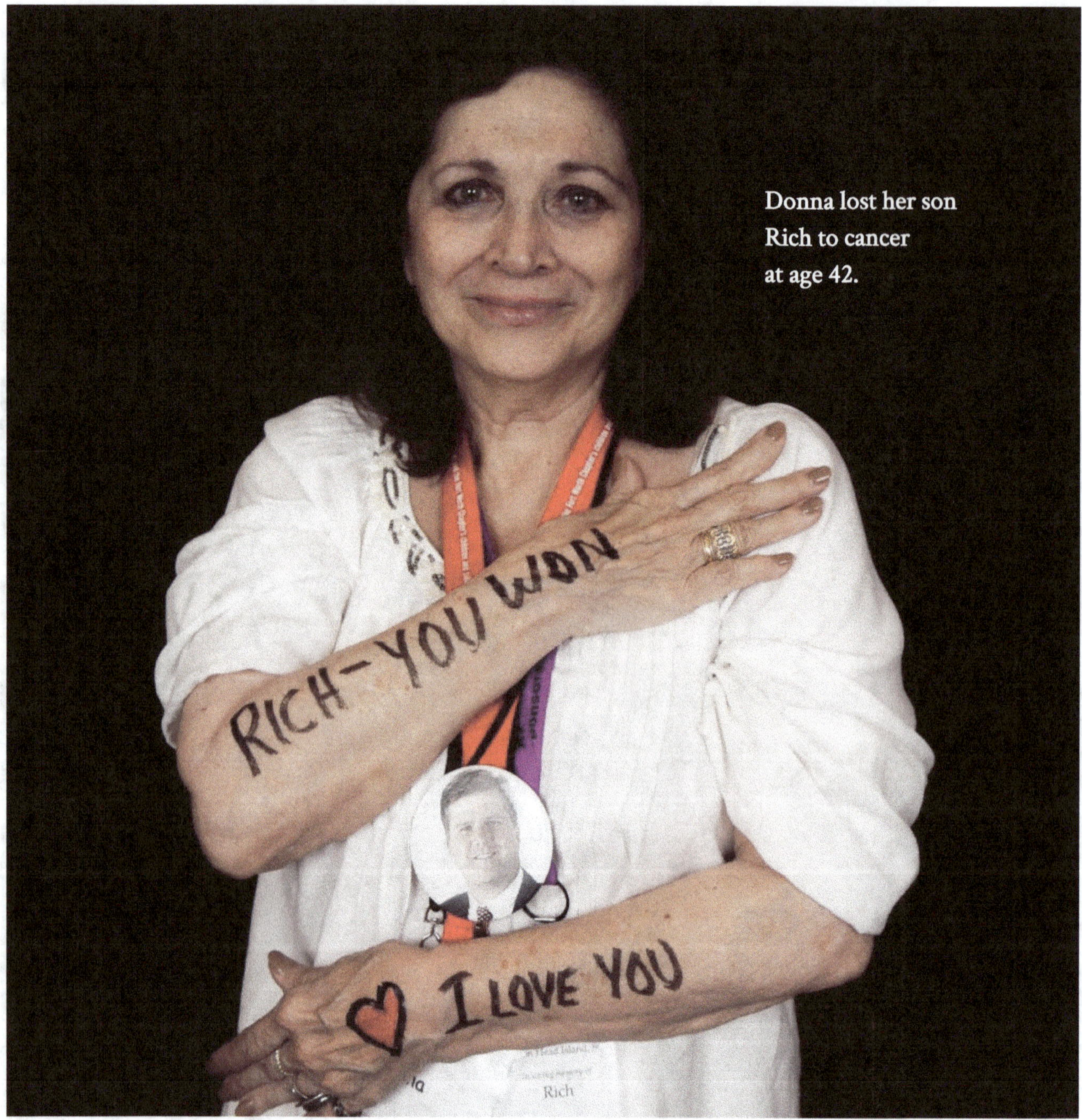

Donna lost her son
Rich to cancer
at age 42.

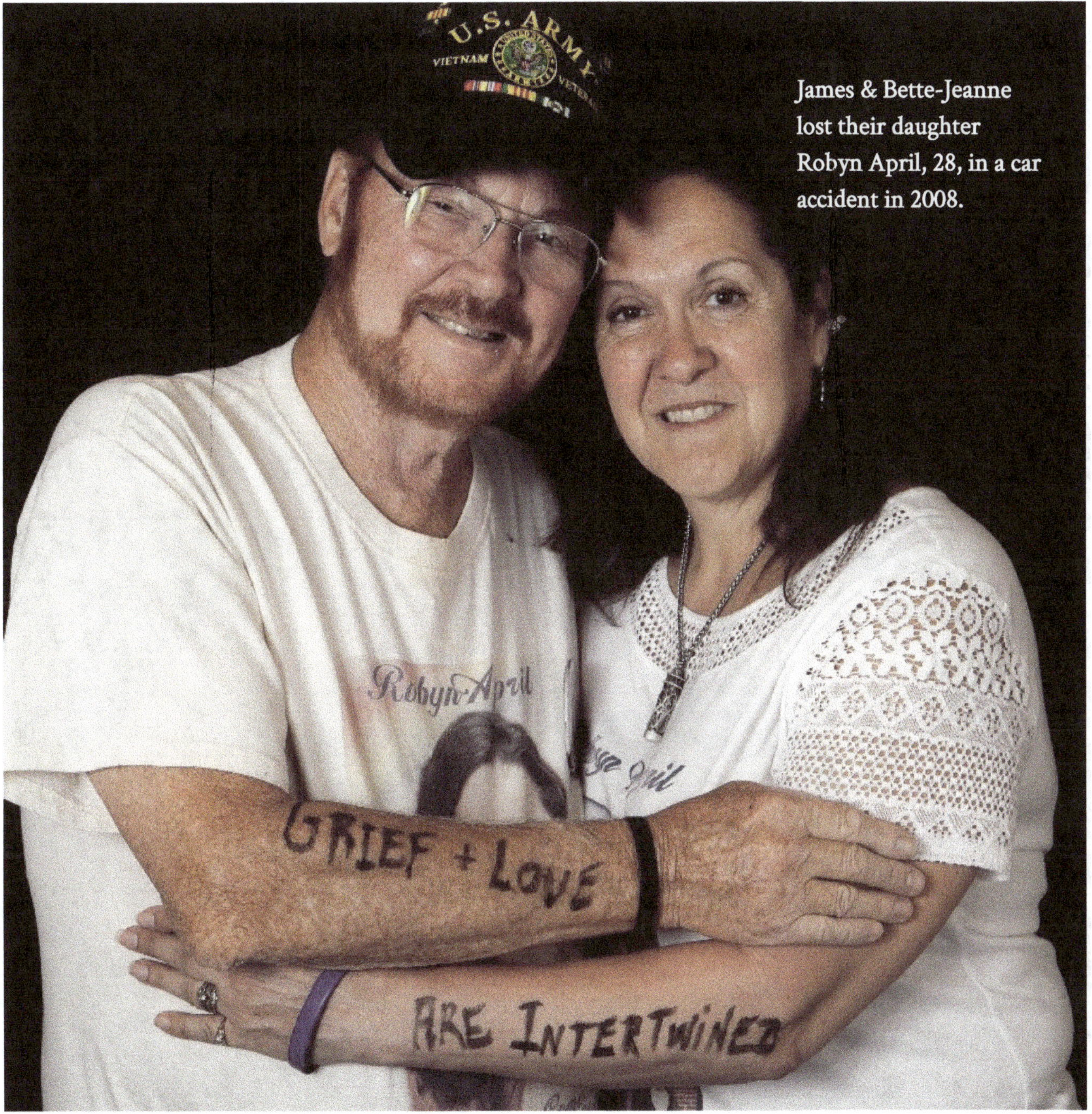

James & Bette-Jeanne
lost their daughter
Robyn April, 28, in a car
accident in 2008.

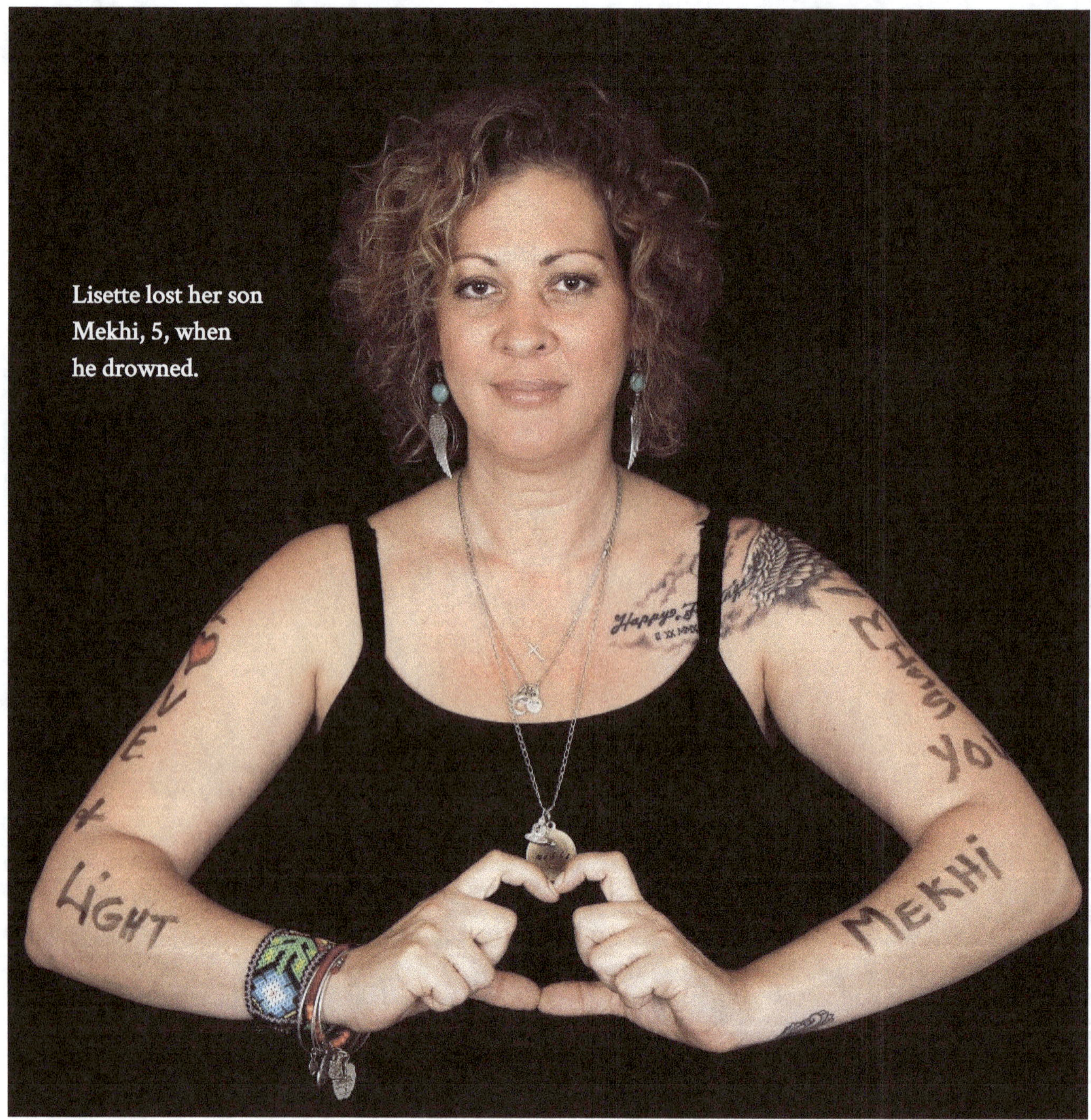

Lisette lost her son
Mekhi, 5, when
he drowned.

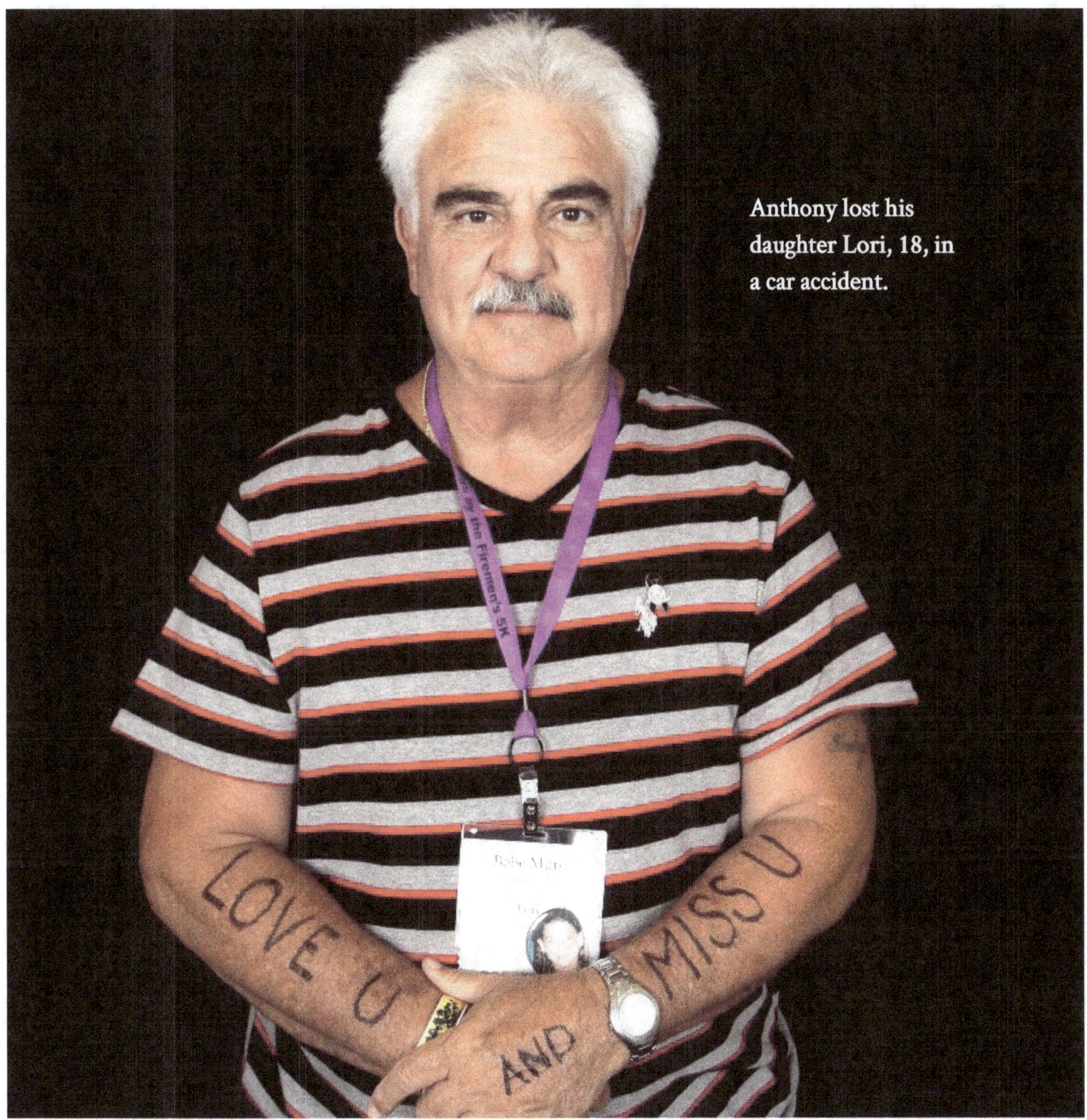

Anthony lost his daughter Lori, 18, in a car accident.

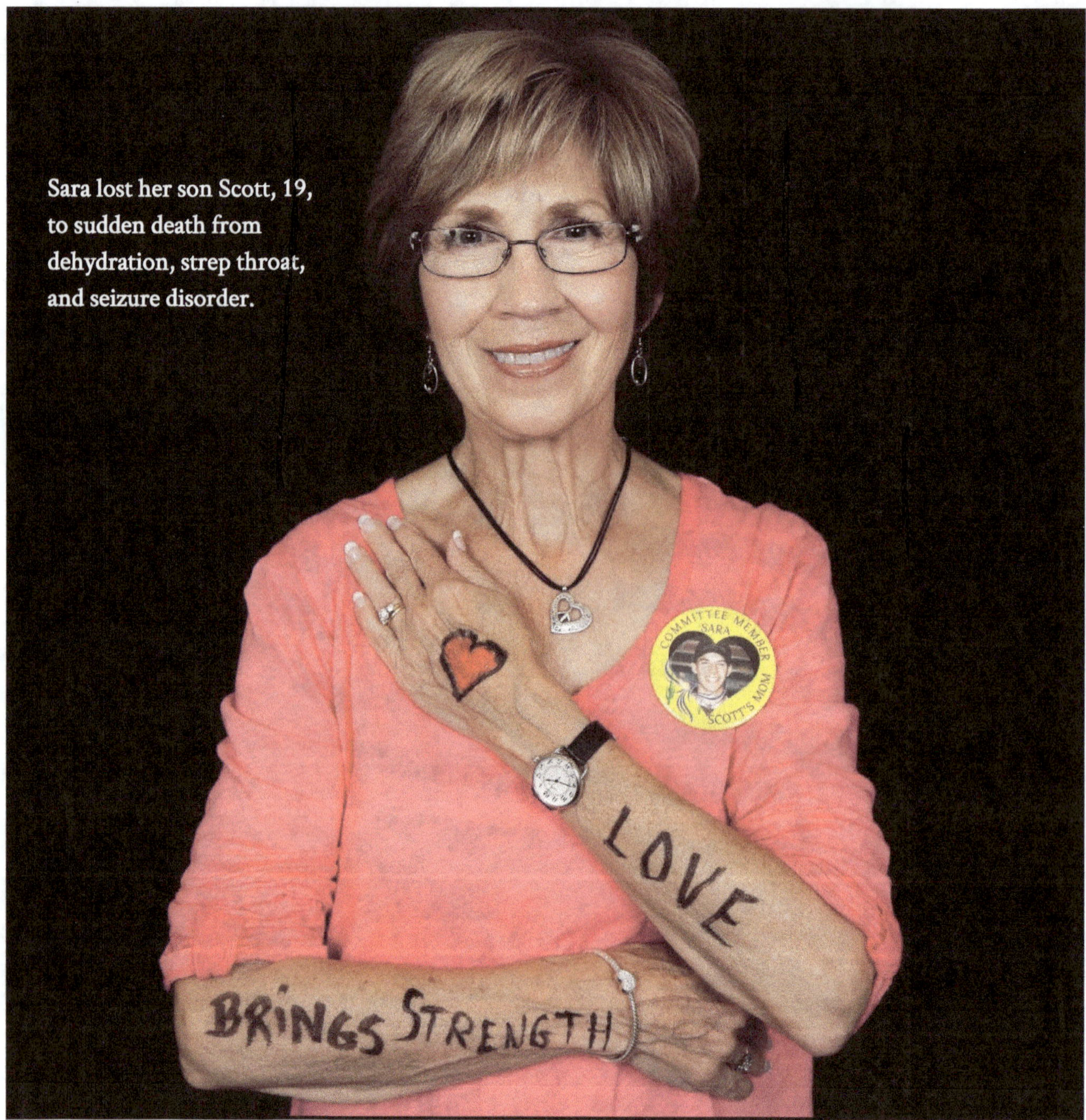

Sara lost her son Scott, 19, to sudden death from dehydration, strep throat, and seizure disorder.

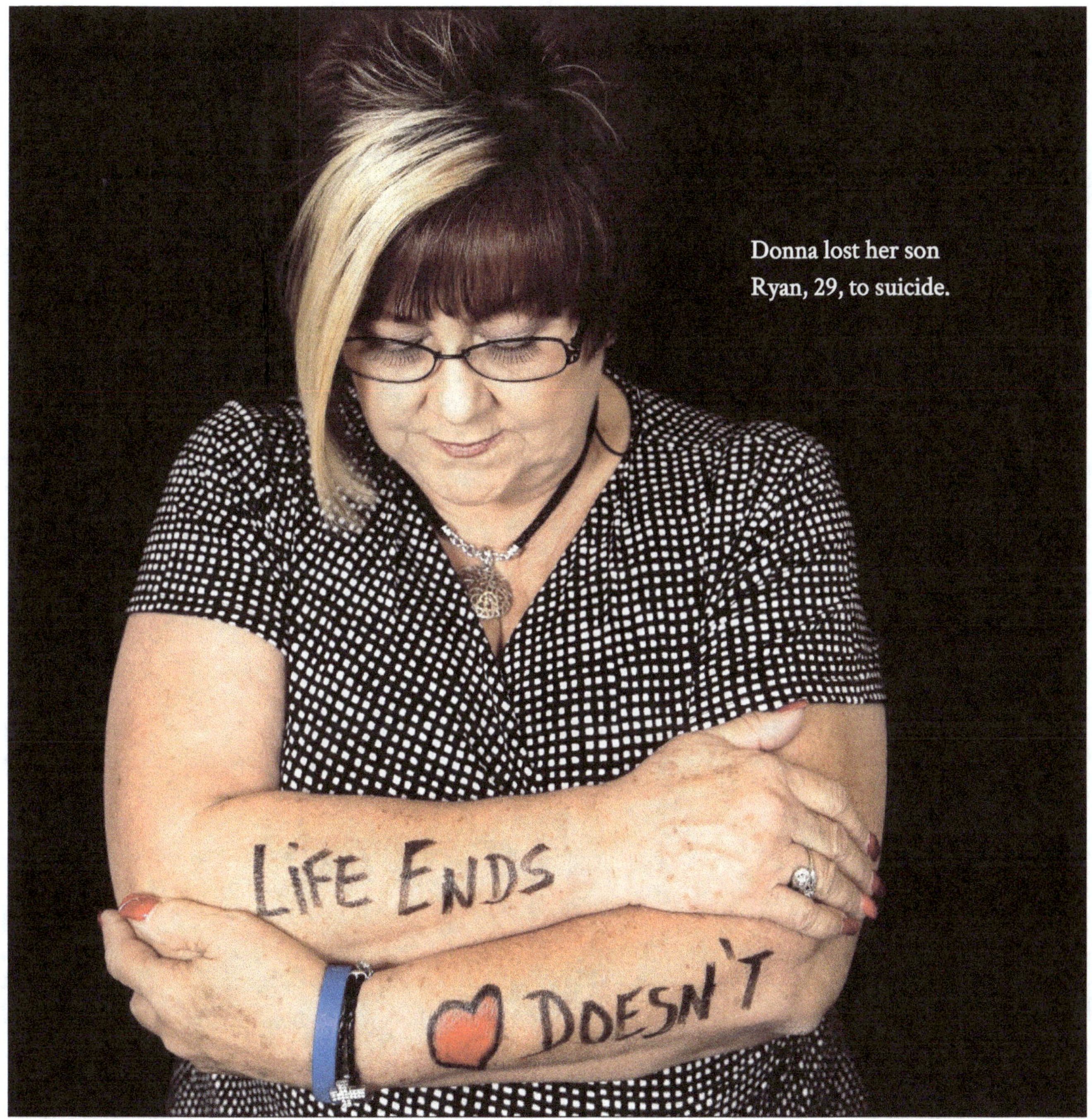

Donna lost her son
Ryan, 29, to suicide.

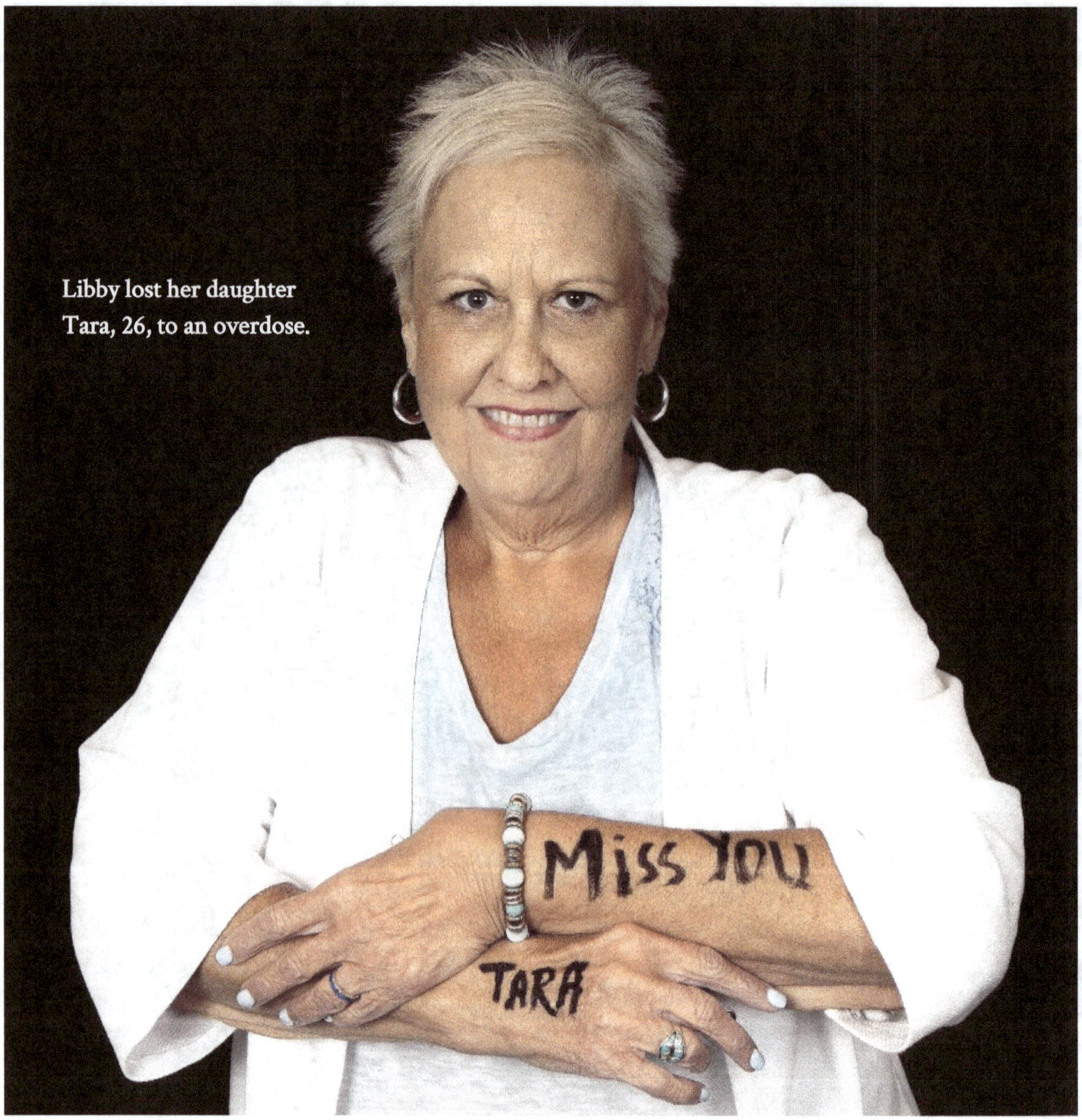
Libby lost her daughter
Tara, 26, to an overdose.
Miss You
TARA

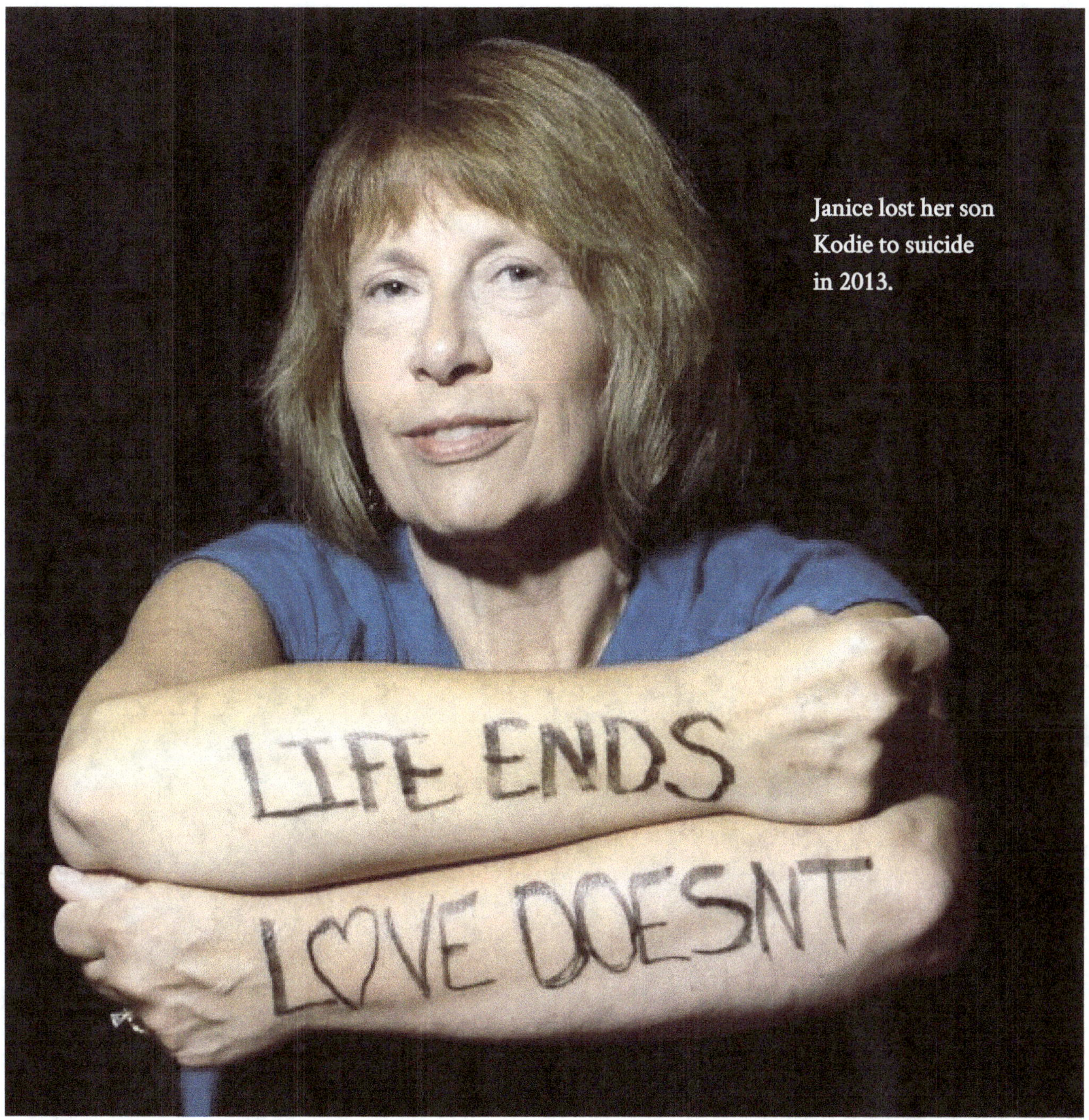

Janice lost her son
Kodie to suicide
in 2013.

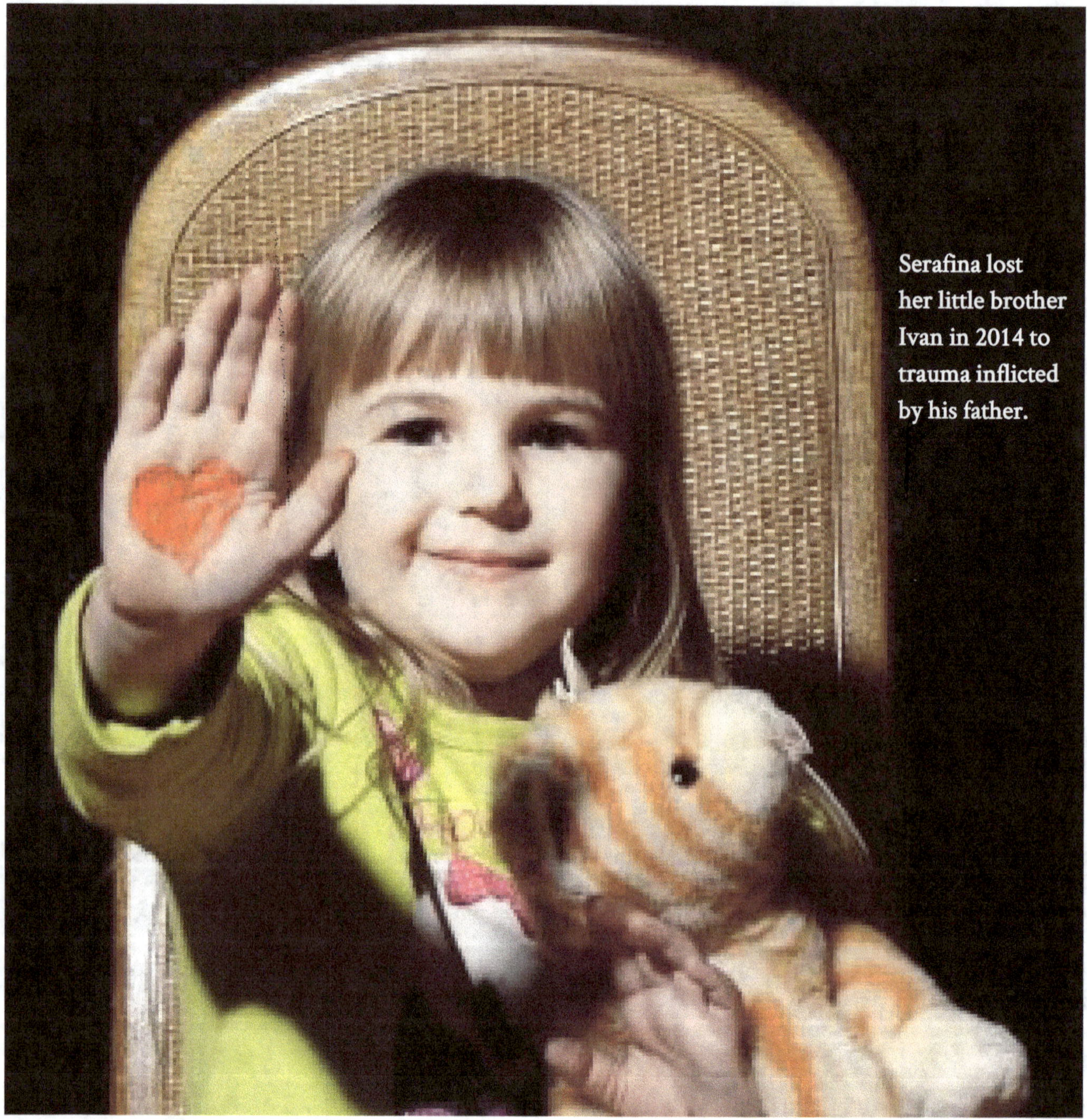
Serafina lost
her little brother
Ivan in 2014 to
trauma inflicted
by his father.

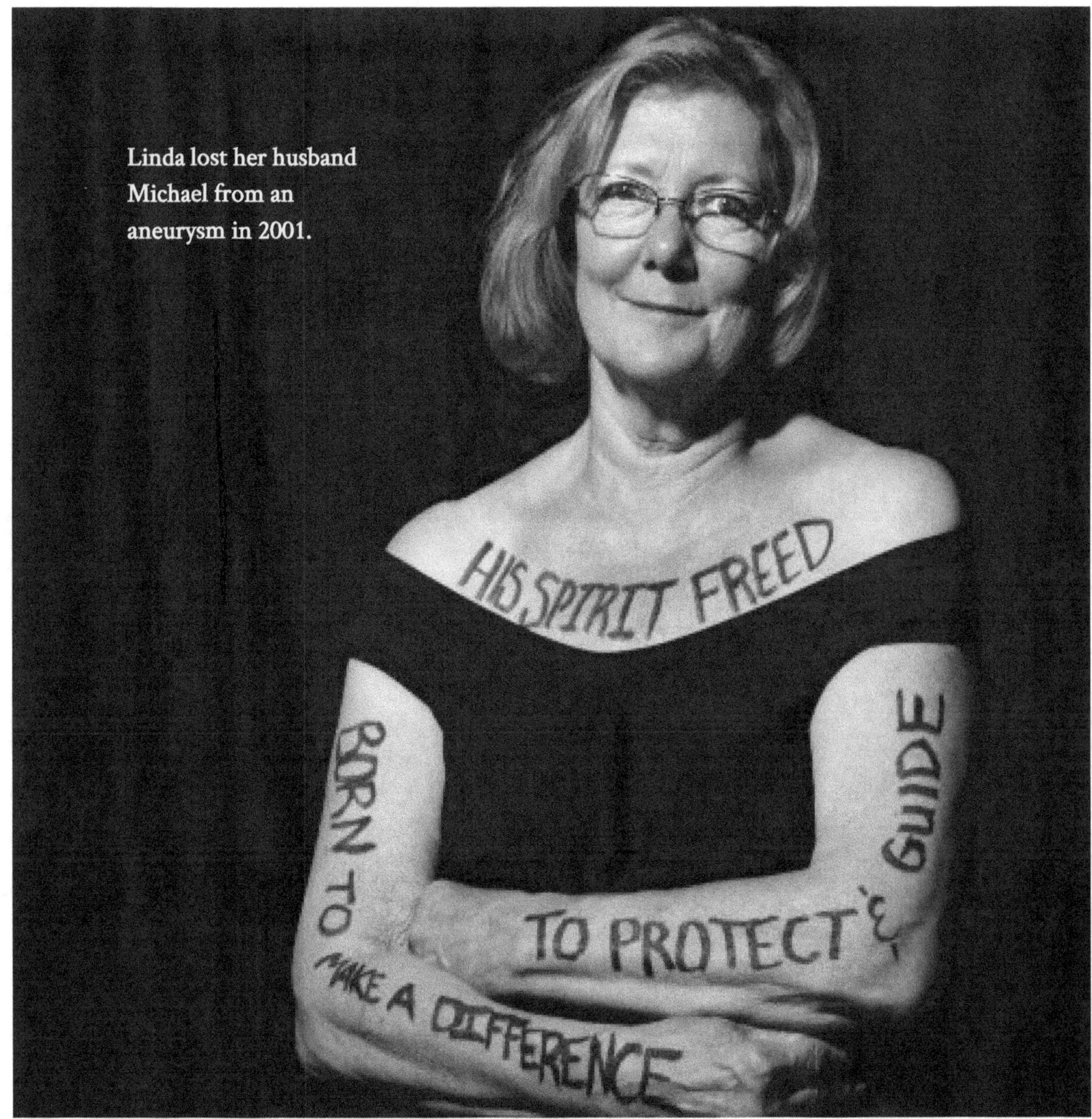

Linda lost her husband
Michael from an
aneurysm in 2001.

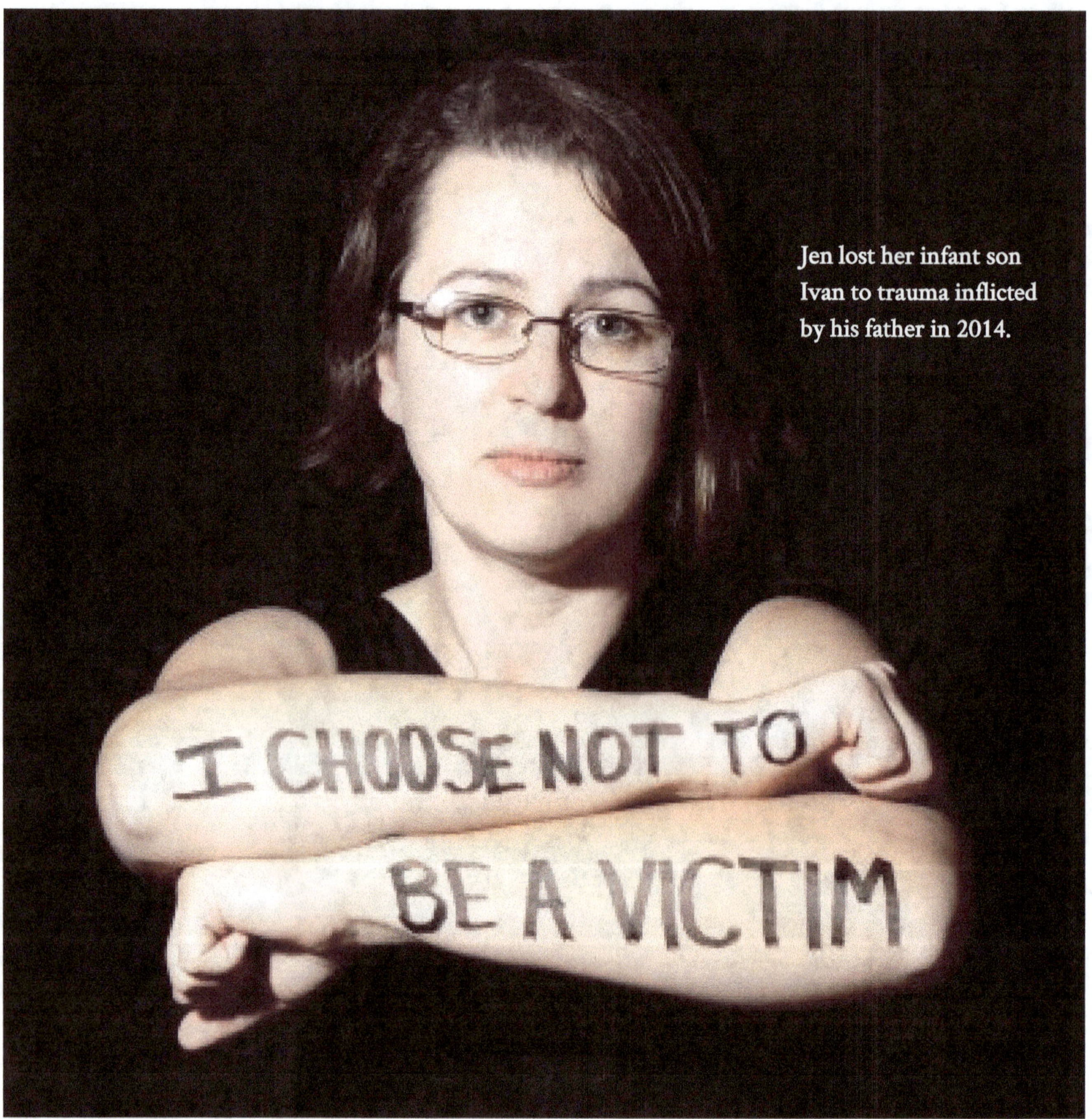

Jen lost her infant son Ivan to trauma inflicted by his father in 2014.

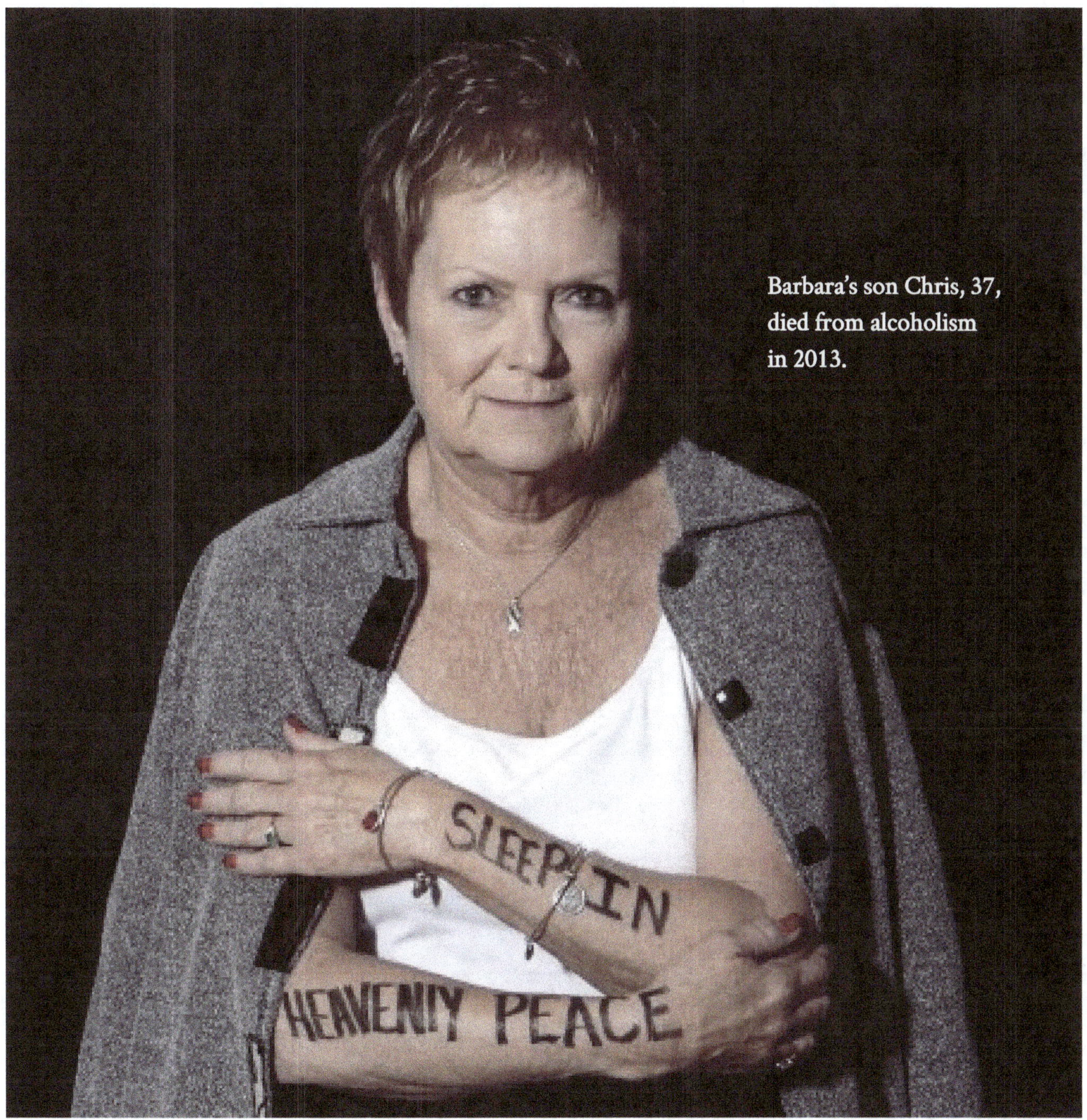

Barbara's son Chris, 37, died from alcoholism in 2013.

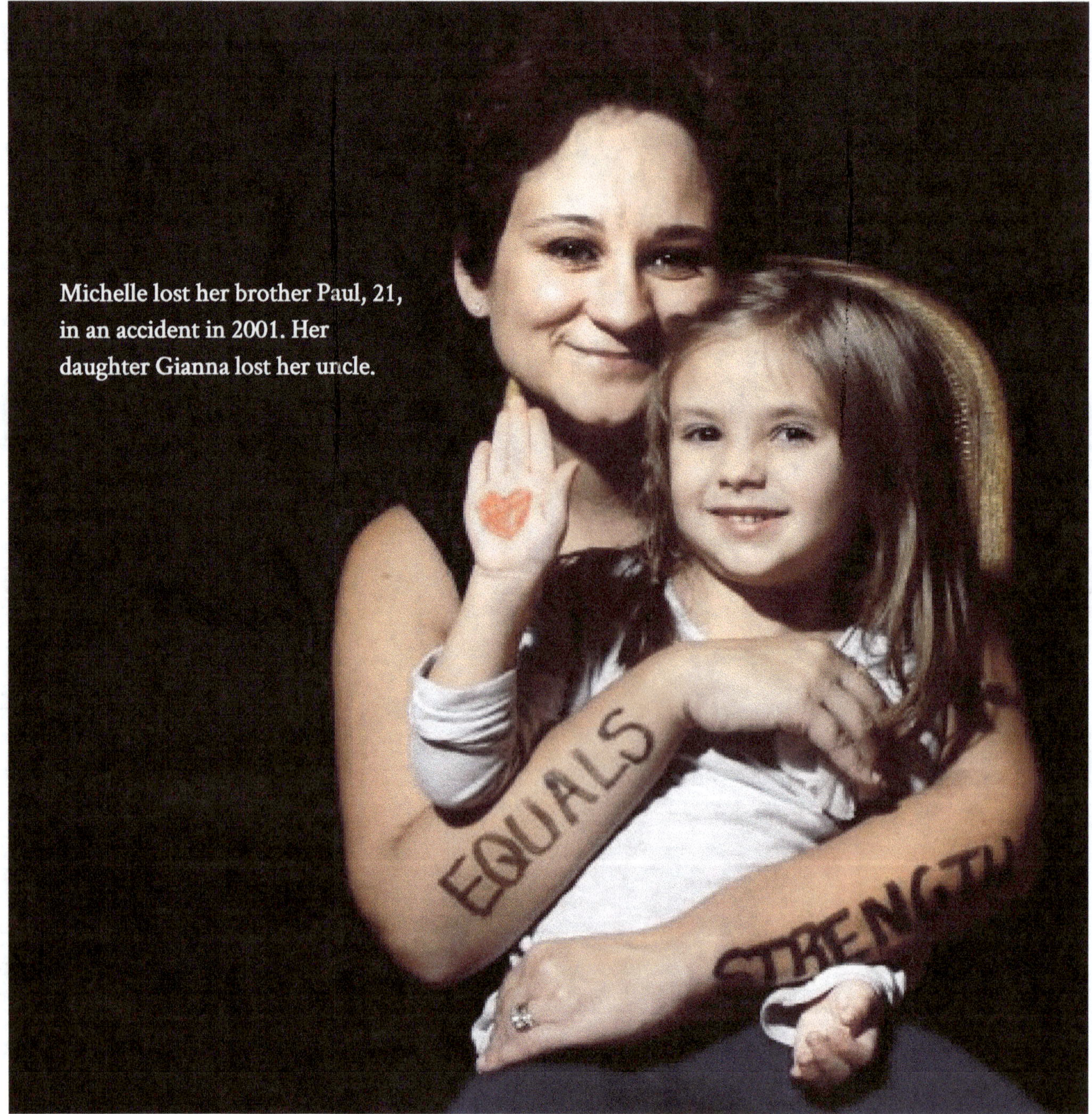

Michelle lost her brother Paul, 21, in an accident in 2001. Her daughter Gianna lost her uncle.

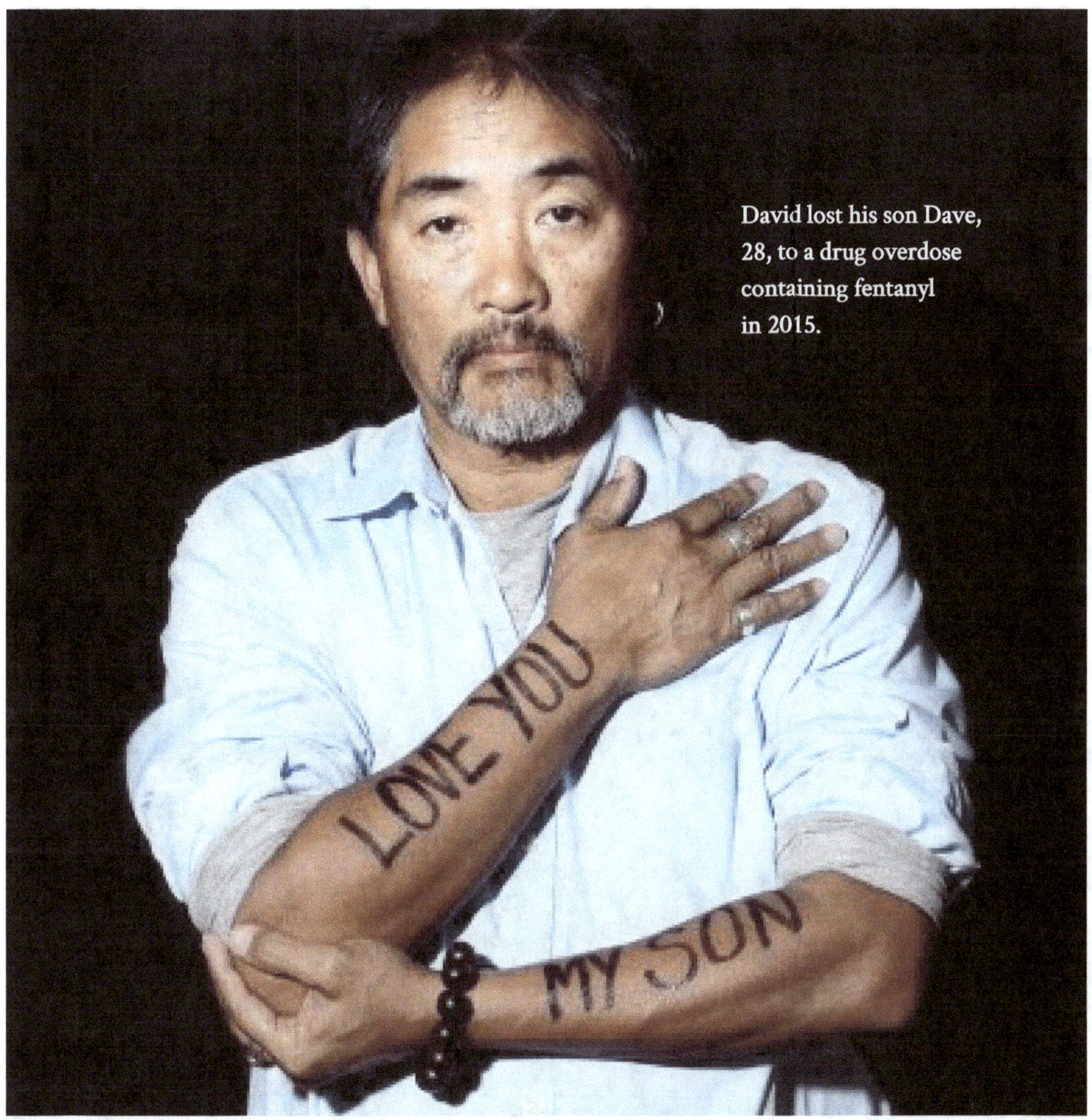

David lost his son Dave, 28, to a drug overdose containing fentanyl in 2015.

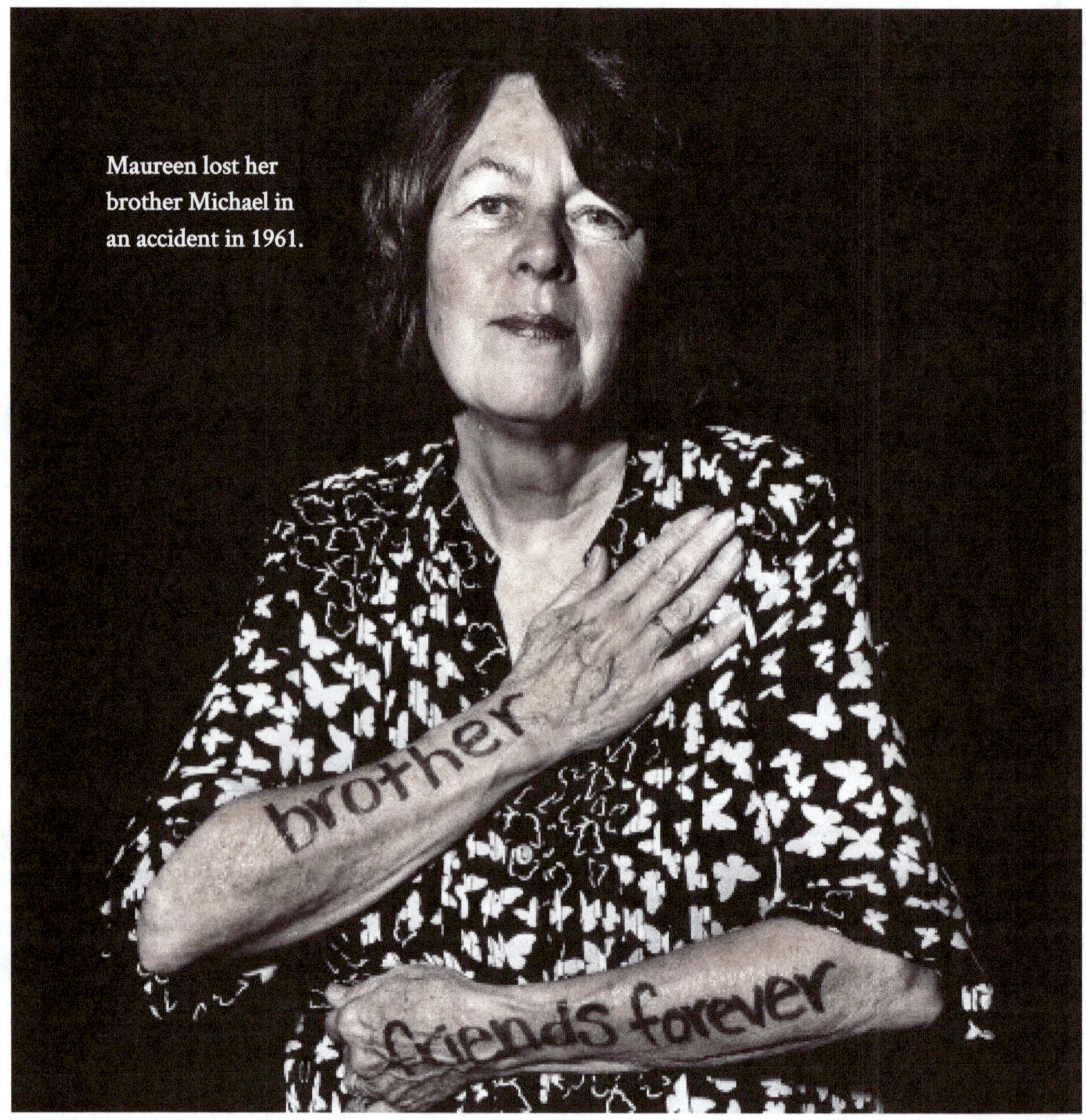
Maureen lost her
brother Michael in
an accident in 1961.
brother
friends forever

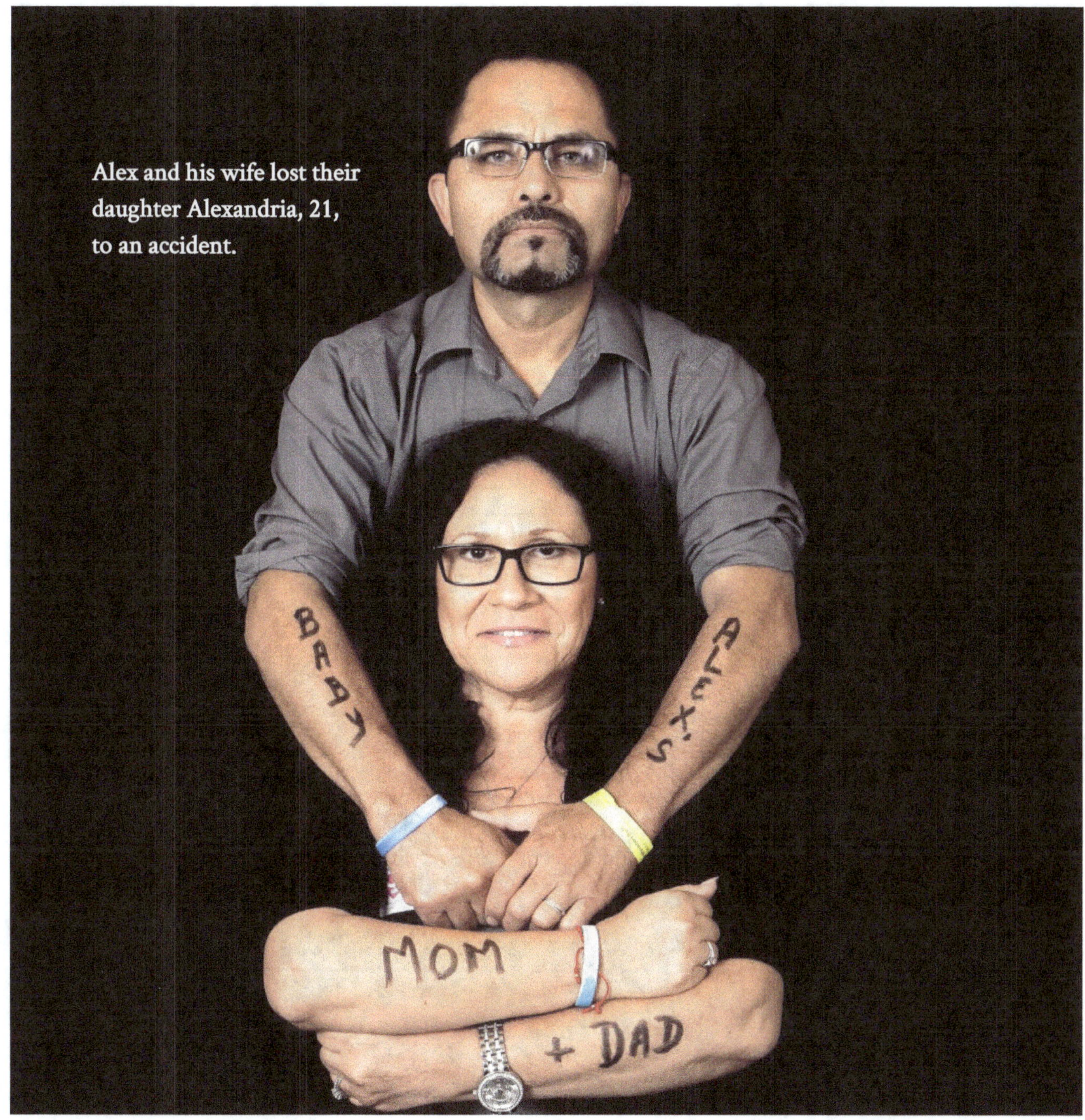

Alex and his wife lost their daughter Alexandria, 21, to an accident.

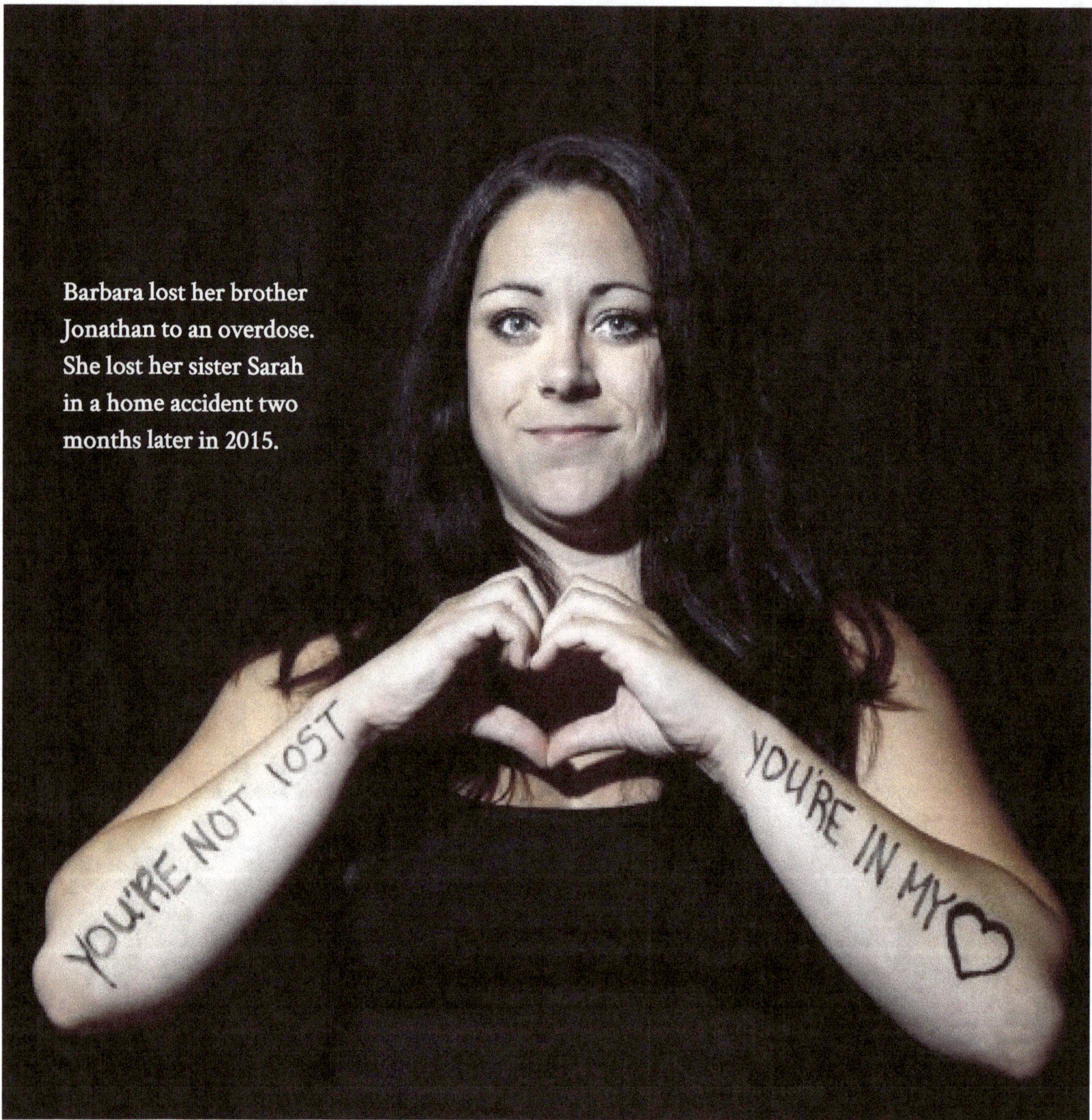

Barbara lost her brother
Jonathan to an overdose.
She lost her sister Sarah
in a home accident two
months later in 2015.

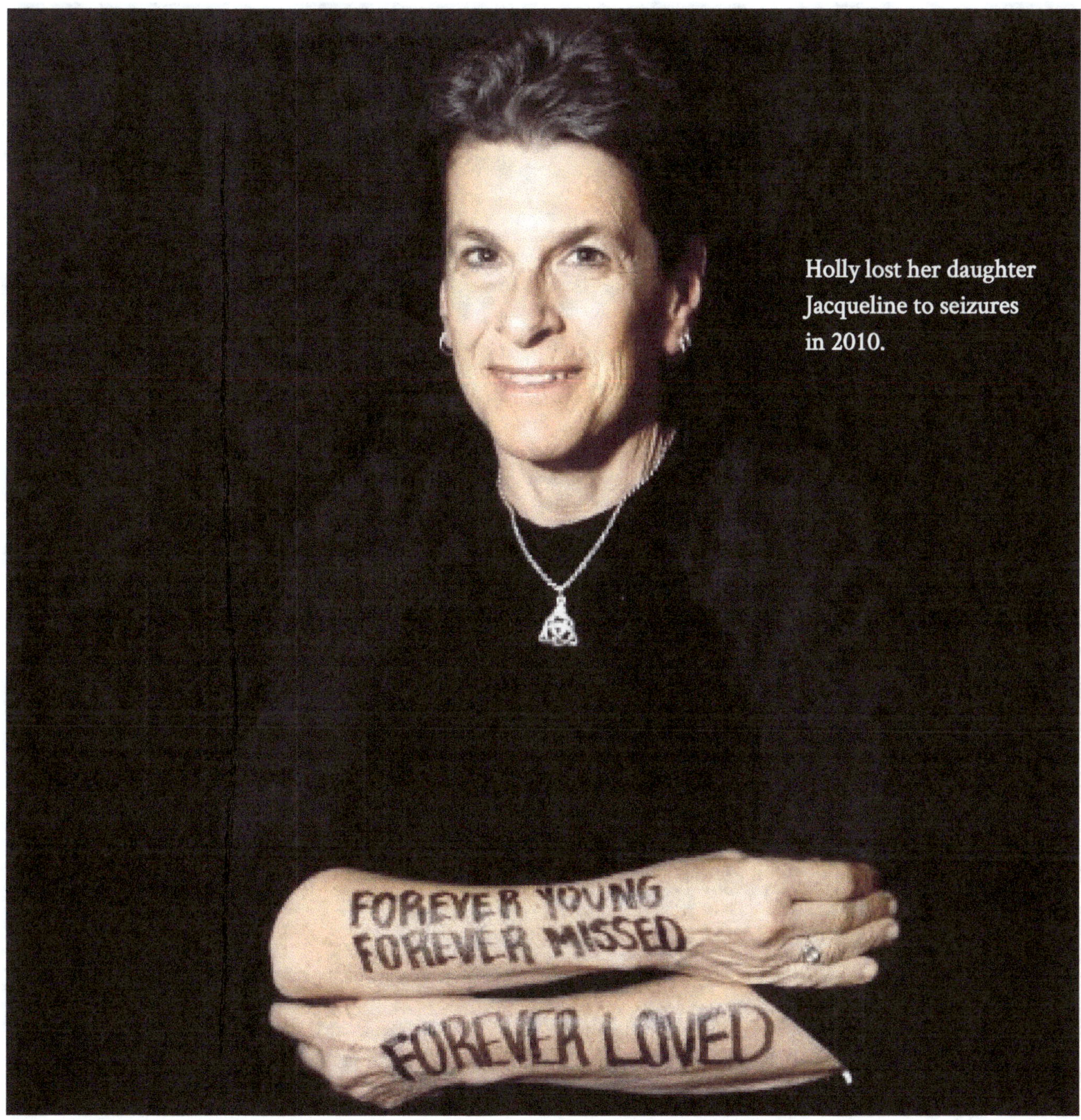

Holly lost her daughter Jacqueline to seizures in 2010.

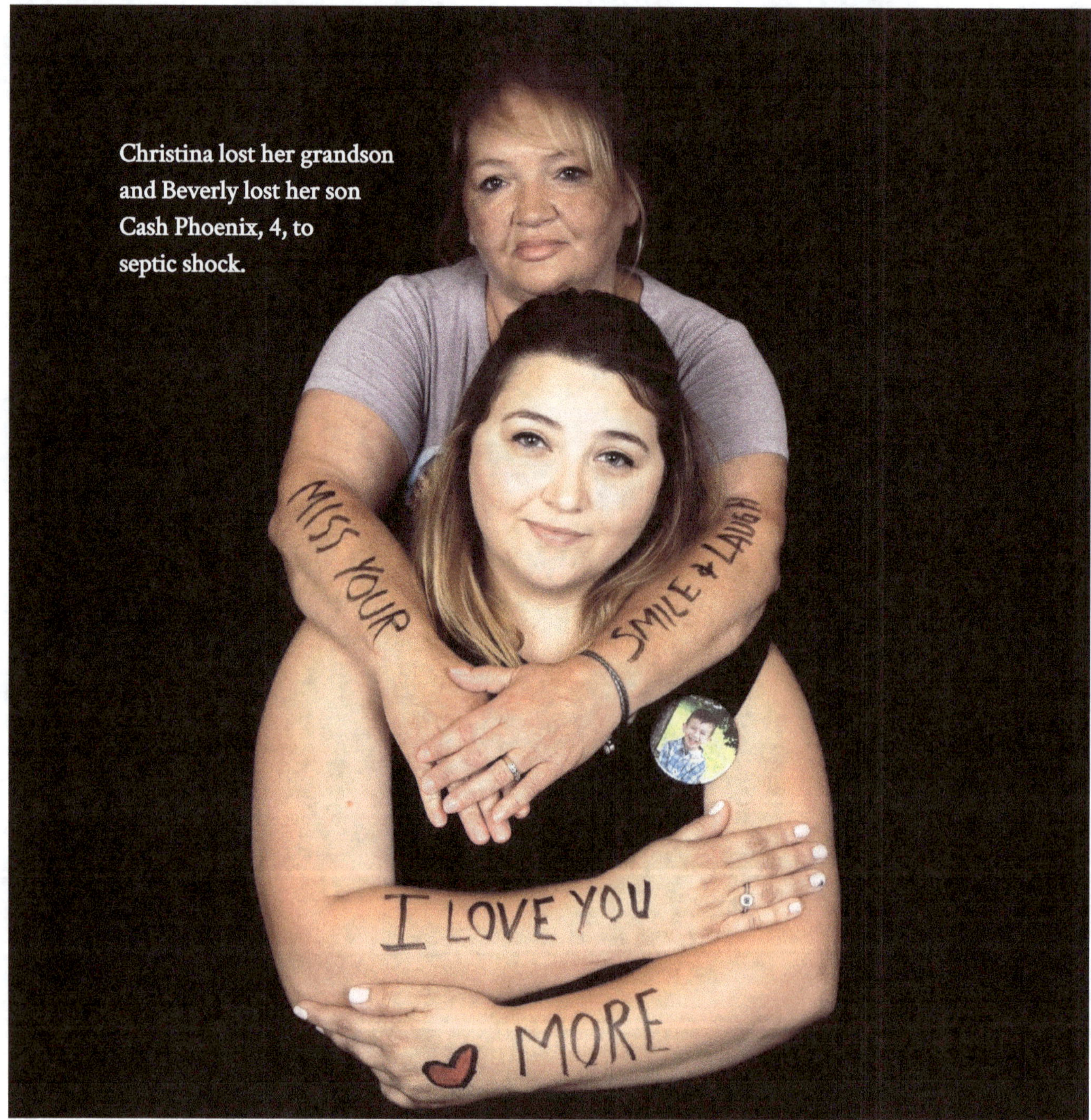

Christina lost her grandson and Beverly lost her son Cash Phoenix, 4, to septic shock.

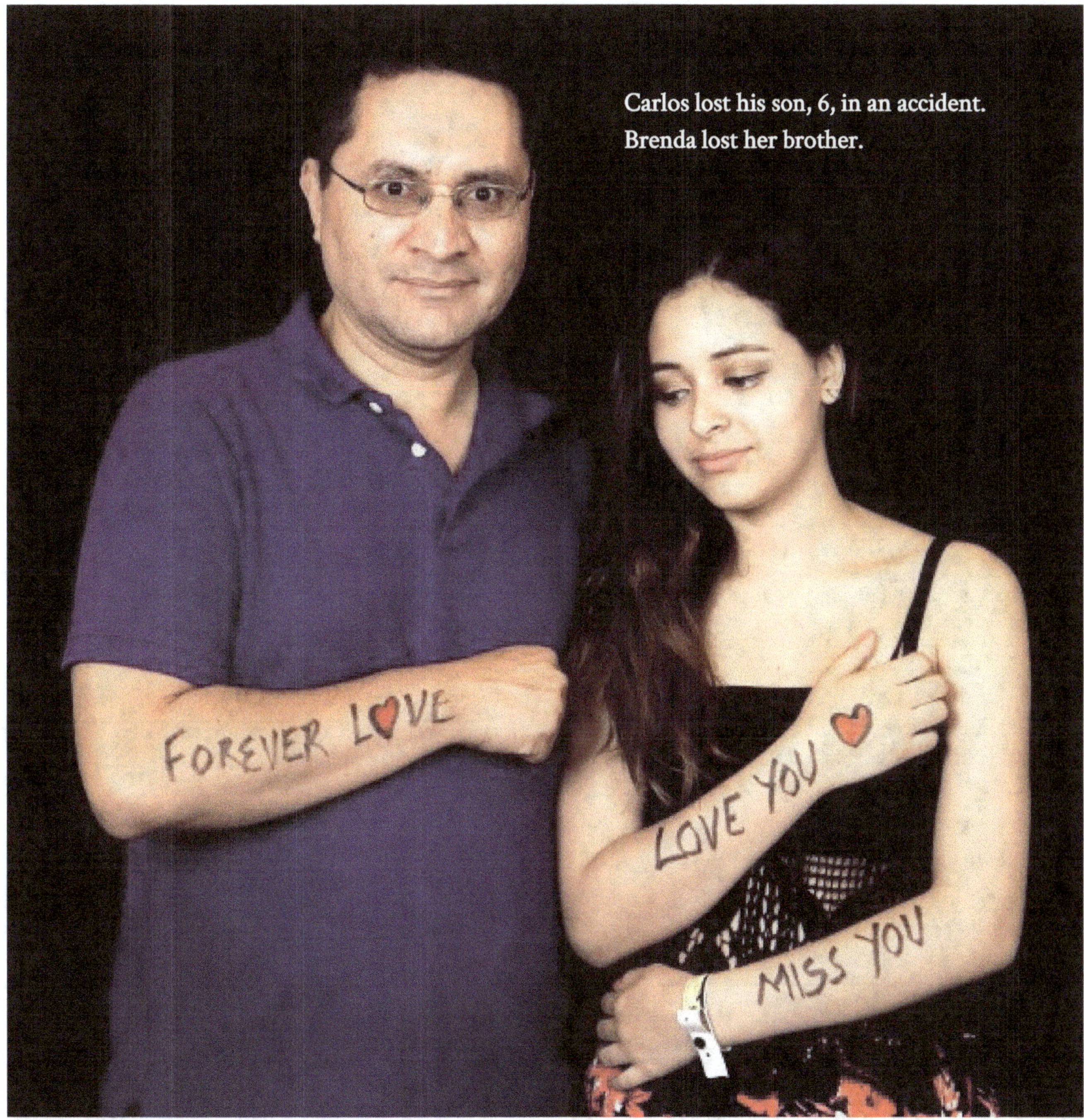

Carlos lost his son, 6, in an accident.
Brenda lost her brother.
FOREVER LOVE
LOVE YOU
MISS YOU

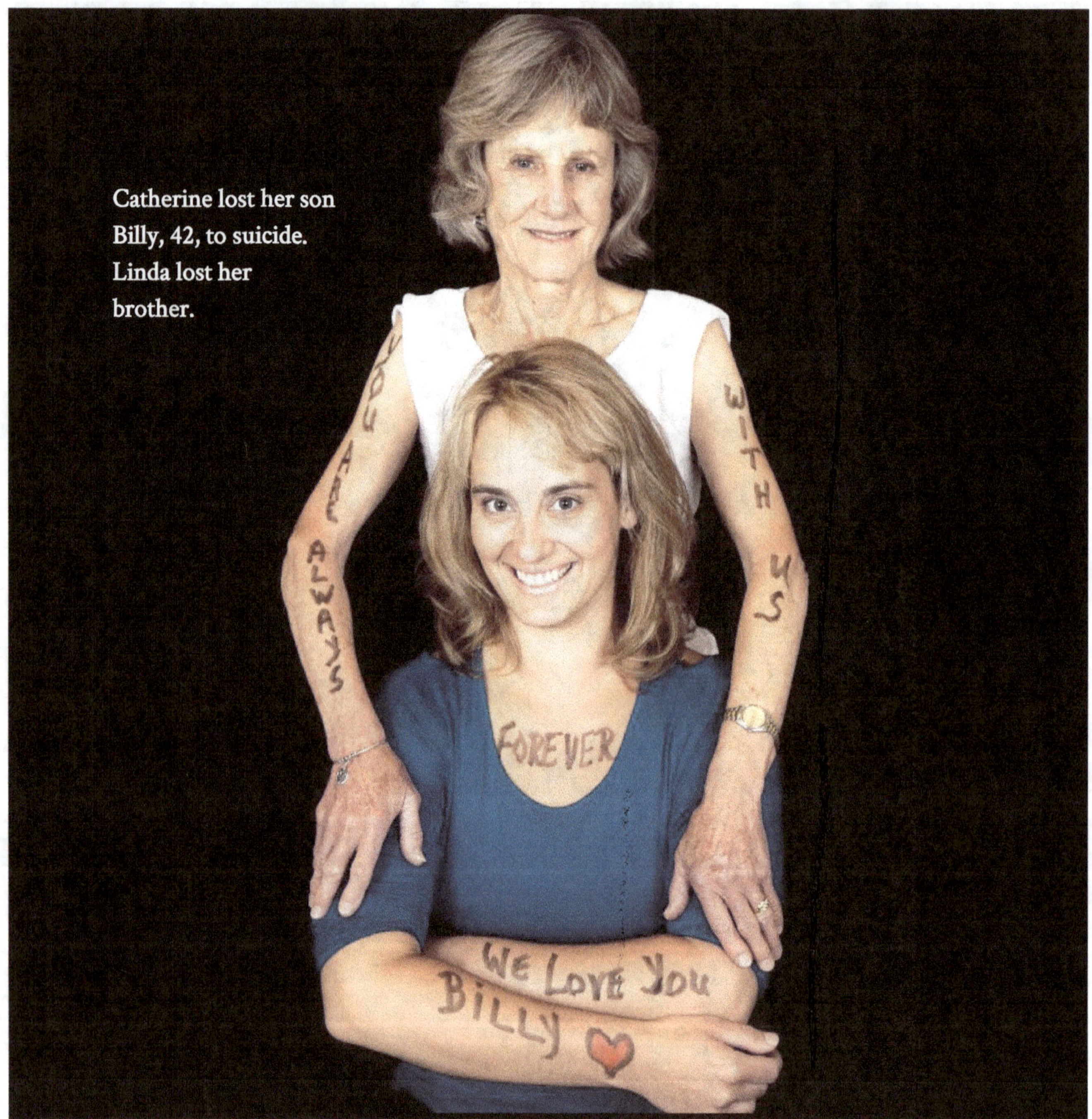

Catherine lost her son Billy, 42, to suicide. Linda lost her brother.

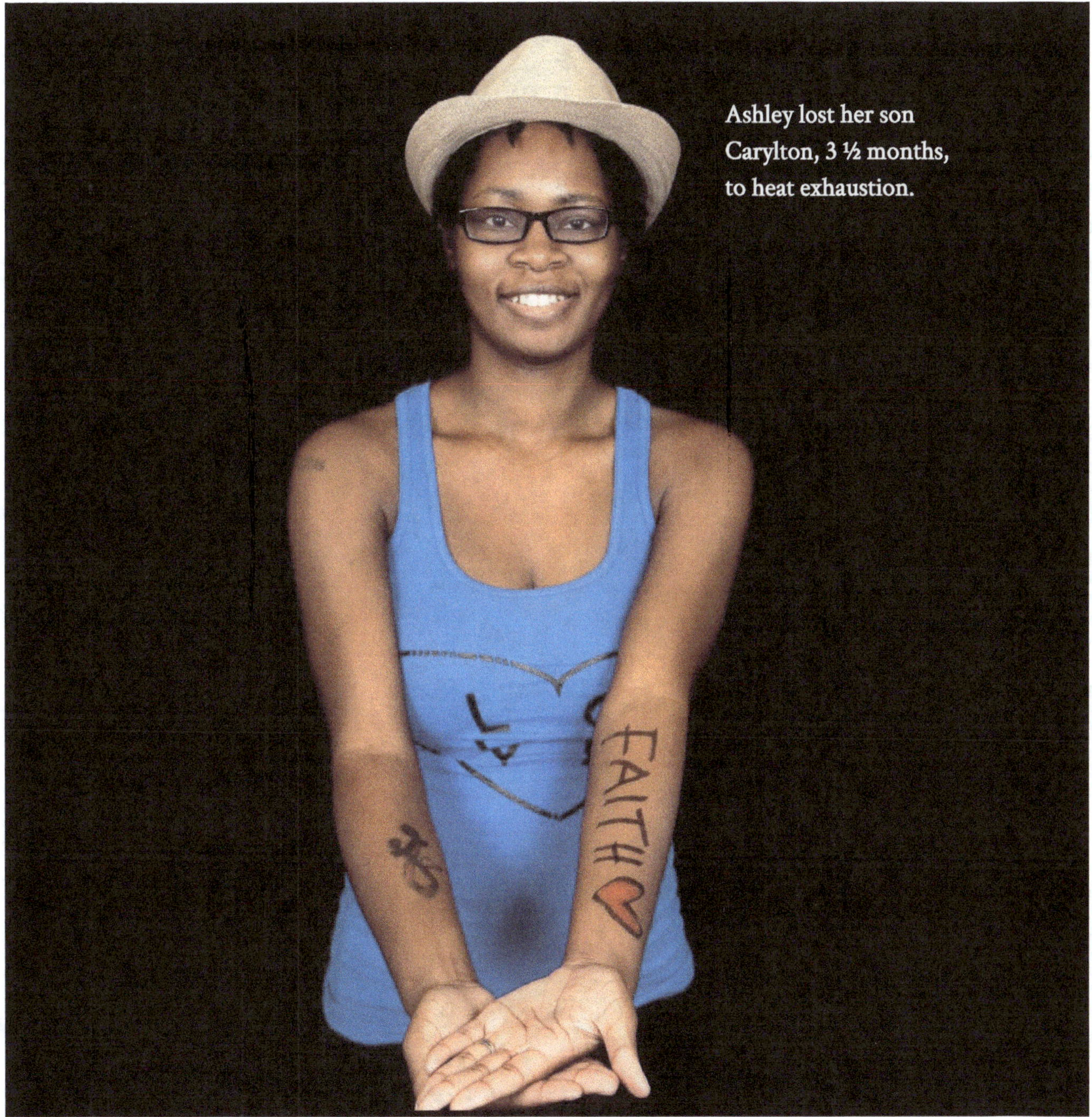

Ashley lost her son
Carylton, 3 ½ months,
to heat exhaustion.

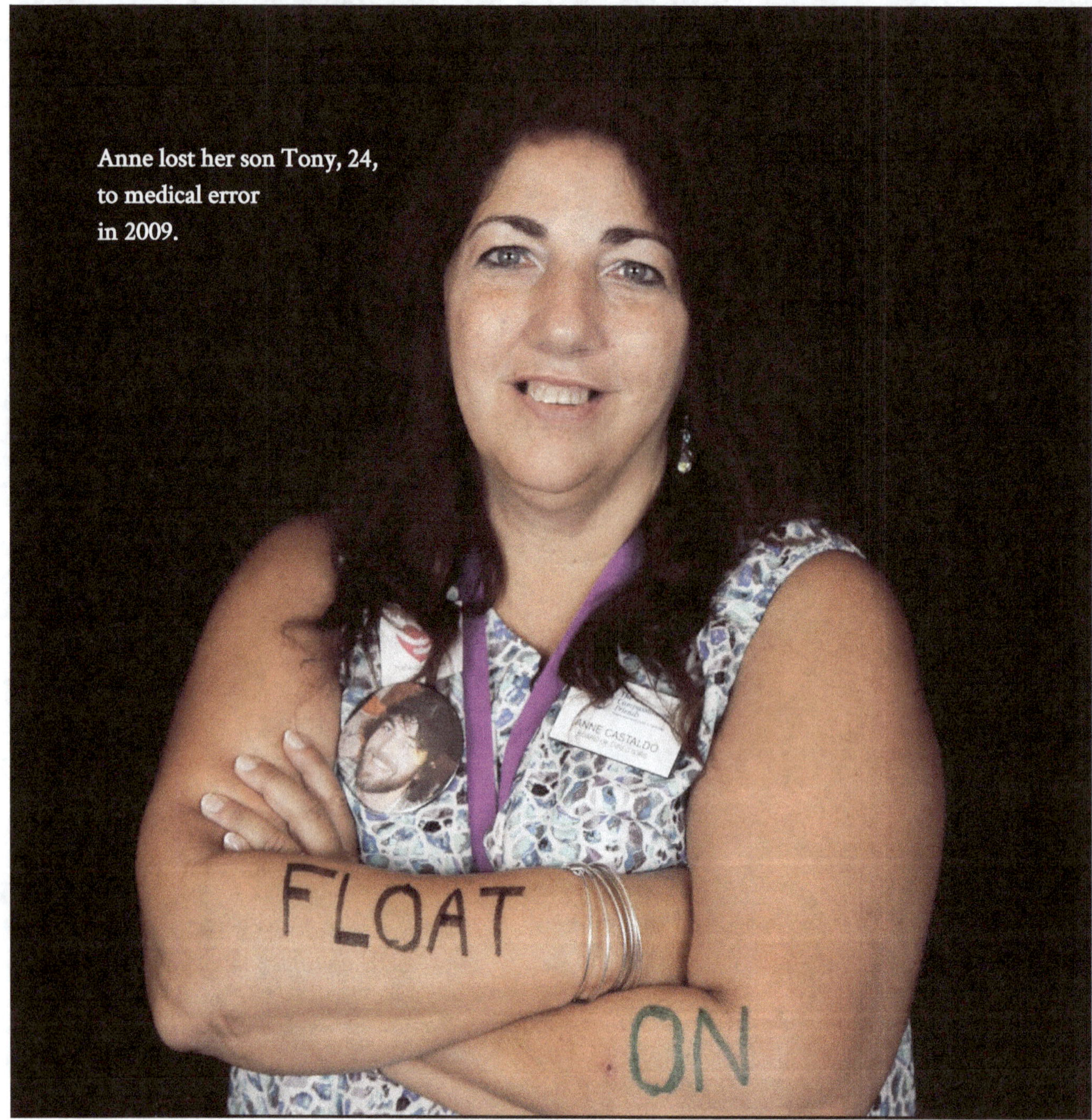

Anne lost her son Tony, 24,
to medical error
in 2009.

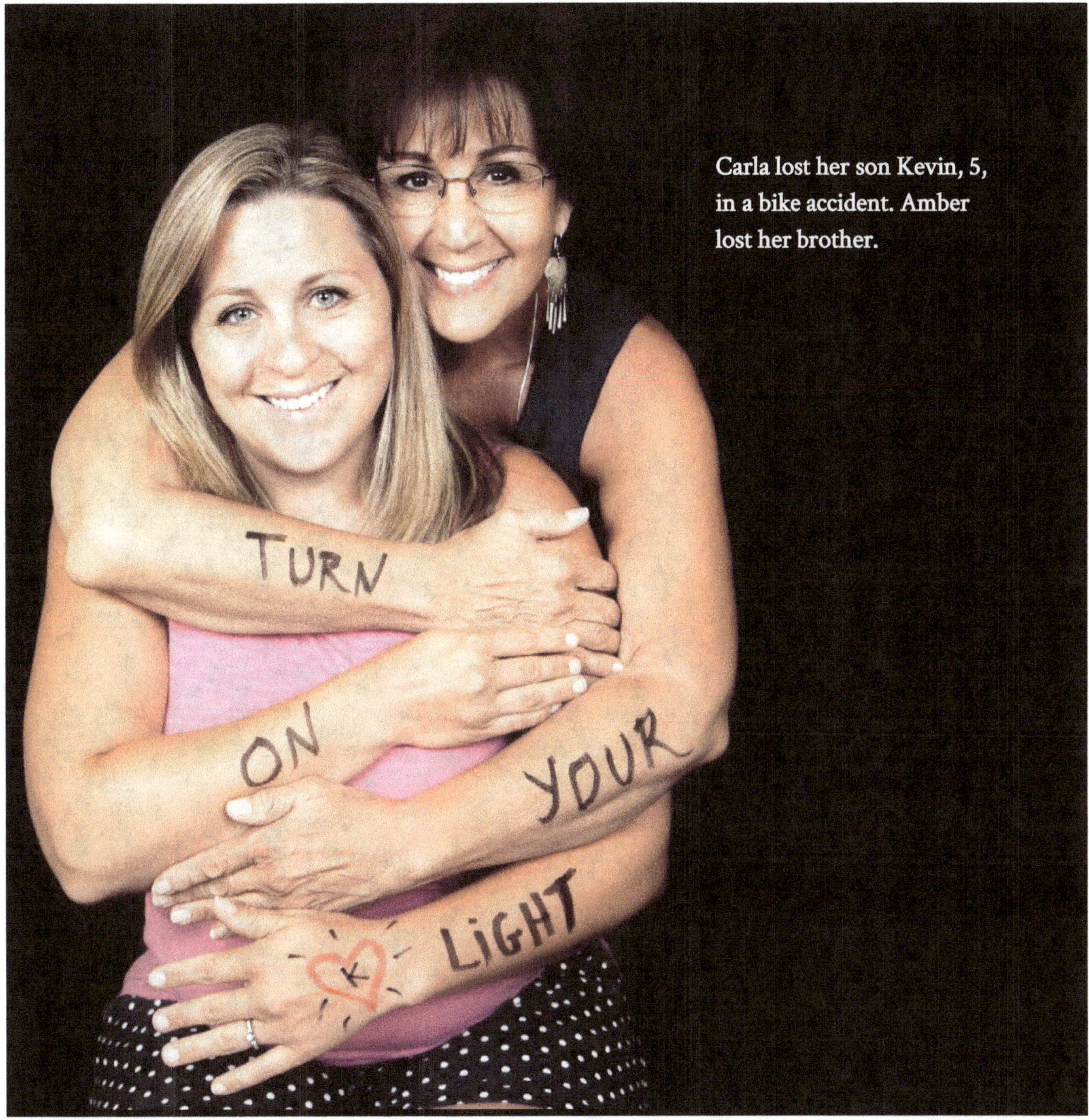

Carla lost her son Kevin, 5, in a bike accident. Amber lost her brother.

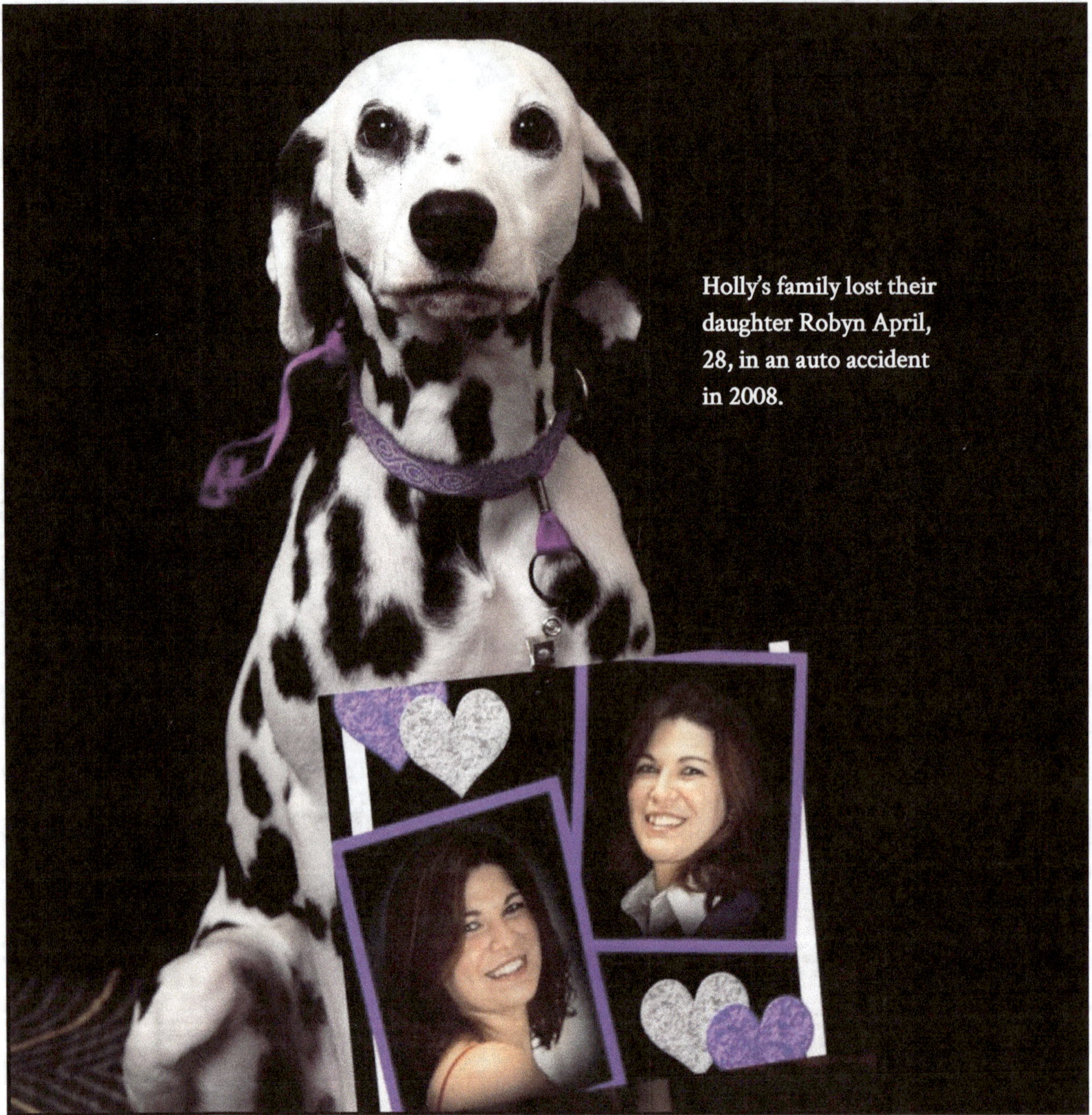
Holly's family lost their daughter Robyn April, 28, in an auto accident in 2008.

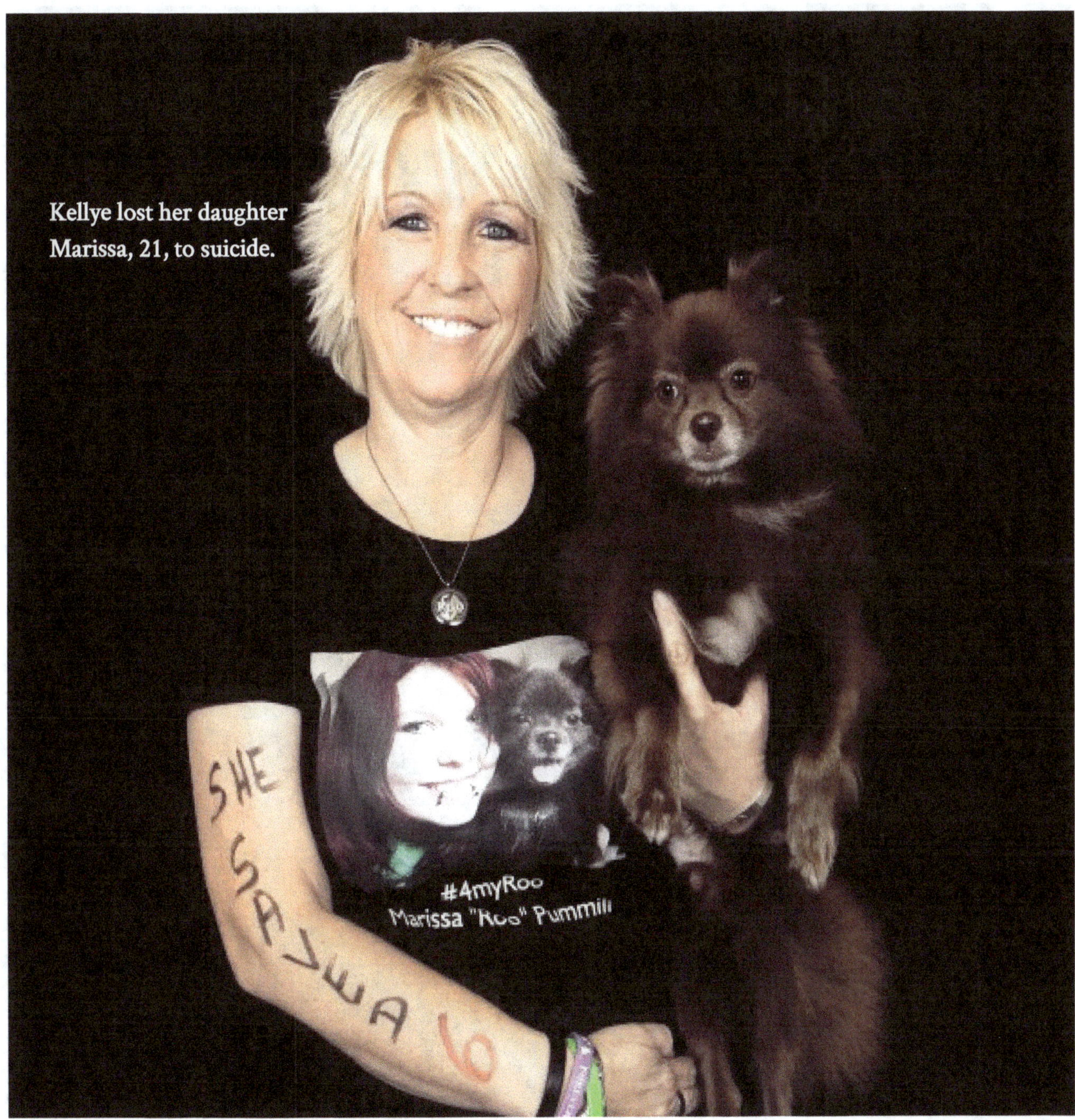

Kellye lost her daughter Marissa, 21, to suicide.

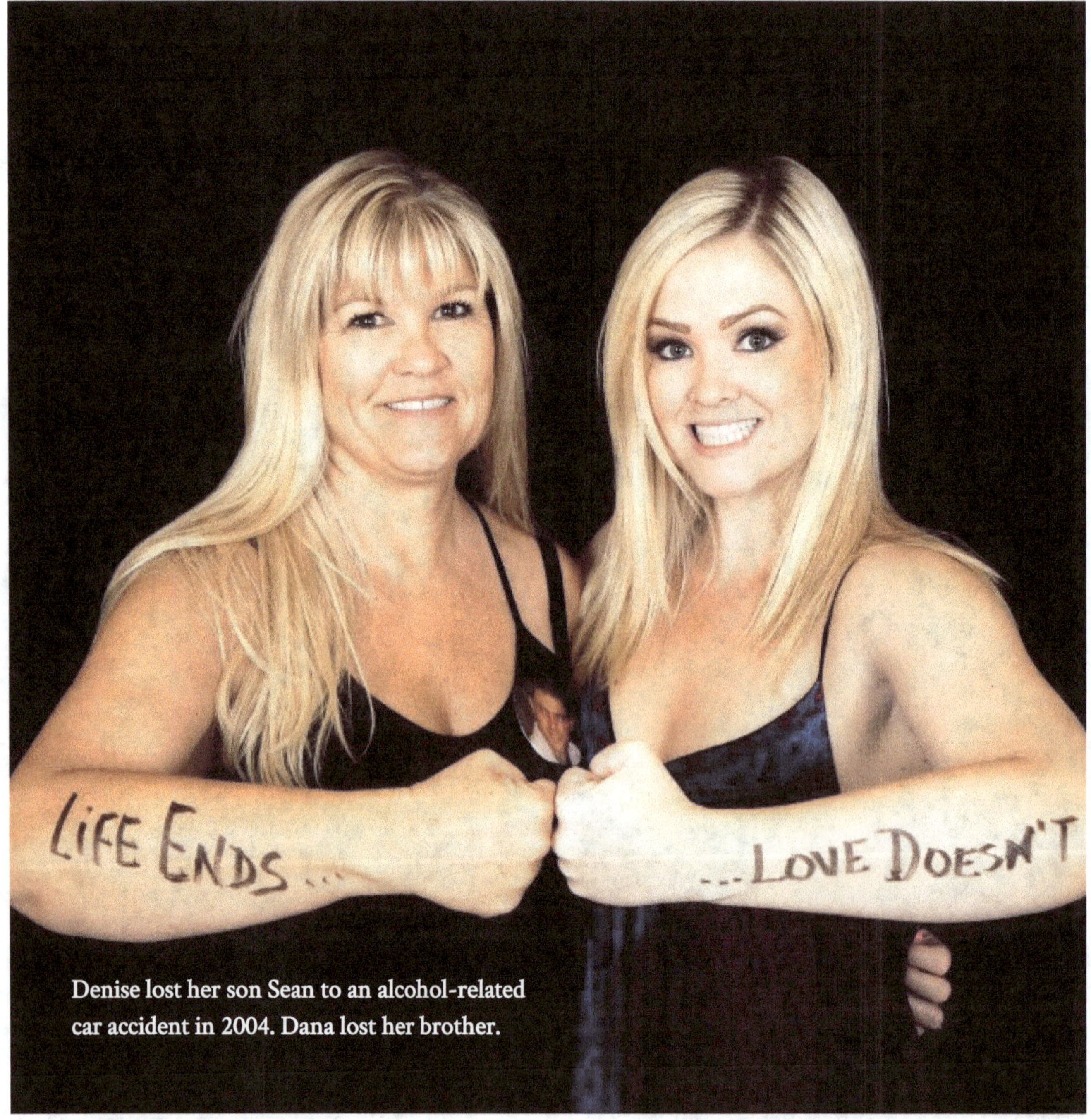

Denise lost her son Sean to an alcohol-related car accident in 2004. Dana lost her brother.

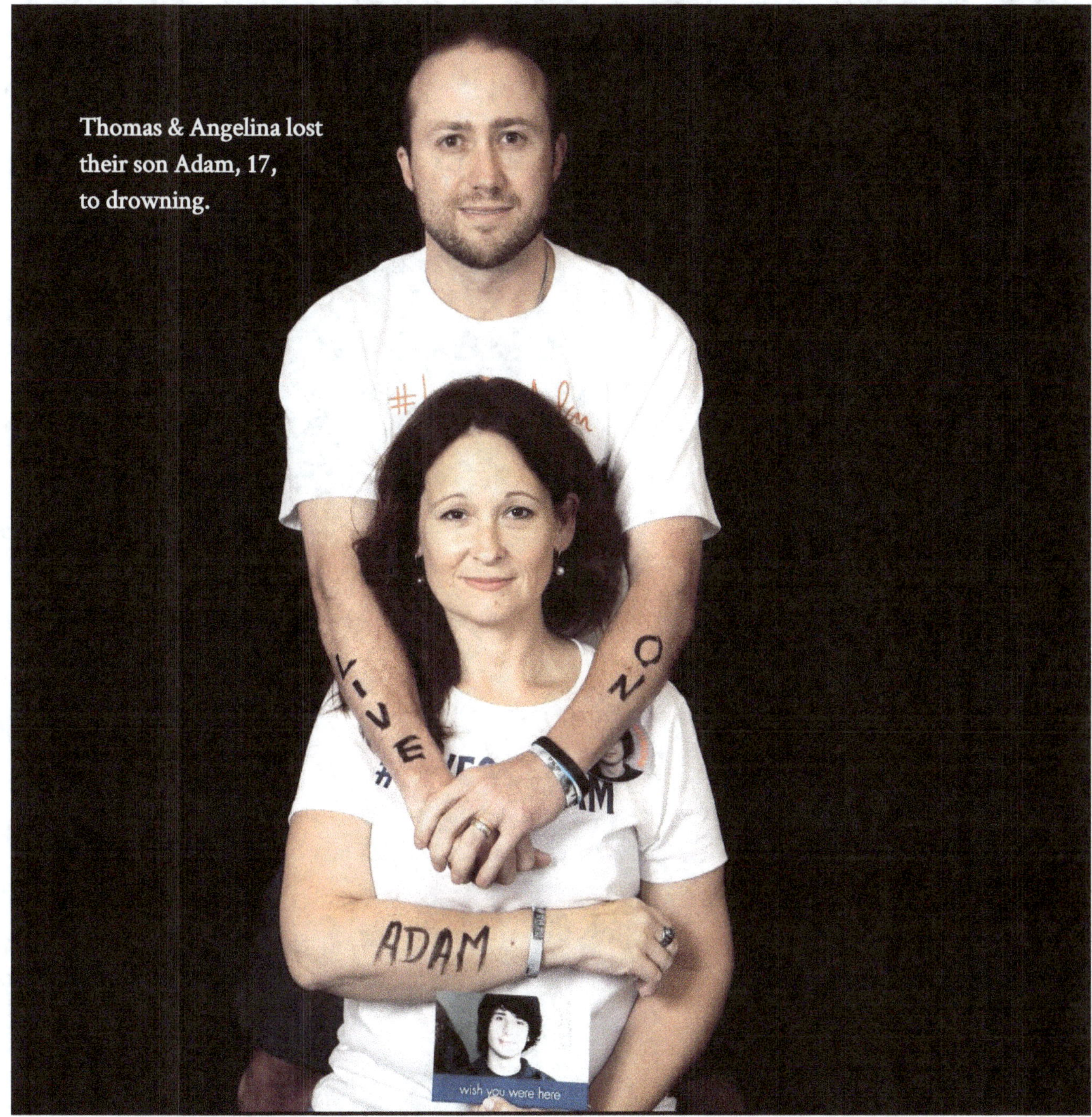

Thomas & Angelina lost
their son Adam, 17,
to drowning.

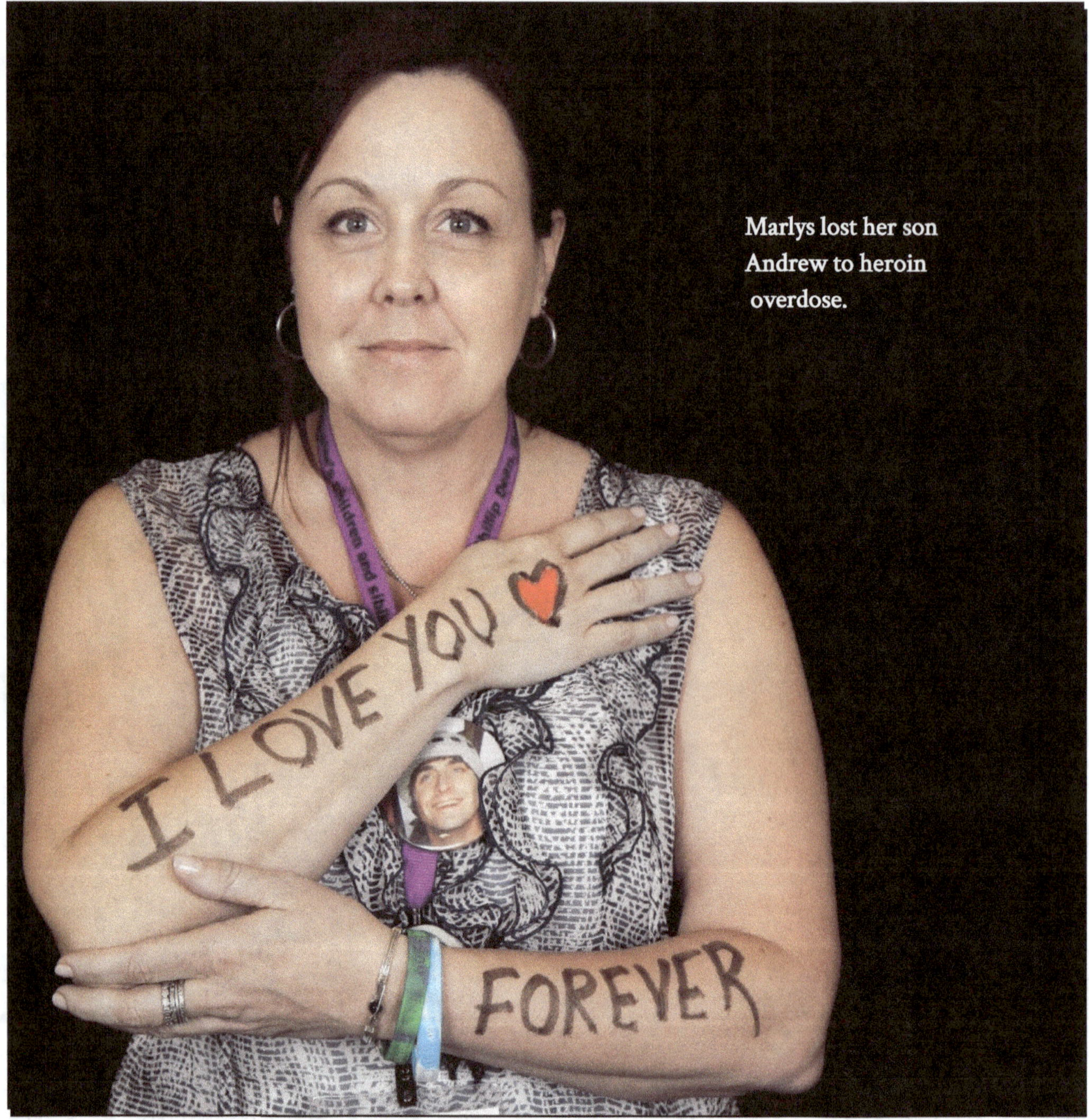

Marlys lost her son Andrew to heroin overdose.

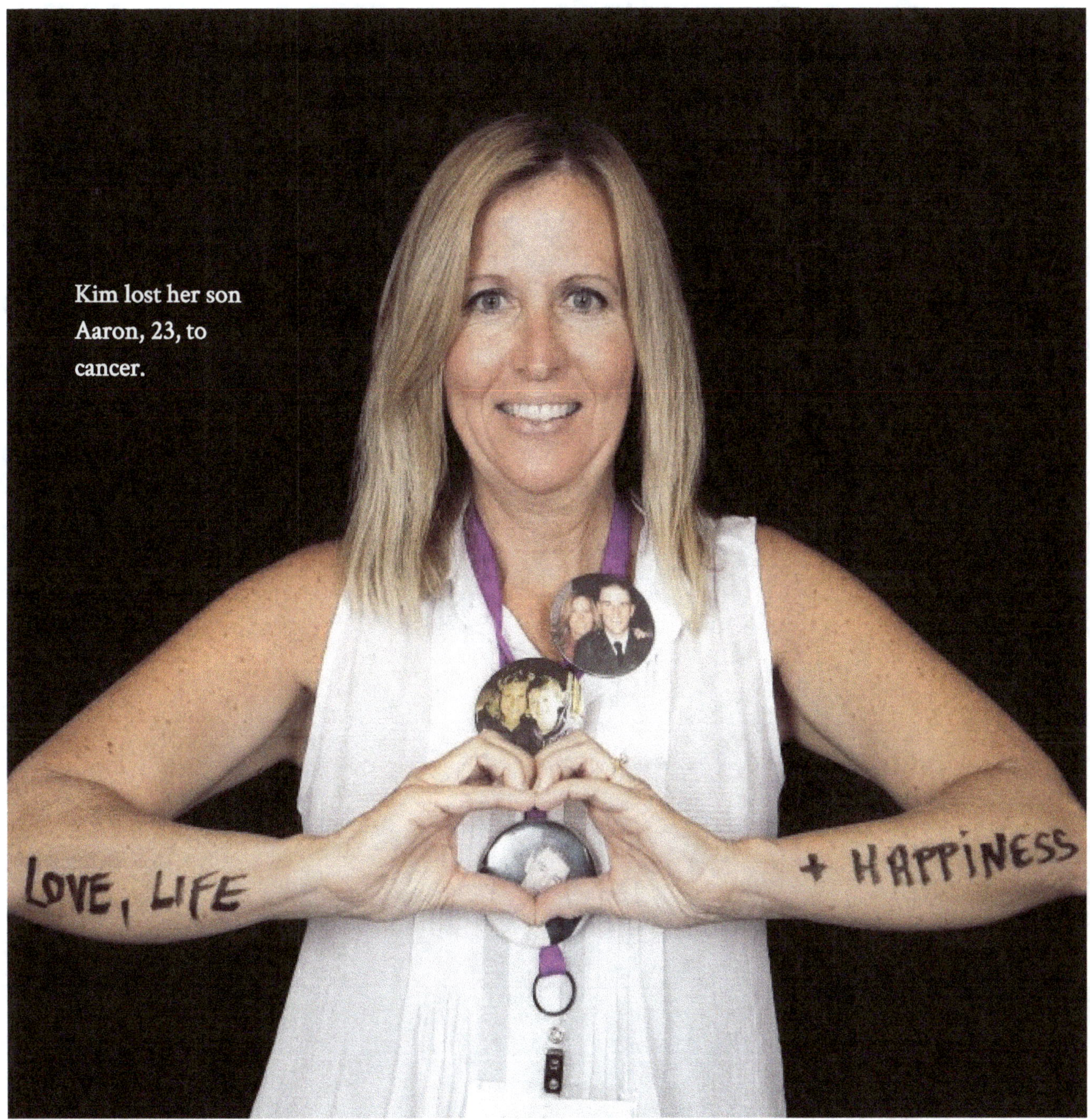

Kim lost her son
Aaron, 23, to
cancer.

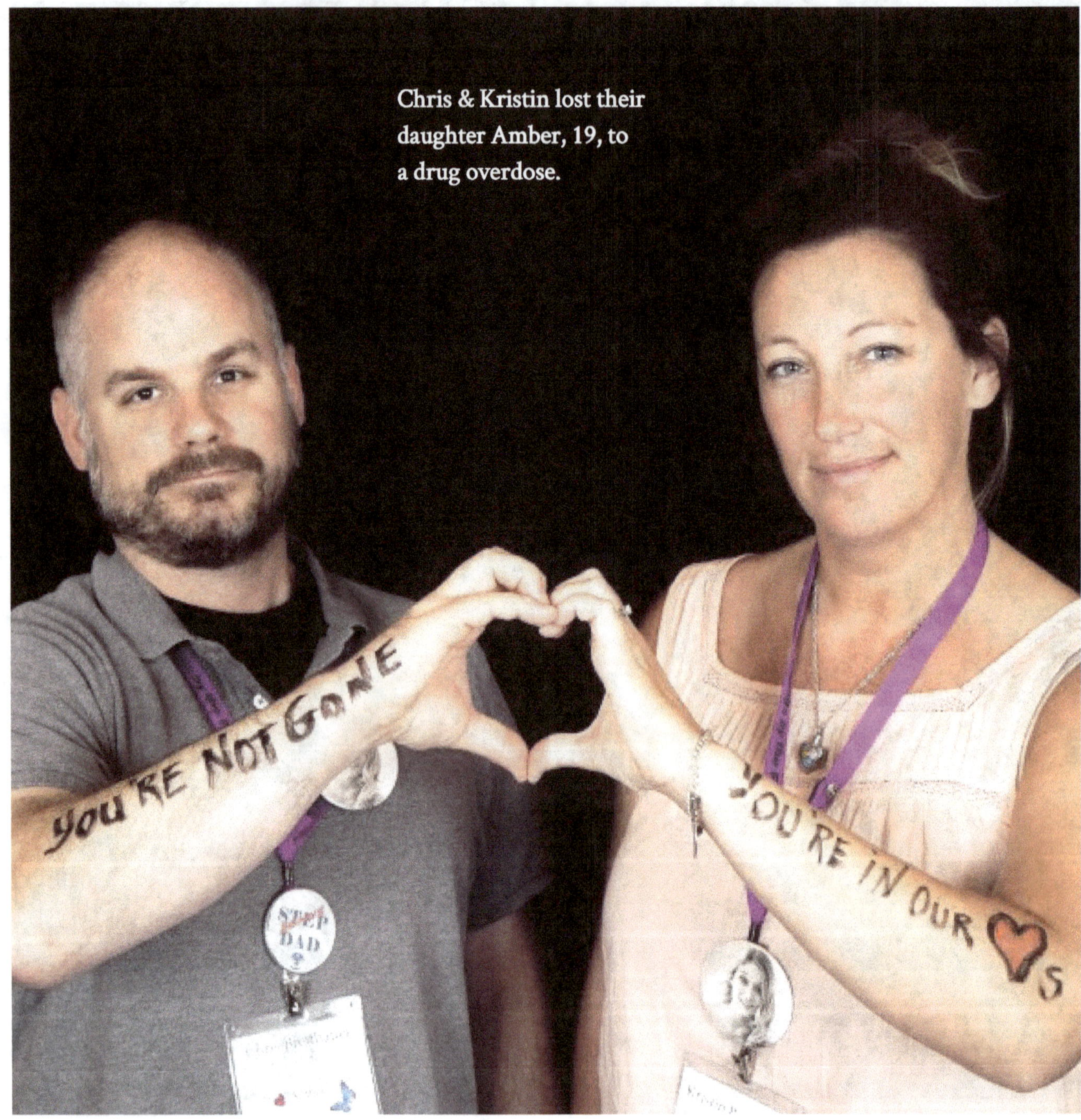

Chris & Kristin lost their daughter Amber, 19, to a drug overdose.

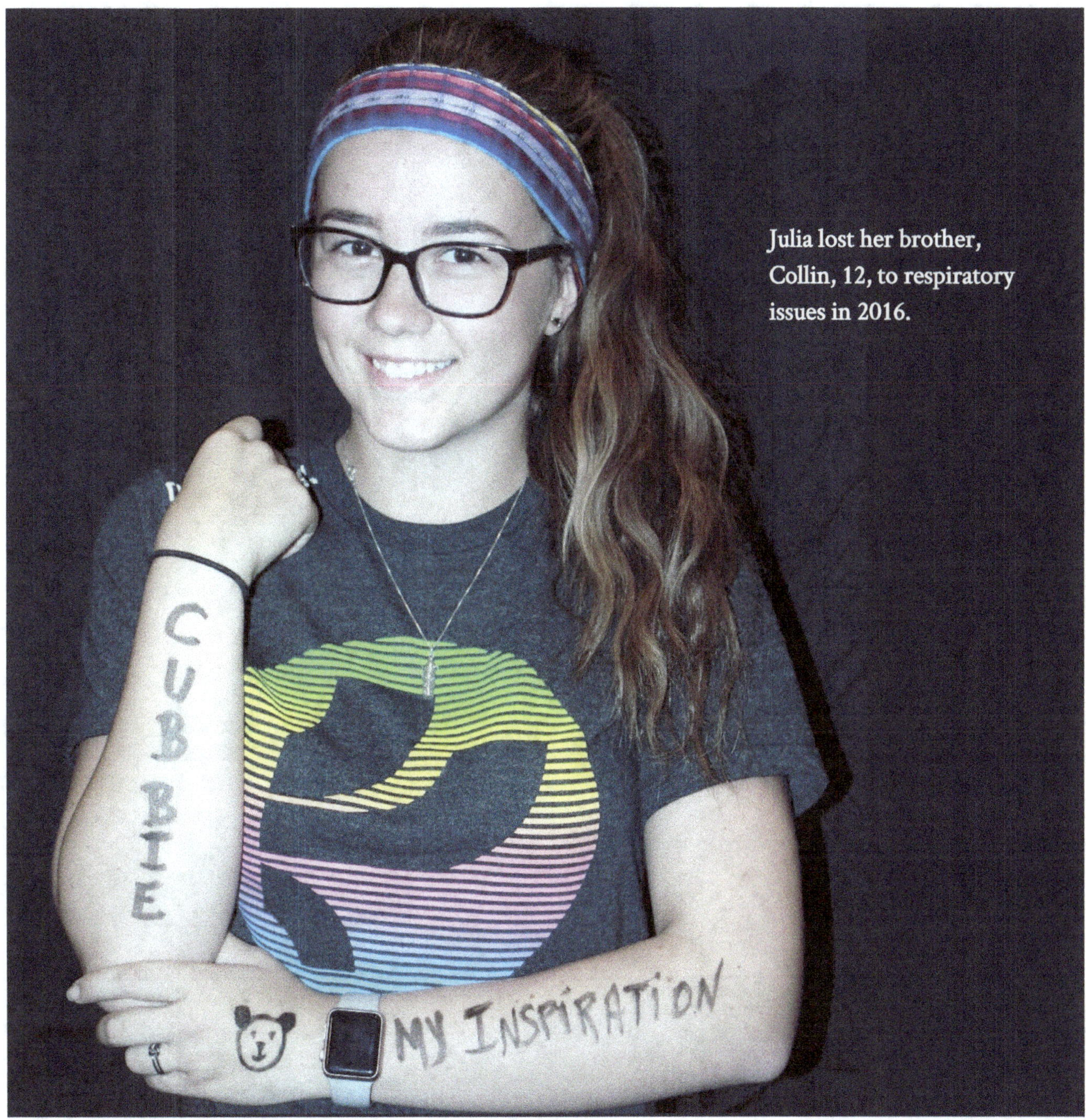

Julia lost her brother, Collin, 12, to respiratory issues in 2016.

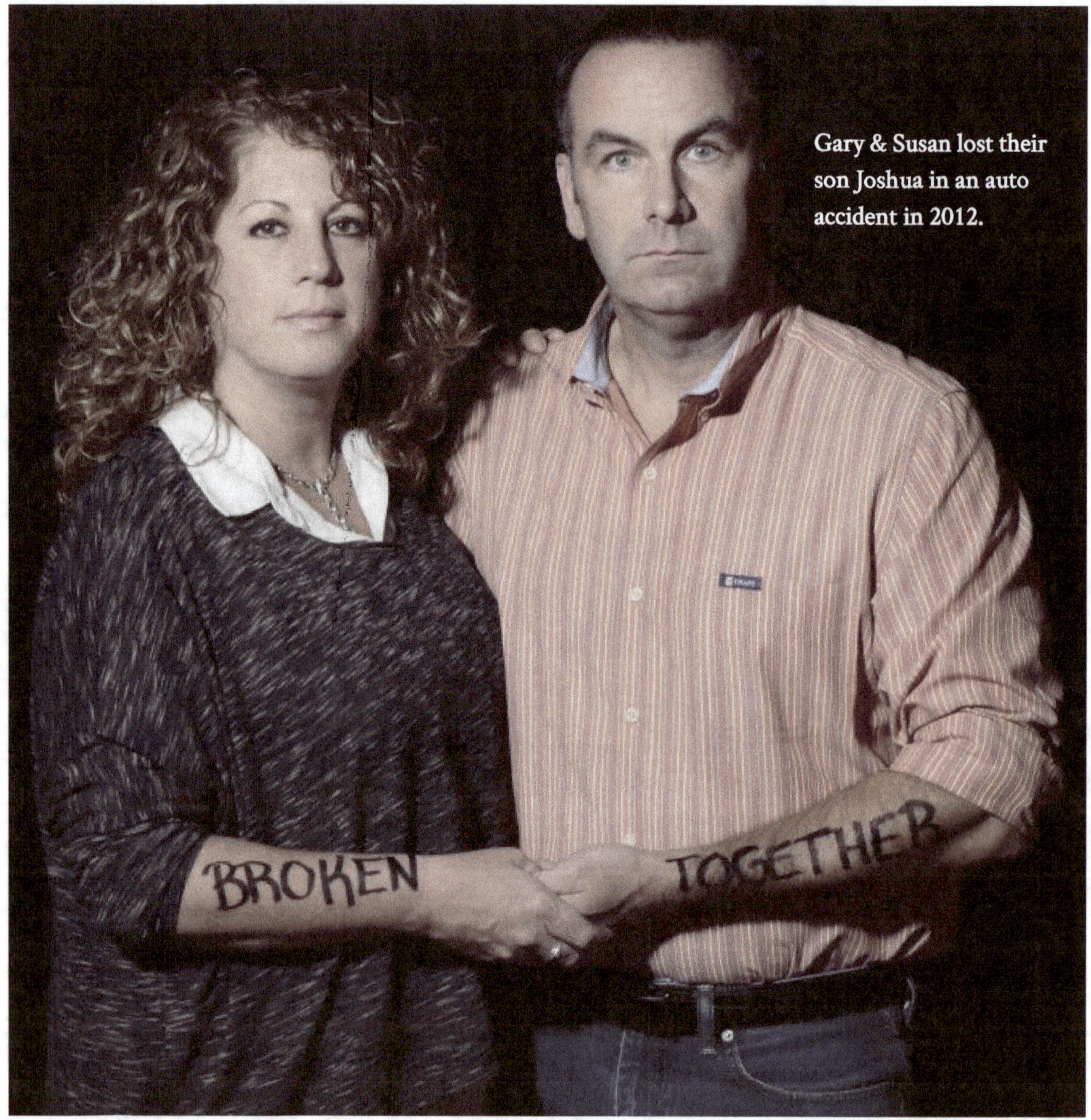

Gary & Susan lost their son Joshua in an auto accident in 2012.

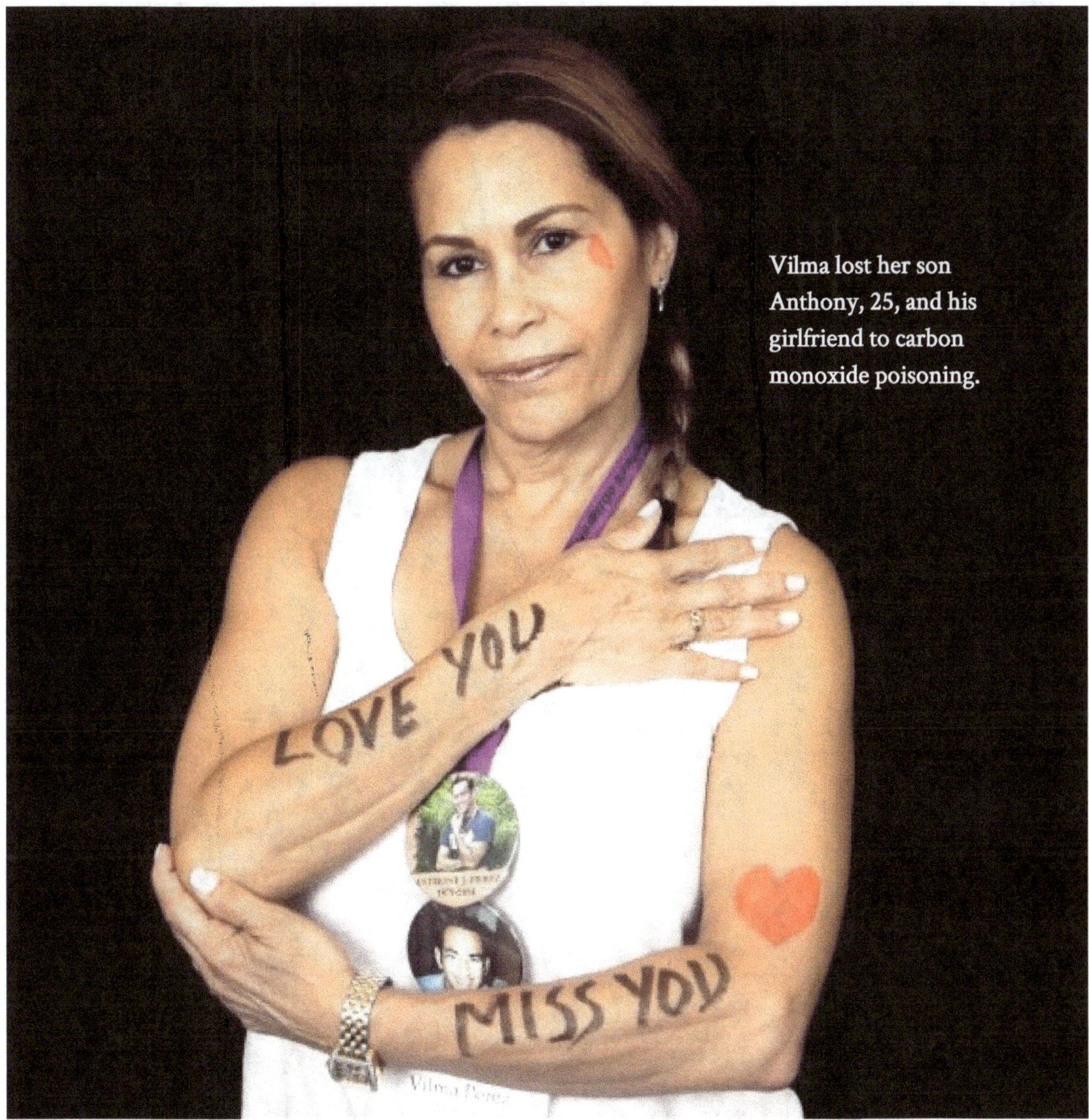

Vilma lost her son Anthony, 25, and his girlfriend to carbon monoxide poisoning.

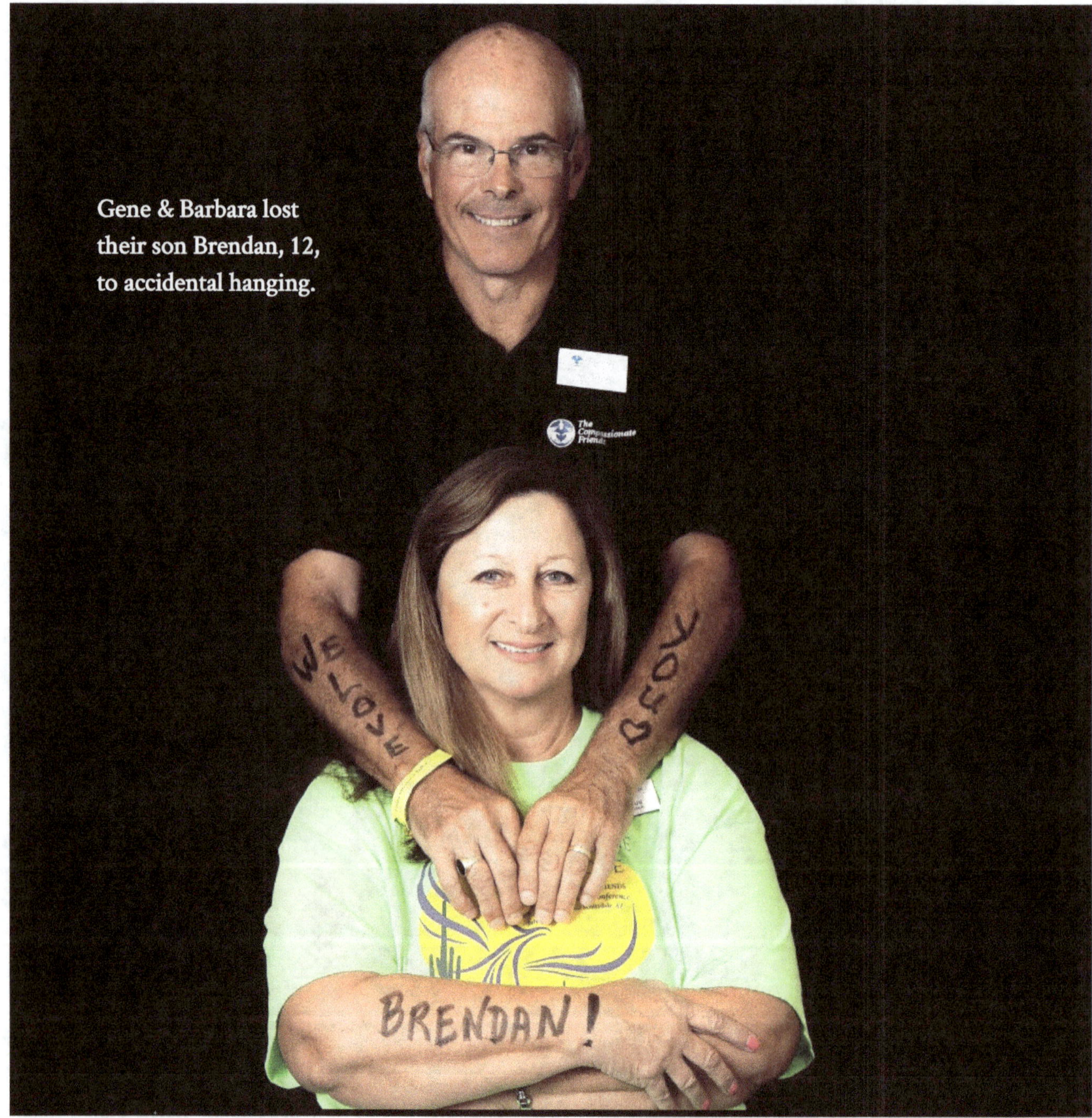
Gene & Barbara lost
their son Brendan, 12,
to accidental hanging.

WE LOVE

JOY ♥

BRENDAN!

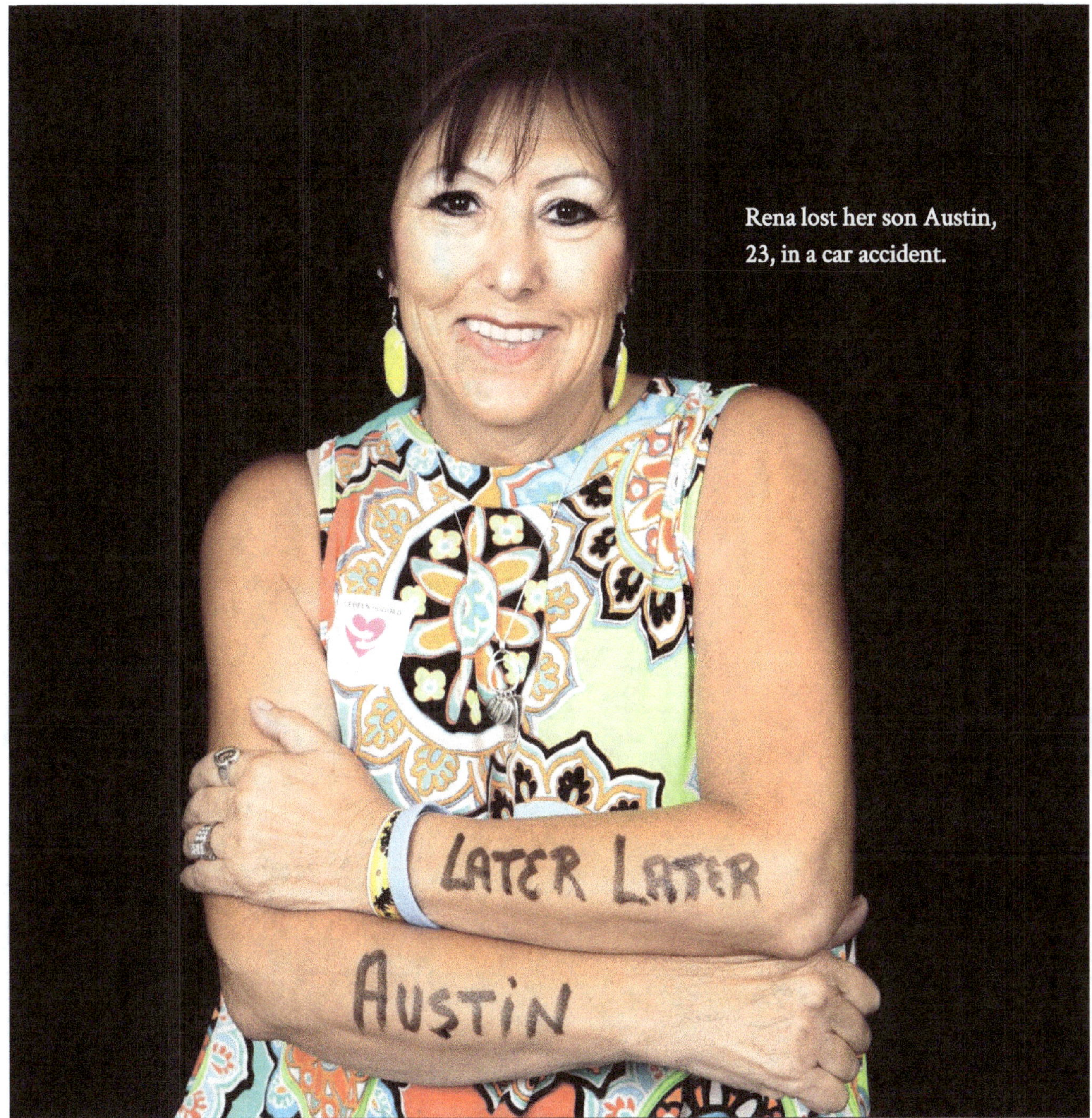

Rena lost her son Austin, 23, in a car accident.

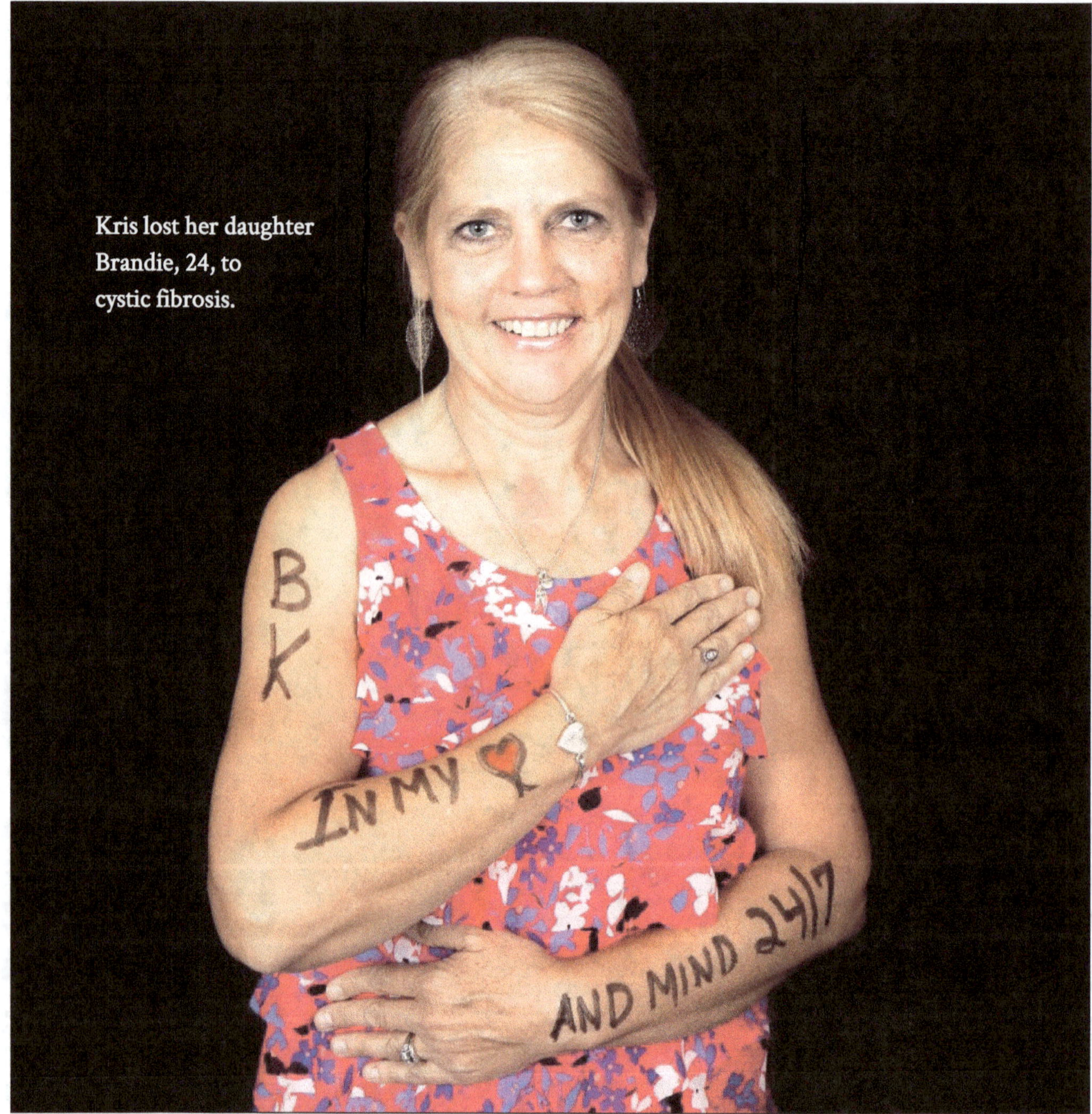

Kris lost her daughter
Brandie, 24, to
cystic fibrosis.

B
K
IN MY ♥
AND MIND 24/7

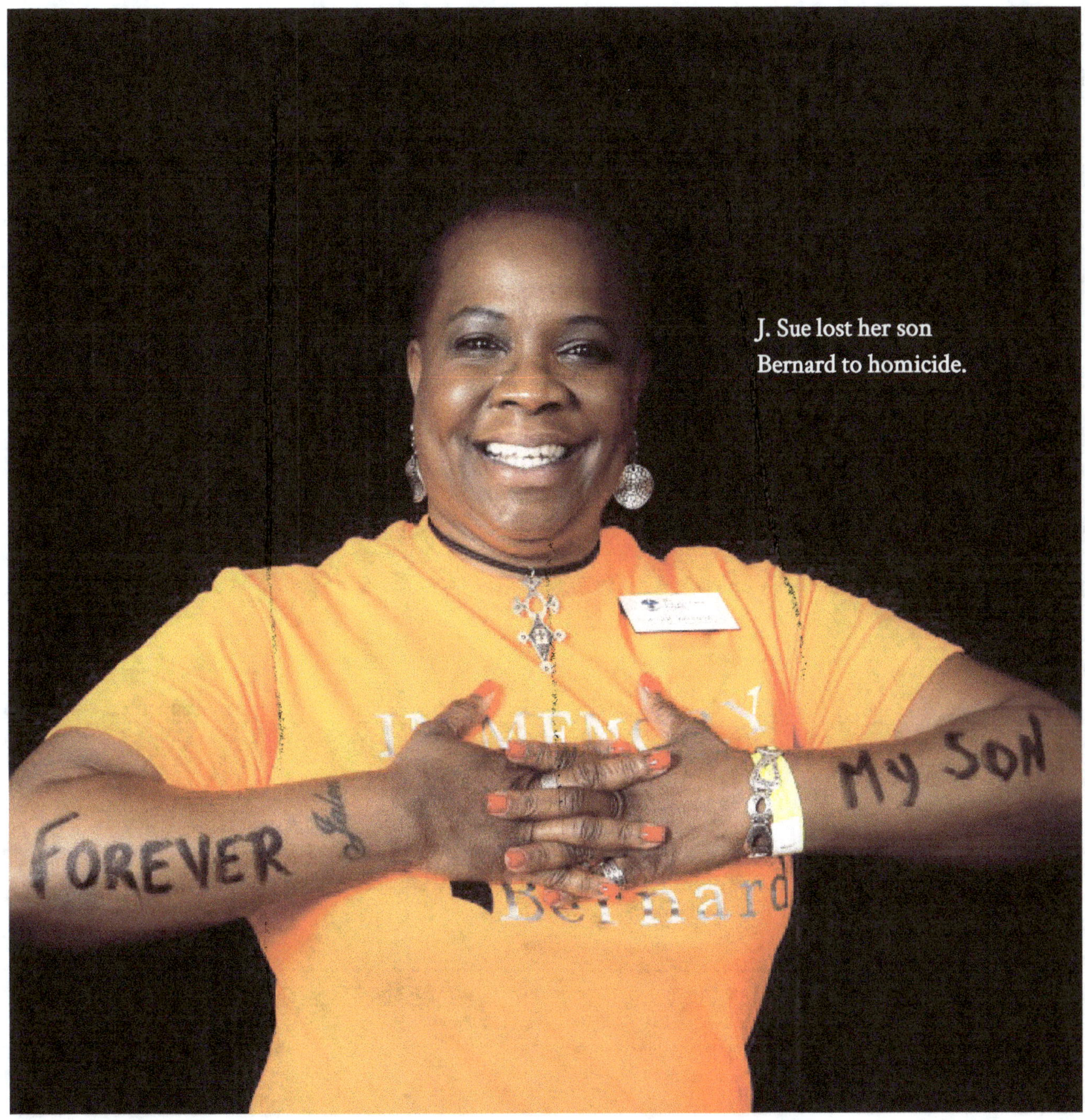

J. Sue lost her son
Bernard to homicide.

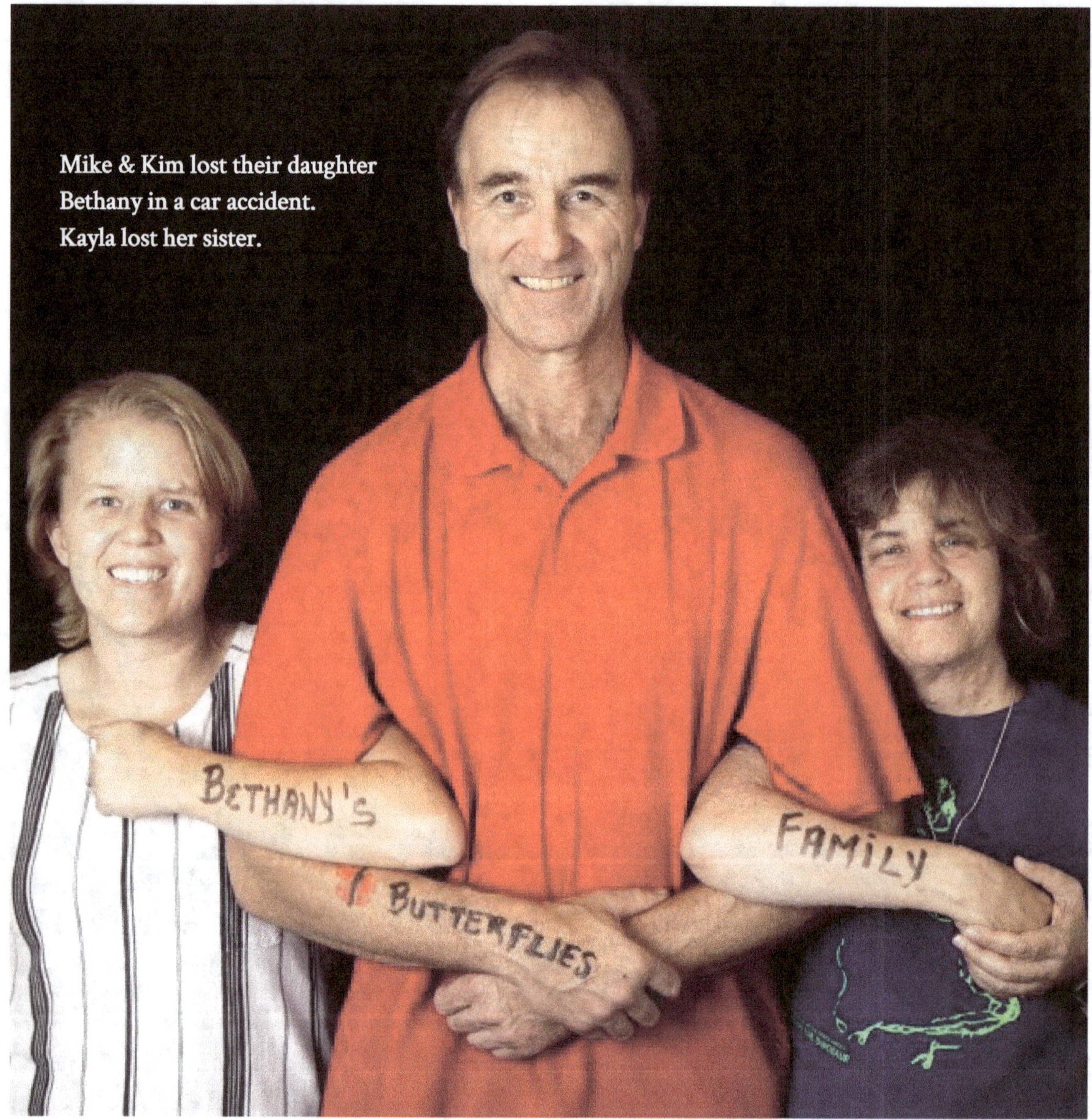
Mike & Kim lost their daughter
Bethany in a car accident.
Kayla lost her sister.
BETHANY'S
BUTTERFLIES
FAMILY

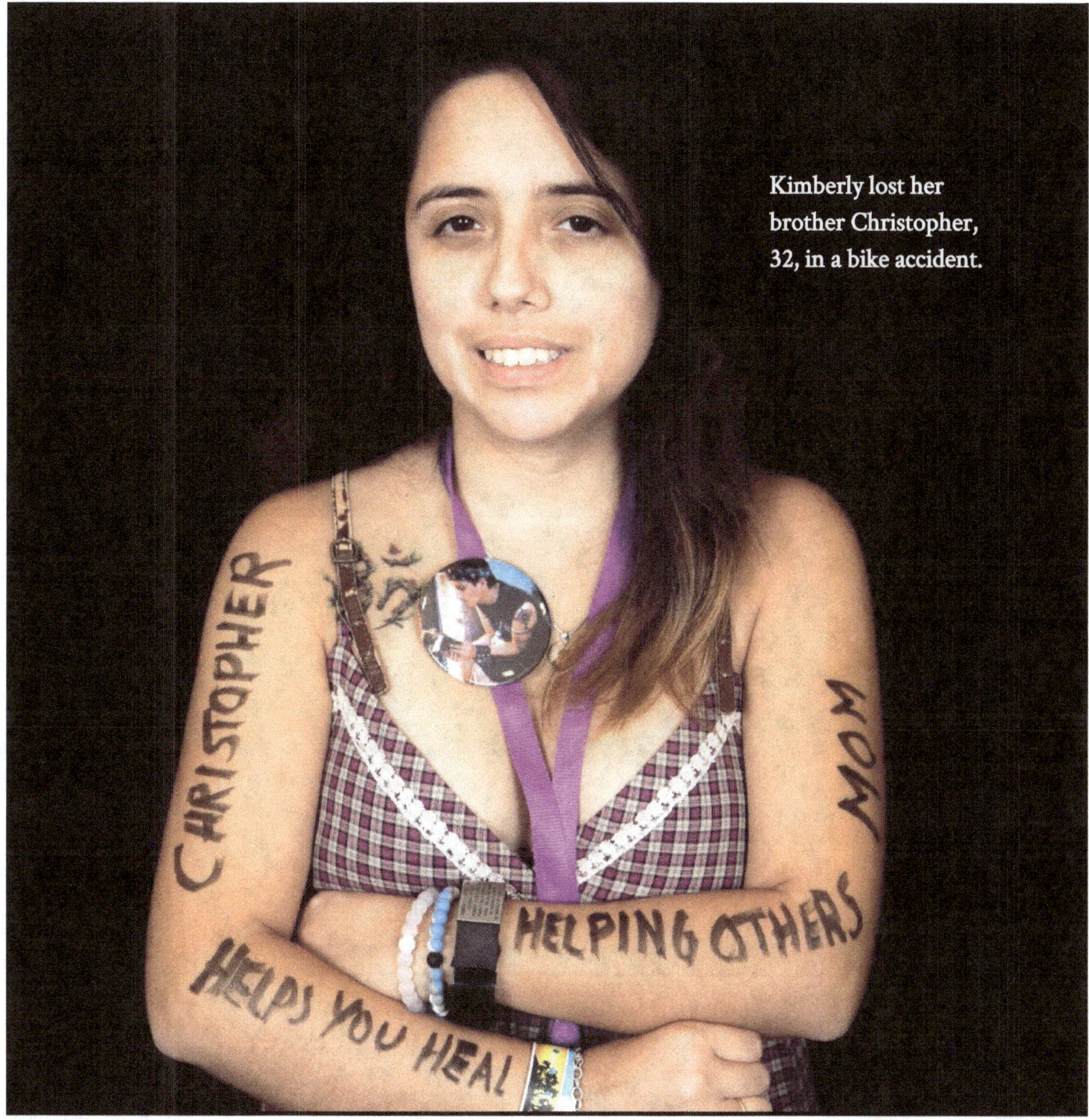

Kimberly lost her brother Christopher, 32, in a bike accident.

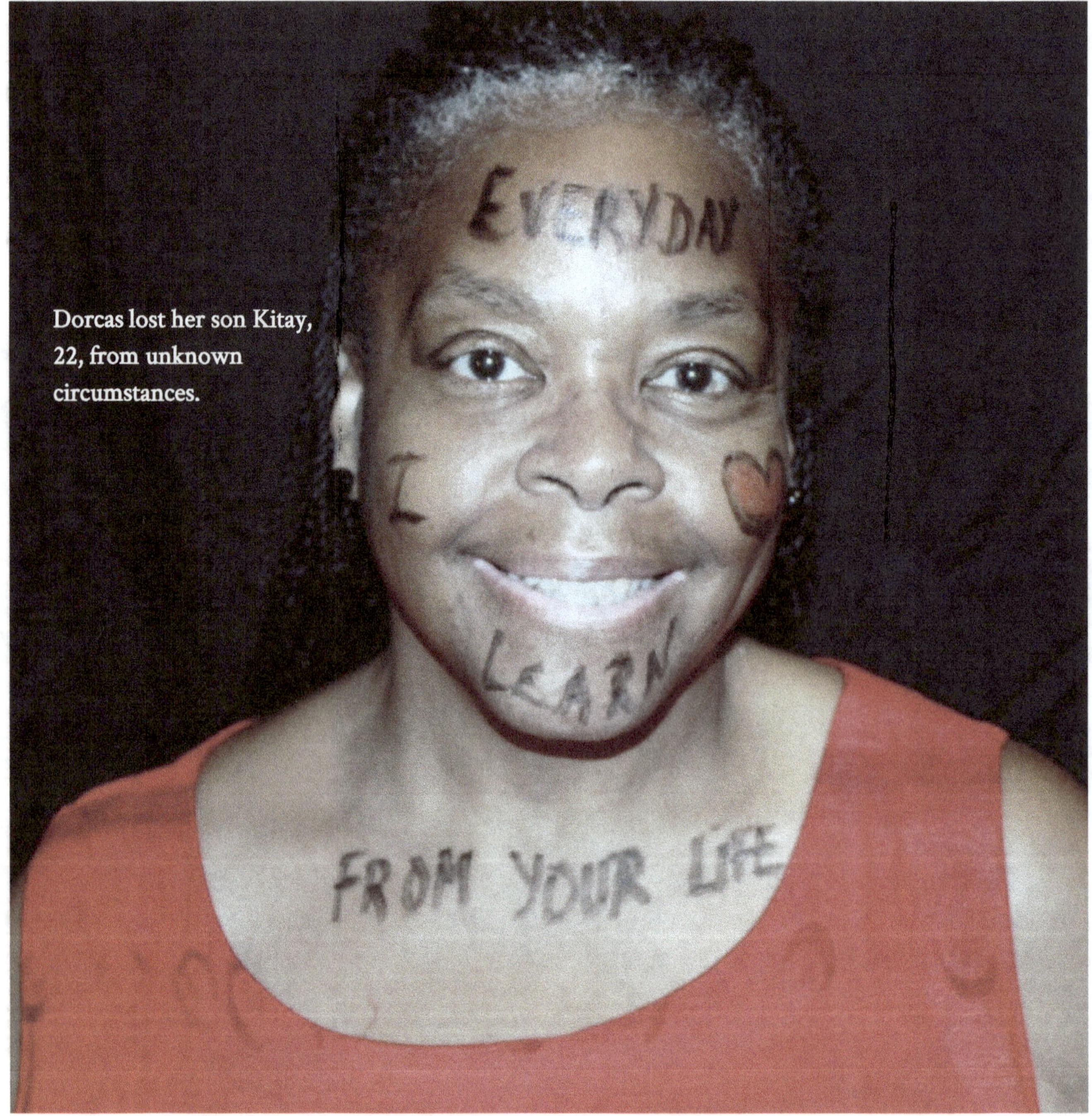

Dorcas lost her son Kitay, 22, from unknown circumstances.

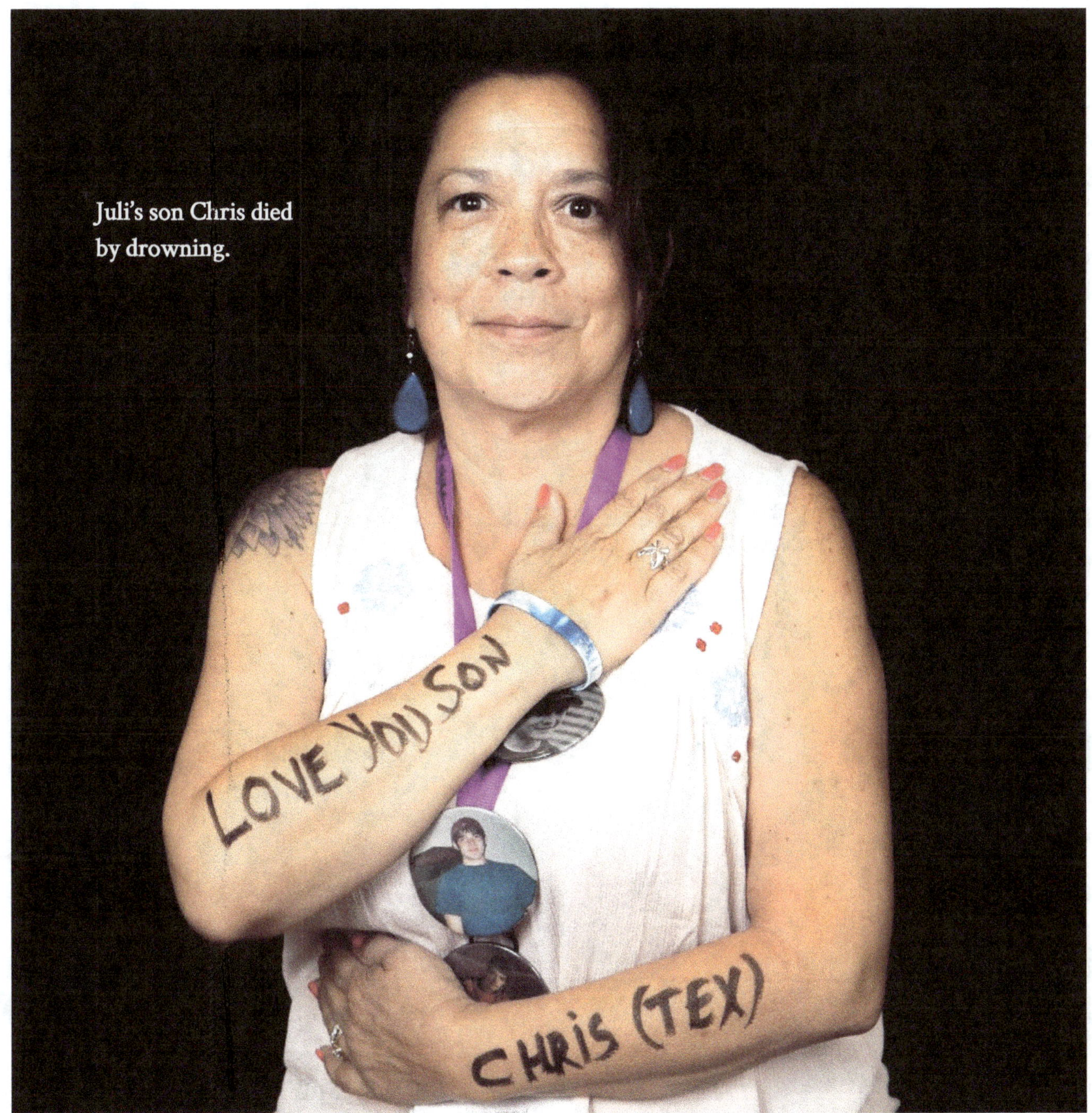

Juli's son Chris died by drowning.

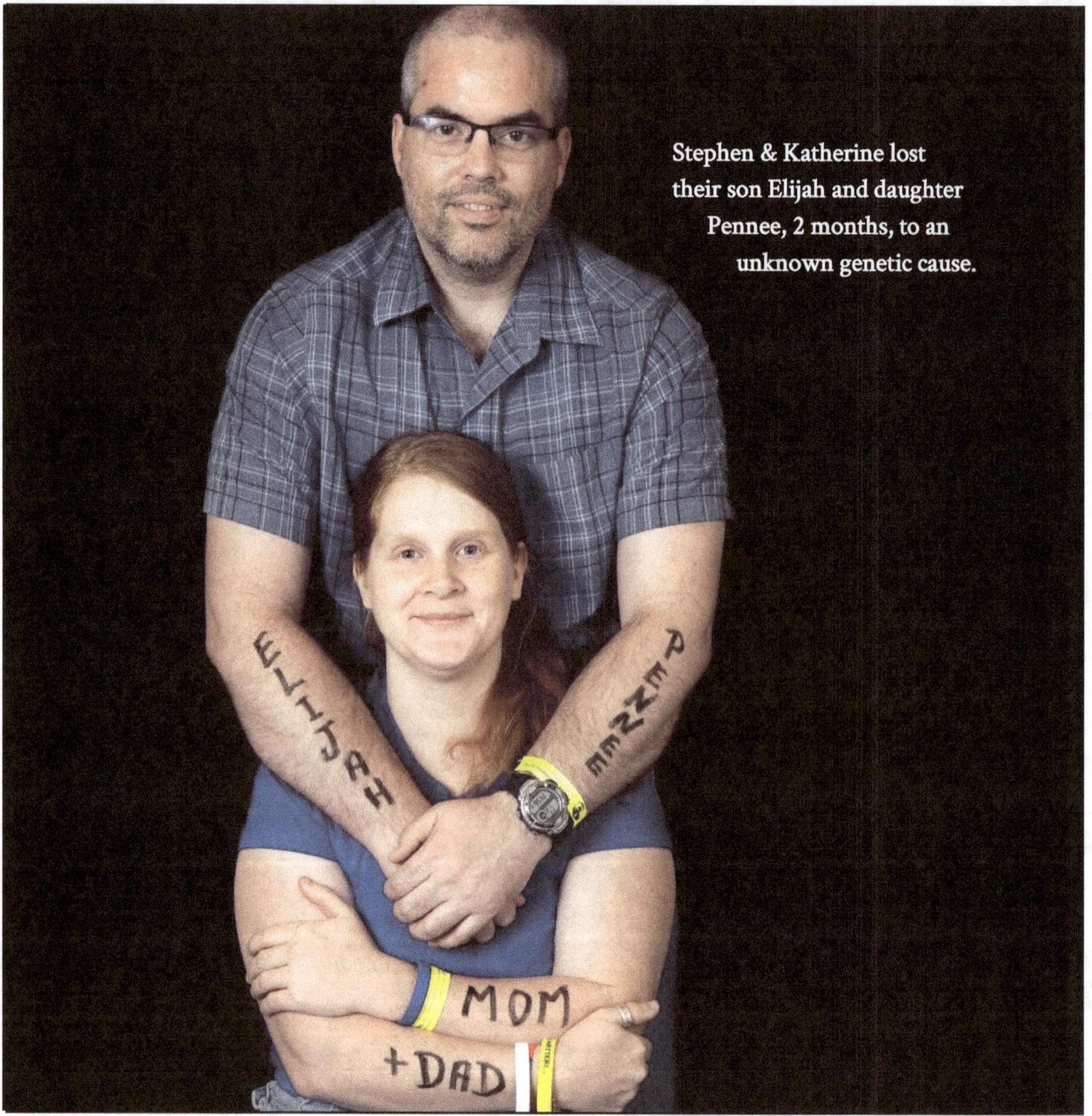

Stephen & Katherine lost their son Elijah and daughter Pennee, 2 months, to an unknown genetic cause.

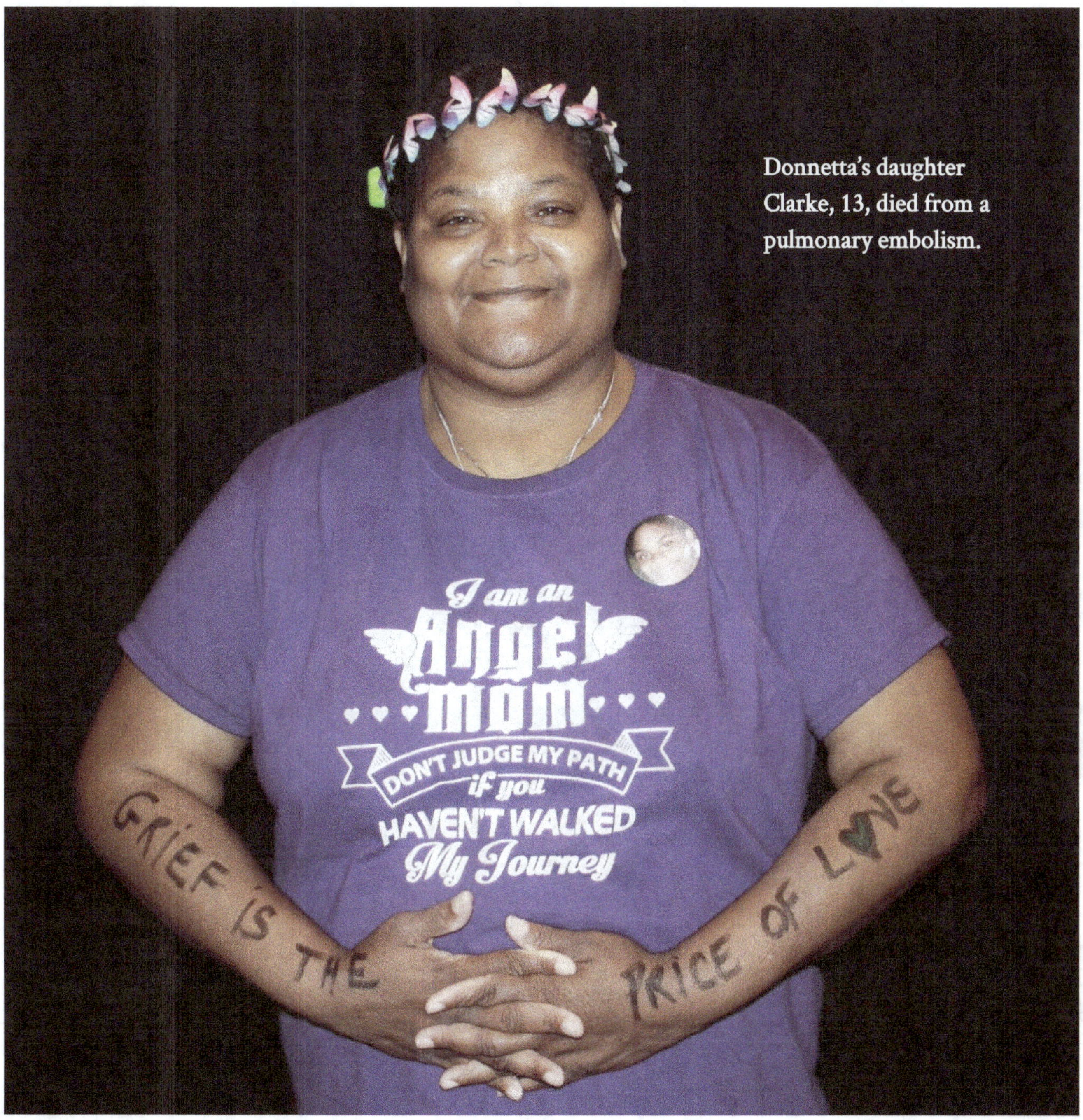

Donnetta's daughter
Clarke, 13, died from a
pulmonary embolism.

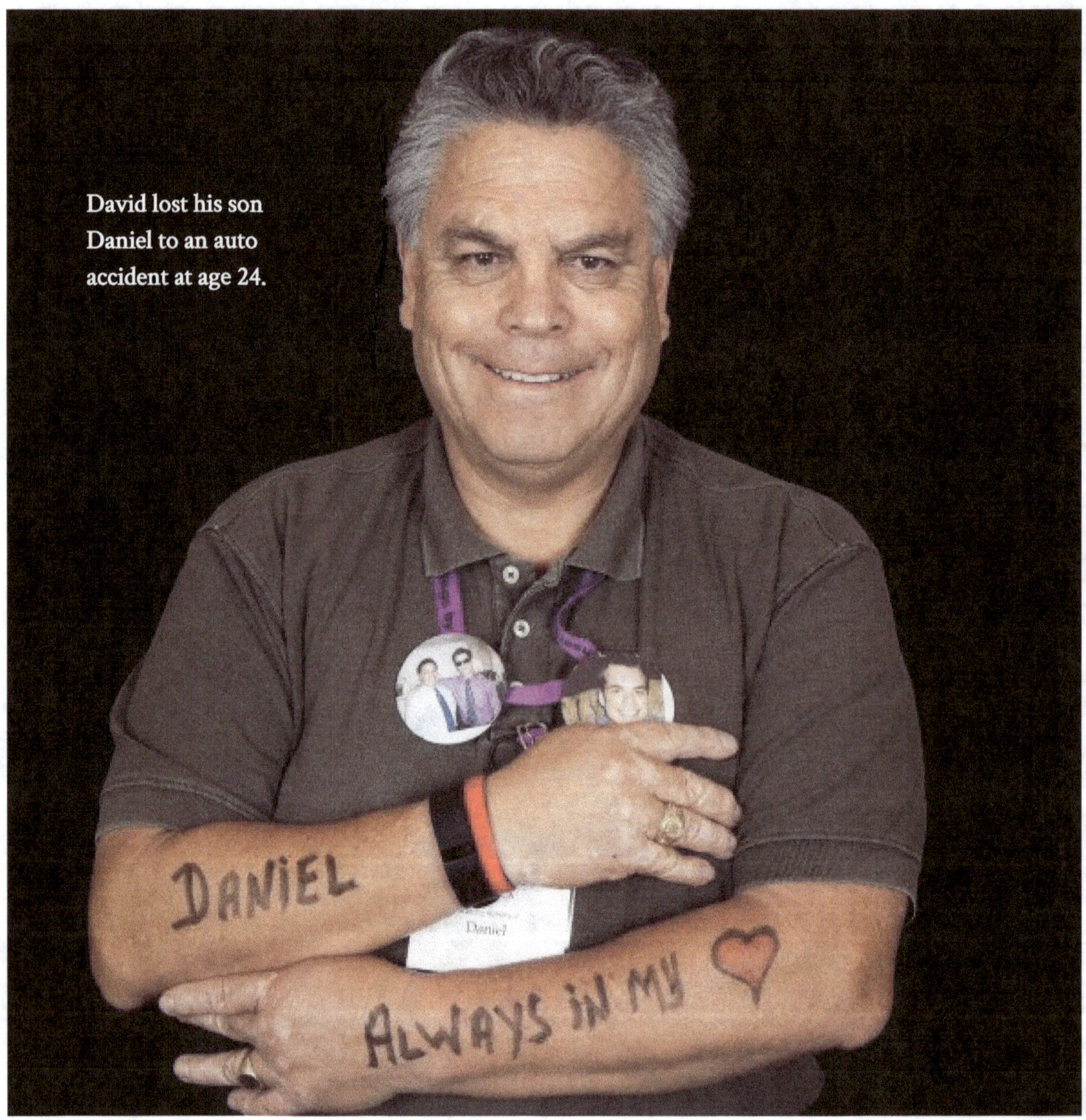

David lost his son
Daniel to an auto
accident at age 24.

DANIEL

ALWAYS IN MY ♡

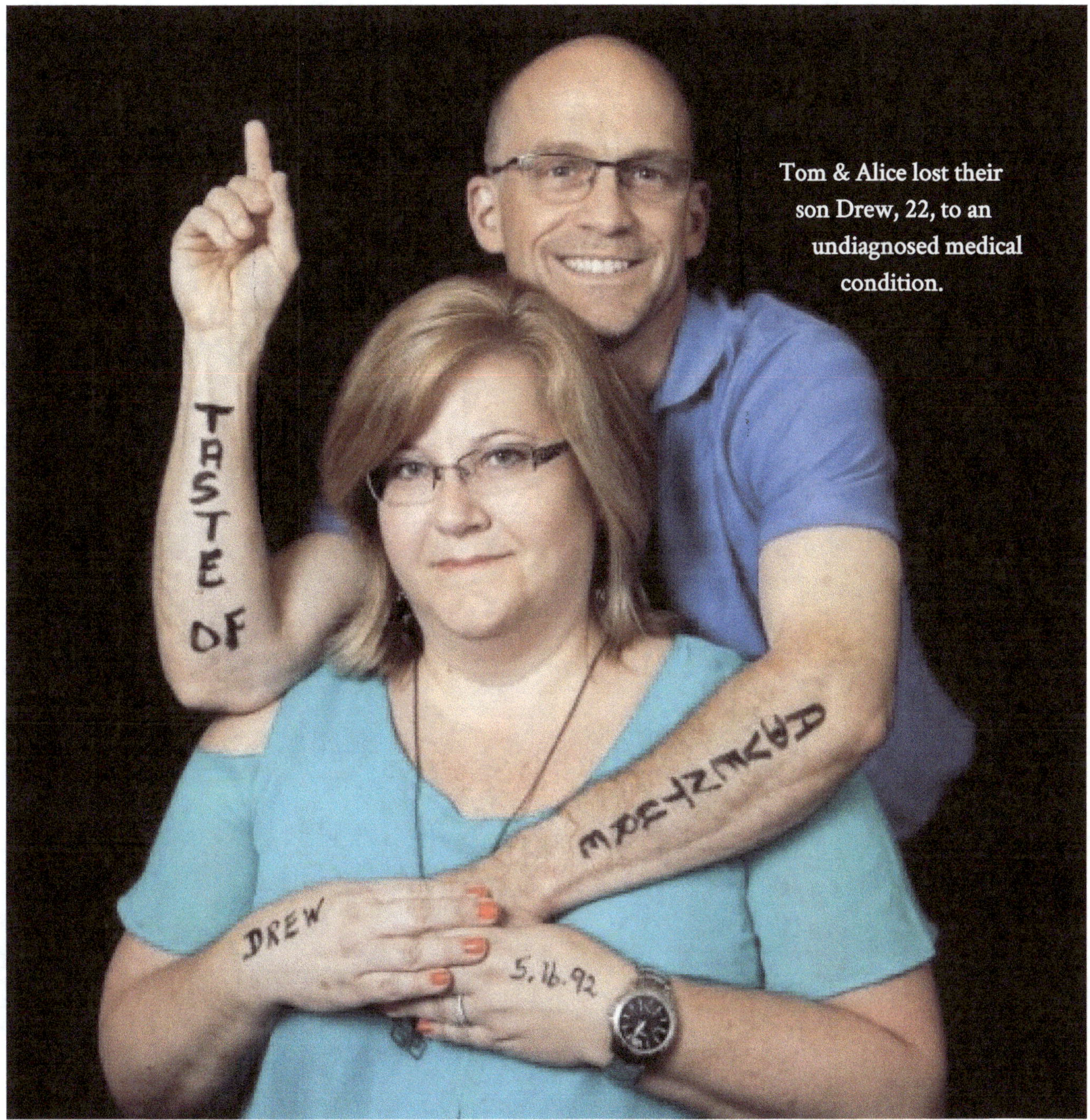

Tom & Alice lost their son Drew, 22, to an undiagnosed medical condition.

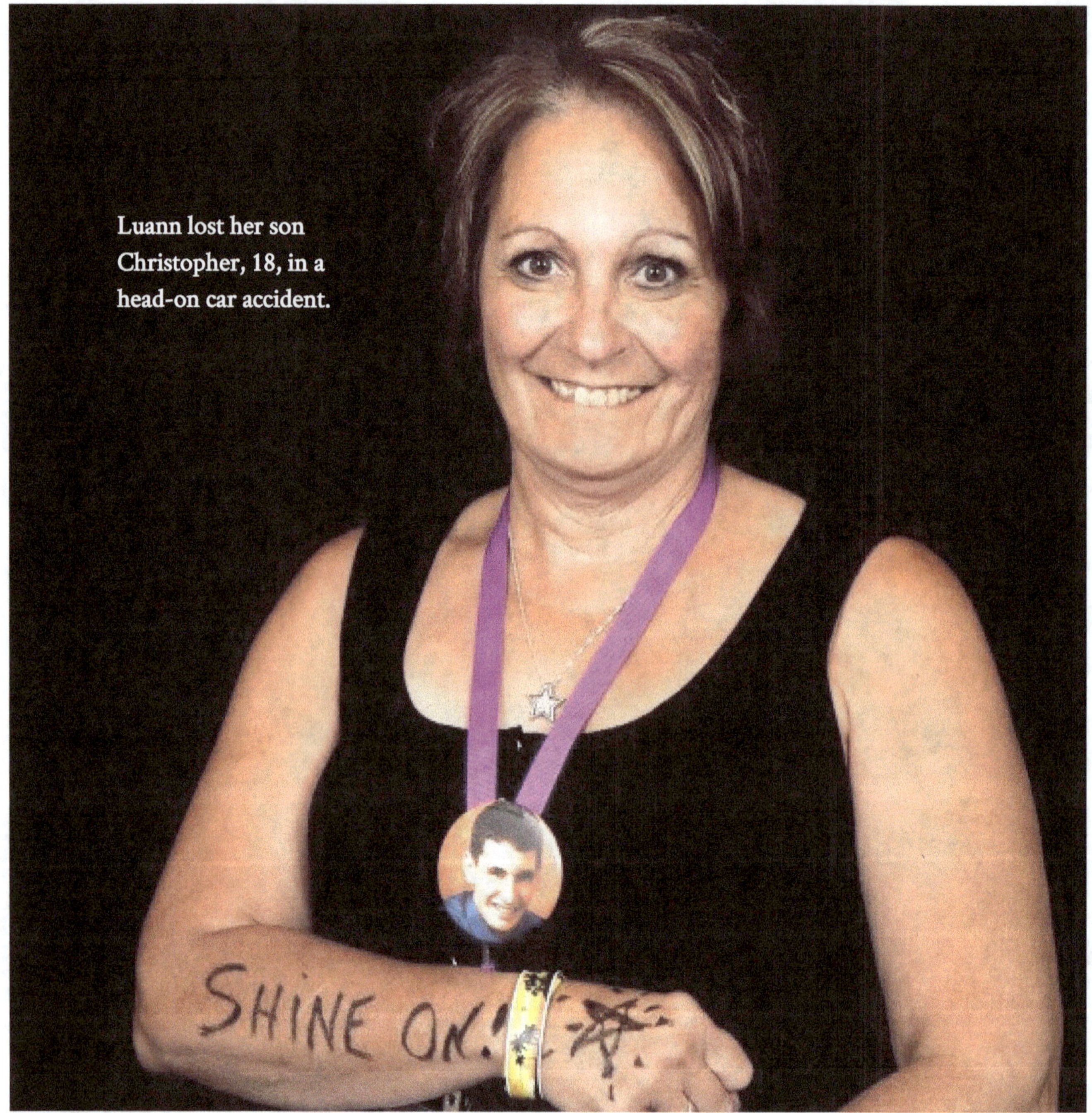

Luann lost her son
Christopher, 18, in a
head-on car accident.

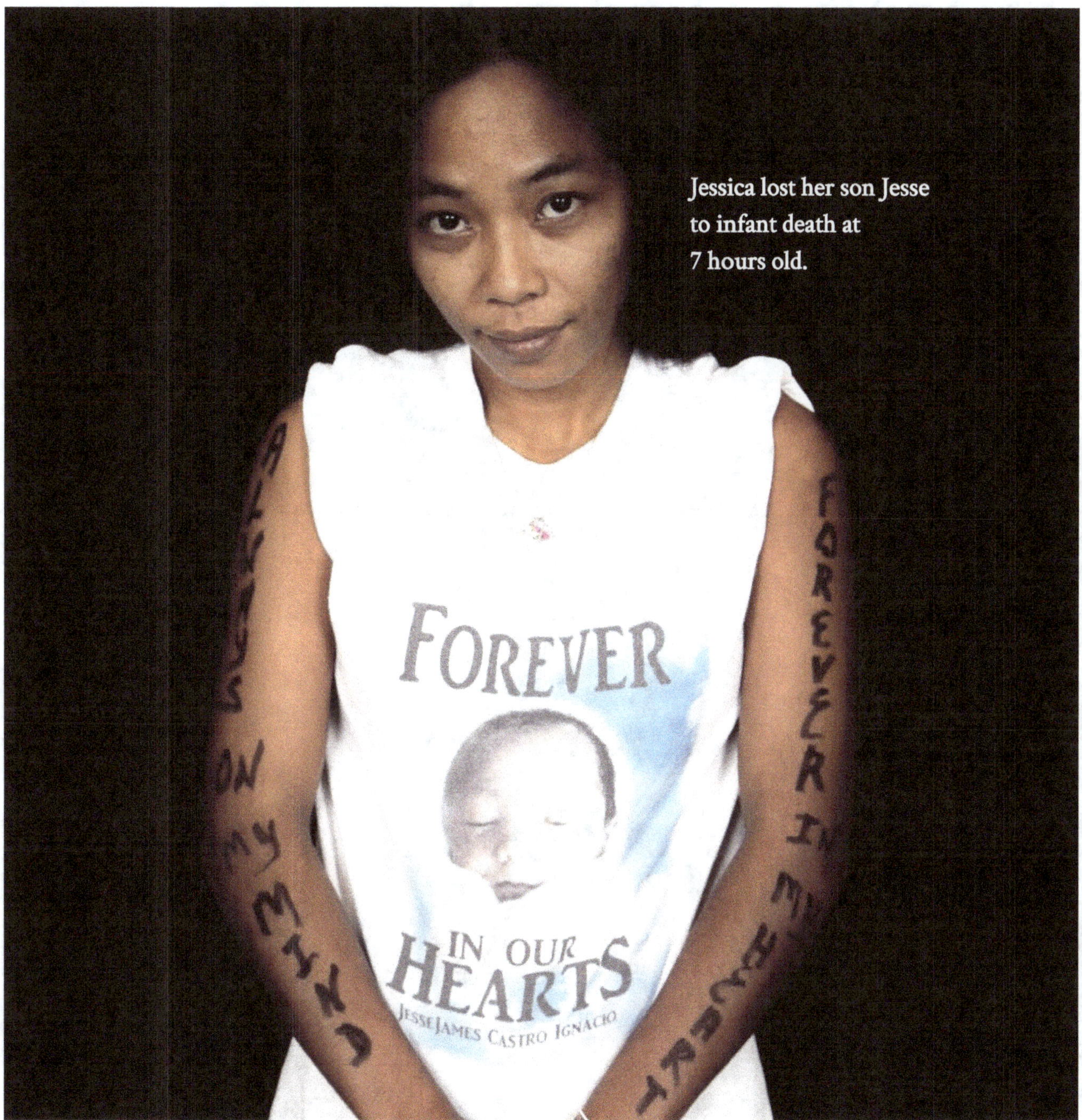

Jessica lost her son Jesse to infant death at 7 hours old.

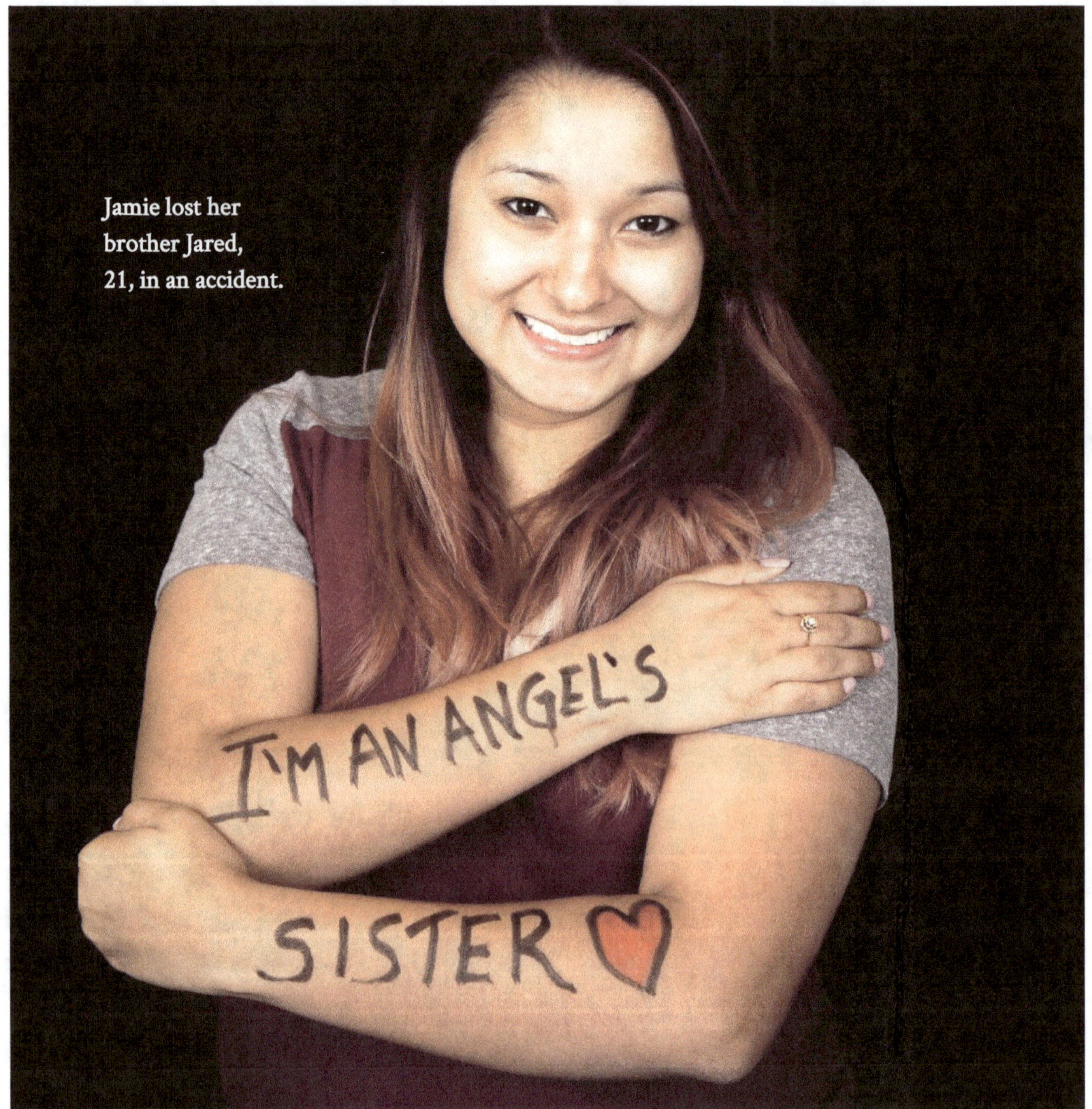
Jamie lost her
brother Jared,
21, in an accident.
I'M AN ANGEL'S
SISTER

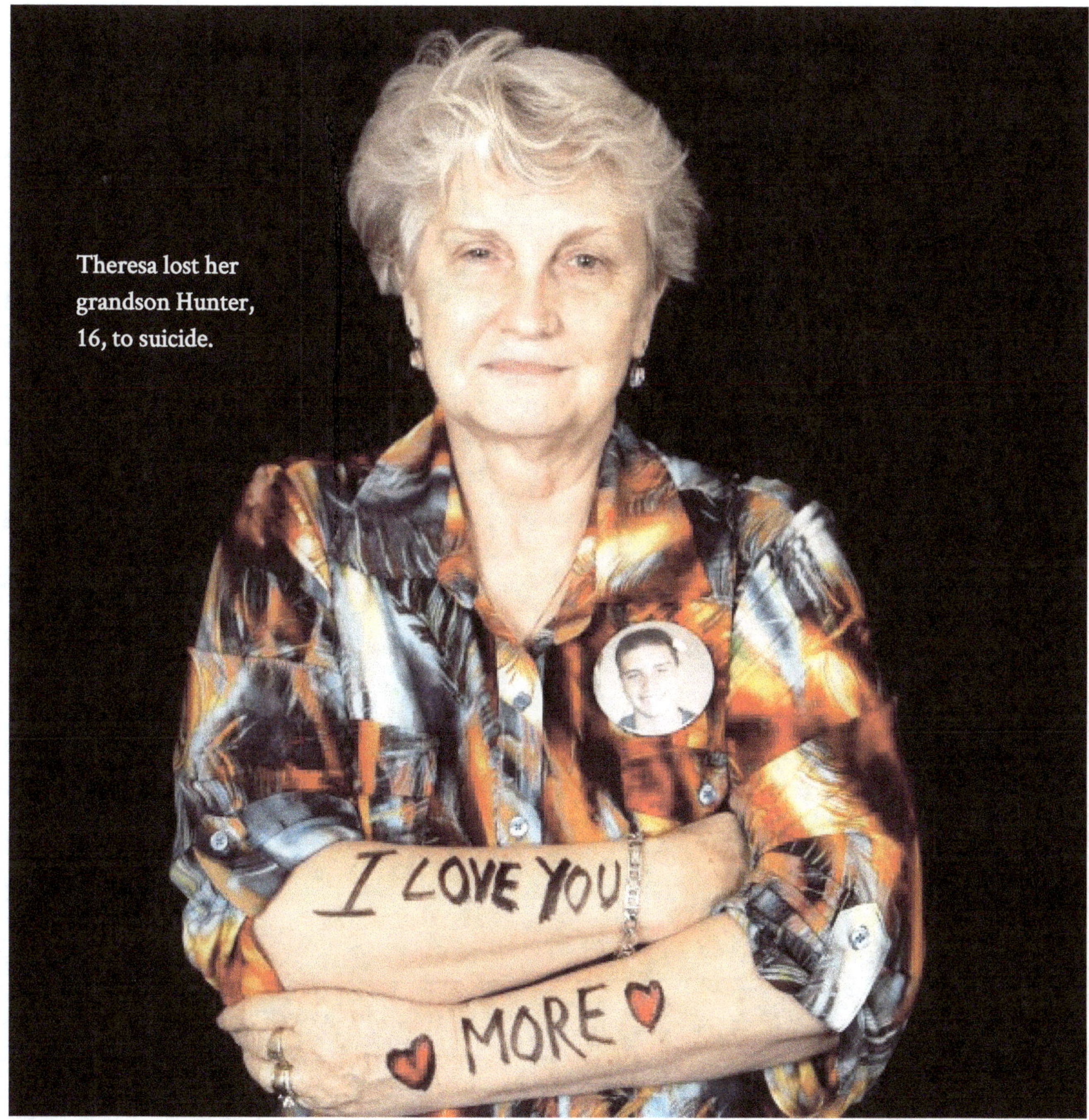

Theresa lost her
grandson Hunter,
16, to suicide.

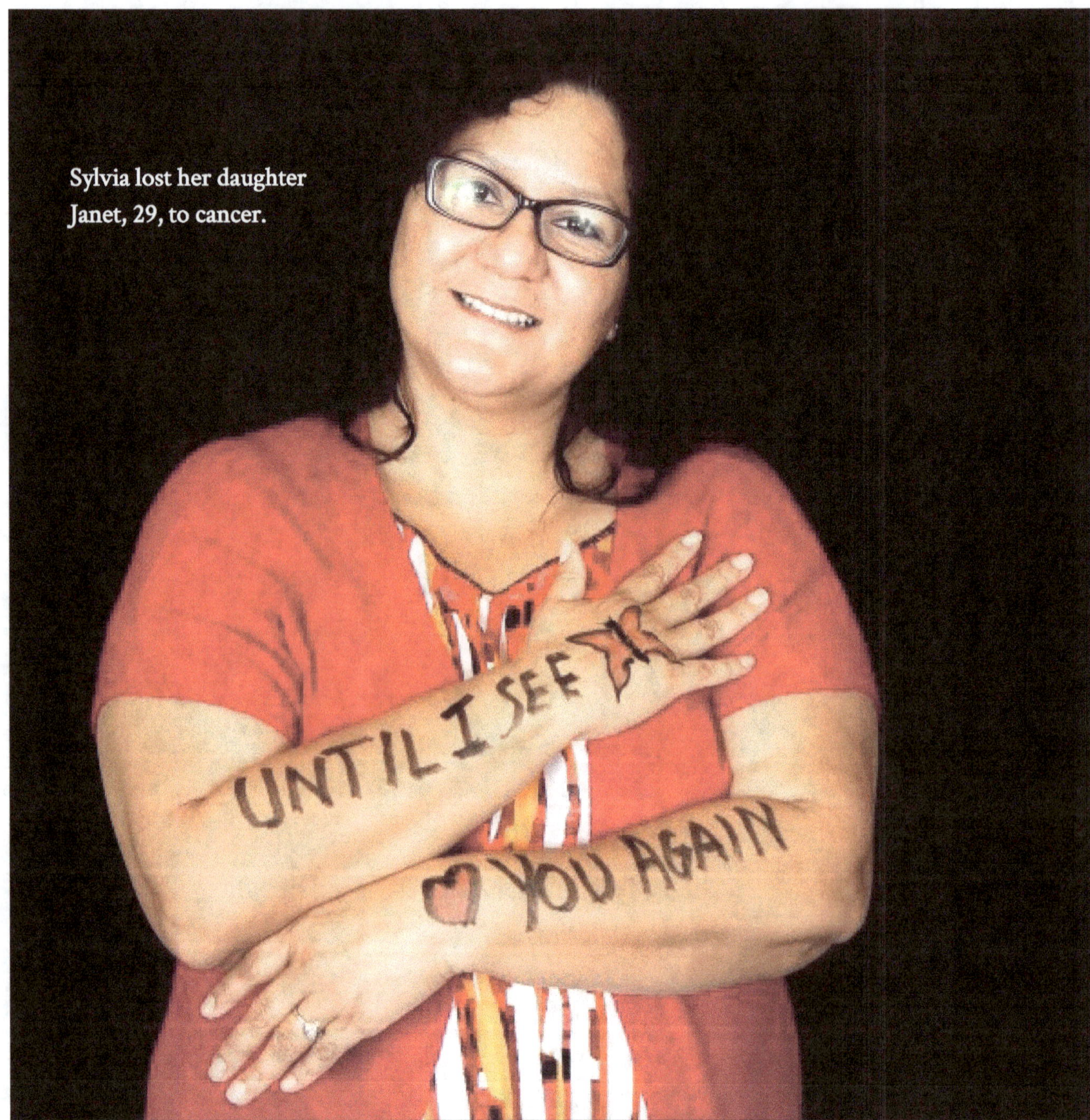

Sylvia lost her daughter Janet, 29, to cancer.

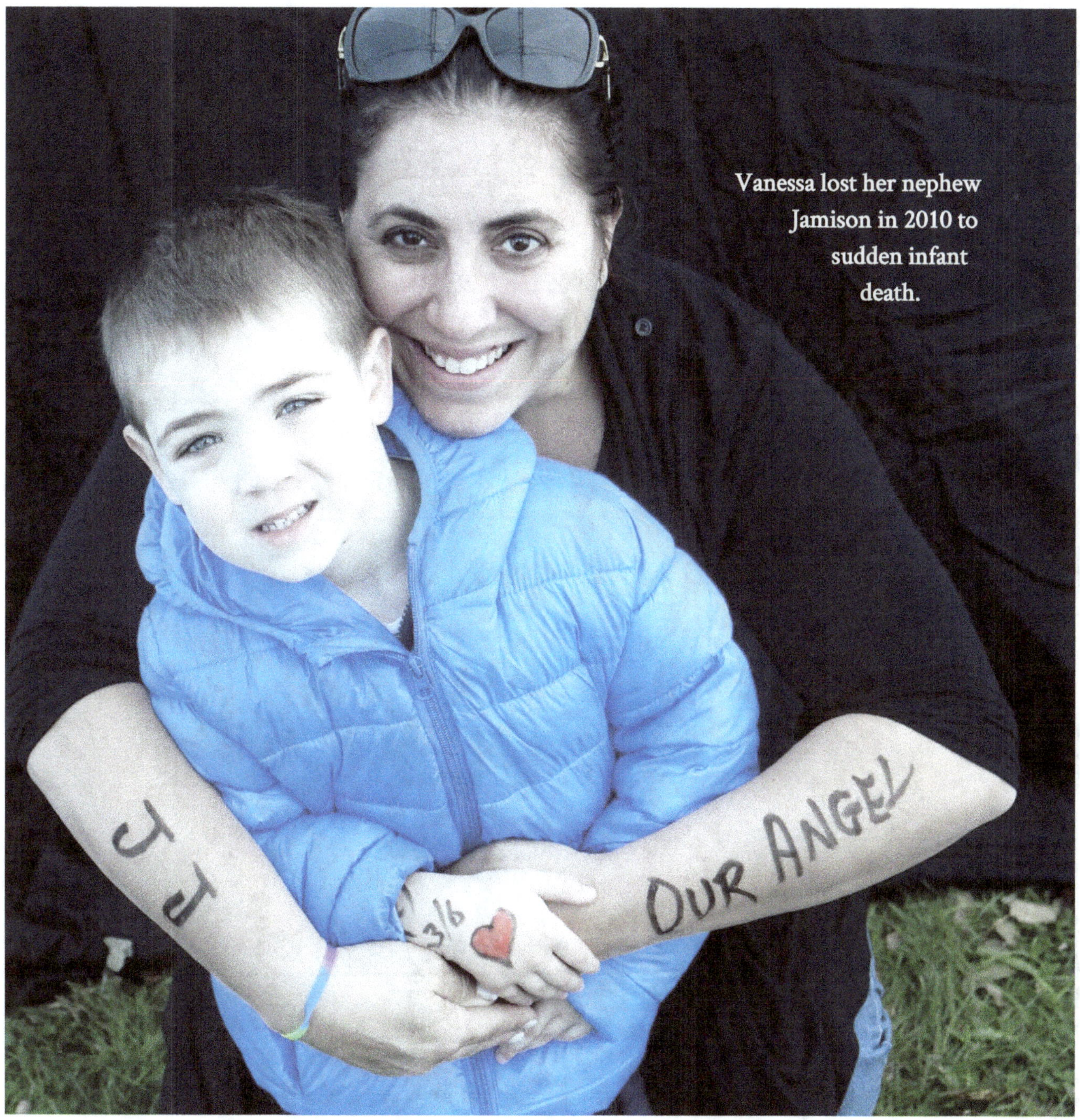

Vanessa lost her nephew Jamison in 2010 to sudden infant death.

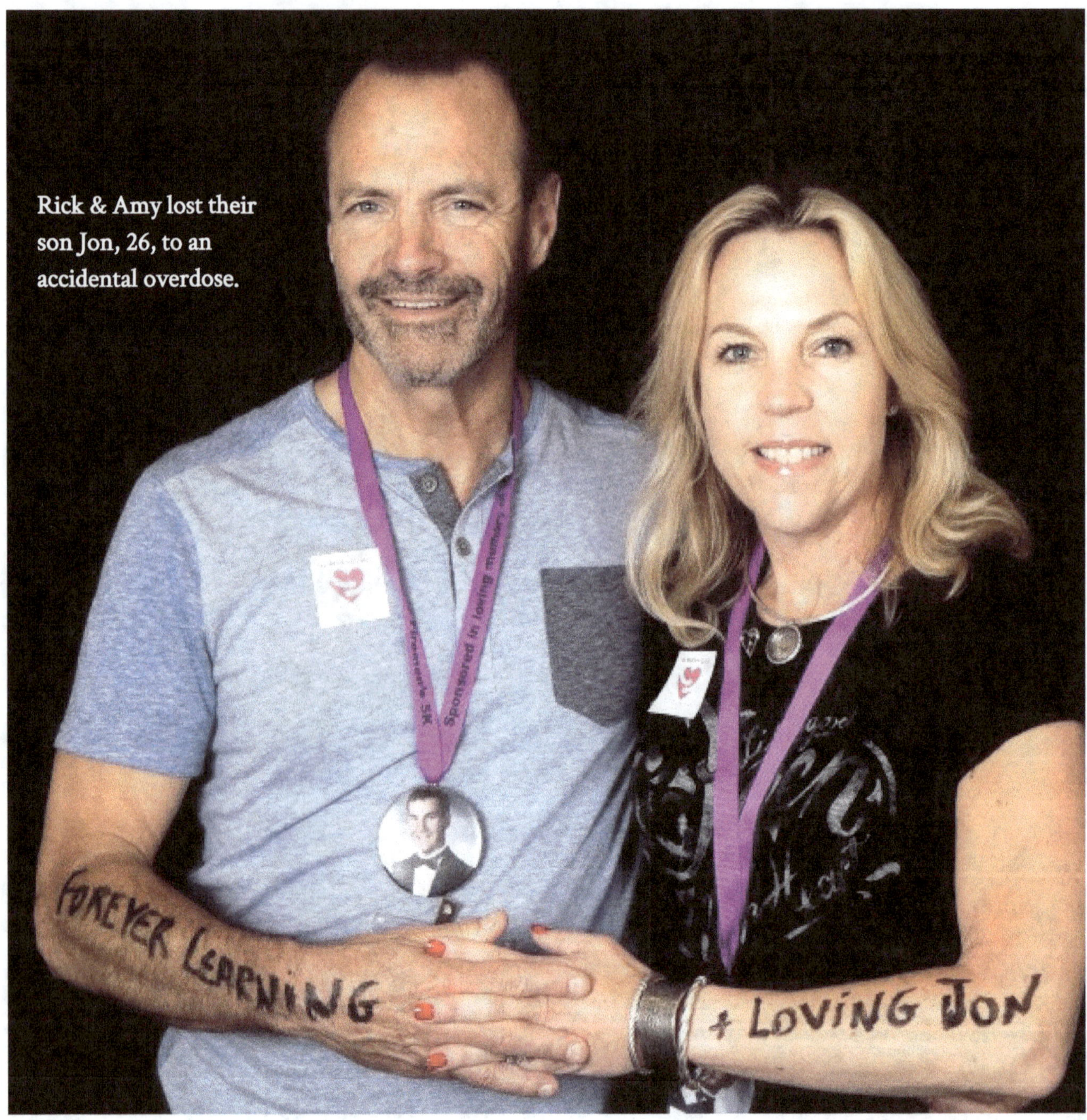

Rick & Amy lost their
son Jon, 26, to an
accidental overdose.
FOREVER LEARNING
& LOVING JON

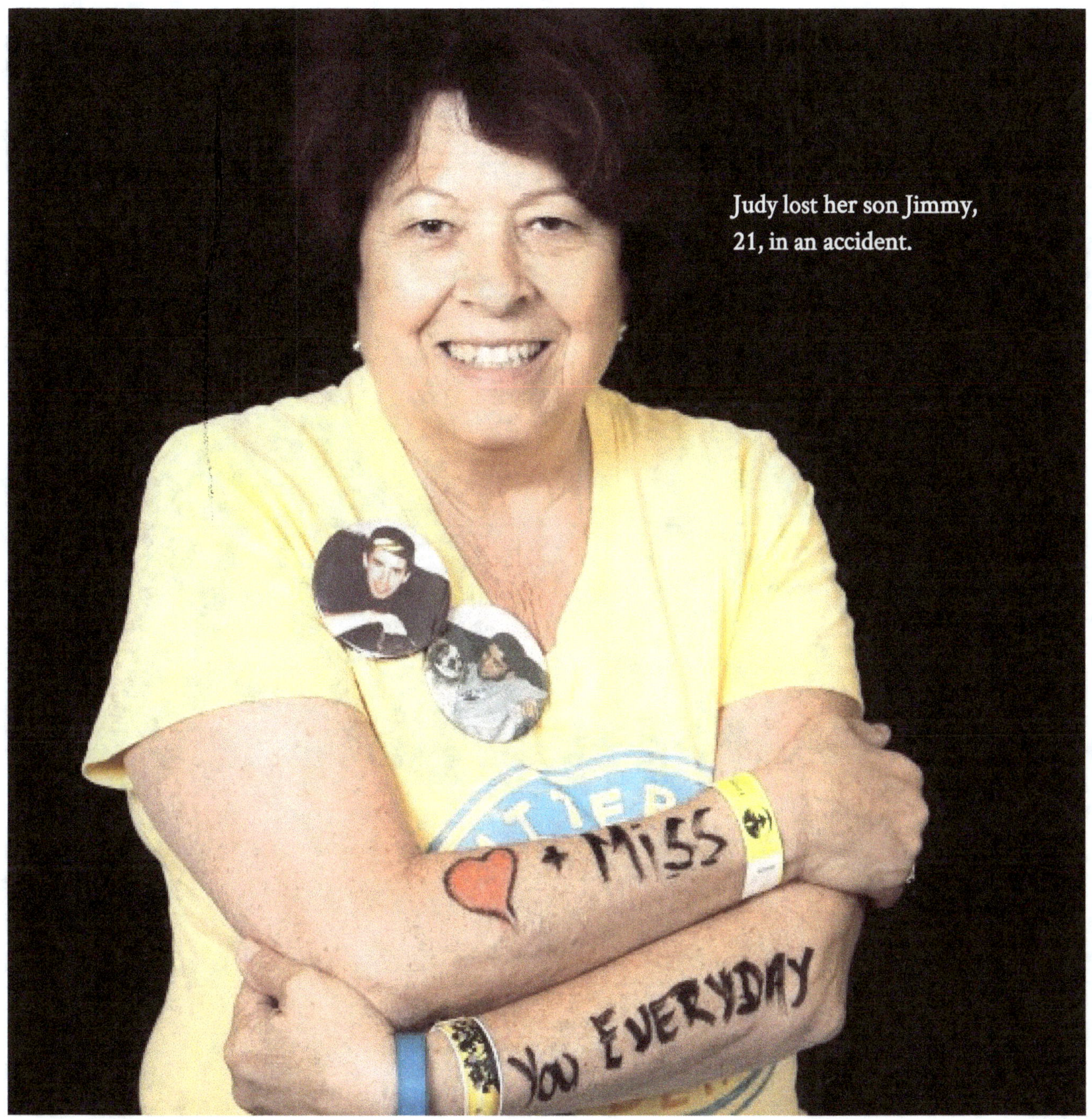

Judy lost her son Jimmy, 21, in an accident.

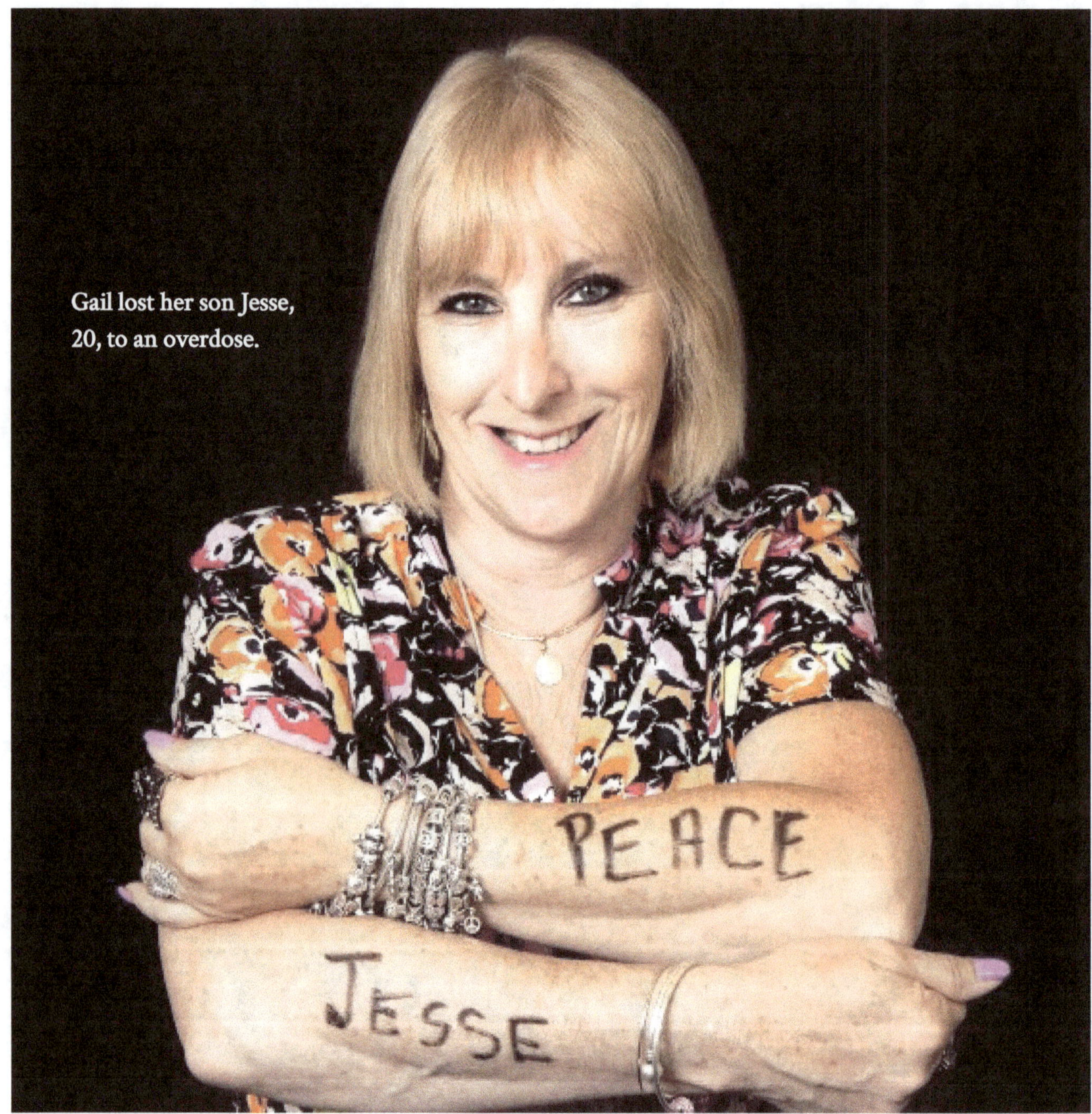

Gail lost her son Jesse,
20, to an overdose.

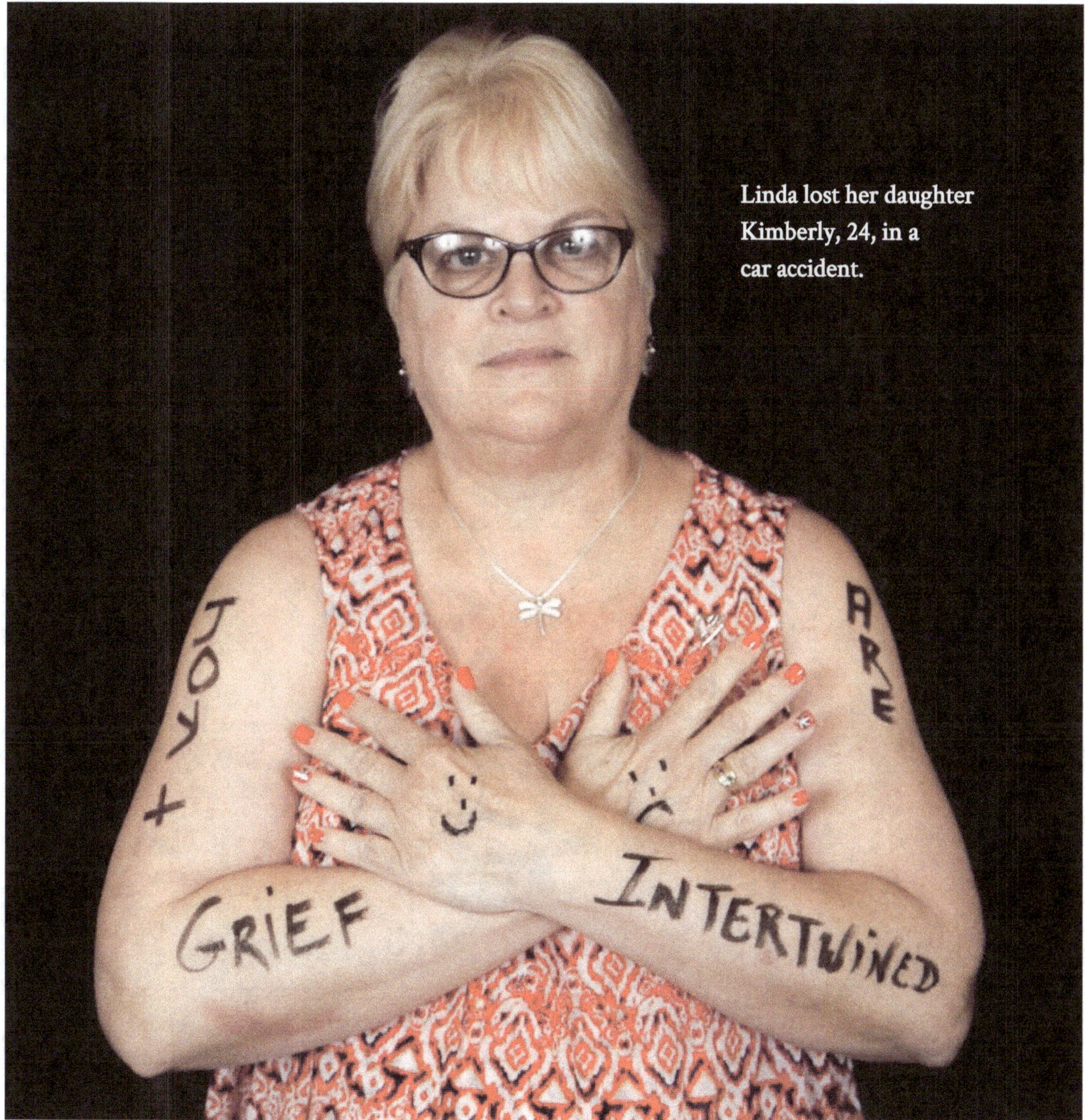

Linda lost her daughter Kimberly, 24, in a car accident.

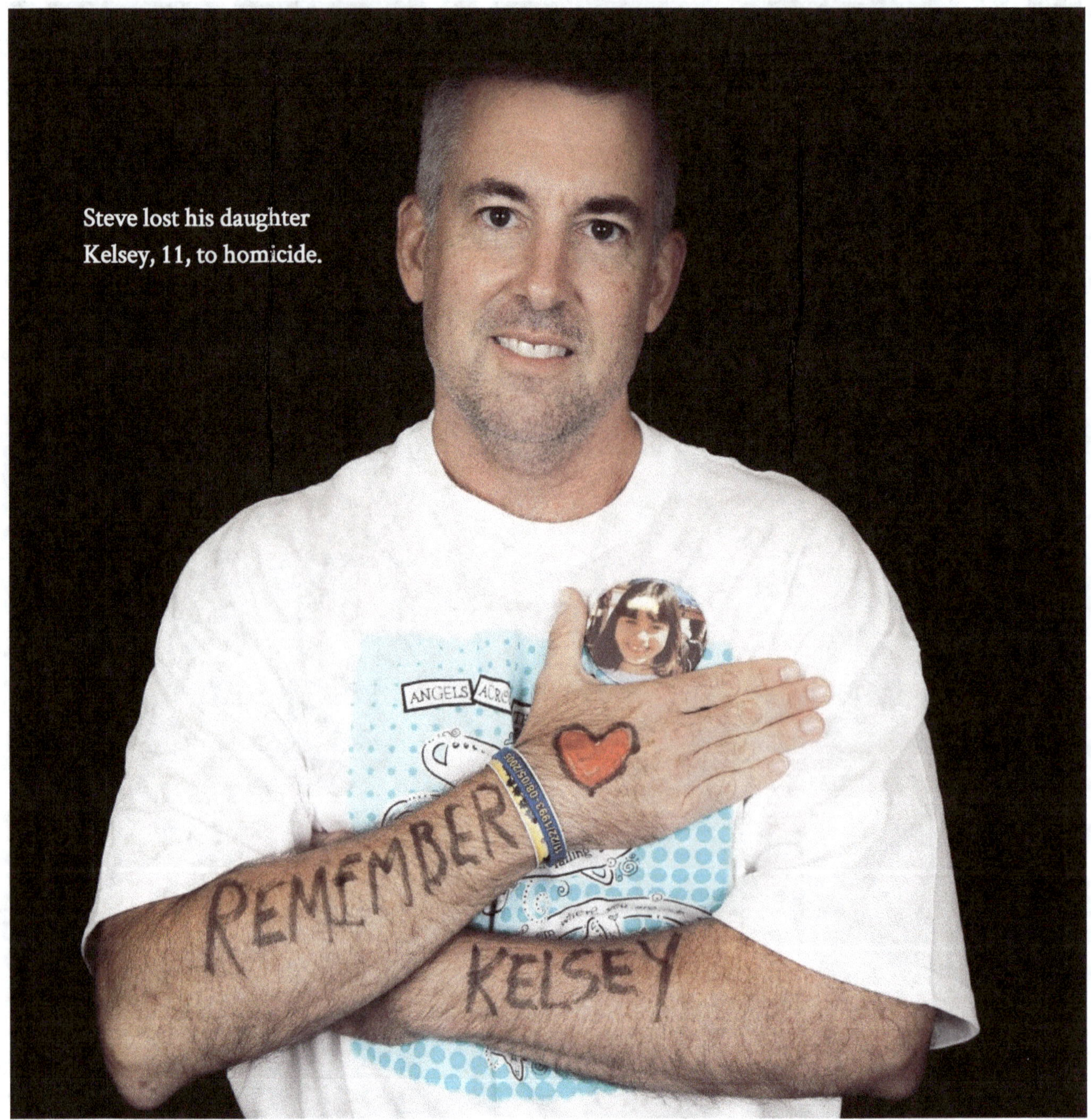

Steve lost his daughter
Kelsey, 11, to homicide.
REMEMBER
KELSEY

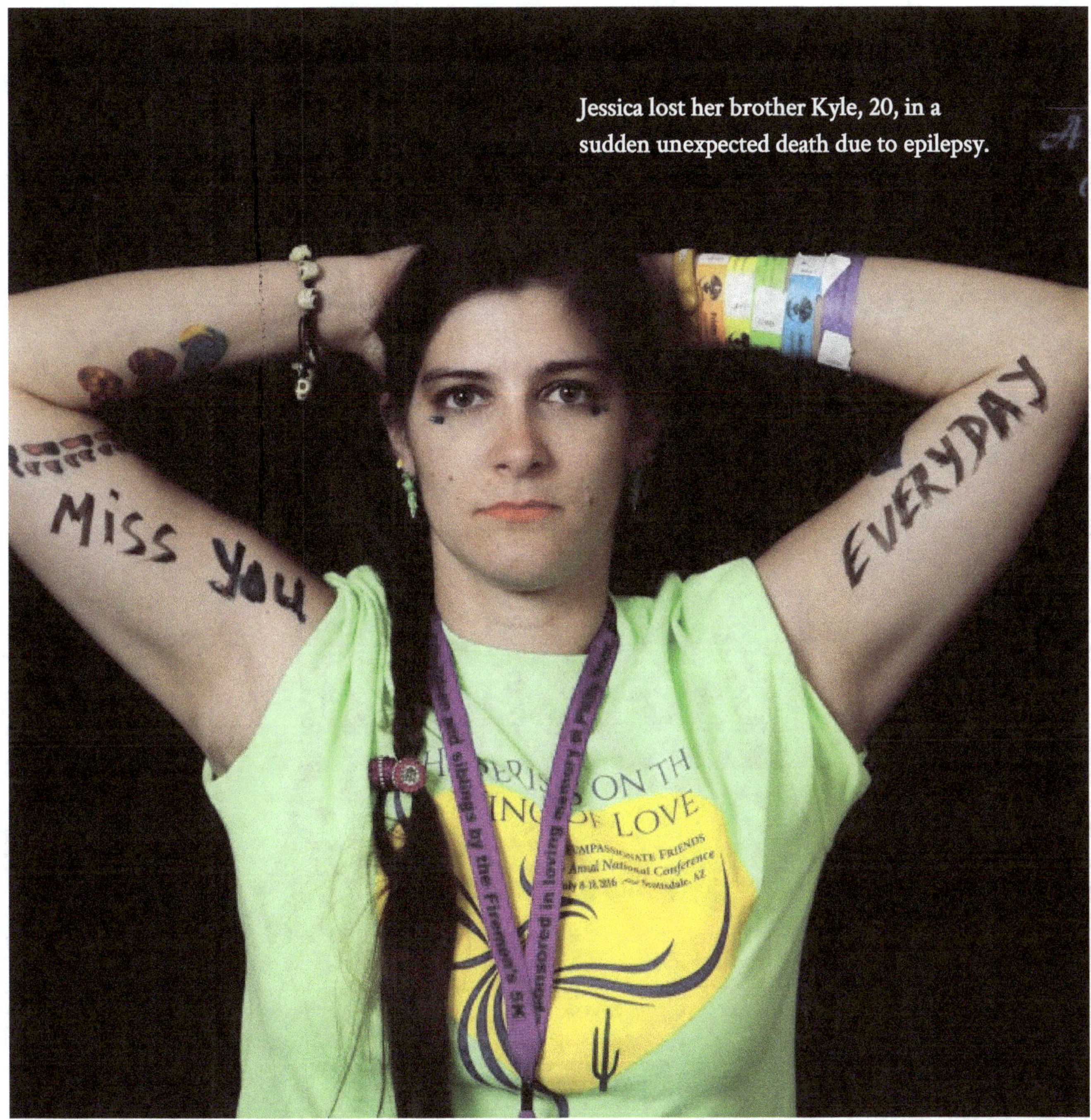

Jessica lost her brother Kyle, 20, in a sudden unexpected death due to epilepsy.

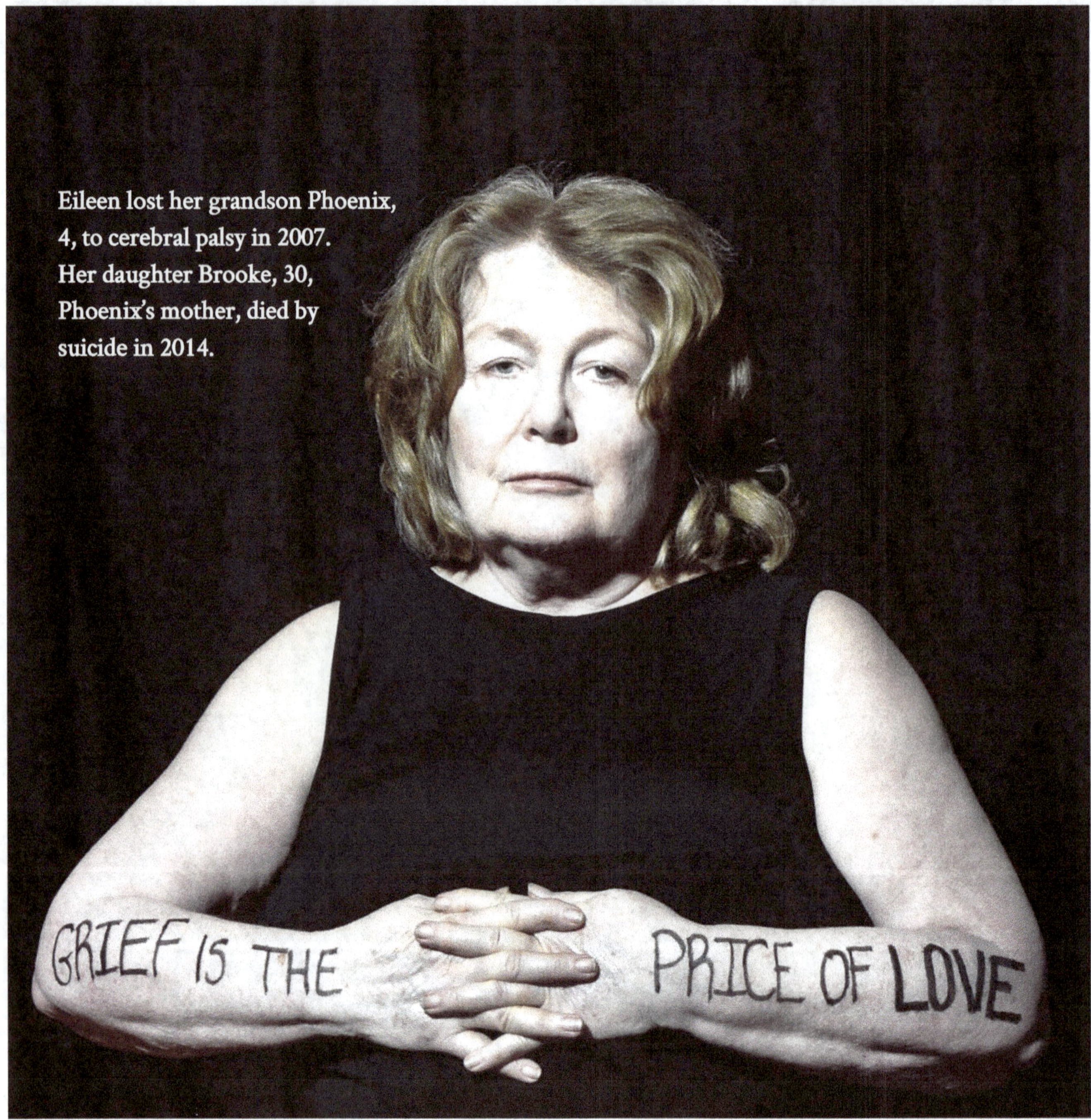

Eileen lost her grandson Phoenix, 4, to cerebral palsy in 2007. Her daughter Brooke, 30, Phoenix's mother, died by suicide in 2014.

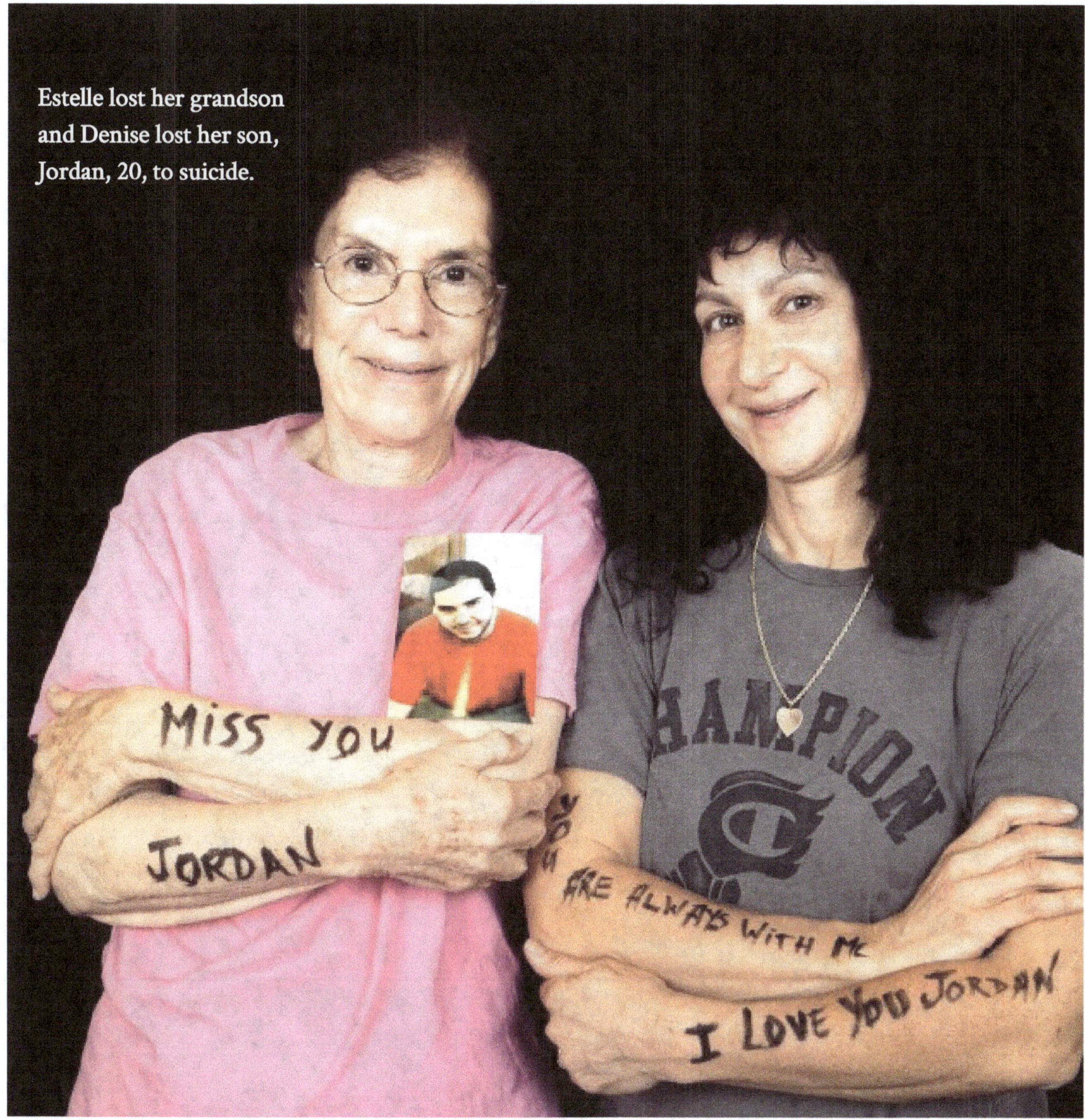

Estelle lost her grandson and Denise lost her son, Jordan, 20, to suicide.

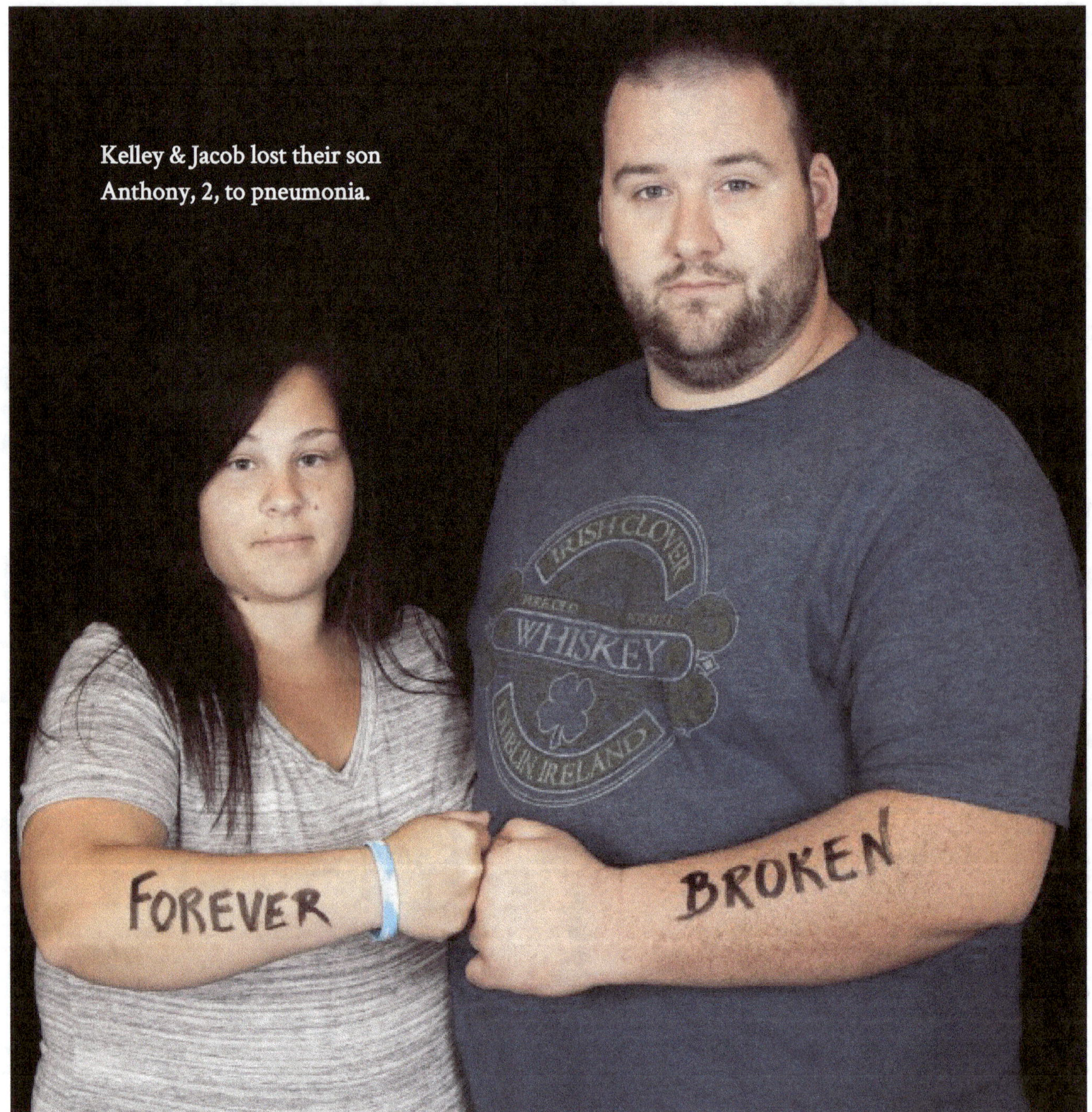

Kelley & Jacob lost their son
Anthony, 2, to pneumonia.

FOREVER

BROKEN

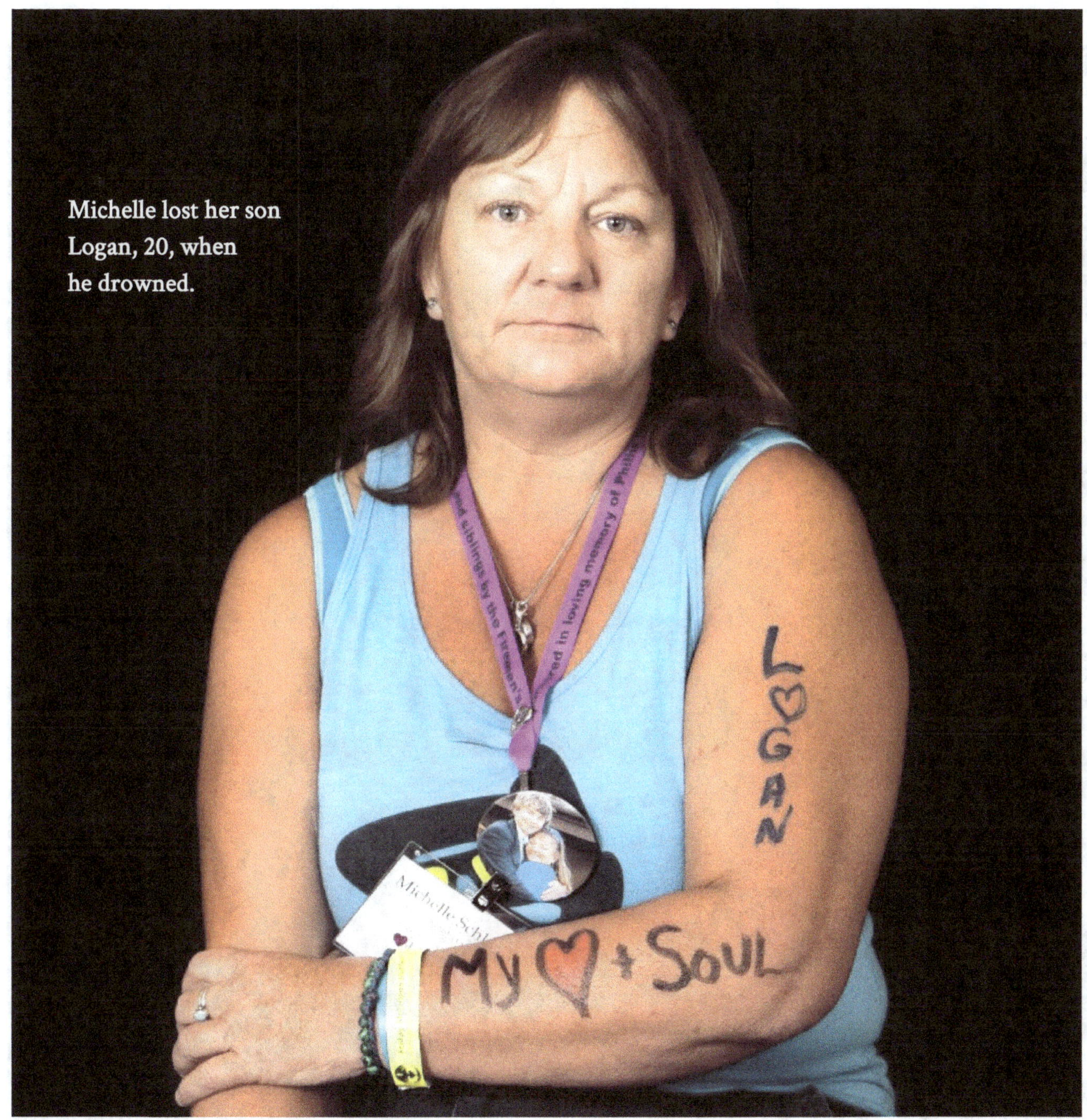

Michelle lost her son
Logan, 20, when
he drowned.

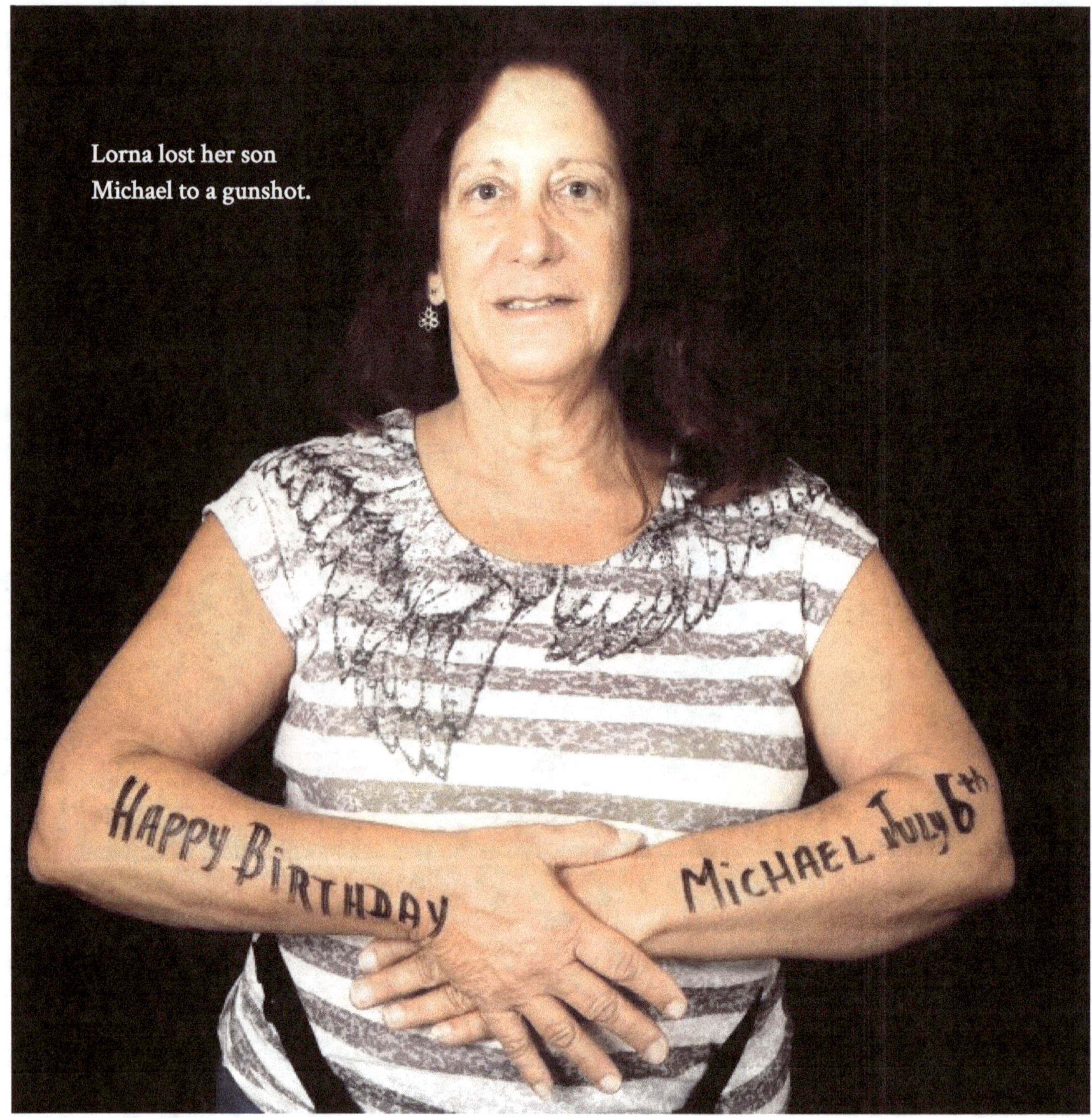

Lorna lost her son
Michael to a gunshot.

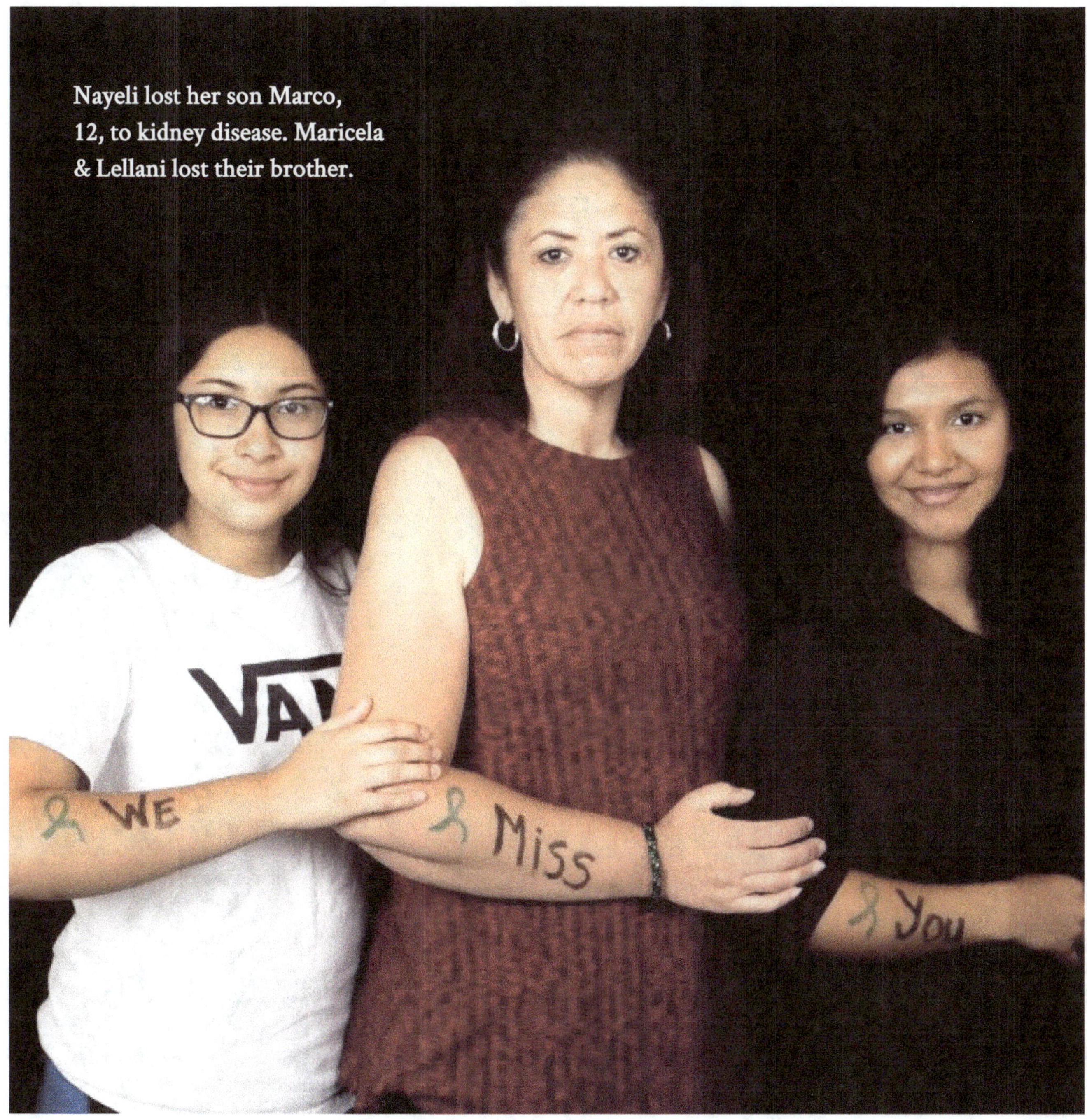

Nayeli lost her son Marco, 12, to kidney disease. Maricela & Lellani lost their brother.

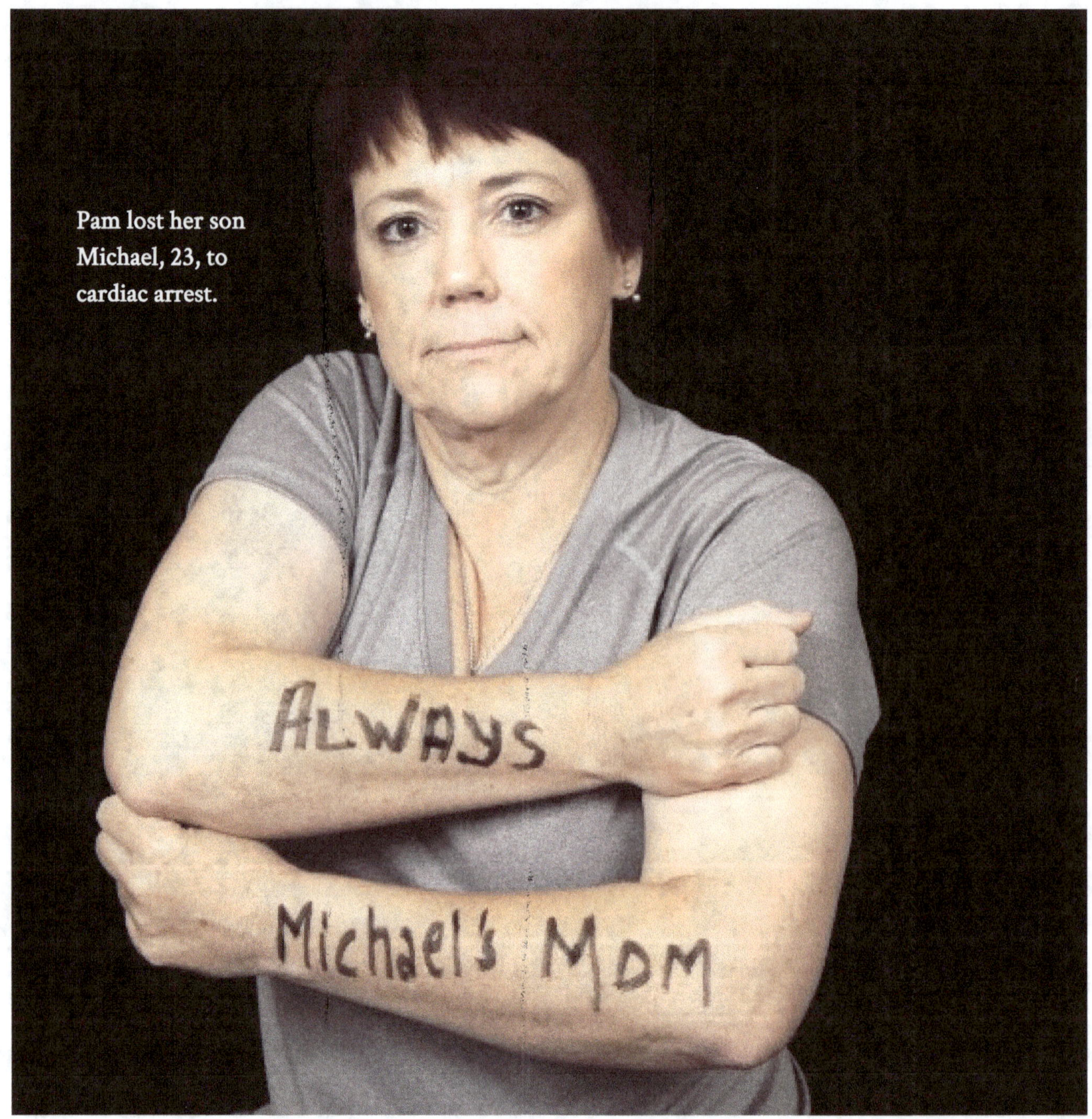

Pam lost her son
Michael, 23, to
cardiac arrest.

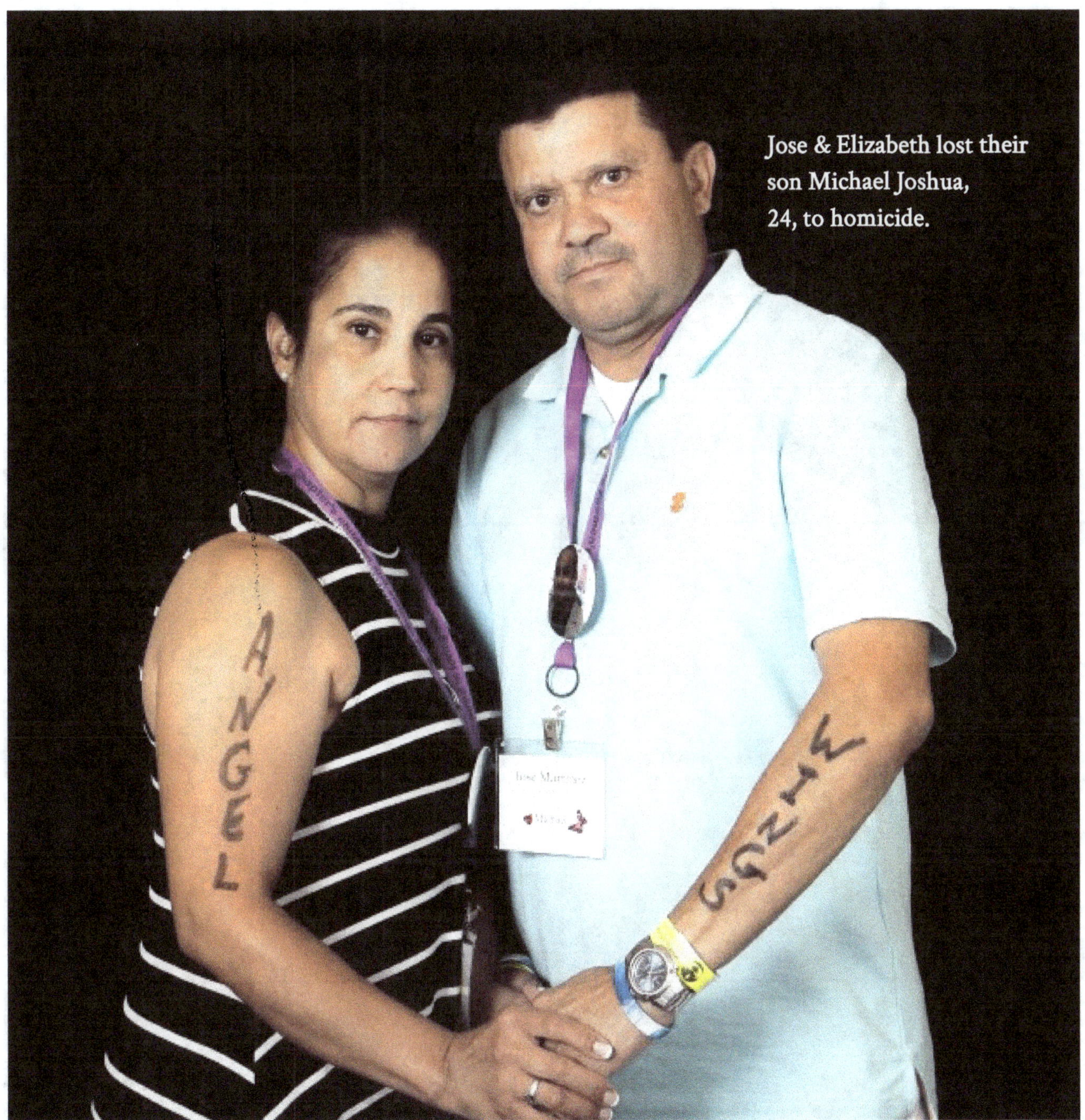

Jose & Elizabeth lost their son Michael Joshua, 24, to homicide.

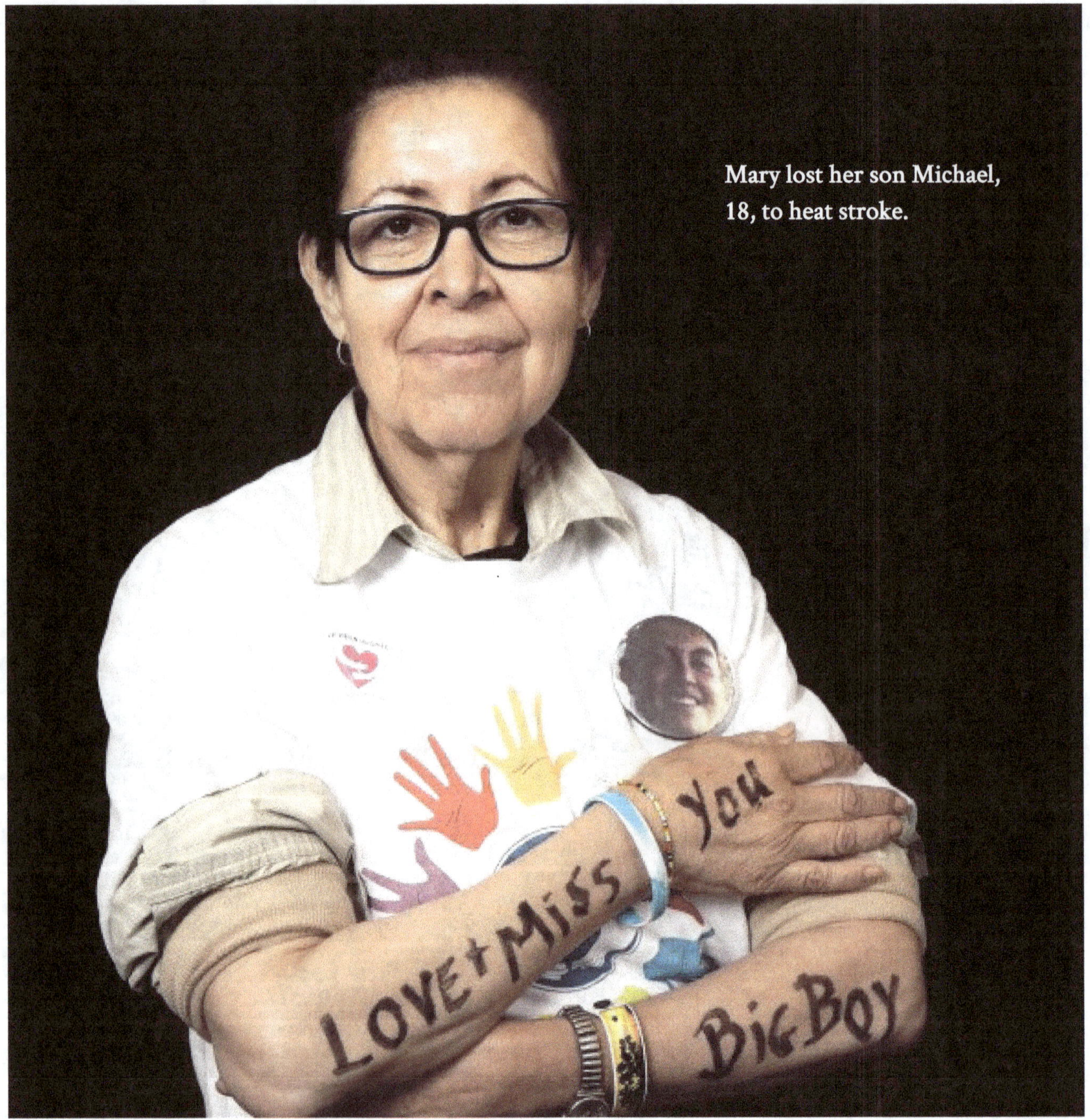

Mary lost her son Michael, 18, to heat stroke.

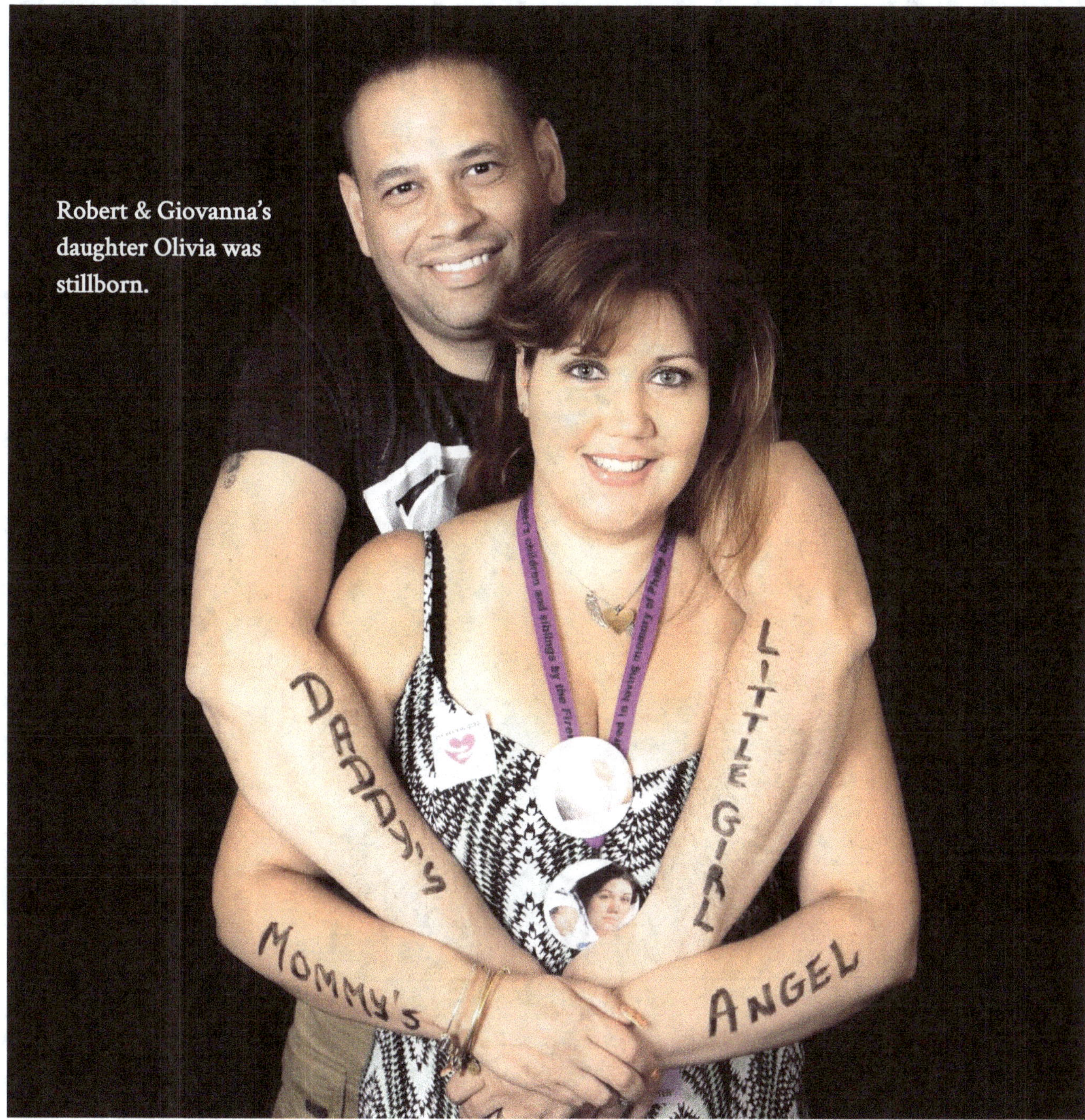

Robert & Giovanna's daughter Olivia was stillborn.

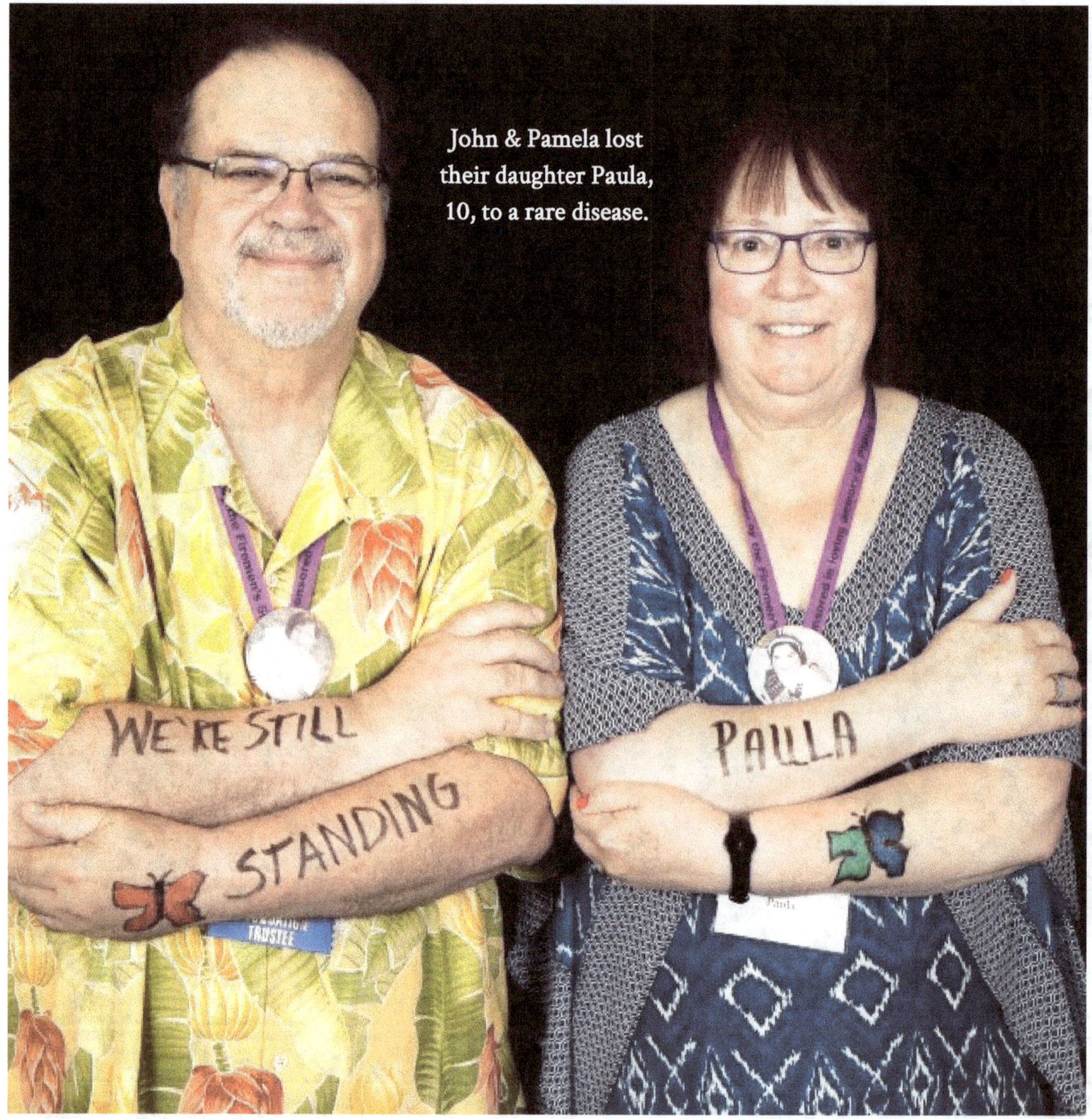
John & Pamela lost their daughter Paula, 10, to a rare disease.
WE'RE STILL STANDING
PAULA

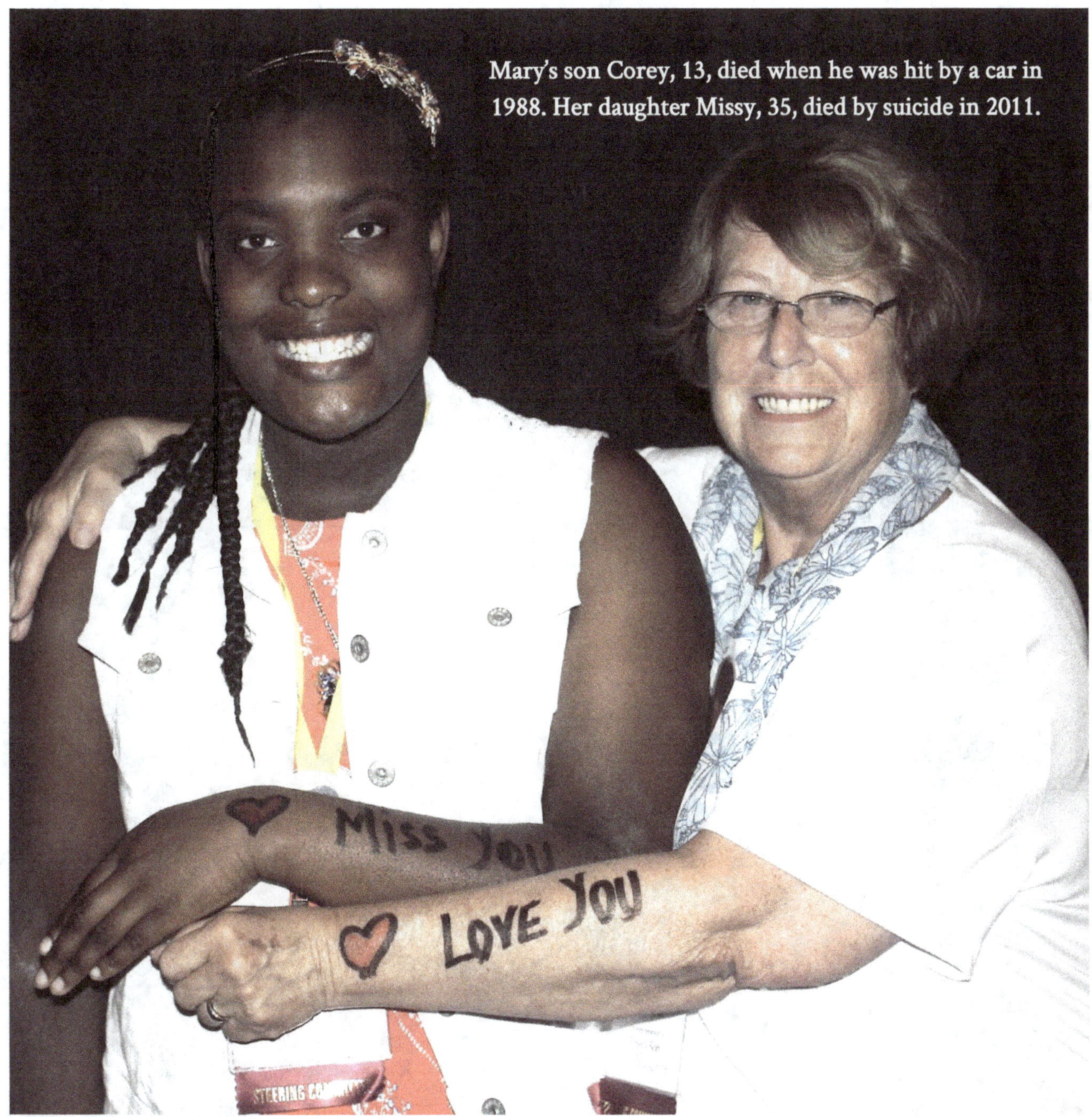

Mary's son Corey, 13, died when he was hit by a car in 1988. Her daughter Missy, 35, died by suicide in 2011.

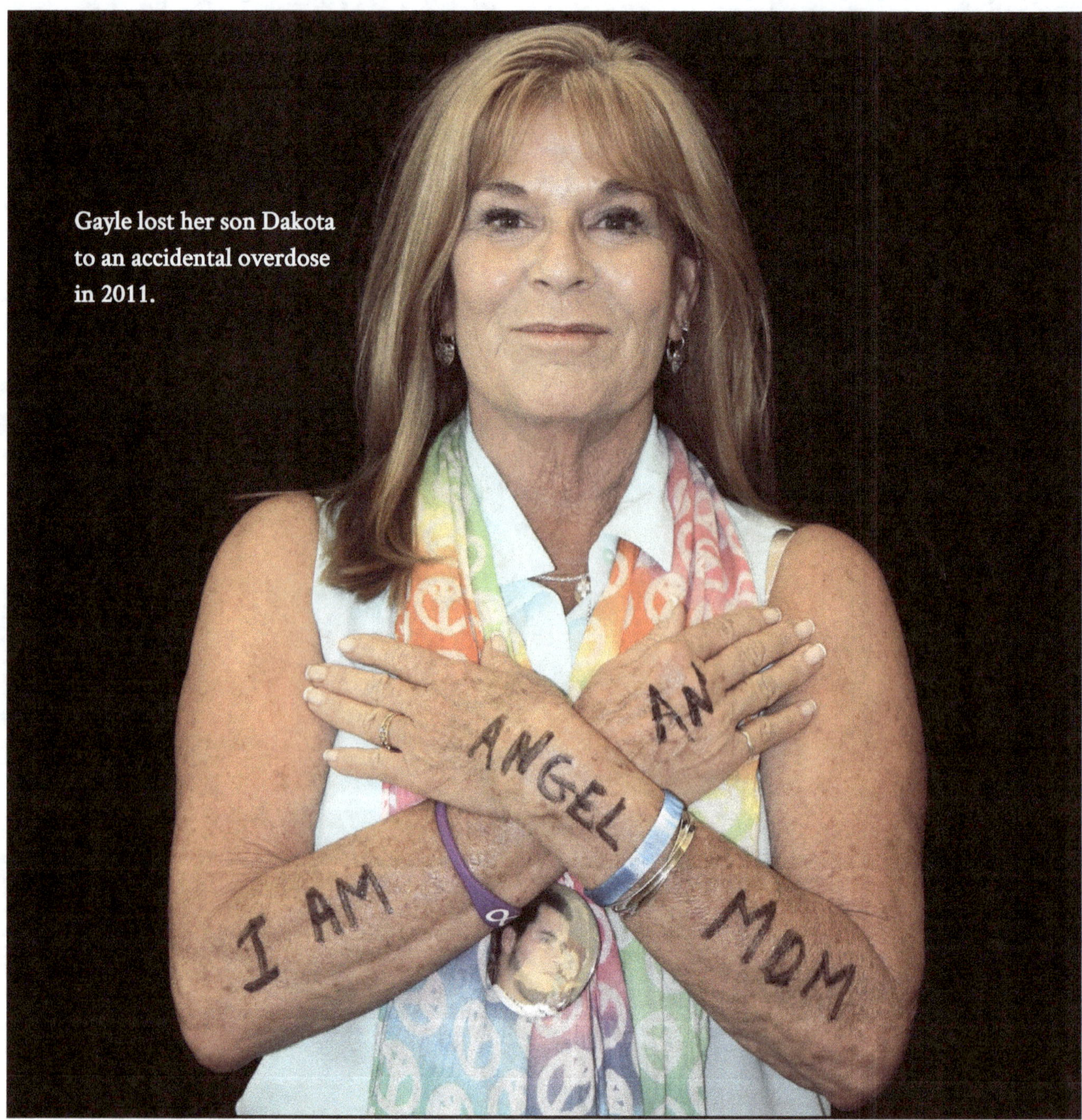

Gayle lost her son Dakota to an accidental overdose in 2011.

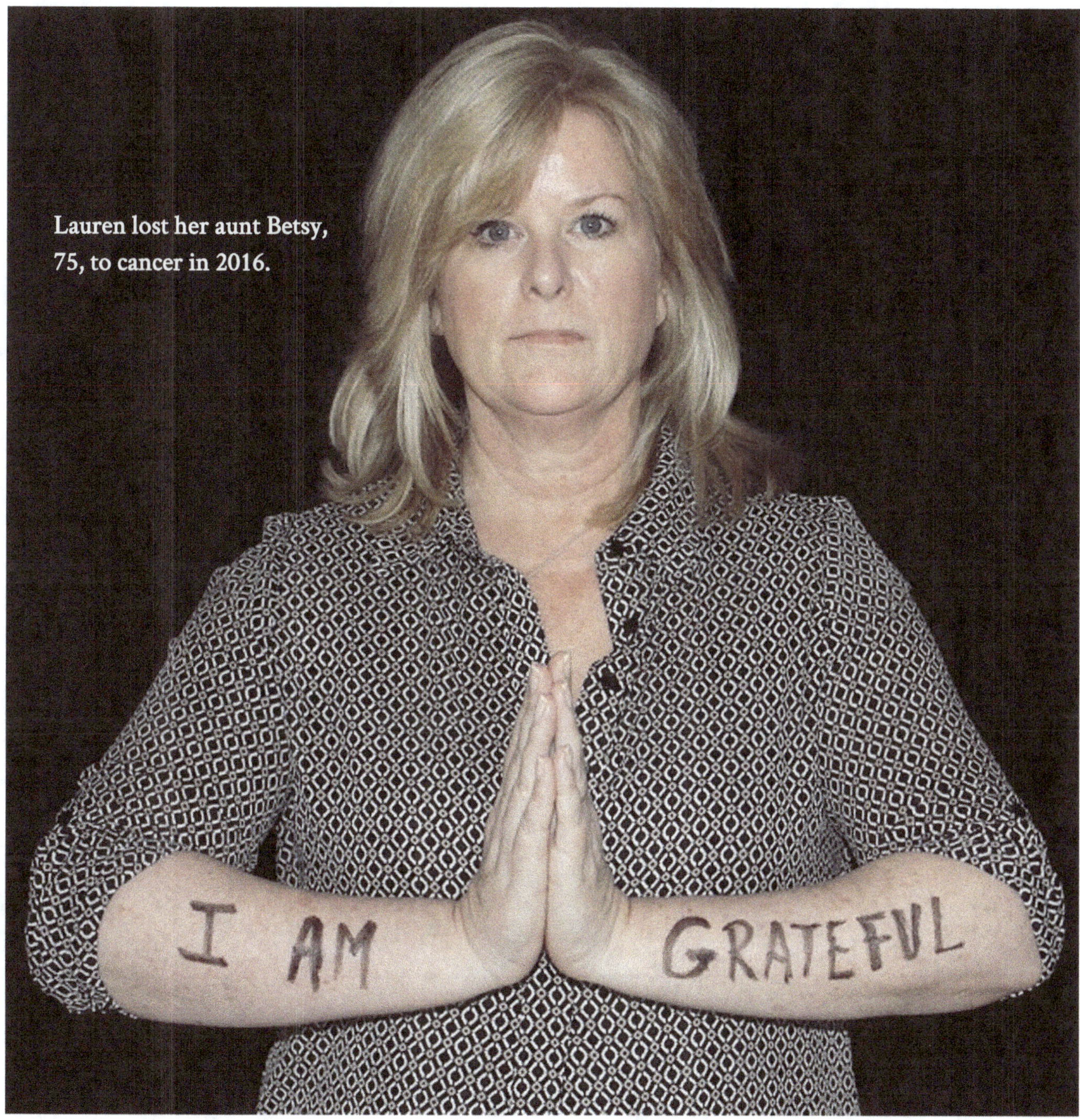
Lauren lost her aunt Betsy,
75, to cancer in 2016.
I AM GRATEFUL

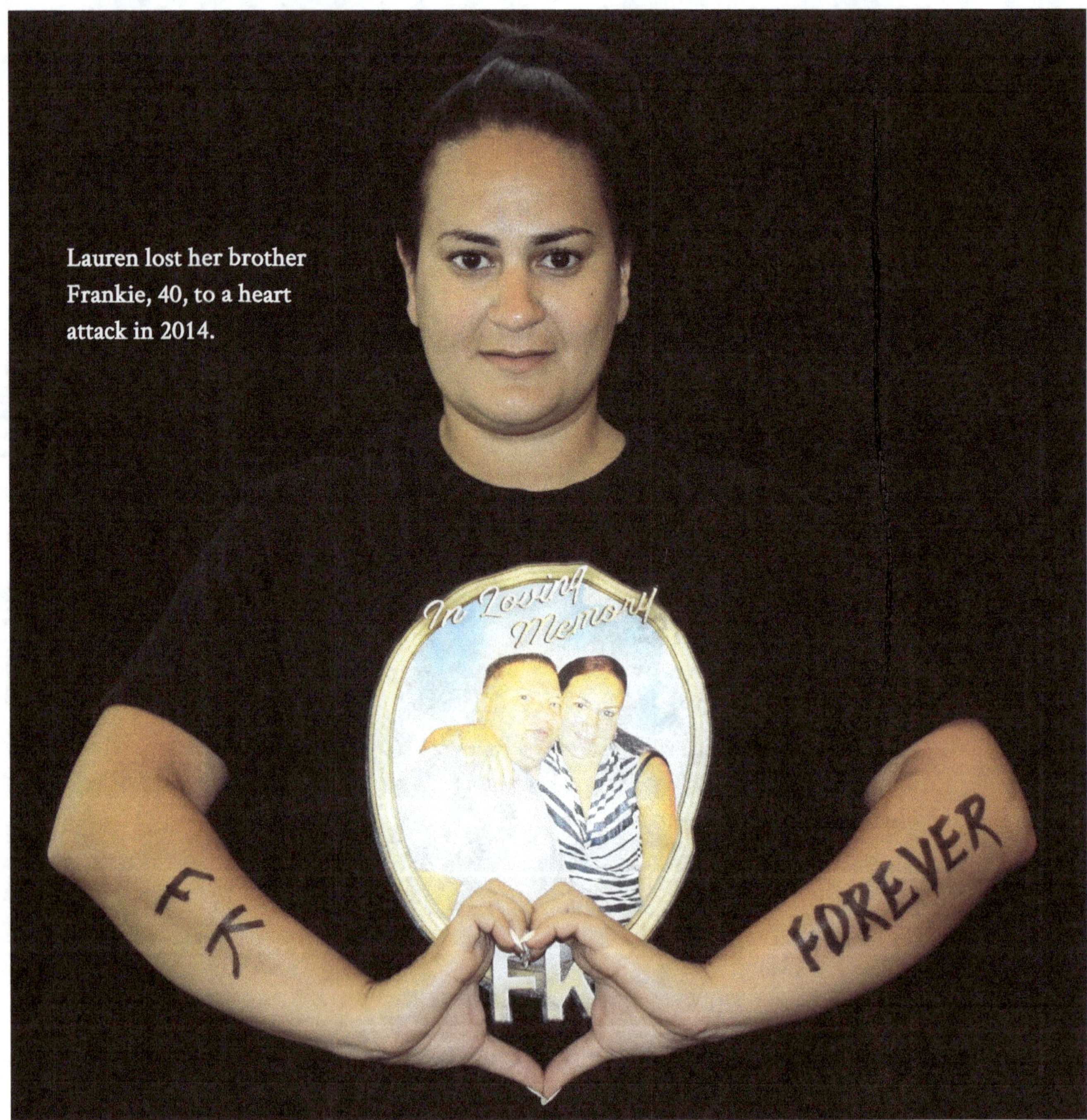

Lauren lost her brother Frankie, 40, to a heart attack in 2014.

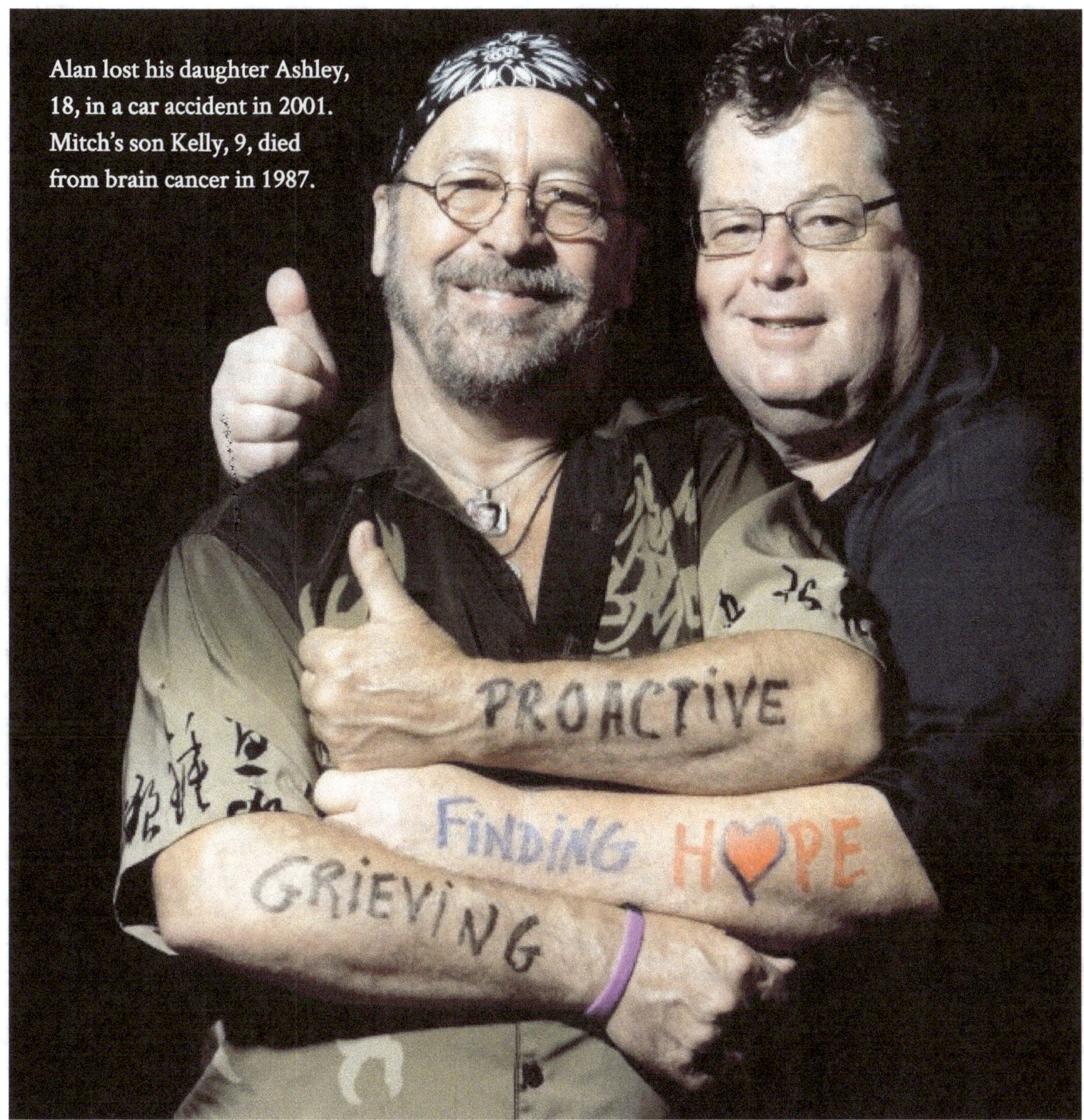

Alan lost his daughter Ashley, 18, in a car accident in 2001. Mitch's son Kelly, 9, died from brain cancer in 1987.

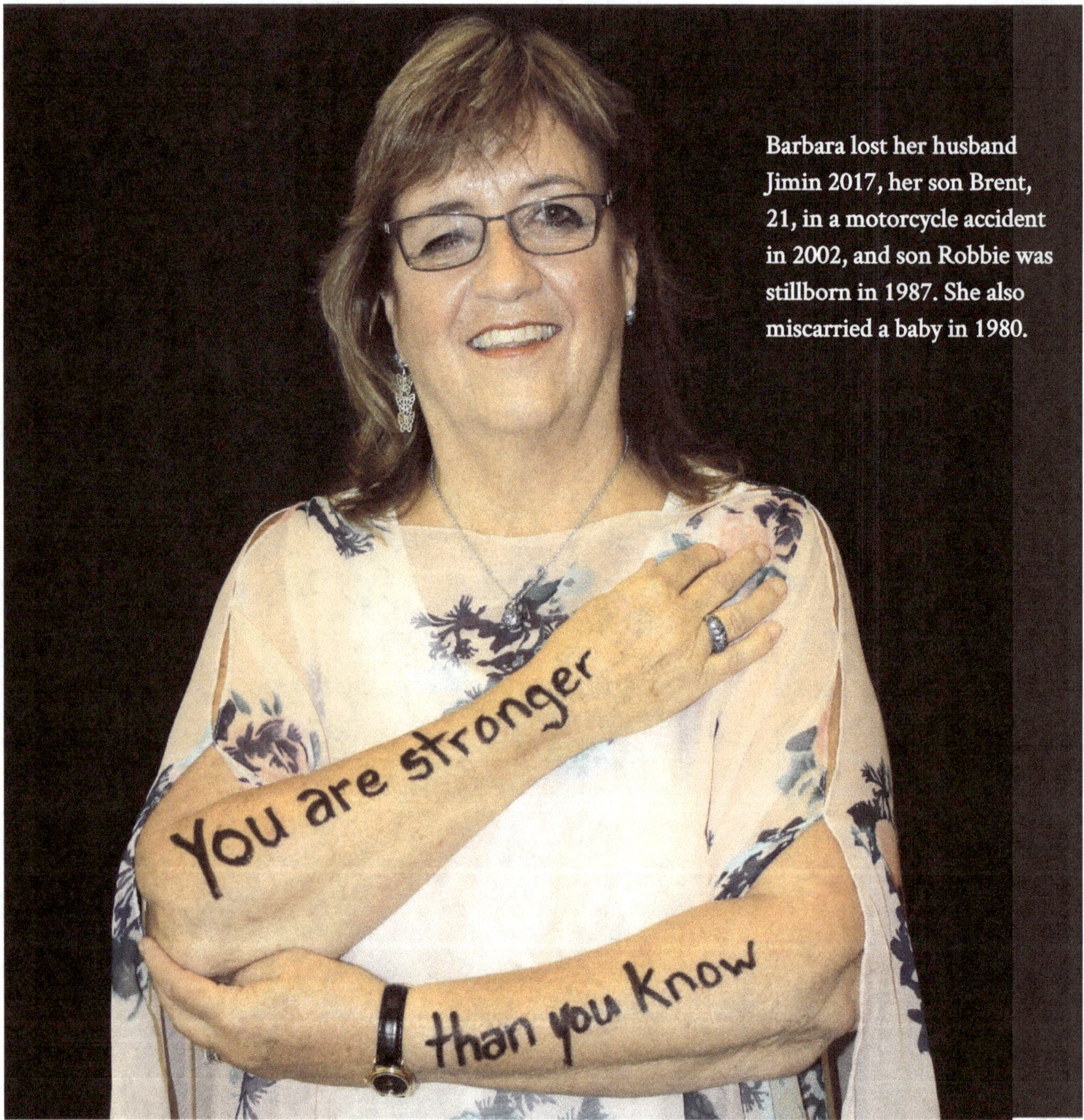

Barbara lost her husband Jimin 2017, her son Brent, 21, in a motorcycle accident in 2002, and son Robbie was stillborn in 1987. She also miscarried a baby in 1980.

BARBARA J. HOPKINSON

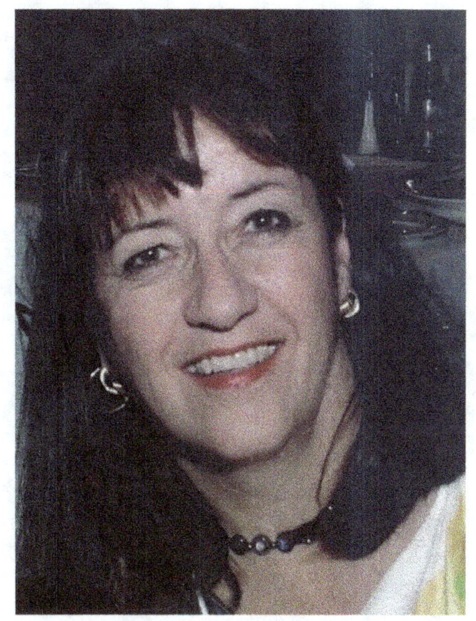

Barbara J Hopkinson is a certified Grief Recovery Specialist, bestselling author, and corporate executive who remains resilient after the loss of 3 children, her husband, both parents, and the sight in her right eye.

Barbara created Faces of Resilience as a traveling photoshoot to encourage open expression of grief, loss and love. She has led families through grief for more than 15 years and founded the nonprofit organization A Butterfly's Journey as well as the chapter of The Compassionate Friends of Greater Newburyport, Massachusetts.

Barbara's unique perspective from being a widow and losing multiple children formed the basis of her books including her first memoir, "*A Butterfly's Journey: Healing Grief After the Loss of a Child,*" as well as the bestselling inspirational collaborative book, *FAITH: Finding Answers in the Heart, Volume II*. Barbara is also coauthor and contributor for multiple books in the award-winning Grief Diaries series.

A Butterfly's Journey began taking emotionally cathartic photos of the bereaved in 2015. To raise awareness and foster discussions about grief, subjects are photographed with a meaningful expression written on their skin. They then receive a copy of the photo to use as a catalyst for discussing grief with family and friends.

Winning multiple awards for her work, Barbara's background encompasses 30 years in corporate technology including 10 years with IBM. She resides north of Boston and enjoys her remaining son and his wife, her grandson, three adult stepchildren and their partners. Passions include travel, photography and cooking.

Barbara J. Hopkinson
Creator, Faces of Resilience
Founder & CEO, A Butterfly's Journey
Founder, The Compassionate Friends of Greater Newburyport, MA
barbara@abutterflysjourney.org / 617-410-6309
abutterflysjourney.org / facesofresilience.org

She who heals others heals herself.
LYNDA CHELDELIN FELL

ABOUT

LYNDA CHELDELIN FELL

Lynda Cheldelin Fell is a certified critical incident stress management educator and international bestselling author of 35 books including the award-winning Grief Diaries series.

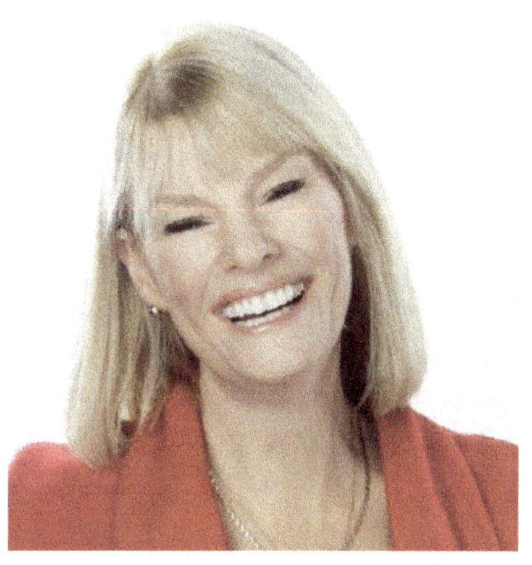

After losing her daughter in a car accident in 2009, Lynda discovered that helping others was a powerful balm for her wounds—a catalyst that changed her world. She first told her story and became an international bestselling author in 2013, and founded AlyBlue Media soon after. She launched Grief Diaries in 2014, founded the National Grief & Hope Convention 2015, wrote the curriculum Managing Grief in the Workplace in 2017, co-founded the International Grief Institute in 2017, and developed Grief's Playbook of Hope in 2018.

Lynda is a national speaker and educator on grief and resilience. She has curated stories and interviewed people around the world including societal newsmakers such as Martin Luther King's daughter, Dr. Bernice King, Pastor Todd Burpo of Heaven is for Real, Trayvon Martin's mother Sybrina Fulton, and more.

Host of the weekly Facebook show Moments of Hope, Lynda has earned five national literary awards and five national advocacy award nominations for her work. Learn more at www.LyndaFell.com.

Lynda Cheldelin Fell
Co-Founder, International Grief Institute
Creator, Grief Diaries brand
lynda@lyndafell.com / 360-510-8590
LyndaFell.com / GriefDiaries.com / AlyBlueMedia.com / InternationalGriefInstitute.com

I will find the courage and strength to be me again.

ALEXANDRA JANE MILIOTIS
*

PATTI RAE MILIOTIS

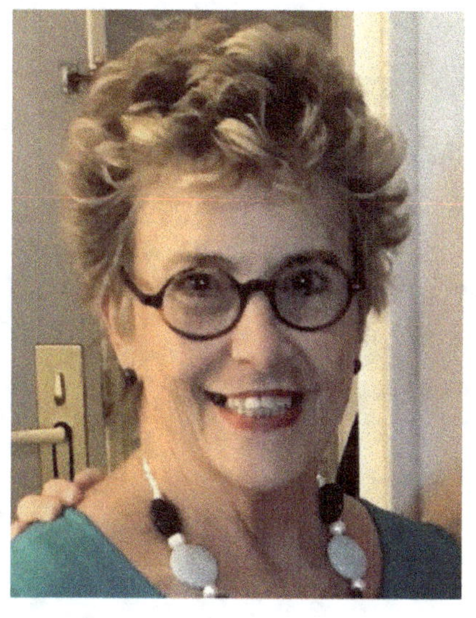

Award-winning photographer and jewelry designer Patti Rae Miliotis began working as an artist in residence at the Nantucket Island School of Design after her sixteen-year-old daughter Alexandra died from a rare form of childhood leukemia in 2002. Seeking solace and survival, Patti began riding her bicycle around the startling beauty of the island, alone and free with grief as her only companion. Her jewelry designs now reflect the winding path of her journey amid nature's elements.

Patti Rae holds a B.A. in Psychology from UCLA and an M.S. in Audiology and Speech Pathology from LSU Medical Center. Her doctoral studies at Boston University Medical Center in Behavioral Neuroscience were interrupted by her daughter's illness. Patti Rae's professional background includes neuropsychology research, as well as programs with autistic children and dementia patients. She co-founded the nonprofit Alex's Team Foundation in memory of her daughter. She joined Barbara Hopkinson in 2016 as part of A Butterfly's Journey, focusing her camera's eye on Faces of Resilience. The chronicling lens of her camera produces emotional portraits for A Butterfly's Journey and images reflecting nature's splendor. She lives north of Boston and enjoys time with her son, daughter, son-in-law and granddaughter.

Patti Rae Miliotis, M.S.
Chair, Alex's Team Foundation
Owner, AlexAria Art
praesarts@icloud.com / 978-502-4548
www.alexs-team.org / www.alexariaart.com

Shared joy is doubled joy;
shared sorrow is half a sorrow.

SWEDISH PROVERB

ALYBLUE MEDIA TITLES

Grief Diaries: Through the Eyes of a Widow
Grief Diaries: Project Cold Case
Grief Diaries: Surviving Loss by Suicide
Grief Diaries: Victim Impact Statement
Grief Diaries: Surviving Loss by Cancer
Grief Diaries: Surviving Loss of a Spouse
Grief Diaries: Surviving Loss of a Child
Grief Diaries: Surviving Loss of a Sibling
Grief Diaries: Surviving Loss of a Parent
Grief Diaries: Surviving Loss of an Infant
Grief Diaries: Surviving Loss of a Loved One
Grief Diaries: Surviving Loss of Health
Grief Diaries: How to Help the Newly Bereaved
Grief Diaries: Loss by Impaired Driving
Grief Diaries: Loss by Homicide
Grief Diaries: Loss of a Pregnancy
Grief Diaries: Hello from Heaven
Grief Diaries: Grieving for the Living
Grief Diaries: Shattered
Grief Diaries: Poetry & Prose and More
Grief Diaries: Through the Eyes of Men
Grief Diaries: Will We Survive?
Grief Diaries: Hit by Impaired Driver
Grief Diaries: Surviving Loss of a Pet
Real Life Diaries: Living with a Brain Injury
Real Life Diaries: Through the Eyes of DID
Real Life Diaries: Through the Eyes of an Eating Disorder
Real Life Diaries: Living with Endometriosis
Real Life Diaries: Living with Mental Illness
Real Life Diaries: Living with Rheumatic Disease
Real Life Diaries: Through the Eyes of a Funeral Director
Real Life Diaries: Living with Gastroparesis
A Child is Missing: A True Story
A Child is Missing: Searching for Justice
Grammy Visits From Heaven
Grandpa Visits From Heaven
Faith, Grief & Pass the Chocolate Pudding
Heaven Talks to Children
After-Death Communication: God's Gift of Love
Grief Reiki
See more titles at www.AlyBlueMedia.com

PUBLISHED BY ALYBLUE MEDIA
Real stories. Real people. Real hope.
www.AlyBlueMedia.com

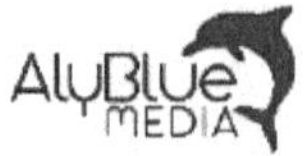